RHYTHMS OF RESISTANCE

Other titles by Peter Fryer available from Pluto Press

Staying Power
The History of Black People in Britain

'An invaluable book, which manages the rare feat of combining scholarship with readability.' Salman Rushdie

'Two thousand years is a long time; Peter Fryer never loses his grip in time or place.' C.L.R. James

'Fryer has performed a splendid service in illuminating this hitherto hidden story.' Francis Wheen, *Literary Review*

'Unquestionably a major work, of importance to all historians of modern Britain.' James Walvin, *Immigrants and Minorities*

'A major contribution to an understanding of the presence, contributions and struggles of black people in Britain over a period of 300 years.' *Sage Race Relations Abstracts*

'Fryer offers several nuggets of historical information, such as on the Africans who came to occupy Britain with the Roman legions nearly 2000 years ago. Even more familiar characters ... seem freshly revived in Mr Fryer's pen portraits.' Trevor Phillips, *The Times*

'A fascinating account of the growth of the black community in Britain over the past centuries.' *Guardian*

Black People in the British Empire

'A grim yet inspiring account of brutal repression and resistance ... Fryer throws the darker side of the empire into graphic and harrowing relief.' *New Statesman*

'Brief, readable, clear ... a persuasive look at racism in the empire filled with telling quotations and well-used data.' *Choice*

'A stupendous feat of scholarship.' *Westindian World*

'Fryer already has the outstanding achievement of *Staying Power* behind him. This new book will prove to be just as useful.' *Tribune*

'An important contribution to the struggle against racism.' *Race & Class*

Rhythms of Resistance

African Musical Heritage in Brazil

Peter Fryer

Pluto Press

First published 2000 by Pluto Press
345 Archway Road, London N6 5AA

British Library Cataloguing in Publication Data
A catalogue record for this book is available from the British Library

ISBN 0 7453 0383 8 hbk

Coventry University

Designed and produced for Pluto Press by
Chase Production Services, Chadlington, OX7 3LN
Typeset from disk by Stanford DTP Services, Northampton
Printed in the EU by TJ International, Padstow

To Raffaella from her *vovô*

Contents

Maps

List of Figures

Map 1 Sketch-map of Brazil

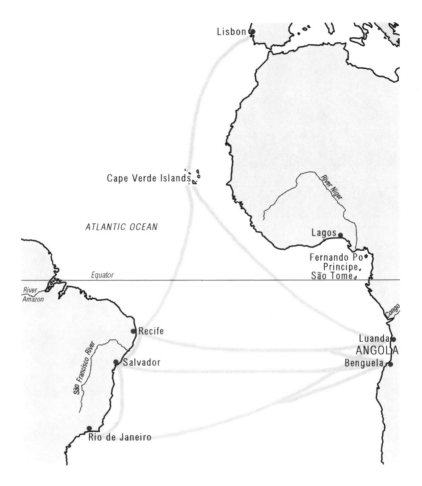

Map 2 Sketch-map of the Atlantic cultural triangle (Mollweide projection)

Preface

This book has developed out of a talk given at the University of Greenwich in March 1998 as part of Terry Cannon's course on World Music and Cultural Imperialism. I thank those who attended for their searching questions and stimulating contributions to discussion.

The study of any aspect of Brazilian traditional and popular music is strewn with pitfalls. The student is faced first of all with innumerable problems of nomenclature. It is hard to think of a musical instrument or musical style or dance style in the vast country that is Brazil which does not rejoice in a multiplicity of names, many of them purely local. Conversely, the same name is sometimes given to quite different instruments, styles or dances. Nearly 200 separate terms exist for various kinds of drum, many referring to identical instruments. There are more than seventy different names for the flute. And there are roughly fifty ways of referring to the fandango – a term which in any case has three distinct meanings in Brazil. I have thought it helpful to give a fair sampling of alternatives, but have tried to avoid sprinkling the text with too daunting a mass of italicised words within brackets. One major source of confusion is the word 'samba', which everyone knows to be the most typical Brazilian dance. There are however not one but many different sambas; and the present-day urban samba does not have a direct relationship, but a complex historical one, with the various forms of rural samba.

In trying to hew a path through this terminological thicket and trace the African musical and dance heritage in Brazil over nearly 500 years, I have been guided above all by the work of Renato Almeida, Oneyda Alvarenga, Mário de Andrade, John Charles Chasteen, Kazadi wa Mukuna and José Ramos Tinhorão.

This book relies heavily on accounts by European and American visitors to Brazil, and I have not hesitated to quote from these at length where they throw a light, however dim or fitful, on the music they heard and the dancing they saw. I have not thought it necessary to shield readers from the cultural prejudices, racist vocabulary, musical deafness, ignorance and prudery of many – though happily not all – of these witnesses.

It is a pleasure to thank those who have so generously given me help, advice and encouragement. I owe special thanks to Louise Meintjes, who made intelligent, penetrating and knowledgeable comments on an early draft; it is no fault of hers if I have failed to meet all her criticisms, and she of course bears no responsibility for the flaws which no doubt remain. The courteous staff of the Music Section of the Biblioteca Nacional in Rio de Janeiro made the three months I worked there in 1994 a most happy and rewarding time. I am indebted to Mercedes de Moura Reis (Mercedes Reis Pequeno) for providing me with an invaluable reading list. In the Rare Books and Music room of the British Library, John Goldfinch, Robert Parker and their colleagues have lightened my labours with many kindnesses, and the helpful attendants there have earned my gratitude day after day. Elsewhere in the British Library, Nina Evans and Nick Chadwick have given me help beyond the call of duty. This book would not have been possible without the elegant translations Bob Archer has made for me of accounts by nineteenth-century German and Austrian travellers. I am deeply grateful to Bridget Leach for her clear and illuminating maps, and to Lúcia Maria Gutierrez for her tireless efforts to procure illustrations of present-day Brazilian music and dance. On various problems of translation from archaic Portuguese and Spanish, my daughter Emily and her husband Jaime Del Cueto have smoothed my path. Luíz Carlos Moreira de Souza has contributed much, above all by showing me something of his country's culture from the inside. I am grateful to Patrícia Lança (Patricia McGowan Pinheiro), who forty years ago guided my first steps in the Portuguese language and in Luso-Brazilian studies and who has generously checked my translation of the key passage that is reproduced, in the original Portuguese, in Appendix E. Sister Catherine Cowley has kindly advised me on Roman Catholic terminology. I am grateful to Pluto Press for their stoical patience, and in particular to their managing editor, Robert Webb, for much sensible advice. This book has benefited greatly from the painstaking and vigilant copy-editing of Véronique Sérafinowicz. I express thanks also to my friends Jeff and Trudi Jackson, Cyril Smith, Rozina Visram and James D. Young for their constant encouragement; to Jeff Jackson for sharing the task of proofreading; to my daughter Frances and my son James for much technical help; and to Norma Meacock for much help of all kinds. Lastly, the person to whom this book is dedicated will realise, when the time comes for her to read it, that writing it has been in every sense a labour of love.

P.F.

New Year's Day 2000

Introduction

Challenge singing and the Atlantic cultural triangle

One morning in February 1994, walking through a big market in the city of Salvador, or Bahia, my head protected against the fierce sun, I heard a black man and a white man singing and accompanying themselves on amplified guitars. My Brazilian son-in-law told me later that from their appearance and accent he knew these were not city-dwellers but men from the *sertão*, the backwoods of north-eastern Brazil. They took it in turns to sing, vying with each other in word play and tongue-twisters and witty comments on local personalities and local events. Like street musicians everywhere, they were asking for contributions from passers-by, and one of them was soon singing: 'Perhaps the *gringo* in the red hat will give us some money; perhaps the pretty little girl with blue eyes will persuade him to.' My four-year-old granddaughter was transfixed and, to her delight, I sent her over with a donation.

This kind of semi-improvised song, known generally in Brazil as *desafio*, or challenge singing,[1] shows how three traditions from two continents, having already merged in Portugal, have merged still more intimately and seamlessly in Brazil. In Portugal such a song is often called a 'duelling song' (*canto a atirar*, literally 'shooting song'), and one variety of it is heard in the Lisbon fado when two singers take it in turns to sing verses (*fado d'atirar* or *desgarrada*).[2] Challenge singing is still a living tradition in the Azores, the second of the three Atlantic archipelagos to be colonised by the Portuguese in the fifteenth century, after Madeira and before Cape Verde.[3] The challenge singing of Portugal, the Azores and Brazil is thought to be related to the Provençal *tenso*, a twelfth- and thirteenth-century verse debate between two troubadours, and to the similar Catalan *partimen*.[4] Luso-Brazilian challenge singing and Provençal and Catalan verse debates share a common ancestor, it seems. That Europe owes troubadour verse and its metrical schemes to the Arabs of the Iberian peninsula is 'no longer seriously in doubt'.[5] Not only the troubadours' sense of form but also their subject matter was borrowed from that source, 'the chief difference being that they put their refrain at the end instead of the beginning'.[6] The very word 'troubadour' is almost certainly derived from one of two related Arabic words: *ṭarrāb* ('minstrel, one who affects listeners with a musical performance') or *ṭarraba* ('to perform musically').[7] And the troubadours' poetic debates probably

1

derived from the Arab literary debates called *munāẓārat*, in which two or more beings, living or inanimate, compete for the honour of which of them has the best qualities.[8] The Moslem occupation of Portugal began early in the eighth century; Lisbon was reconquered in 1147, the Algarve in 1249–50. Thus more than half of Portugal was home for about 500 years to Arabs (as well as Syrians, Persians, Jews, Egyptians and Berbers from Morocco), and I am inclined to think that it was the Arabs who took challenge singing to Portugal along with the water-wheel, rotation of crops, the orange tree, the silkworm and cotton.[9]

Much of Portugal's traditional music, like that of Spain, shows a certain Arab influence, though how much is a matter of dispute. According to one authority, 'From the musical point of view, the Moors left no traces which predominate in our [Portuguese] music. Portuguese popular music is in no way similar to Arab music and retains no kind of element from it, not even in the rare songs of melismatic type' (i.e. where a single syllable is spread over several notes).[10] Another authority takes a different view: 'Portuguese music ... quite regularly uses drums, tambourines and triangles – a legacy, along with some of the rhythms, of the Arab period ... [T]he music of Portugal, especially southern Portugal, was influenced by the Arab domination (though not as fundamentally as southern Spain).'[11] What is beyond dispute is that the Portuguese tradition of songs accompanied by percussion instruments (e.g. the Arab-derived *adufe*, a hand-beaten double-membrane square frame drum with metal jingles, which the Arabs call *al-duff*)[12] helped make Portuguese colonisers in Brazil and their African slaves markedly receptive to each other's music. Much of what the transported Africans sang and played was compatible with the music of the Portuguese settlers; and that music in turn, both traditional and otherwise, was largely accessible to the slaves. A significant number of captive Africans in Brazil were indeed soon being trained as instrumentalists or singers, and by the early seventeenth century Africans were playing in the plantation-owners' prestigious, and profitable, orchestras or singing in their choirs. This mutual musical compatibility, as well as the rapidly acquired musical literacy of slave instrumentalists and vocalists, hastened the emergence in the second half of the eighteenth century of a national popular music that was no longer either Portuguese or African but distinctively Brazilian. Many of the early Portuguese colonisers in Brazil were in fact Mozárabes from the southern part of Portugal, where Arab cultural influence was strongest, and this too must have favoured, and helped to shape, the acculturation process.[13]

There can be little doubt that in Lisbon at least there was some African as well as Arab influence on Portuguese challenge singing. African slaves were transported to Portugal from 1441 onwards. Before long, about 700 or 800 slaves were being imported from West Africa each year, and by the middle of the sixteenth century Lisbon's black community numbered about 10,000 (approximately 10 per cent of the city's population);[14] some 200 years later it was estimated to be about 15,000 (around 6 per cent).[15] Verbal contests – contending or duelling with words, often in song – are an important means of communication and entertainment in many parts of sub-Saharan Africa. One example is the practice of 'mother-rhyming' – licensed abuse between age-mates of each other's parents and grandparents – among the Yoruba and Efik of Nigeria, the Dogon of Mali, the Gogo of Tanzania, and other ethnic groups.[16] Another is the *halo* competition of the Ewe of Ghana, in which two villages compete for several years in making up elaborate insulting songs about each other, based on the recollections of old men, a practice which has been described as a sort of protracted village opera.[17] Verbal-contest traditions, often in song and serving as entertainment, are found throughout the African diaspora, e.g. in Puerto Rico (*controversia*),[18] Trinidad (*picong*)[19] and the United States ('playing the dozens', a form of 'mother-rhyming').[20] Lisbon's black community is unlikely to have been an exception.

That community was in no sense isolated. A German visitor to Lisbon commented in 1801 on the city's 'negroes, of whom there is a greater number here perhaps than in any other city of Europe, not excepting London', adding: 'Great numbers of them are employed as sailors.'[21] Thanks largely to those seafarers, Lisbon's black community was in close and constant touch with the music and dances of Angola (and of Luanda and Benguela in particular) and with the music and dances of Brazil (and of Salvador, Recife and Rio de Janeiro in particular). The ships that linked these ports with each other and with Lisbon carried this music and these dances round and round the Atlantic trade triangle – which from as early as the sixteenth century functioned also as a cultural triangle. Though stylistic differences were never fully ironed out, there was a constant circulation of musical styles and of dance fashions. (The Atlantic dance tradition is discussed in Chapter 7.)

At the same time Lisbon's black community was in close and constant touch with the rest of the city's 'lower orders': the working people, beggars and other poor inhabitants of Alfama, on whose quays the ships from Angola and Brazil tied up, of Mouraria, and of the other lower-class districts of the city. A social historian of Lisbon, summing up the eighteenth century, tells us: 'No dance … was so favoured by Alfama-dwellers, fishwives, vagrants, all the riff-raff of the city, as the dances of black influence: lewd, funky [*catingueiras*], hip-swinging, belly-shaking [*quebradas de rins*].'[22] Lisbon's African population, who included dancers and musicians taken to Portugal for their entertainment value, brought from Angola lively dances called, in Portugal and Brazil, *batuque* and *lundu*; the latter may possibly have got its name from the Angolan port of Luanda.[23] And those black people who were taken to Portugal from Brazil – they started arriving at least as early as the first decade of the seventeenth century[24] – eventually brought with them two popular African-influenced Brazilian dances which were either close relatives of the *lundu* or perhaps just variants of it: the fado, which in Lisbon became a kind of song rather than a dance, and the hip-shaking *fofa*. The latter was such a popular import that some foreign visitors in the second half of the eighteenth century took it to be Portugal's national dance. Four centuries before jazz came to Europe, Portugal felt 'a significant African influence at the very heart of its popular music and dance',[25] and not only in Lisbon. *The New Grove Dictionary of Music and Musicians* tells us that African rhythms and instrumentation were

> a feature of Portuguese folk music apparently since the beginning of the 16th century ... The *guineos* and *negros* are usually responsorial [i.e. in call-and-response form] and feature hemiola shifts [i.e. duple and triple rhythmic divisions alternate] to 3/4 within a 6/8 metre; their texts, usually on the Christmas theme, mention African place names and African as well as European instruments, and use vocables such as 'gulugá, gulugué'.... In 20th-century Portugal African traces survive in such dances as the *cana-verde* [see p. 181], the *bailes de escravos* (a shuffling chain-dance in imitation of slaves) and the *bailes dos pretos*, a circle-dance featuring a solo imitation of black African dancing, with appropriate costume, make-up and instruments providing 'African' rhythms.[26]

It should be added that from the seventeenth century onwards, to an increasing extent, the African influence on Portuguese music and dance was mediated through Brazil.

A final word on challenge singing in Brazil. Highly stylised, it has no fewer than ten clearly defined types: *martelo* (literally 'hammer', though it is said to take its name from an eighteenth-century professor of literature who is supposed, rather improbably, to have invented it);[27] *galope* ('gallop'), *martelo agalopado* ('galloping hammer'), *galope a beira-mar* ('seashore gallop'), *colcheia* ('quaver'); *carreta* ('truck') or *carretilha* ('little truck'); *mourão* ('stake'); *ligeira* ('quick'); *quadrão* ('eight-verse stanza'); and *quadra* ('four-verse stanza'). The last of these is said to be the oldest type. Each type has a certain number of stanzas which are distributed between the singers (*repentistas*, literally 'improvisers') in a specific way and are rhymed also in a specific way; each stanza has lines containing a specific number of syllables, usually ten, seven or five. To take just one example: each stanza of the *martelo agalopado* has ten lines each of ten syllables; the fourth and fifth lines rhyme with the first, the third with the second, the seventh and tenth with the sixth, the ninth with the eighth, giving the rhyming formula ABBAACCDDC; it is a 'difficult and beautiful genre'.[28] The strictness of these formulas – reminiscent of the *décima* ten-verse poetry of the Iberian peninsula, written by the great Spanish novelist and dramatist Miguel de Cervantes Saavedra (1547–1616) among others – clearly points to Portugal and its Arab conquerors.[29] And the rather high, nasal, vocal tone points no less clearly to the Arab presence in Portugal.

The instruments which traditionally accompany challenge singing in the north-east of Brazil are the *viola* and the *rabeca* (rebec). The *viola* is a traditional guitar with five, six or seven pairs of strings; it may derive from the Iberian *vihuela*, a plucked lute with a guitar-shaped body which was popular during the Renaissance. The *rabeca* is a kind of fiddle with three or four strings which evolved from the *rabāb* bowed lute of the Arabs and was known in Europe from the thirteenth century.[30] Also formerly in use, especially by black *desafio* singers, was the *pandeiro* tambourine, a circular frame drum with jingles, whose name derives from the Arabic *bandīr* (or *bandair*).[31] In the north-east of Brazil the accompaniment is for the most part prominent in the intervals between verses but rudimentary during the singing, in the sense that the rhythm is barely, if at all, sketched in, though sometimes there is heterophony, i.e. a variant of the melody, differently accented, is played against the vocal line. Elsewhere in Brazil the verses are fully accompanied. In the southern state of Rio Grande do Sul the accompaniment is usually played on the *sanfona* button accordion, brought to Brazil by Italian settlers from about 1836 and soon to become the favourite – some say the indispensable – instrument of the Brazilian *gaúchos*.[32]

The African presence in Brazil

Brazil was 'discovered' in 1500, and within sixty years Portuguese settlers were using African slave labour there on a vast scale. They began to colonise Brazil from about 1530, and before long the coast had been divided into fifteen hereditary *capitanias* ('captaincies', i.e. administrative provinces). In a curious amalgam of feudalism and colonialism, these were granted to rich Portuguese who began to develop them in their own interests. The Portuguese were above all looking for gold, silver and precious stones, but it would take them another 160 years to find significant amounts of these. Meanwhile they turned to growing sugar cane and manufacturing sugar, a hugely profitable enterprise on which they embarked soon after the colony's first governor-general was appointed in 1549.[33]

Amerindians were found to decline rapidly under the working conditions the Portuguese imposed on them, so the colonists had recourse to Africans, the first of whom may have been landed in Brazil as early as 1532.[34] It was said that when the Portuguese adventurer arrived in Brazil the first thing he did was neither kiss the earth nor give thanks to the Virgin for a safe passage, but buy a slave.[35] From the 1690s Africans were working not only on the sugar plantations and in the sugar mills but also in the gold and later the diamond mines of Minas Gerais. And towards the end of the colonial period (i.e. before 1822) they were working on the expanding coffee plantations of São Paulo and Rio de Janeiro, too.

These slaves were transported mainly from West Africa in the second half of the sixteenth century; from Angola during the seventeenth century; from the Mina coast (which the English called the 'Gold Coast') from about 1700 to 1770; from the Bight of Benin (i.e. Nigeria and Benin, formerly Dahomey) from 1770 until the 1850s.[36] That, at any rate, was the provenance of Africans landed at Salvador. The provenance of Africans landed at Rio de Janeiro and the north-eastern port of Recife probably showed the same changes over time, but details are sparse because many documents relating to the slave trade were destroyed by government decree in 1890–91.[37] To replace the many slaves who died from overwork, undernourishment, disease and ill-treatment – the annual mortality rate of African-born slaves is estimated to have been about 10 per cent in the first half of the nineteenth century[38] – and also the many who fled into the forest, more captive Africans were transported to Brazil than to anywhere else in the Americas, so that today Brazil has the second largest black population of any country in the world.[39] It was reckoned in 1681 that about one million slaves – referred to, and valued as, 'pieces' (peças)[40] – had already been shipped from Angola to Brazil, in ships known colloquially as 'coffin-bearers' (tumbeiros).[41] This figure cannot have been far off the mark, for the most generally accepted modern estimate puts the total number of Africans transported to Brazil, over a period of 350 years, at about 3,600,000.[42] One scholar, however, holds out for a higher figure: 'probably more than 5,000,000'.[43]

Portugal's Brazilian colony was being called a 'new Guinea' – i.e. a new West Africa – as early as 1618.[44] Visiting Salvador in 1714, Louis XIV's military engineer Amédée François Frézier (1682–1773) reported that '19 in 20 of the People we see there, are Blacks ...; so that the City looks like a new *Guinea*'.[45] The poet Robert Southey (1774–1843) echoed this in his *History of Brazil* (1810–19): 'The black population in Bahia was so numerous that it is said a traveller might have supposed himself in Negroland.'[46] By 1775 half the population of Minas Gerais were slaves.[47] Reasonably reliable official statistics for 1817–18 gave Brazil's slave population as 1,930,000, or about half the colony's total population of 3,817,900,[48] and in 1819, according to an unofficial contemporary estimate, no region of Brazil had fewer than 27 per cent of slaves in its population.[49] Clarke Abel (1780–1826), an English botanist who visited Rio de Janeiro in 1816, reported that 'a stranger unacquainted with the slave-trade ... might imagine that the slaves were its proper inhabitants, and their masters its casual dwellers';[50] Otto von Kotzebue (c. 1787–1846), a captain in the Russian imperial navy who visited the city seven years later, was another who testified that 'the blacks are so numerous, that one might fancy oneself in Africa'.[51] By 1849 there were more than 78,000 slaves living and working in Rio, out of a total population of 206,000, and 60 per cent of them were of African birth; this was the largest urban slave population in the Americas.[52] Visiting Recife in 1852, the English chemist Charles Blachford Mansfield (1819–55) reported that '[t]wo-thirds of the population seem to be naked Negroes, in cotton drawers; most of them are slaves'. The first thing that struck him about these slaves, he added, was 'the dignity and independent look which they preserve'.[53]

Though the Brazilian slave trade was outlawed in 1830 it was not stamped out until the 1850s: between 1831 and 1851 at least half a million slaves were illegally imported into Brazil from Africa,[54] and captive Africans were landed in Brazil as late as 1855.[55] Between 1851 and 1885 there was a massive inter-provincial slave trade: a forced internal migration by whose means a great number of slaves were transferred from the north-east to the coffee-producing states of Rio de Janeiro, São Paulo and Minas Gerais. It is reckoned that 'more than 400,000 slaves were victims of this traffic during those three decades'.[56] While slaves in Ceará and Amazonas were freed in 1884, and all slaves over the age of sixty in the following year, Brazil did not finally abolish slavery until 1888.[57] It was the last country in the western hemisphere to do so.

Africans from different culture areas had at first been distributed for the most part in different parts of Brazil. West Africans, including Moslems (Hausas, Mandings and Fulas) as well as Yorubas and Fon, ended up mainly in the north-eastern states of Bahia, Alagoas and Pernambuco – though there was also a nucleus of Yoruba culture, including descendants of people from the Òyọ empire, in Rio Grande do Sul.[58] People from Angola, Kongo[*] and Mozambique were also taken to Bahia and Pernambuco, but many of the slaves from those parts of Africa were sooner or later transferred to the states of Rio de Janeiro, São Paulo, Minas Gerais, Mato Grosso, Goiás and Alagoas, as well as the northern state of Pará. The distribution pattern changed steadily over the centuries; it changed more rapidly after emancipation, when there was an intensified drift to the cities, especially to Salvador and Rio de Janeiro in the late nineteenth and early twentieth centuries.[60] Until the late nineteenth century people of African descent in Brazil still traced their ancestry to various African *nações* (nations), but these were defined, as the ethnomusicologist Gerhard Kubik points out, by 'a curious assortment of African names which were not always ethnic'. 'Benguela', for instance, is not an ethnic group but an Angolan port from which many people from south-western Angola were shipped to Brazil. 'Angola', 'Benguela', 'Cambinda', 'Congo' and 'Monjolo' were in fact trademarks – 'labels with which the prospective buyer in Brazil associated certain qualities in appearance and character'.[61] According to José Honório Rodrigues,

> Imprecise geographical definitions prevent cultural classification of the African ethnic groups that populated Brazil. Modern classifications are based upon only modern data; the lack of decisive documents leaves the limits of the regions uncertain and prevents knowledge of the history of the cultural groups that here had intercourse with one another and with whites and Indians.[62]

This slightly overstates the case. Although between the sixteenth and nineteenth centuries the boundaries of many African polities were indeed imprecise, the boundaries of many ethnic groups still less precise, the distinction between Nigeria-Benin and Kongo-Angola culture areas in that period is quite

---

[*] I have adopted the practice now followed by many Africanists of spelling 'Kongo' thus when it refers to 'the traditional, unitary civilization and way of life of BaKongo peoples', and using 'Congo' to indicate 'the political shift that occurred with white colonial penetration and participation in Central Africa'.[59]

clear. And, in discussing the lineaments of African traditional music when it was transplanted to Brazil, this is the distinction that matters.

The African cultural heritage in Brazil

The fact that Brazilian challenge singing has a triple ancestry – African and Arab as well as Portuguese – is one indication that the African musical heritage in Brazil is not solely a question of African and African-derived musical instruments (though, as we shall see, there are many of those). Nor is it solely a question of the musical styles and functions which John Storm Roberts has called 'neo-African', 'with elements still totally or very largely African'[63] (though, as we shall see, this 'neo-African' layer is a living tradition in Brazil). Some, including many Brazilians, see no need for the prefix 'neo-'. A weekly class called simply 'African Dance', which my daughter was attending in Rio de Janeiro in 1994, turned out to be teaching pupils the sacred dances of the African-Brazilian candomblé religion (see Chapter 1). All the 'neo-' really signifies is that an African tradition is being carried forward, but not on African soil. And this is an aspect of their culture that Brazilians feel increasingly proud of.

It was not always so. In 1929 a Brazilian journalist could write of his great compatriot, the composer Heitor Villa-Lobos (1887–1959), that this 'propa-gandist degrades us in Paris by insinuating that we are a nation of black people, and that our art does not go beyond an African drunkenness'.[64] Half a century ago it was commonplace for a learned British writer on Brazilian music to dismiss the 'African element' in it as something that 'scarcely requires describing'; to assert that 'the African blood beats too loud to heed the significance of melodic thought'; to claim that 'the roots of Brazilian music are Portuguese'; even, almost unbelievably, to class the African-Brazilian *atabaque* drums, which are of the West African hollow-log type, as deriving from 'the Portuguese instrumental family'.[65] Another scholar, equally unable or unwilling to see what was before his eyes, stood things on their head in the 1950s by asserting that 'the outstanding role which Negroes play in the [Brazilian] *congadas* [see pp. 67–8] and *moçambiques* [see pp. 73–4] may have something to do with the Portuguese *dança dos Pretos* [black men's dance] wherein "men with blackened faces were dressed in red and hung with little bells"'.[66] Nowadays the African contribution is seen as a prominent and essential strand that can be traced throughout Brazilian popular music and dance and is in fact central to them. The African element has not merely enriched the whole of Brazilian popular music: it has decisively shaped it.

In this essentiality and centrality of its African element, Brazilian music is no different from any other part of Brazilian culture. African languages have made an immense contribution, and not solely in vocabulary, to the Portuguese spoken in Brazil.[67] The Brazilian diet was Africanised from early times.[68] The African presence in Brazil is prominent also in oral literature, children's games and the techniques of artisans. As early as the second half of the seventeenth century, the greatest of classical Portuguese prose writers, the essayist, preacher and missionary António Vieira (1608–97) – a man of mixed ethnicity who, born in Portugal, was educated in Brazil, joined the Jesuit order, and became a professor of theology before he was 30 – declared that 'Brazil has its body in America and its soul in Africa'.[69] And by the first half of the nineteenth century a Brazilian senator, Bernardo Pereira de Vasconcelos (1795–1850), had reached the conclusion that 'Africa has civilised America'.[70] In short, both people of European descent and many Amerindians in Brazil underwent 'a decisive Africanization of their cooking, dress, language, music, religion and folklore'.[71] Dancing and making music with Africans and their descendants, the 'lower classes' – low-paid Portuguese artisans and clerks – were the first to experience this acculturation. But by the second half of the eighteenth century it had spread to the middle and even the upper classes of the Portuguese colonists, many of whom, born in Brazil, already thought of themselves as Brazilians.

'Neo-African' music in Brazil

Within the 'neo-African' layer of traditional music in Brazil, in which European influence is either absent or negligible, five types and functions of music can be distinguished, of which one is now something of a 'neo-African' borderline case. The present book discusses each of these five types of 'neo-African' music in turn:

1) The music that is an essential component of various African-Brazilian religious ceremonies (Chapter 1). In the classical African-derived rituals known as candomblé the music is played on instruments of purest West African provenance, and many of the songs are sung in Yoruba or in the Fon language. Originally this was a music of resistance, whose primary function in the teeth of persecution was to keep Africa and African deities alive in the minds and hearts of captive Africans.

2) The music that is an essential component of the capoeira fighting game: songs, many of which include words in various languages of Angola, accompanied on an African-derived gourd-resonated single-string musical bow called *urucungo* or berimbau (in full, *berimbau de barriga*, 'belly-bow') (Chapter 2). This too was at first a music of resistance, which helped young African slaves in Brazil prepare for rebellion by clandestinely learning and practising fighting skills.

3) Worksongs and venders' street cries of various kinds (Chapter 3). Before Brazilian slaves were emancipated in 1888, their worksongs had several distinct resistance functions: they enabled the slaves to pace their labour to some extent; and those sung in African languages, as most were until well into the nineteenth century, often had a markedly satirical or political content or were used to transmit warnings, other signals, messages and news. The *jongo* riddle

songs in particular, sung both as worksongs in the fields and at *jongo* and *caxambu* dances, were songs of protest, phrased as a rule with considerable subtlety and ambiguity.

4) The music that accompanies certain dramatic dances (Chapter 4), to use the term coined by the great Brazilian musicologist Mário Raul de Moraes Andrade (1893–1945).[72] These are folk plays, or pageants, in which bygone customs or events are remembered or relived in song, dance and theatre. For the most part they represent a fusion of African and European traditions. One of these, known variously as *Congos* and *Congadas,* features the coronation of a Kongo king or queen or both. Another, the *Quilombo*, celebrates the free state of Palmares, a liberated area in the Brazilian interior held by fugitive slaves for almost the whole of the seventeenth century against incessant attacks. Yet another, though its precise origins are in dispute, bears the name *Moçambique*. And the best-known and most widely surviving of these dramatic dances, *Bumba-meu-boi*, is now known to have been 'created by African slaves in colonial Brazil ... to denounce and ridicule colonial slave owners'.[73]

In general, although the rhythmic patterns of the music accompanying these dramatic dances remain clearly African-derived, European musical structures and instruments are increasingly used. So from the strictly musical point of view these must now be called at best borderline examples of the 'neo-African' classification. However, the music of the most important dramatic dances, whether remembering and honouring Africa or Palmares, or condemning and satirising the Portuguese masters, was in its origins a music of resistance.

5) The music that accompanies various African-derived secular dances (Chapter 6), among them the dance from the Kongo-Angola culture area that was formerly often called *batuque* but is today generally known as samba, a word which has various meanings in a number of Angolan and other African languages. Different in many ways from the modern dance that has taken the name samba, the traditional African-Brazilian dance of that name varies in its choreography in different regions of Brazil. Celebrating and perpetuating African culture in captivity, these dances and the music that accompanied them were originally yet another expression of resistance.

Musical instruments of African provenance which are played in Brazil today are described where appropriate in the chapters summarised above, and three African instruments which came to Brazil but are no longer found there – the lamellophone, known in Brazil as the marimba; the pluriarc, or compound bow-lute; and the resonator xylophone, also called marimba in Brazil – have a chapter to themselves (Chapter 5). The first two of these originated in the Kongo-Angola culture area, continuity and change in whose music is the subject of Appendix A. Some other African musical instruments which migrated to Brazil, but are either not mentioned elsewhere in the book or are referred to only briefly, are listed in Appendix B.

Acculturated music in Brazil

As has been pointed out, the 'neo-African' layer by no means exhausts the African contribution to Brazilian music. The present book also discusses that portion of the African musical heritage which, through the acculturation process, has been central to Brazil's traditional and popular music and has had a marked influence on many composers of what Brazilians call 'erudite' music.

Fundamental to the acculturation process in Brazil was the widespread adoption and adaptation by Brazilians of European descent of two dances that originated in the Kongo-Angola region of Africa: the *batuque*, mentioned above, and the *lundu* (Chapter 7). By the early nineteenth century European visitors were referring to these as the national dances of Brazil. The *lundu* seems to have been a variant of the *batuque*, to some extent 'polished', Iberianised – it owed something, but by no means everything, to the Iberian fandango – and Atlanticised: it was the Luso-Brazilian form of a dance tradition carried round and round the Atlantic triangle and extremely popular among black people and white people alike in many parts of the New World, as well as in Portugal, from the sixteenth century onwards. As was stated above, two dances very similar to the *lundu* migrated from Brazil to Portugal: the *fofa* (Chapter 7 and Appendix E) and the fado (Chapter 7), which in Portugal became a song rather than a dance. The *lundu*, as both dance and song, was central to the emergence of distinctively Brazilian popular music in the eighteenth century (Chapter 8). Central also to this process was the *modinha*, a love song in which a European type of melody, transplanted to Brazil and written by Brazilian composers, was for the first time systematically syncopated. With the sung *lundu* and the *modinha*, African musical influence, however attenuated, entered the salon for the first time. A further major contribution to the emergence of Brazilian popular music was the widespread use of black musicians to provide entertainment, in town and country alike.

In the second half of the nineteenth century the Brazilian *lundu* merged with the imported polka and Cuban *habenera* to become the *maxixe*, a dance which was eventually re-Africanised as the modern urban samba, nowadays regarded as Brazil's national dance (Chapter 9).

Appendix C outlines the contribution of African-Brazilian resettlers to the music of Nigeria and Benin, and Appendix D gives a summary account of the music and dance of Cape Verde, that crossroads of the Atlantic.

The sources of Brazil's 'neo-African' music

'Neo-African' music heard in Brazil today shows stylistic traits that can be traced to two main areas of Africa: south-west Congo-Kinshasa and Angola; and south-west Nigeria and Benin, formerly known as Dahomey. (There are also stylistic traits which can be traced to Mozambique and to the Hausa and Manding of

West Africa, but these are less prominent.)[74] Why this musical predominance of the Kongo-Angola and Nigeria-Benin culture areas?

On the one hand, during the whole of the seventeenth century, as we have seen, Angolan arrivals in Brazil outnumbered everybody else. In Brazil – as in Cuba, Haiti, New Orleans and South Carolina – people from Kongo and Angola made up the majority culture among the African captives. They brought with them to Brazil 'a mixture of Kongo and Kongo-related cultures', which 'reinforced the more salient and important of shared general Bantu cultural traits. In this fusion, memory and grandeur and the name of Kongo itself were maintained'.[75]

On the other hand, Yoruba and Fon people had been the first on the scene. While Yoruba people from what is now Nigeria were scattered through vast areas of the New World, Salvador was their most significant, distinct and identifiable concentration, permitting unbroken religious and musical traditions.[76] There was a comparable though lesser concentration of Fon from Dahomey, and perpetuation of their traditions, in the northern port of São Luís de Maranhão. The most important drum rhythms of these two ethnic groups, used for summoning the gods, have been passed down unchanged in Brazil, from generation to generation, for some 450 years. It is this musical heritage from Nigeria and Benin that we examine first.

1

The Heritage of Nigeria and Benin: Music for Worship

African-derived religions in Brazil

The African-derived Brazilian religions have been called 'the main matrix of Afro-Brazilian identity',[1] and I refuse to belittle them with the disparaging term 'cults'. For they are not, as many suppose, a mere collection of superstitions; they furnish 'a coherent philosophy of man's fate and the cosmos'.[2] But they are not one homogeneous whole. They are an entire cluster of belief systems, differing in all sorts of detail from area to area and even from house of worship (*terreiro*) to house of worship within one and the same city – and in Salvador alone there are (or were in the early 1980s) over 900 registered houses, though many of them have departed from tradition in one way or another.[3] It had been estimated in 1942 that there were then 67 *terreiros* in the city, divided among 17 different *nações* (the average number of devotees per *terreiro* was put at 300).[4] Such a remarkable growth rate suggests that, together, the African-Brazilian faiths, in their various forms, must have constituted one of the world's fastest-growing religions for at least 40 years of the twentieth century.

These faiths have complete local independence, there being no central authority to co-ordinate their activities or to rule on tradition.[5] And they display varying degrees of syncretism with Roman Catholicism, to whose more flamboyant aspects they have proved highly receptive. At first, such syncretism had the purpose of camouflaging African forms of worship and thus limiting persecution by Roman Catholic priests and by police of what was for long a major focus of slave resistance and therefore a forbidden faith in Brazil,[6] prohibited as mere witchcraft and rendering its adherents liable to excommunication, refusal of communion, arrest and imprisonment. As Roger Bastide puts it: 'Originally the saints were merely white masks placed over the black faces of the ancestral deities ... [T]he whites had to be given the impression that the members of the 'nations' were good Catholics.'[7] In Brazil the African deities are called *orixás* (from Yoruba *òrìṣà*); each is identified with one or more Catholic saints,[8] each saint being essentially 'the Portuguese name of the *orixá*'.[9] These identifications are not at all consistent from area to area: in Salvador, for instance, Ogun, Yoruba god of iron and war (Ògún), is identified with St Anthony, in Rio de Janeiro and Recife with St George; in Salvador Oxóssi, Yoruba god of hunters (Ọ̀ṣọ́ọ̀sì), is identified with St George, in Rio with St Sebastian, in Belém not only with the latter saint but also with his sixteenth-century namesake King Sebastião of Portugal (1554–78). In both Salvador and Rio de Janeiro, the Yoruba arch-divinity Orixalá (Òrìṣàálá or Ọbàtálá), is identified with Our Lord of Bomfim (Jesus Christ). Each *orixá* is characterised by particular symbols: colours, songs, anecdotes, objects, animals, plants and atmospheric phenomena. And each devotee has a guardian *orixá* which he or she 'receives' while in trance.

It is impossible to draw hard-and-fast dividing lines between the various African-Brazilian religions, many of which are fluid and still evolving. There has been, and there still is, much borrowing and exchange of ritual and songs. The least affected by such borrowing and exchange is candomblé, which may be called the classical African-Brazilian religion. It is the one closest to Africa in language, pantheon, liturgy, musical instruments and musical styles. One widely accepted explanation of its name is that it combines three African words: *ka*, which in the Kimbundu language of Angola means 'custom'; *ndombe*, which in the same country's Kikongo language means 'a black person'; and *ilé*, the Yoruba word for 'house'. Together these give the meaning: 'house of black customs'. There is however an alternative, though similar, explanation: that it combines the word *candombe* (from Kimbundu *kanome*, a kind of drum dance, and a word still used in Uruguay) with Yoruba *ilé*.[10] In some ways candomblé resembles *vodoun* in Haiti, which is largely Dahomean (i.e. Fon);[11] but, being largely Yoruba, candomblé is still more closely paralled by *Santeria* (properly, *Regla de Ocha*) in Cuba,[12] especially by the Lucumi tradition, and by Shango in Trinidad.[13]

The latter takes its name from Ṣòngó, Yoruba deity of thunder and lightning, as does the *Xangô* tradition in Pernambuco, Alagoas and Sergipe, one of four regional variants in Brazil of the classical candomblé of Salvador. The earliest known picture of black musicians and dancers in Brazil (Fig. 1), dating from *c.* 1640, portrays what is probably a *Xangô* ceremony in Pernambuco. This watercolour was painted by the German traveller Zacharias Wagner or Wagener (1614–68), who lived in Brazil from 1634 to 1641, during the quarter-century (1630–54) of Dutch rule over the north-eastern part of the colony. It shows an orchestra of two drums and what appears to be a notched scraper. One of the participants in the counter-clockwise ring dance is shaking a tambourine. Wagner wrote of this 'Negro Dance':

> When the slaves have performed their very arduous task for a whole week they are allowed to do as they please on the Sunday. Usually they gather in certain places and, to the sound of pipes and drums, spend the entire day in disorderly dancing among themselves, men and women, children and old people, amidst continual drinking of a very sweet beverage called *Grape* [i.e. *garapa*]: they spend all the holy day dancing thus without stopping, frequently to the point where they no longer recognise each other, so deaf and drunk have they become.[14]

But what the seventeenth-century German observer interpreted as deafness and drunkenness was more probably the state of possession attained by devotees at the *Xangô* ceremony.[15] Although the last speakers of Yoruba in Recife died some fifty years ago, many of the songs in the *Xangô* ritual are still sung in that language. An important part of the ritual involves the washing of the devotees' heads with the juice of sacred leaves.[16]

Each of the other three regional variants of candomblé has a large admixture of Fon (Dahomean) beliefs and practices. One of these, in the northern state of Maranhão, is known as *casa das minas* or *tambor-de-mina*. In the state capital São Luís and the surrounding area there is an enclave of Fon influence. Here, besides a large number of Catholic saints, African deities known as *budus* or *voduns* are worshipped, one as Legba Bogui, others under such Brazilian names as Pedro Angaço and Maria Barbara.[17]

Another regional variant of candomblé is the highly syncretised *batuque* of Pará and Amazonas (not to be confused with the secular dance of the same name). Yoruba-derived, but with much Fon influence, this faith is said to have been taken to Belém around the beginning of the twentieth century from São Luís de Maranhão. Originally called *babaçuê* or *babassuê*, *batuque* admits Amerindian and vulgarised Roman Catholic elements, besides certain traditions which can be traced to the Iberian peninsula. African deities are here joined by

Figure 1 The earliest known picture of black dancers and musicians in Brazil, this watercolour by the German traveller Zacharias Wagner or Wagener, dating from *c.* 1634–41, depicts what is probably a *Xangô* ceremony in Pernambuco. There are two hand-beaten hollow-log drums of different sizes and what seems to be a notched scraper. (Thomas Thomsen, *Albert Eckhout ein niederländische Maler und sein Gönner Moritz der Brasilianer: Ein Kulturbild aus dem 17. Jahrhundert* Copenhagen, Levin & Munksgaard, 1938)

Amerindian spirits called *encantados*. Umbanda and, through umbanda, spiritism (both to be described later) have also had a major influence on *batuque* since the 1950s; in the past 50 years personages and rituals have been freely borrowed from the umbanda faith of Rio de Janeiro, and correspondingly greater emphasis has been placed on healing. *Batuque* rituals begin with a ceremony called *bater-cabeça* ('knocking the head'), in which devotees salute a food offering placed in the centre of the room by kneeling and touching their heads on the floor.[18]

Lastly, a variant of candomblé in the southern state of Rio Grande do Sul is also called *batuque* by outsiders, but devotees themselves call it *pará*. Far from Brazil's main centres of African settlement and therefore relatively isolated, *pará* retains in its pantheon some Dahomean deities little known in the northeast, such as Mawu and Aïdo Wëdo, the rainbow serpent.[19]

In one direction candomblé shades off into macumba. This fusion of Yoruba, Kongo-Angola, Roman Catholic and Amerindian influences is strongest in the states of Rio de Janeiro, Espírito Santo and São Paulo; its name, confusingly, is sometimes used as a synonym for candomblé or indeed for any African-Brazilian religion. Originally called *cabula*, macumba is a twentieth-century development reflecting 'a new social structure born of industrialisation and the rise of great sprawling cities after the First World War'.[20] In some areas the macumba deities have lost their African names: in the Espírito Santo city of Vitória, for instance, only the *exús* – incarnations of Exú (Yor. Èṣù), messenger

Figure 2 At this present-day candomblé ceremony in Brazil the three drums are each encircled with a band of coloured cloth, adorned with beads and shells, called *ojá*. A symbol of nurturing and care, this is the sash that Yoruba women tie around the waist to honour the gods and to carry a child against the mother's body. (Rogério Reis/Tyba Agência Fotográfica, Brazil)

of the gods, trickster, and guardian of crossroads and entrances – retain such names.[21] In Rio, on the other hand, according to Robert Farris Thompson, 'the ecstatic songs of the *macumba* cult ... are peppered with Ki-Kongo healing terms and phrases', and Kongo charms (*minkisi*) are called by such names as Zambi, Bumba and Lemba.[22]

In another direction candomblé shades off into umbanda, a tradition which emerged in the 1920s and is seen by some nowadays as Brazil's national religion. In the Kimbundu language the word *umbanda* means 'the art of healing' or 'traditional medicine' or, perhaps more precisely, 'to work positively with medicines', and Brazilian umbanda was originally a largely Angolan tradition but gradually came under Yoruba influence.[23] It also borrowed from astrology and from the 'spiritism' of the French engineer Allan Kardec (1804–69), who claimed that spirits had dictated his books to him, and whose teachings had begun to attract middle-class followers in Brazil in the 1860s. Umbanda adds to the African pantheon various Brazilian personages, notably the *pretos velhos* ('old black men'), whose names, such as Pai Kongo de Arunda and Pai Joaquim de Angola, sufficiently indicate their origins. These souls of dead Kongo-Angola slaves are portrayed in statues and statuettes as elderly pipe-smoking black men and are seen as the embodiment of meekness, wisdom, kindness and forgiveness, and the givers of good advice. There are female black elders, too, such as Maria Konga and Maria Kambinda. Umbanda's Pomba-Gira, wife of Exú, takes her name from the Kikongo expression *mpamba nzila* ('crossroads').[24]

In yet another direction candomblé shades off into *candomblé de caboclo*, whose pantheon includes Amerindian deities with names in the Tupí language or in Portuguese.[25] Variants of *candomblé de caboclo* include *catimbó* (or *catimbau*; originally *santidade*) in the north-eastern states and *pagelança* or *pajelança* in Piauí, Pará and Amazonas.[26] In 1977 the term *candomblé de caboclo* was said to be 'far less definite' than it had been 30 years before,[27] and in the subsequent 20-odd years it has no doubt become less definite still.

Little seems to be known about the *tambor-de-crioulo* of Maranhão, one of Brazil's least studied popular religions. It is said to show much Dahomean influence and to use hymns in the Portuguese language, 'with texts of an essentially secular nature', resembling in mood and structure the rural samba of São Paulo state (see p. 102).[28]

At the most obviously African end of this enormous and variegated spectrum – or perhaps I should say at its centre, where the closest linguistic, liturgical, musical and choreographic links with Africa are maintained – is what I have been calling the classical candomblé faith practised in the city of Salvador.[29] This comprises six distinct traditions, four of which derive from the Yoruba of Nigeria and Benin:

1) *The Nagô or Ketu tradition.* This is the candomblé ritual claiming the largest number of followers and includes songs sung in archaic Yoruba. Many people of Yoruba descent in Benin describe themselves by the Fon term Nago or Anago; Ketu refers to the ancient Yoruba kingdom of Kétu.

2) *The Ijexá tradition*. This ritual, too, includes songs sung in archaic Yoruba and takes its name from another ancient Yoruba kingdom: Ìjẹ̀sà.

3) *The Egba tradition*. This minor Yoruba ritual takes its name from the Yoruba sub-group known in Nigeria as Ègba.

4) *The Efan tradition*. Another minor Yoruba ritual, named after the Yoruba sub-group known in Nigeria as Èfòn.

5) *The Gêge (i.e. Ewe) tradition*. This derives from the Fon of Benin and includes songs sung in the Fon language, which is closely related to Ewe and is sometimes classified as one of its dialects.

6) *The Kongo-Angola tradition*. Known in Salvador and Rio de Janeiro as Angola, this ritual in fact borrows much from Yoruba practice.[30]

Of all the *orixás*, the one whose influence has spread most widely in Brazil is Yemanjá. A great many inhabitants of Rio de Janeiro throw flowers into the sea for her on the last night of each year, and many young Brazilian women of European descent will tell you: 'Eu sou uma filha de Yemanjá' ('I am a daughter of Yemanjá'), a statement which does not necessarily connote active participation in her rituals. She is Yẹmọnja, Yoruba goddess of waters both fresh and salt, from whose body flow all rivers and lagoons and the sea itself. At the same time she is an Angolan water spirit and is identified variously with Our Lady of the Conception and Our Lady of the Navigators; outside candomblé, her icons generally portray a young woman of decidedly Marian and European appearance. She also has something about her of the mermaid and the European water-sprite, though she does not wholly share the Lorelei's malevolence. Her dance represents the sea's tumbling movements, and she rustles her skirts to imitate the waves. She is Brazil's goddess of the sea.[31]

African-Brazilian religious music

In all African-Brazilian religious ceremonies, wherever they are located on this spectrum, music is of supreme importance. Its primary function is to summon the gods, and without it worship could not take place.[32] Three conical drums known collectively as *atabaques* are used in candomblé ceremonies: the largest, about 1.1 to 1.4 metres high, is called *rum* (Fon *hun*, and pronounced 'hum' in north-east Brazil) or *ilú* (Yor. *ìlù*); the medium-sized one is called *rumpi* (Fon *hunpevi*); and the smallest is called *lé*. As was said in the Introduction, these drums are of the West African hollow-log type, though nowadays in Brazil they are usually made from barrel staves. The largest drum has a head of deer- or calf-skin about 35 to 40 cm in diameter; goatskin is used for the other two. For Nagô (Ketu) and Gêge rhythms the drumheads are secured with pegs inserted in the body of the drum near the top and are struck with sticks (*oguidavis*, from Yor. *ò igi dá wiwọ*), usually made of hardwood. For Kongo-Angola and *caboclo* rhythms,[33] where the drums are struck with the hands, the drumheads are secured with cords fixed halfway down the drum to a skin-covered cord or hoop, held in place and tuned by wedges driven between it and the wood; thus secured, the drumheads are better able to withstand the heavy battering they receive.

The drums are treated with great reverence. They are 'baptised' soon after being made, with a godfather and godmother to sponsor them.[34] They are 'dressed', or encircled with a long band of coloured cloth, adorned with beads and shells, called *ojá* (Yor. *òjá*, the sash that Yoruba women tie around the waist, both for ornament and to honour the gods; it may also be used to suspend a child against the mother's body and is thus 'a sign of nurturing, care, and life'; in Salvador it decorates altars as well as drums).[35] To renew their power, the drums are 'fed', with chicken's blood, oil, honey and holy water, at an annual ceremony. The master drummer (*alabê*, from Yor. *alá agbè*) plays the largest drum; his part is relatively intricate, while the two smaller drums generally repeat a single steady rhythm. Though the drums are made by a cooper, the master drummer has to know how to repair them when necessary, and it is said that an *alabê* who cannot head a drum, or take it apart when it must be repaired, is unworthy of being a drummer.[36]

Two other traditional Yoruba instruments are also used in candomblé ceremonies. One is the *agogô* (Yor. *agogo*) or *gã* (Fon *ga*) clapperless double bell, which generally sets the fundamental pulse at the start of each song and seldom changes it in the course of a song; the *agogô* is struck with a metal stick. The other traditional instrument is the *aguê* (Yor. *agè*) or *xequerê* (Yor. *sèkèrè*) or *piano-de-cuia* (or, in Pernambuco, *obe* or *xere*). This is a rattle consisting of a large gourd containing cowries, pebbles, or dry seeds (*contas de Santa Maria* or *contas de Nossa Senhora*) and with a net covering made of cotton thread, to which shells, beads, or nuts are fixed at the intersections, acting as strikers when the gourd is shaken.[37]

The candomblé orchestra is a formidably complex percussion ensemble. It has at its disposal an enormous number of different rhythmic patterns, and the differences between them are often extremely subtle. Throughout candomblé ceremonies, as in similar ceremonies in Africa, Cuba, Haiti and Trinidad, there is a continuous exchange of energy between musicians and dancers, with the master drummer always in ultimate control. Sheila S. Walker has described this relationship in general terms, and what she writes about such ceremonies applies to some extent to candomblé:

> The dancers dance with great violence, energy, and concentration, getting really involved in the rhythm and movement ... The drummers ... can play certain signals in the rhythmic pattern to cause the dancing to take a violent turn ... One method is for one drum to syncopate the rhythm slightly (another one maintaining it) such that a strong beat falls just before the main beat ... This gives the impression of increased speed when this is not really the case, and creates tension and a feeling of imbalance in the listener or dancer.[38]

This is correct so far as it goes, but two observations should be made. First, the relationship between musicians and dancers in African and African-derived traditions is deeper than Walker suggests. It is a reciprocal relationship. As John Miller Chernoff puts it, 'A dancer *converses with* the music ... a dancer and an orchestra cut across each other's movements, as if the dancer is a part of the ensemble.'[39] Second, Walker alludes to only one aspect, and not a major one, of the master drummer's shaping of the rhythm in candomblé. His signals to the dancers determine not merely the pace of the dancing but also the arrival of the various deities. The master drummer is 'the mainspring of the ritual, its focal point'.[40] Cutting across the established beat with the rhythm of a particular *orixá*, he is able to trigger in the dancer's brain the learned response that expresses itself in the state of 'possession'. From that moment on, the dancer *is* the *orixá*, and behaves accordingly. He or she first salutes the drums, and is then dressed in the appropriate costume and handed the appropriate accoutrements: emblems, arms or ritual tools.

In some houses, if the summoned *orixás* are slow to arrive, a specially strong and supposedly irresistible fast-tempo rhythm called *adarrum* is played, invoking the entire pantheon at once. This can be heard on an LP containing Gerard Béhague's recordings of classical African-Brazilian drumming and singing at Salvador candomblé ceremonies, including several songs sung in Yoruba and Fon.[41]

Béhague's recordings reveal a rich texture of contrasting timbres arranged polyrhythmically, with five discernible strands: the deep-voiced *rum*; the other two drums, which for practical purposes can be considered as a single strand; the *agogô* bell; the male solo singer; and the female chorus. The singers make much use of call-and-response and of heterophony (i.e. different voices sing the same melody, but with individual variations). They accompany the drums rather than the other way round: from the musical point of view the drums are most important, though the song plays the leading role liturgically.[42] If you were to make a tape of the drumming used in present-day Nigeria to invoke, for instance, Òg̣ún, and intersperse it with the song to Ogun heard on Béhague's LP, moving backwards and forwards between them, you would find that there is no difference at all in the invocation played by the master drummer; whatever else has changed in African-Brazilian musical practice, the rhythms associated with particular African deities have stayed exactly the same, after anything up to fifteen generations.[43] It is thought that the specific drum pattern used to summon each deity was originally a rendering of a 'praise name': an expanded version of the deity's name in Yoruba, which is a tonal language.[44]

Alan P. Merriam has studied Nagô songs in detail. Two-thirds of them use the pentatonic (five-note) scale. All are in call-and-response form – the most common structural device in African traditional music – with slight overlapping between leader and chorus in more than half the songs studied. There is consistent anticipation of the established pulse by a fraction of a beat, the singer reaching the final note of the phrase slightly ahead of the expected arrival, giving the whole line a 'rushed' feeling. The melody accent normally falls between the percussion beats. To heighten the interest of the melodic line, entire phrases are sometimes moved forward or back by as much as half a beat or an entire beat. About half the songs repeat the same phrase with significant variation; the rest use contrasting phrases. Three ornamental devices are used: rising attack, where the singer starts below the proper note and rises to it in a short glissando; falling release, where the singer lets the final note fall downwards in a short glissando; and portamento, where the singer slides the voice from note to note without gaps.[45] Gerard Béhague points out that melodic intervals in classical candomblé singing are often quite large, and that where there is call-and-response the melodic phrases tend to be quite short, though in solo songs the melodic line lengthens and becomes more complex. He adds that singing styles 'are essentially similar to the relaxed, open manner of singing common in West Africa. Female voices present a characteristically hard, metallic quality, with a preference for the upper range of the voice'. Falsetto however 'is not as common nowadays as it used to be'.[46]

Melville Herskovits and R. A. Waterman, analysing 21 Gêge songs, found a tendency to vary between the minor and major third of the scale, and sometimes to sing a note between the two, a practice which calls to mind the use of so-called 'blue notes' in African-American blues.[47]

The music of *Xangô* has two distinctive features. First, the conical *atabaques* of Salvador are less commonly used. In the older Recife houses there can still be heard a trio of *batá* (Yor. *bàtá*) drums, such as are also played in Cuba and were formerly believed to have fallen out of use in Brazil. Played on the musician's lap, these two-headed drums are almost goblet-shaped, with goatskin heads wrapped round hoops and fixed in place by cords or leather thongs laced tightly between the hoops. More widely used are barrel-shaped two-headed drums called *ilús*, played with wooden sticks, and single-headed hand-played drums called *ingomba* (or *ingome* or *ingone*; cf. Kimbundu *mungumba* and *ngoma*, both meaning 'drum', as well as the now famous stick-beaten *ingoma* drums of Burundi, 25 of which are played at a time). Second, there is a striking contrast between the style of the songs dedicated to the older *orixás*, Orixalá and Yemanjá, and those sung for the younger ones: the former are markedly melismatic (i.e. a single syllable is spread over several notes), while the latter are for the most part syllabic.[48] A piece of *Xangô* music recorded in Recife in 1938 has recently become available.[49] It is a song cycle for the *orixá* Euá (or Ewá), a river deity from south-western Nigeria, who in Recife seems to be a local avatar of Yemanjá. The singers are accompanied by three *ingomba* drums, an *agogô* double bell, and a *xere* shaker. Four *Xangô* songs recorded in Ceará in 1943, accompanied by an unspecified drum, *cuíca* friction drum, shaker, and *gonguê* iron bell, have also been issued recently.[50]

Dr Morton Marks has recorded the music used in *batuque*, the syncretised African-Brazilian religion practised in the northern states of Pará and Amazonas.[51] A large hollow-log drum known as *carimbó*, with deerskin head, can be heard; it is used, too, in the Pará dance of the same name, also recorded by Dr Marks, as is a song for Yemanjá. This beautiful song, which diffused to Belém from the Nagô houses of Salvador, is sung in Yoruba; the *batuque* drummers do not, however, try to reproduce Nagô drumming style but play it in their own way. Now also available is a 1938 recording of a *babaçuê* song for the spirit Doçu, accompanied by three drums (an *abadão* and two *abatás*).[52]

In the *casa das minas* or *tambor-de-mina* of Maranhão, where the master drummer bears the title *run-tó*, three drums are used: *hum*, *gumpli*, and *humpli*. The latter, the smallest, is played with two sticks, the others with stick and hand. A *ferrinho* triangle and a shaker are also used. There are dances in honour of the musicians, and the devotees give them small presents. When a devotee dies, a special drum lament (*sirrum* or *sihun*) is performed, and gourds and jars, associated with the world of the dead, are used as musical instruments.[53] Recordings made in 1938 of five *casa das minas* songs have recently been issued.[54]

Two drums only, not three, are generally used in the *pará* of Rio Grande do Sul. Called *iniam* and *yabaniam*, these are smaller than the *atabaques* of Bahia and are played on the lap.[55] They are barrel-shaped, with a head at either end, the heads being held in place not by pegs but by strips of leather laced diagonally the length of the drum. Rattles and gongs are also played. Melville Herskovits heard songs in Pôrto Alegre that were 'in the striking Dahomean musical style seldom encountered in the North':

> The outstanding characteristic of Dahomean music is its use of the falsetto, and this was specifically named as such by one singer, who, contrasting it with Oyo [Yoruba] music[,] said that while Dahomean songs are more easily remembered, they are harder to sing; that is, while they are 'without the cadenzas' the Oyo songs have, their falsetto 'tears the throat'.[56]

The music of macumba and umbanda has been less studied than that of Bahian candomblé and its variants in the north and south of Brazil. Judging by available recordings, macumba music is consistent with ritual practice in showing varying degrees of acculturation.[57] Much umbanda music is hardly less eclectic than the tradition's beliefs and practices. With *chocalho* rattles, *reco-reco* notched bamboo scrapers, and even guitars added to – or, more and more, replacing – *atabaque* drums and *agogô* double bells, umbanda music has taken the acculturation process further still, and is said to resemble modern samba music, with rarely any use of hemiola (i.e. a pulse structure where duple and triple rhythmic divisions alternate).[58] This tendency is less evident, however, in the most easily accessible umbanda singing, recorded by Dr Morton Marks in Belém in 1975. His remarkable recording of an umbanda 'possession sequence' includes a trumpet fanfare greeting the arrival of the personage who is at once Oxóssi, St Sebastian and King Sebastião.[59] Umbanda songs, unlike those in candomblé, use a placement of the voice that 'tends to follow that of

Luso-Brazilian folk traditions, with an occasional use of vibrato', while soloists like to use 'a ringing voice'. Umbanda songs have a characteristically short melodic range, often using smooth, conjunct motion. Heterophony is often heard but consists mainly of parallel thirds at the end of choral phrases.[60] Some umbanda houses have abandoned all percussion except for handclapping.[61]

The Maranhão *tambor-de-crioulo* is said to resemble the *casa das minas* of that state in using an orchestra of three drums, a gourd rattle and a triangle. The dancers make periodical rotations (*gingas*) as they dance counter-clockwise, and we shall meet these spinning figures again in a Rio funeral procession (see p. 48) and in the *Boi de Zabumba* dramatic dance (see p. 76).[62]

Candomblé and carnival

Brazil imported carnival from Europe in the nineteenth century to replace the old Portuguese-derived *entrudo*. In this revelry, held on the three days starting on the Sunday before Ash Wednesday, people threw wax water-bombs and dust at each other and sprayed water at each other with large syringes. Banned in 1853, *entrudo* is said to have 'withered away' by the 1860s, and for some 20 years carnival was largely the preserve of parading societies.[63] The European accretions – masked balls modelled on those of Paris, first staged in 1846, then, somewhat later, parades imitating the royal courts of Europe – were intended as a sign of *civilidade*: politeness, breeding, good manners. But from the 1880s carnival was in a sense an annual battlefield. Especially after emancipation in 1888, the black population of Salvador and other cities insisted on celebrating carnival in their own, highly African, way, by dancing and singing through the streets as they had done for generations, with bands known as *charangas* playing candomblé instruments: *atabaque* drums, *agogô* double bells, and *aguê* (*xequerê*) large gourd shakers. The rich saw black people enjoying themselves in their own way as anything but polite, well bred or well mannered. There were protests in the newspapers about unseemly black participation in the Salvador carnival. In 1901 an incensed citizen wrote as follows to a leading newspaper:

> I refer to the great festival of Carnival and to the abuse which has been introduced with the presentation of masks that are badly made, filthy and even ragged [*maltrapilhos*], and also to the way in which this great festival of civilisation has been Africanised amongst us … The authorities ought to prohibit these *batuques* and candomblés which litter [*alastram*] the streets in abundance, producing this enormous uproar [*baralhuda*] … since all this is incompatible with our state of civilisation.

Three days later, a supporting letter complained that 'Africanised' carnival groups 'debase the name of Bahia with these irksome and tasteless displays' (*esses espetáculos incômodos e sensaborões*).[64] These protests seem to have had some success. Between 1905 and 1914 'the exhibition of Negro costumes with *batuques'* was banned.[65] But the anxiety-makers were not satisfied. A newspaper expressed horror in 1913 at 'young people of both sexes practically wrestling in the middle of the street, without modesty or shame, in the most scandalous contact, without distinction of race, colour, or education'.[66]

But it was not so easy to take the streets away from black people in Brazil. And one of their responses was the creation of *afoxés* (Yor. *àfọṣe*, 'priest who can foretell the future'): semi-religious carnival groups composed of candomblé devotees wearing white tunics of West African style and singing songs in Yoruba. This 'street candomblé', as the *afoxé* movement has been called,[67] took shape in Salvador in the 1920s. In the following decade there were *afoxés* in the city with such names as Otum Obá de África, A Folia Africana ('African Merry-making'), A Lembrança Africana ('African Remembrance'), Lutadores de África ('Fighters of Africa') and Congos de África.

In the mid-1970s an African-Brazilian cultural movement arose in Salvador which found its first expression in the revival of the *afoxé* movement and the emergence of new *afoxés*. The oldest then existing *afoxé*, Filhos de Gandhi, had been formed in 1949 by stevedores on the Salvador docks, candomblé devotees. Now it was joined by Badauê, Oju Obá, Olori, and other groups. The upsurge of the *afoxé* movement in the 1970s began a new stage in the re-Africanisation of the Salvador carnival and led to the formation of a number of parading groups (*blocos afro*) which consciously sought to re-Africanise their music. The first of these, Ilê Aiyê ('House of Life') was founded in 1974, in the Salvador working-class district of Liberdade. In Larry N. Crook's words, it 'touched a nerve deep in the Brazilian psyche' by focusing on black identity and thus refuting 'the myth of Brazil as a racial democracy'. For five years this was the only *bloco afro* in Salvador, and each year it paid homage to a single African country or ethnic group. Although its costumes, lyrics, and music were 'not always geographically, historically, or stylistically authentic', they captured people's imagination:

> Rather than a romanticized return to an idealized 'tribal' Africa or a frozen folkloric Africanity, this process [of re-Africanisation] involved the reinvention of Africa and the construction of a socially engaged image of Brazilian identity that celebrated African heritage and black distinctiveness but ... was rooted in the social, cultural, and economic realities of blacks in contemporary Brazil.[68]

Or, as Ilê Aiyê's president put it, 'We are rewriting history from our point of view and not from the colonisers' point of view.'[69]

In 1979 former members of Ilê Aiyê founded Grupo Olodum in the Pelourinho district of Salvador. Malê Debalê was formed in Itapuã in the same year; Ara Ketu in Periperi in 1980; and Muzenza in Liberdade in 1981. Of the new *blocos afro* Olodum emerged as musically the most powerful. This was a consciously innovative group, whose creative innovations were widely copied. From 1986 it mixed candomblé rhythms – notably those of the *Ijexá* tradition – as well as *salsa*, *merengue* and reggae rhythms, into the basic samba beat. The new drumming patterns were called *música-afro*, *afro-primitivo* and, later, *samba reggae* – though one percussionist at least, Ubaldo Waru, took the view that the new rhythms were not in fact a fusion of samba and reggae but a mixture of various African rhythms, to which samba and reggae are both heirs.[70] Instead of thick wooden drumsticks Grupo Olodum used thin, flexible switches, 'giving the drums a sharp attack and a crackling timbre'. And they borrowed from the popular music of Cuba and Puerto Rico a set of three *timbales* – drums tuned like bongos, and not unlike them in timbre. This eclectic, assertive and compelling music soon became 'a force of resistance and source of self-confidence'. In 1988 *blocos afro* helped persuade thousands of Bahians to turn their backs on the official celebrations of the centenary of abolition. By now there were about 40 *blocos afro* in Salvador,[71] and many similar groups had sprung up in São Paulo, Rio de Janeiro, Recife and other cities. And this, as Crook makes clear, was a musical and political force to be reckoned with.[72]

Figure 3 The outstanding musical result of the re-Africanisation of Salvador carnival has been the new importance attached to drums, which reaffirm and continue a centuries-old African-Brazilian rhythmic tradition. *Blocos afro*, some of which mix candomblé rhythms into the basic samba beat, are both source and symbol of black pride and self-confidence. The group shown here is Olodum.
(Jeremy Horner/Panos Pictures)

Though candomblé has not been the only factor in this re-Africanisation of carnival, its importance should not be underestimated. Of the 23 *afoxés* which took part in the 1983 Salvador carnival, writes Daniel J. Crowley,

> fourteen had as their themes subjects derived directly from Candomblé ... Their younger female parallel, Filhas de Gandhi, chose as subject the local Candomblé ritual of washing the steps of the Bonfim Pilgrimage Church which takes place in early February ... Of the nine remaining groups, the theme of one was about Candomblé ..., four were about Africa and enslavement, and two were about Black liberation in Brazilian history ...
> Blocos Afro ... differ somewhat from *afoxés* in their greater freedom of organization and variety of costumes ... The largest Blocos Afro are even more spectacular than *afoxés* in their costume and float design and in the wider range of their themes: not only African nationalism and identity, the Black experience in Brazil, Black racial solidarity, pleas for better racial integration in Brazil, and a certain consciousness of Black political and cultural achievements in the Caribbean and the United States.[73]

The most important musical result of the re-Africanisation of carnival in Salvador has been the way drums have acquired a new dignity and a new importance there; this is of course also a political result. As Goli Guerreiro puts it:

> Drums acquire in this context an unsuspected status, through the expansion of their use and through the validation [*valorização*] of the player, since from 'drummer' [*batuqueiro*] he has turned into 'percussionist' – and this is not just a matter of semantics. There is no doubt that the rise of *blocos afro* and of Olodum in particular – which, through the use of Pan-Africanist colours, has made each drum a banner of Negritude – was basic in acquiring not only affection for, but also pride in handling, an instrument which has become an Afro-Brazilian symbol, which reveals and reaffirms a rhythmic tradition.[74]

When the ethnomusicologist Gerhard Kubik visited Salvador in 1975, in the company of the Malaŵi musician Donald Kachamba, they attended a candomblé ceremony together. The next day, hearing the music of samba street bands, Kachamba exclaimed: 'Now Nigeria is finished; we are in Angola.'[75] How could he tell? Candomblé has a twelve-pulse time-line pattern, the rhythmic 'backbone', as it were, that is characteristic of much West African music.[76] Street samba in Salvador and Rio de Janeiro has a sixteen-pulse time-line pattern, such as is commonly found in the music of the Kongo-Angola culture area. An important part of the Angolan heritage in Brazil, the martial art, sport, performance, ritual and drama known as capoeira, is the subject of the next chapter.

2

The Angolan Heritage:
Capoeira and Berimbau

Training for resistance

Very different from the African-Brazilian religious music described in the previous chapter is the music which accompanies the capoeira fighting game in Brazil. Capoeira is a martial art, providing a complete system of self-defence. It is also a sport. With its 'dancelike, acrobatic movement style' and its songs accompanied on the *berimbau de barriga* gourd-resonated single-string musical bow (usually known simply as berimbau) and often on various other instruments too, it is also 'a kind of performance'. Nor is this all: it is ritual and drama besides, and has been described as a *'theater of liberation'*. And each of these essential aspects 'comes to the fore at various moments during a typical event'.[1]

The tradition of training for a war of resistance in Angola dated from the first arrival of the Portuguese in the late fifteenth century.[2] And originally, accompanied by drums and handclapping, capoeira continued this tradition: it was a means whereby young black men in Brazil could learn and practise fighting skills in preparation for insurrection or guerrilla warfare against their oppressors. This early stage in the development of capoeira was illustrated by the German artist Johann Moritz Rugendas (1802–58) during his first visit to Brazil in 1821–25. He titled his picture 'Jogar Capoëra ou danse de la guerre' (Fig. 4).[3] This picture of a 'war dance' shows two young men who at first glance seem to be squaring up to each other, while a musician sits astride a cylindrical drum whose skin he beats with his hands. On closer inspection however the protagonists are also clearly dancing, as are two of the spectators, one of whom is also clapping the rhythm. This ambiguity is at the very heart of the 'capoeira game'.

According to Rugendas there were in fact two kinds of 'military dance' among black men in Brazil in the early nineteenth century. In the first variant, which seems to have closely resembled the *calenda* (or *calinda*) stick-fighting dance of Trinidad,[4] two groups armed with sticks stood face to face, and the object was to dodge the opponent's thrusts. From this may have evolved the present-day Bahian fighting game called *maculêlê*, practised with sticks but played in earnest with matchets that emit showers of sparks as the steel blades clash, and said to resemble both initiation ceremonies in Angola and a sham stick-fight by men recorded in 1965 among the Ngumbi of south-western Angola.[5] Rugendas describes the second variant thus:

> The Negroes have another, much fiercer, war game, the *Jogar capoera*: two champions rush at each other, each trying to strike with his head the chest of the opponent he is aiming to knock down. The attack is thwarted by leaping sideways or by equally skilful parrying; but in springing at each other, pretty much like goats, they now and again butt each other's heads very roughly; so one often sees jesting give place to anger, with the result that the sport is made bloody with blows and even with knives.[6]

JOGAR CAPOÉRA
ou danse de la guerre.

Figure 4 Dance or fight? Capoeira is both – and performance, ritual and drama besides. In slavery days it prepared young black men in Brazil for insurrection or guerrilla warfare against the Portuguese colonists. Rugendas shows capoeira accompanied by a drum in the 1820s, before the berimbau gourd-resonated musical bow became its chief accompaniment. (Moritz Rugendas, *Malerische Reise in Brasilien* Paris, Engelman; Mülhausen, Ober-Rheinisches Dept; 1835)

The unpaid – and on this matter uninformed – British vice-consul in Salvador, James Wetherell (1822–58), wrote in 1856:

> Negroes fighting with their open hands is a frequent scene in the lower city. They seldom come to blows, or at least sufficient to cause any serious damage. A kick on the shins is about the most painful knock they give each other. They are full of action, capering and throwing their legs about like monkeys during their quarrels. It is a ludicrous sight.[7]

These references to 'fighting with ... open hands' and 'capering and throwing ... legs about' point unerringly to capoeira.

What Rugendas and Wetherell give us are of course merely outsiders' impressions. It is clear from J. Lowell Lewis's illuminating and enthralling account by a self-styled 'semi-insider'[8] (*Ring of Liberation*, 1992) that one of capoeira's chief functions is precisely to teach young men how to control their anger, whatever the provocation:

> [C]apoeira teachers say that one should play with a 'cool head' ..., which may be the survival of [an] African value ... [S]uperior emotional control is an example of a kind of one-upmanship available to the slave, through which he could demonstrate his power over the master by making him angry and frustrated while the slave smiled inwardly.[9]

Yet the essence of capoeira lies not in keeping cool, important though that is, but in the appropriate and quick-witted use of *malícia*. This is not to be understood as malice but rather as cunning, 'a lesson learned in slavery but still valuable in the modern world'.[10] In capoeira, being cunning entails deceiving the expectations of the onlookers as well as of one's opponent. And that includes being able both to feign anger and to throw off the pretence at the appropriate moment.

In Salvador and Rio de Janeiro there is a simplified variant of capoeira, known variously as *pernada*, *batuque*, *batuque-boi* and *banda*.[11] In Recife there is a modified, more individualistic, form of capoeira called *passo,* from which developed *frevo*, a frenetic, improvisatory and often comical carnival dance in which the participants carry open umbrellas.[12] Besides the Trinidad *calenda*, analogues of capoeira elsewhere in the New World include the Martinique martial art called *ladjia* in the south of the island, *damié* in the north; its sister martial art in Guadeloupe, called *chat'ou*;[13] the Cuban martial art known as *maní* or *Bombosá*, which may have died out;[14] a martial art known as 'knocking and kicking', reported from the Sea Islands off Georgia and South Carolina;[15] and *broma*, a martial art practised by black men in Venezuela.[16]

The primary meaning of the word *capoeira* in Portuguese is 'large chicken coop', and it probably served Angolans in Brazil as a code word for their clandestine military training. There are similar-sounding words in Angolan languages: two possible sources, not necessarily mutually exclusive, are

Umbundu *kupwila* ('to rush headlong into, to cause to fall') and Kimbundu *kapwela* ('to clap hands').[17] Kubik comments:

> If *capoeira* is indeed an Angolan word its coincidental phonemical identity with the Portuguese word meaning 'chicken coop' could have been accepted by the freedom fighters with a great laugh. In this case they could speak the word into the White Man's face and enjoy the fact that he was only able to know the stupid meaning it had in his own language, unable to discover what it meant to the Angolans in Brazil.[18]

Though capoeira seems to have evolved into its present form in Brazil, many of its elements are clearly of African origin. For instance, the money game, where *capoeiristas* bend over backwards to pick up coins or notes from the ground with their lips, is identical to an acrobatic initiation ritual among the Makonde of Mozambique and coastal Tanzania.[19] Again, there is a capoeira 'flourish' called *relógio* ('clock'), where the player tucks his elbow into his side and spins his whole body on one hand, moving like the hand of a clock; similar figures are seen in several Mozambique dances.[20] Acrobatic dances are part of male initiation ceremonies in many African ethnic groups. Several writers have noted striking similarities between capoeira and the *ngolo* zebra dance of the Mucope of Angola, who live near Luanda, and there is an oral tradition in Salvador according to which capoeira originated in just such an Angolan dance. A painting of the *ngolo* dance is proudly displayed on the wall of the Salvador building where a prominent local capoeira group works and plays.[21] Lewis calls attention also to a young men's dance among the Kuanyama Ambo – many of whom used to live in south Angola but moved south about 85 years ago to what is now Namibia – where the dancers jump out from their group and kick as high into the air as possible, to the admiration of the young women.[22] The traditional form of capoeira is properly called *capoeira Angola*, as opposed to the modified *capoeira regional*, and it uses many Angolan words in its songs.

But nowadays capoeira is by no means practised only by Brazilians of African descent. It has become part of general Brazilian culture. This was brought home to me when I spent a day in the Rio de Janeiro suburb of Niterói with some friends of my daughter; after lunch, the teenage son and daughter of this middle-class family of European descent, knowing of my interest in capoeira, asked if I would like to see them perform it – or play it, for, as has been said, it is sport as well as performance. So they pushed back the furniture, put on a tape of berimbau music, and danced capoeira with immense grace and skill. They were attending a capoeira school on Saturday mornings, where they and scores of other young people in Niterói were learning to play both berimbau and capoeira. Nor is this a wholly new phenomenon: white people's participation in capoeira over the past hundred years or so has helped to check persecution and establish the practice as part of Brazilian national culture.[23]

Present-day *capoeiristas* indeed display a marked generosity and hospitality to all those from outside Bahian culture, including foreigners, who sincerely want to learn and master capoeira. Nowhere has this acceptance been more instructively described than in the story J. Lowell Lewis tells about himself in the preface to *Ring of Liberation*. It happened in the Bahian town of Santo Amero de Purificação, during a contest between an expert player, *Mestre* Nô, and a former pupil of his, Braulio, now himself a *mestre*:

> Even though the masters had paused several times to find their wind, they were demonstrating extreme endurance given the intensity of their struggle and the difficulty of their moves ... Experts and casual observers alike were fascinated with the variety of attacks and defenses, the beautiful yet deadly moves these two could improvise, and everyone wanted to see the resolution ... [T]he audience had thrown quite a bit of paper money into the ring. If the players chose to, they could begin a variation of the game by competing to pick up the money, thereby claiming it for themselves. So far ... they had been ignoring the money ...
>
> I myself was a fledgling player, a student of the older master for some months ...
>
> Without warning, Braulio did a cartwheel into the center ... and picked up the pile of money with his mouth ... The crowd exploded with laughter and approval ...
>
> After some negotiations, Braulio was convinced to return the money to the center of the ring and the game was restarted ... As they crouched there, *Mestre* Nô suddenly leaped backwards into a double backflip, lowering himself on the second revolution to pick up the money in *his* mouth. He came to rest on his haunches, mouth stuffed with bills, looking like the cat who ate the canary. This time it was Braulio's turn to look sheepish as the crowd laughed approvingly. Excited and moved by this inspired trickery, without stopping to consider the consequences, I burst into song:

s[olo]:	ô me dá o meu dinheiro	oh give me my money,
	ô me dá o meu dinheiro	oh give me my money,
	valentão	tough guy,
	ô me dá o meu dinheiro	oh give me my money,
	valentão	tough guy,
	porque no meu dinheiro	because on my money
	ninguém ponhe a mão	nobody puts a hand

As I started singing, many of the players looked up to see who it was, especially since I obviously had a foreign accent. Although it is accepted for anyone to join in on a chorus in capoeira singing, even audience members who are not participating in the physical contest, usually only masters or respected senior players initiate songs, since the soloist must carry the song, giving a clear indication of pitch and rhythm. Therefore as I was ending the verse I became quite nervous as I realized what I had done. Would anyone respond to my call, or would they all keep silent, a snub to the pretentious foreign novice who dared to interfere in the creation of this exceptional game?

It was with relief and thankfulness, then, that I heard a full chorus come in on the refrain:

c[horus]:   ô me dá o meu dinheiro   oh give me my money,
            ô me dá o meu dinheiro   oh give me my money,
            valentão   tough guy

I didn't try to continue the song for more than a few repetitions, since I realized that I only knew that one solo verse, but as I sang I understood that the reason the chorus had responded enthusiastically was that I had done the most important thing right. I had chosen an appropriate song to capture that moment in the game, to highlight the action and allow the audience and players a chance to express their delight in the quality of play.[24]

This anecdote illustrates the supreme importance of music in capoeira. But still more important than the songs commenting on the action is the accompaniment provided on the berimbau, which is played throughout every contest.

African prototypes of the berimbau

A learned Frenchman once said loftily that the berimbau 'could well be "antediluvian"'.[25] Those who regard it as a 'primitive' instrument should try playing it. In an expert player's hands it is capable of nuances which call for high skill and dedication. Properly called *urucungo* or *berimbau de barriga* (belly bow)[26] – to distinguish it from the *berimbau de boca* (mouth bow, for which see p. 168) and *berimbau de bacia* (basin bow, for which see p. 168–9) – it consists of a braced bow with a single string made from steel wire (in colonial times cord twisted from plant fibre was used).[27] The string is struck with a little stick (*vaqueta* or *vareta*), and the player has a small plaited rattle (*caxixi*) suspended from one finger of the playing hand. A gourd resonator is tied to the bow, and the player obtains subtle changes in timbre by pressing the open end of the gourd against chest or stomach at various angles and with various degrees of pressure, as well as by varying the distance between the body and the opening of the gourd, thus reinforcing certain harmonics.[28] Further variations in timbre are obtained by striking the string at different heights. Most players prefer to perform shirtless, since clothing absorbs much of the sound. The berimbau has eight basic notes, and changes in pitch are obtained by stopping the string, formerly with a coin, nowadays generally with a coin-shaped device (*dobrão*, literally 'doubloon').

Just as the elements of capoeira are clearly of African origin, so the berimbau, though it has evolved to its present form in Brazil, clearly derives from various Angolan gourd-resonated single-string musical bows played with a thin cane stick. It has several notable precursors.

According to Gerhard Kubik, who has done fieldwork in both Angola and Brazil, the *mbulumbumba* bow used by the Ngumbi and Handa of south-western

Angola is 'virtually identical' to the berimbau, though it is slightly smaller.[29] It is made and tuned in the same way. And it is played in the same way: as with the berimbau, the musician produces 'floating, vibrato sounds' by slightly varying the pressure of the gourd against the chest and thus stressing certain harmonics.[30] Moreover, some of the basic patterns played are identical on both sides of the Atlantic, so that Bahian berimbau players, when Kubik played them tapes recorded in Angola, recognised and 'understood' what the Ngumbi musicians were doing. The only difference in playing practice is that 'the Angolans stopped the string with the *nail* of the thumb in a kind of pincer movement of thumb and index finger, while the Brazilians had adopted a coin instead'.[31] This bow is known in Cuba as *burumbumba*,[32] and an Angolan bow identified by that name was illustrated, with *marimba* xylophone and three-string *kissumba* pluriarc (compound bow-lute), in a travel book published in 1859.[33]

A broadly similar Angolan musical bow, the *humbo* or *hungi* of Luanda, was twice mentioned by the Portuguese traveller Ladislau Batalha (1856–c. 1939). In 1889 he wrote of it:

It generally consists of a half-calabash, hollow and well dried. It is bored in the middle at two adjacent points. They make separately a curved bow with a suitable string. They fasten the end of the bow to the calabash with a small piece of fibre string threaded through the two holes; then, leaning the instrument against the skin of the chest, which acts here as a sound-box, they make the bowstring vibrate by means of a small reed.[34]

In the following year Batalha told how he had heard one of these bows played by a 'big Negro' (*negralhão*); he described it as 'a kind of guitar with only one string, for which the artist's naked body serves as a sound-box'.[35] The *humbo*, which has been called a 'twin brother' of the berimbau,[36] has been documented in Peru as well as Brazil.[37] Among the Mbunda of south Angola, a similar bow is called *nhungo*.[38]

A third such bow, the *rucumbo*, found among the Kongo-speaking peoples along the Angola-Congo border, was described and illustrated in 1890 by a Portuguese writer who said of it:

This instrument is well known in our province of Angola. They take a stick of a particular pliable wood and bend it into a bow, joining the ends with a thick string which is made beforehand from cotton fibre and stays very taut. On the lower part of the bow is fixed a small gourd with an opening of a size calculated to secure good vibrations. This opening is turned outwards [*sic*] and the string goes above it.

The bow is held between the body and the left arm, using the left hand to hold it at the right height. Touching the string at different heights with a stick held in the right hand produces good sounds which recall those of a violin and are altogether pleasant. The Loandas [i.e. Lunda] call it *violâm* [guitar]. They play it when they walk around and also when they are lying in their huts. It is very handy and portable.[39]

According to José Redinha, the *rucumbo* musical bow is used not only by the Lunda but also by the Shinje and Mbangala of west central Angola.[40]

A similar bow, the *ombumbumba* of the Ovimbundu (Mbunda) of central Angola, was described and illustrated in 1934 by an American anthropologist who wrote of it: 'The player holds in his right hand a reed which is tapped lightly on the bowstring, while the thumb and forefinger of the left hand are used occasionally in pressing the string to alter its vibrating length.'[41] Yet another such bow, illustrated in a travel book published in 1881 and described and illustrated by Redinha, is the *oburububa* of the people of Benguela.[42]

One of these Angolan bows, or perhaps a different but certainly a very similar one, was described in 1875 (but not named) by Joachim Monteiro, a long-term resident in Angola, who wrote that it was

> made by stretching a thin string to a bent bow, about three feet long, passed through half a gourd, the open end of which rests against the performer's bare stomach. The string is struck with a thin slip of cane or palm-leaf stem held in the right hand, and a finger of the left, which holds the instrument, is laid occasionally on the string, and in this way, with occasional gentle blows of the open gourd against the stomach, very pleasing sounds and modulations are obtained.[43]

This description resembles the near-contemporary one by Herman Soyaux, who was in Angola between 1873 and 1876 and gave the name 'N-kungu' to the gourd-resonated bow he described:

> a string made of twisted plant fibres is stretched between the two ends of a gently-bowed sapling and drawn somewhat tighter near the thicker end by a thread acting as a sort of bridge. On the opposite, weaker end of the sapling however a gourd is fixed. The player holds the N-kungu upright in his left arm, so that the gourd rests on the left hip, and presses more or less firmly with the index finger of the left hand on the thread, while causing it to vibrate by means of a little stick held in the right hand.[44]

There is in Zimbabwe a musical bow, the Shona *chipendani*, which is said to be almost identical to the Brazilian berimbau.[45] Other broadly similar African bows, recorded in recent years, include the *makeyana* (or *umakweyana*) of the Swazi and Zulu of South Africa (where it is a women's instrument);[46] the *shitendé* (or *chitendé*) of the Chopi and Hlengwe of Mozambique;[47] the *munahi* of the Hutu of Rwanda;[48] the *umuduri* (or *umuduli*) of Burundi;[49] the *dienguela* of the Bisa of Burkina Faso;[50] and the *gingeli* (or *jinjelim*) of the Dagomba of Ghana.[51]

The berimbau in Brazil

From the rich store of Kongo-Angola prototypes there emerged in Brazil, in the course of the nineteenth century, the modern berimbau, rather bigger and rather louder than any of its predecessors. Those immediate predecessors in Brazil were described and illustrated several times. In 1813 Henry Koster (1793–*c.* 1820), the Portugal-born son of a Liverpool sugar dealer, heard one of them at Jaguaribe in the province of Ceará. It was one of the 'extremely rude' (i.e. crude) musical instruments played by the slaves. He described it as 'a large bow with one string, having half of a coco-nut shell or of a small gourd strung upon it. This is placed against the abdomen, and the string is struck with the finger, or with a small bit of wood'.[52]

The English visitor Lieutenant Henry Chamberlain (1796–1844), an artillery officer and amateur artist who spent time in Rio de Janeiro in 1819–20, left two pictures of the gourd-resonated single-string musical bow. Each shows a street vender playing a musical bow while carrying on his head a large covered basket. One of these pictures, dated 1819, is included in Chamberlain's album of colour aquatints, *Views and costumes of the city and neighbourhood of Rio de Janeiro* (1822). He calls the instrument *madimba lungungo*, a name quite close to two names it has it in parts of the Congo – *lungungu* (Mbala and Sonde) and *lukungo* (Luluwa, Mwanza, and Bapende)[53] – and refers to it as

> an African musical instrument in the shape of a bow, with a wire instead of a string. At the end where the bow is held is fixed an empty calabash or wooden bowl, which being placed against the naked stomach enables the performer to feel as well as to hear the music he is making. The manner of playing is very simple. The wire being well stretched, it is gently struck, producing a note, which is modulated by the fingers of the other hand pinching the wire in various places according to the fancy; its compass is very small, and the airs played upon it are few; they are generally accompanied by the performer with the voice, and and [*sic*] consist of ditties of his native country sung in his native language.[54]

Chamberlain's other picture showing the musical bow, a watercolour on paper entitled *Street Vendors*, is in the Museu de Arte de São Paulo.[55]

In his celebrated portrait of *L'Aveugle Chanteur* ('The Blind Singer', Fig. 5), the French artist Jean Baptiste Debret (1768–1848), who was in Brazil from 1816 to 1831, shows two musicians, one of whom is playing a musical bow with gourd resonator, the other a portable African lamellophone (US lamellaphone) with gourd resonator (for the lamellophone in Brazil, see Chapter 5). Debret also included in the second volume (1835) of his *Voyage pittoresque et historique au Brésil* (1834–39) a brief but closely observed account of what he correctly called the *oricongo*:

> This instrument consists of half a gourd attached to a bow formed by a curved stick with a stretched brass wire which is lightly struck.

The performer's aptitude for music is immediately apparent; with one hand he holds the gourd against his bare stomach so as to procure through resonance a deeper and more harmonious sound. The effect, at its best, is comparable only to the sound of a dulcimer string, since it is obtained by tapping lightly on the string with a small cane held between the index and middle fingers of the right hand.[56]

In about the year 1819 the Austrian botanist Johann Emanuel Pohl (1782–1834) heard the 'twanging' (*Geklimper*) of a 'simple string stretched on a bow and fixed to a hollowed-out gourd, yielding at most three notes';[57] he seems not to have been a very attentive listener, unlike the Englishwoman Maria Graham (1785–1842), later Lady Maria Callcott, who in 1822 heard what she called 'uncouth airs, played on rude African instruments' in Rio de Janeiro. She found these instruments 'the most inartificial things that ever gave out musical sounds', adding, 'yet they have not an unpleasing effect'. A musical bow, to

Figure 5 Debret's famous picture of a blind street-singer playing the berimbau gourd-resonated musical bow, *c.* 1816–31, shows also a musician playing a lamellophone with half-gourd resonator. Both instruments came to Brazil from Angola. (J[ean]. B[aptiste]. Debret, *Voyage pittoresque et historique au Brésil, ou Séjour d'un Artiste Français au Brésil depuis 1816 jusqu'en 1831 inclusivement*, Paris, Firmin Didot Frères, 1834–39)

which she gave no name, was 'simply composed of a crooked stick, a small hollow gourd, and a single string of brass wire. The mouth of the gourd must be placed on the naked skin of the side; so that the ribs of the player form the sounding-board, and the string is struck with a short stick.'[58]

Travelling through Minas Gerais in the late 1820s, an Irish clergyman, the Revd Robert Walsh (1772–1852), was having his breakfast at a place called Chepado do Mato – and was successfully resisting the landlady's efforts to make him wash it down with wine rather than coffee – when

> there stood in the hall a poor black minstrel boy, who played a very simple instrument. It consisted of a single string stretched on a bamboo, bent into an arc, or bow. Half a cocoa nut, with a loop at its apex, was laid on his breast on the concave side; the bow was thrust into this loop, while the minstrel struck it with a switch, moving his fingers up and down the wire at the same time. This produced three or four sweet notes, and was an accompaniment either to dancing or singing. He stood in the porch, and entertained us like a Welsh harper, while we were at breakfast, and he was so modest that when we praised his music, he actually blushed through his dusky cheeks. It was the first time that a branco, or white, had ever paid him such a compliment.[59]

The *caxixi* basket rattle is used as a separate instrument in the Kongo-Angola culture area. The Baluba people of Lunda call it *cassaca*, the Libolos *quissaca*. Containing small pebbles or dried seeds, it is used with other instruments to mark the beat in dances and songs.[60] But it is unknown in Africa as a permanent adjunct to the musical bow. It is thought to have been incorporated into the berimbau's playing technique in Brazil, though not until the mid-nineteenth century.[61] The earliest reference to it in this context that can be found was made by the British vice-consul James Wetherell in 1856, when he described the berimbau as follows:

> It is a long stick made into a bow by a thin wire, half a gourd to serve as a sounding board is attached to this bow by a loop, which, pushed up or down, slackens or tightens the wire. The bow is held in the left hand, the open part of the gourd pressed upon the body. Between the finger and thumb of the right hand is held a small stick with which the wire is struck, producing a tinkling sound; on the other fingers is hung a kind of rattle made of basket-work, confined in which are some small stones which are made to rattle as the hand moves to strike the string. A very monotonous sound is produced, but, as usual, seems to be much appreciated by the negroes.[62]

None of these early descriptions of the African-derived musical bow in Brazil associates it with capoeira. The French journalist Charles Ribeyrolles (1812–60), who reached Brazil in 1858, described capoeira as 'a kind of pyrrhic dance, with daring and combative manœuvres, to the sound of the Congo drum', and mentioned the *urucongo* only as an instrument accompanying the *batuque* dance (see pp. 95–102).[63] Kubik suggests that the berimbau was not incorporated into capoeira until about the end of the nineteenth century, and certainly not until after emancipation (1888), when 'what had been a systematic training for possible insurrection ... gradually became an acrobatic game'.[64]

Just as music plays a central role in the religious faiths described in the previous chapter, so music is essential to capoeira. 'There can be no capoeira without music', writes Lewis, adding, 'During a performance, there is an intimate interplay between the musicians and the contestants in the ring, a relation of interdependence.' As the nature of the contest changes, so the music must change; conversely, if the music changes 'the contestants should take note and respond in kind'.[65] Kathleen O'Connor puts it like this:

> The music guides and is guided by the play; it begins and ends the competition; it slows the game when players are in danger of losing their tempers; it speeds the game up if it lags; it pokes fun at a poorly executed move or a spoilsport; it lauds virtuosic or amusing play. To regard *capoeira* as merely a martial art ... is to miss the main point of the game: the creation and solidification of community, which is initiated and strengthened by music performance.[66]

According to oral tradition in Salvador, a special pattern (*toque*) of rhythm and melody, called *Aviso* ('warning'), nowadays played on the berimbau, is said to derive from drum patterns used to warn those taking part of an approaching white man or black overseer (*capataz*) or hunter of runaway slaves (*capitão-do-*

Figure 6 Berimbau-players and tambourine accompany present-day capoeira,
(Julio Etchart/Panos Pictures)

mato). Another celebrated berimbau pattern, called *Cavalaria* ('cavalry'), almost certainly imitating the sound of horses' hooves, was used in the 1920s to warn of the approach of the notorious *Esquadrão de Cavalaria*, whose duties included suppressing both candomblé and capoeira; this unit of mounted police was headed by the hated Pedrito Gordo (Pedro de Azevedo Gordilho), about whom songs are still sung in Salvador.[67] Besides *Aviso* and *Cavalaria*, there are many other berimbau patterns, known to expert players, who usually play them with slight individual variations. These patterns are listed by Waldeloir Rego under the names of various *mestres*,[68] and Kay Shaffer provides musical transcriptions of 13 of them: *Amazonas, Angola, Angolina, Aviso, Banguela, Cavalaria, Iuna, Muzenza, Pone a Laranga no Chão Tico-Tico, Samba de Angola, Santa Maria, São Bento Grande* and *São Bento Pequeno*.[69] Lewis stresses, however, that *Angola* and *São Bento Grande* are by far the most common patterns; that a player who can play those two can accompany 99 per cent of the capoeira contests in Brazil; and that 'there is really only one basic capoeira rhythm' and 'named *toques* are all variations on it'.[70] On playing techniques, Lewis draws attention to the way that feints in the ring are echoed by 'deceptive' playing of the berimbau. This is done in two main ways. The player can trick the listener's ear into expecting a high note but then produce a low note instead (or vice versa). Or he can lay down a rhythmic pattern and then skilfully break it in a way that involves the alternation of two distinct pitches.[71] Lewis makes an interesting comparison between the vocal tone used in capoeira songs and that used in African-American worksongs and 'hollers': the capoeira singer's voice must be 'loud and strident', but 'should be clearly melodic as well'.[72]

There are several excellent modern recordings of the berimbau. Outstanding among these is an LP recorded in 1990 by the Bahian *Mestre* Paulo dos Anjos (b. 1936); many of his accompaniments include melodic variations played during the singing, which frequently uses overlapping call and response between soloist and chorus.[73] A rare recording of the berimbau being used not for capoeira but to accompany the *carimbó* dance of north Brazil has recently been issued; it was made in 1938 in São Luís de Maranhão, where the berimbau was called by the local name *marimba*.[74] Other local names for it include *berimbau-de-vara* (Ribeira do Itapagipe, Bahia) and *marimbau*.[75]

The berimbau was one of several African-derived instruments which were adopted by various groups of Amerindians. It diffused from Brazil to Uruguay and to the Guaraní Amerindians of Paraguay, who, having no *r* sound in their language, called it *gualambau*.[76] However, it is said to be no longer played in Paraguay.

Other instruments were, and some still are, often used with the berimbau to provide music for capoeira. The *adufe* square frame drum with metal jingles is no longer used; but the *pandeiro* tambourine, *agogô* double clapperless bell and *reco-reco* notched bamboo scraper are often heard, and of late years the *atabaque* drum has been introduced, or reintroduced, into the capoeira repertoire. These additional instruments do not play cross-rhythms, but reinforce the beat laid down by the berimbau.

3

The 'Angola Warble': Street Cries and Worksongs

The cities

The captive Africans sang as they trooped off the slave ships and stepped on the soil of Brazil for the first time. Hearing them in Salvador in 1821, Maria Graham wrote in her journal: 'This very moment, there is a slave ship discharging her cargo, and the slaves are singing as they go ashore … [A]t the command of their keeper, they are singing one of their country songs, in a strange land.'[1] This is the poignant detail the future Lady Callcott adds to our aural picture of early-nineteenth-century Salvador, Recife and Rio de Janeiro as cities alive from dawn to dusk with the cries of black street-sellers and the songs of black porters.

Not every European or American visitor found the street cries and worksongs of Brazil agreeable; some heard them as groans, moans, howls, screams or grunts rather than as music of any kind. Mrs Nathaniel Edward Kindersley, a much travelled Englishwoman who spent two months in Salvador in 1764, about a year after it had ceased to be Brazil's capital city, was carried about by two black slaves in a sedan chair, from which 'a stranger is in danger of being thrown out at every step'.

> The chair is carried by two negro slaves on their shoulders; at every step the foremost gives a groan, which the other answers: this helps to make them keep an equal pace; but it is a melancholy disagreeable noise, and when we first came on shore, hearing the slaves, who were in parties, carrying any thing from one place to another, utter these kind of moans, we thought they were oppressed with burdens beyond their strength; which excited in us much pity for the slaves, and accordingly great contempt for their masters.[2]

When the ruler of a petty German state, Prince Maximilian of Wied-Neuwied (1782–1867), arrived in Rio de Janeiro in 1815, he noticed

> Negroes, some of them half naked, … drawing heavy burdens; and this useful race of men convey all the merchandise from the harbour into the city: united

in parties of ten or twelve, and keeping time together by a kind of song, or rather howl, they carry ponderous loads, suspended from long poles.[3]

Two years later, an uncomprehending American who spent a few weeks in Rio – he was Henry Marie Brackenridge (1786–1871), lawyer, author and secretary to a US government commission sent to study the political situation in South America – wrote that black water-carriers in Rio 'relieved the bodily pain of suffering, by a kind of harsh noise, not unlike that made by a flock of wild geese', while 'others hitched to carts or carrying burthens', were 'all screaming in the same style'.[4] In 1819–20 the German visitor Friedrich Ludwig von Rango heard continually in Rio the 'monotonous songs' of black people accompanying themselves on 'self-invented' [*selbst erfundenen*] instruments: 'One seldom sees, even during the hardest tasks, three of them together of whom one is not singing or strumming on a string.'[5] William Webster, an English surgeon who paid the city a brief visit in 1828, was hardly more impressed by what he heard (it should perhaps be pointed out that the chains referred to in the following passage were those with which the slaves pulled the carts):

A stranger on landing at Rio Janeiro is immediately struck by the great number of slaves, which may be said to infest the streets. As he leaves the landing-place, his ears are assailed by their monotonous shouts and the rattling of chains which proceed from the various parties of them as they perform their work. These unfortunate creatures supply the place of the beasts of burden to the people of Rio, and are to be seen linked together drawing carts and sledges [i.e. low-wheeled carts], and performing other laborious duties, with an apparent unconcern and a degree of hilarity which are hardly credible.

It is the custom of the slaves, and it appears to be general among negroes, to accompany their labours with their own native music, at least with such as their voices afford. This has no doubt the effect of inspiring them to greater efforts, and the streets resound with the echo of their uncouth song and the rattling of their chains.[6]

Two other Englishmen, briefly glancing at Brazil on their way to Paraguay in the 1830s, dismissed the songs of black slaves as 'howlings as they work'.[7] A US naval officer, William Ruschenberger (1807–95), visiting Rio de Janeiro in the early 1830s, found the street cries of the city 'indescribable', since 'the ears are assailed with the shrill and discordant voices of women slaves vending fruits and sweetmeats; and of the water-carriers crying "agua", which they carry about on their heads in large wooden kegs, filled at the different fountains'.[8] In 1856 an English midshipman wrote of black porters in Rio 'trotting along to the tune of a loud monotonous howl, with a heavy cask hanging from a pole that runs from shoulder to shoulder of the group'.[9]

Other visitors were less dismissive. John Luccock (1770–1826), a Yorkshire merchant who lived in Brazil from 1808 to 1818, tells of slaves sent into the streets, with empty baskets and long poles, to seek employment for their owner's benefit. Heavy goods were conveyed between two, by means of these poles laid upon their shoulders; then a pair of slings was attached, by which the load, raised a little above the ground, was carried to its place of destination. If the burden were too heavy for a couple of men, four, six, or even more were united, and formed a gang, over which one of the number, and generally the most intelligent of the set, was chosen by them to be their captain, and to direct the labour. To promote regularity in their efforts, and particularly a uniformity of step, he always chaunted an African song to a short and simple air; at the close of which the whole body joined in a loud chorus. This song was continued as long as the labour lasted, and seemed to lighten the burden, and to cheer the heart ... It is certain that their songs gave a cheeriness to the streets which they would otherwise have wanted.

Luccock also reported that when a dozen or so black men yoked themselves to 'a clumsy truck', with four very low wheels, they sang 'their usual favourite airs' while hauling it forward 'with their utmost might'.[10]

Maria Graham's 'country songs', William Webster's 'their own native music' and John Luccock's 'African song' clearly indicate the use of African languages in urban worksongs, as does the English artillery officer Lieutenant Henry Chamberlain's description in 1819–20 of 'Pretos de ganho, or black porters':

[To] maintain the regularity of step, so necessary to produce uniformity of effort, the Capataz [foreman] chants a few African words, at the close of which the whole body joins in chorus, and thus singing, and stepping together, they perform the service undertaken ... The Capataz generally contrives to get behind, and push the load forward, saving himself, at the expense of his people, to whom he sings, and by whom he is answered in chorus.[11]

The African languages used in such songs would most likely have been Yoruba, Kikongo and Kimbundu, which were those in which slaves generally conversed.[12] But there is evidence from the early nineteenth century about the use of the Portuguese language, too, in such songs. This is not surprising, for Portuguese was not only the dominant language of Brazil but had been a trading language along the West African coast since the fifteenth century, and *fala de Guiné* – so familiar in Lisbon, and so fascinating to the Portuguese playwright Gil Vicente (*c.* 1470–1536) – was a Portuguese-based creole.[13] The chief witness for the early use of Portuguese in Rio de Janeiro worksongs is the orientalist Sir William Ouseley (1767–1842). On his way to Persia in 1810 he spent ten days in Rio de Janeiro, where he watched slaves dragging 'an immense cask of water from the public fountain to their master's house, ... five or six pulling the vessel on a sledge, or low four-wheeled frame'. Already, he tells us, some Rio worksongs were sung in Portuguese, and he points to a significant difference in function between those and the ones sung in African languages:

During this exertion, they cheered each other by singing short sentences, either in the language of their own country, or in Portuguese. There was a pleasing kind of melody in this simple chant; and a gentleman who had resided many years at Rio de Janeiro, informed me that the usual burden of their Portuguese song, was little more than an address to the water-cask, 'come load, come soon home!'; but that if they belonged to a cruel master or mistress, their own language served as a vehicle for lamentation and condolence, and for imprecations on their oppressor.[14]

Captain Otto von Kotzebue of the Russian imperial navy, who visited Rio in 1823, either did not hear or did not recognise the use of Portuguese or *fala de Guiné* in slaves' worksongs. He reported that the 'immense weights' they carried 'are usually fastened on a plank, each end of which is borne by a negro, keeping time to his steps by a monotonous and melancholy song in his native language'.[15] But a Brazilian writing in 1896 quoted a few words in *fala de Guiné* from the song of the Prince Regent's 'black guard', twelve strong black men in green uniforms and large military caps decorated with the royal arms, who carried the prince around the Rio streets in a sedan chair in the 1830s, and whom he held in high regard. They 'sang and danced a fado' (*sic*) which included what on the surface seems to have been a reference to Brazil's then recent declaration of independence from Portugal in 1822. But, with emancipation still half a century in the future, this verse may also have a deeper, ironic meaning:

> Our master has come,
> Captivity is over.[16]

Somewhat earlier, the German visitor Theodor von Leithold testified to the slaves' 'extraordinary agility and physical strength', and their ability to 'carry unbelievably heavy loads on their heads', adding: 'The harder the work seems that they have to perform, the more readily do they burst into wild song which, like our woodcutters' "Hm!", seems to stimulate or fire their strength.'[17] The blind traveller James Holman (1786–1857), who visited Rio de Janeiro in 1828, took note of both the porters' 'national' songs and the street cries:

[E]ach group of porters as they pass along with their heavy loads, chant their peculiar national songs, for the double purpose of timing their steps and concentrating their attention on their employment. To these sounds are added the variety of cries, uttered in an endless alternation of tones, by the pretty negress fruit venders, who, smartly dressed, and leering and smiling in their most captivating manner endeavour so to attract the the attention of the sons of Adam.[18]

According to Debret, the sound of the songs regulating the steps of the black men who hauled huge carts (*cangalhas*) around the Rio streets 'warns from afar absent-minded coachmen and horsemen to respect their laborious and fettered progress'.[19] 'When those of the same caste [i.e., presumably, *nação*] work together', wrote the Revd Robert Walsh in 1830,

> they move to the sound of certain words, sung in a kind of melancholy cadence, commenced in a tenor tone by one part [i.e. party], and concluded in a base [*sic*] by the other. A long line of negroes, with burdens on their heads, sing it as they go along, and it is heard every day, and in almost every street in Rio.[20]

Like Luccock's 'loud chorus' in which 'the whole body joined', this obviously refers to call-and-response singing, as does the account of Rio de Janeiro porters' songs, accompanied by rattles but sung in Portuguese, given by Dr Melchior-Honoré Yvan (1803–73), physician to the French embassy in London for several years, who visited Rio de Janeiro in 1844 (the call quoted here may have meant 'How hard! How bad!'; the response means 'It's good!'):

> I could not suppress a feeling of amazement on seeing the streets completely filled with negro population, and involuntarily stopped to gaze on the half-naked and noisy throngs of beings around me, who frisked about in the rays of a burning sun, as blithely as so many devils in a furnace. I shall never forget the impression made upon me by this band of strange looking creatures, as I watched them passing to and fro before me, laden with heavy burdens, continuously singing in a monotonous tone '*Que calo! que malo!*' whilst some of their companions replied in a grave serious tone, '*Esta boa! esta boa!*' at the same time shaking about a noisy sort of rattle which they held in their hands. I really could have imagined myself present at some mysterious ceremony, or some rite of infernal worship.[21]

Less excited by what he saw and heard, as befitted a sober American theologian, the Revd Walter Colton (1797–1851), who was in Rio in 1845, wrote that the porters 'carry ... enormous burdens on their heads, and trot along with a *sonorous grunt*, which works itself off into a sort of song. You wonder how they can have so much wind to spare for their tune.'[22]

Three years earlier the 'sad and monotonous song' of the Rio coffee-carriers had made a 'painful impression' on the Comte de Suzannet[23] (about whom nothing is known except that he wrote a book about his travels in the Caucasus and Brazil). In 1850 the Austrian globe-trotter Ida Pfeiffer (1797–1858), who visited Rio de Janeiro in 1846, wrote disparagingly of the coffee-carriers' songs, but agreed with Debret that they did perform one useful function:

> The greatest amount of noise is made by those negroes who carry burdens, and especially by such as convey the sacks full of coffee on board the different vessels; they strike up a monotonous sort of song, to the tune of which they keep step, but which sounds very disagreeable. It possesses, however, one advantage; it warns the foot passenger, and affords him time to get out of the way.[24]

To the Belgian Count Eugène de Robiano, the black porters he heard in Rio in the 1870s were 'singers whom nothing can keep silent' and who always had 'some ancient song which they readily repeat in chorus when they go in step through the city streets, carrying heavy loads'.[25]

The Revd Charles Samuel Stewart (1795–1870), an American ex-missionary who was in Rio de Janeiro in 1851–52, seems to have been the only nineteenth-century foreign visitor to Brazil to attempt any kind of taxonomy of the street cries and worksongs he heard, and his account is therefore especially valuable. After mentioning 'the rapid lope and monotonous grunt of the coffee-bag carriers', Stewart went on to describe

> the jingling and drumming of the tin rattles or gourds borne by the leaders of gangs, transporting on their heads all manner of articles – chairs, tables, sofas and bedsteads, the entire furniture of a household; the dull recitative, followed by the loud chorus, with which they move along; the laborious cry of others, tugging and hauling and pushing over the rough pavements heavily laden trucks and carts, an overload for an equal number of mules or horses …
>
> [T]he first sight which arrests the eyes of the stranger on landing in Rio is the number, varied employments, and garb of the negroes. The first and chief human sounds that reach his ears are also from this class. Their cries through the streets vary with the pursuits they follow. That of the vegetable and fruit venders is monotonous and singular; but so varied, that each kind of vegetable and fruit seems to have its own song. The coffee-carriers, moving in gangs, have a tune of their own to which they keep time, in an Indian-like lope, with a bag of one hundred and sixty pounds' weight, poised on their heads. The bearers of furniture form a regular choir. One or two, with rattles of tin in their hands, resembling the nose [sic] of a watering-pot, perforated with holes and filled with shot, lead the way in a style truly African. To this is allied, with full strength of lungs, a kind of travelling chant, in which at times all join in chorus. It is full and sonorous, and rendered pleasant, if from no other cause, by the satisfaction from it visible, in the shining and sweating faces of the poor blacks.[26]

That Rio porters often used rattles, and that they sang in call-and-response form ('at times all join in chorus'), is confirmed by several other mid-century visitors. The British 'sketcher' Robert Elwes, who was in the city in 1848, wrote:

> The best and strongest negroes not brought up as servants or to any trade are employed in carrying coffee from the stores to the custom-house, where it is shipped. They work in gangs of ten or twelve, each carrying a bag of coffee on his shoulder. They … work cheerfully, one singing a song and often carrying a rattle, whilst the others join in chorus, and always go at a jog trot.[27]

Two more American clergymen, the Revd Daniel Parish Kidder (1815–91) and the Revd James Cooley Fletcher (1823–1901) described what they heard in the same decade as a 'wild Ethiopian ditty': the singing of the Rio coffee-carriers, who usually go in troops, numbering ten or twenty individuals, of whom one takes the lead, and is called the captain. These are usually the largest and strongest men that can be found ... Each one takes a bag of coffee upon his head, weighing one hundred and sixty pounds, and when all are ready they start off upon a measured trot, which soon increases to a rapid run.

As one hand is sufficient to steady the load, several of them frequently carry musical instruments in the other, resembling children's rattle-boxes: these they shake to the double-quick time of some wild Ethiopian ditty, which they all join in singing as they run [Fig. 7]. Music has a powerful effect in exhilarating the spirits of the negro; and certainly no one should deny him the privilege of softening his hard lot by producing the harmony of sounds, which are sweet to him, however uncouth to other ears. It is said, however, that an attempt was at one time made to secure greater quietness in the streets by forbidding the negroes to sing. As a consequence they performed little or no work, so the restriction was in a short time taken off. Certain it is that they now avail themselves of their vocal privileges at pleasure, whether in singing and shouting to each other as they run, or in proclaiming to the people the various articles they carry about for sale. The impression made upon the stranger by the mingled sound of their hundred voices falling upon his ear at once is not soon forgotten.[28]

COFFEE-CARRIERS.

Figure 7 Rio de Janeiro coffee-carriers, as sketched by the US clergymen Kidder and Fletcher in the 1840s. Each carried on his head a bag of coffee weighing 160lb. As they ran through the streets they sang to the rhythm of tin rattles known as *ganzá* or *canzá* (from Kimbundu *nganza*, 'gourd'). (Revd D. P. Kidder and Revd J. C. Fletcher, *Brazil and the Brazilians, portrayed in historical and descriptive sketches*, Philadelphia, Childs & Peterson, 1857)

Kidder's and Fletcher's sketch of Rio coffee-carriers (Fig. 7) shows two of them carrying what seems to be the egg- or pear-shaped tin rattle known in Brazil as *ganzá* or *canzá* (from Kimbundu *nganza*, 'gourd') or *xeque-xeque*. The German visitor Hermann Burmeister (1807–92), professor of zoology at Halle University – who would lose that job in 1860 for having voted against Bismarck – found the coffee-carriers' responsorial song monotonous. Heard every day in the Rio streets, it consisted of three quavers and a crotchet;[29] unfortunately Burmeister did not or could not say what notes were sung to this rhythm.

Thomas Ewbank (1792–1870), Durham-born inventor and manufacturer of lead, tin and copper tubing, who had emigrated to the USA in 1819 and was later to become Commissioner of Patents, called the singing of a group of over twenty black porters carrying household furniture through the Rio streets in the 1840s 'a yell and *hurlement* [howling] ... that made me start as if the shrieks were actually from Tartarus', adding:

> Chanting only at intervals, they passed the lower part of the Cattete in silence, and then struck up the Angola warble that surprised me. There they go, jog-trotting on! The foremost, with pants ending at the knees, a red woolen strip round his waist, upon his head a mop, whose colored thrums play half way down his naked back, and in his hand a gourd-rattle, fringed with carpet-rags, beats time and leads the way.

Ewbank thought London street cries were 'bagatelles' compared with those of the Brazilian capital: 'Slaves of both sexes cry wares through every street. Vegetables, flowers, fruits, edible roots, fowls, eggs, and every rural product; cakes, pies, rusks, *doces* [sweetmeats], confectionery, "heavenly bacon", etc., pass your windows continually.'[30]

The porters' use of rattles is mentioned also by the French journalist Charles Ribeyrolles, who arrived in Brazil in 1858,[31] and by the French painter François Biard (1798–1882), who was there about two years later. Biard saw a rattle shaken by one of six slaves who were carrying a grand piano on their heads. Like Stewart, he described the rattle as being like the rose of a watering can and as having little pebbles inside; with it the black porter 'joyfully beat time'.[32] The American naturalist Herbert Huntington Smith (1851–1919), who visited Brazil three times in the 1870s and 1880s, described the black porters as

> great, brawny fellows, who run in gangs through the streets, each one with a hundred and thirty pounds of coffee on his head. Sometimes we see five or six of them, trotting together, with a piano; the weight evenly distributed on the wooly craniums; the men erect, moving in time to the leader's rattle, and to a plaintive chant.[33]

Besides worksongs, the American clergyman Kidder also heard, in the streets of the Rio suburb of Engenho Velho, a kind of song that is mentioned by no other traveller. He saw a funeral cortège consisting of about twenty negresses, and a number of children, adorned most of them with flaunting stripes of red, white, and yellow. They were all chanting some Ethiopian dirge, to which they kept time by a slow trot; the bearer of the deceased child pausing, once in one or two rods [i.e. about every 5–10 metres], and whirling around on his toes like a dancer.

The procession then returned [from the churchyard], chanting and dancing, if possible, more wildly than when they came.[34]

In Salvador, where carts or wagons were seldom used to carry loads before the middle of the nineteenth century, Kidder and his colleague Fletcher saw

[i]mmense numbers of tall, athletic negroes ... moving in pairs or gangs of four, six, or eight, with their loads suspended between them on heavy poles ... Like the coffee-carriers of Rio, they often sing and shout as they go; but their gait is necessarily slow and measured, resembling a dead march rather than the double-quick step of their Fluminensian colleagues.[35]

Another American visitor to Salvador saw 'twelve strong muscular slaves' carrying a heavy hogshead suspended from the pole borne on their shoulders, 'and in order to mark time they have a singular sort of cry as they proceed along the streets, sung in a kind of melancholy cadence, that proceeding from those in front being on a higher key than from those behind'.[36] In 1851 the British vice-consul James Wetherell reported on the Salvador *ganhadores* (porters):

The black carriers, 'Ganha dores' [*sic*] are a fine race of men of athletic form, when employed they are as nearly naked as possible, their only dress being the scantiest pair of coarse cotton drawers. They carry all the smaller things upon their heads, whilst large objects, such as pipes of wine &c., are slung between two poles which are carried on the shoulders. I have seen immense blocks of wood, with thirty blacks and upwards carrying them, for all the world like an immense centipede.

During the time of carrying those heavy burdens through the streets they sing a kind of chorus, a very useful manner of warning persons to get out of the way, as the footfall is not heard in the surrounding bustle. This chorus generally consists of one of the blacks chaunting a remark on anything he sees, and the others come in with a chorus of some ridiculous description, which is seldom varied, however much the recitative solo part may. Thus a kind of march, time and time, is kept up. I have noticed, too, that when the work is heavy, or the burden is being carried up hill, that they become much more vigorous in their shouts, aiding their labour and varying their song with an expressive longdrawn grunt.[37]

The Revd Hamlet Clark (1823–67), an entomologist who visited Salvador in 1856, noted that the black stevedores loading coal and unloading cargo, working twenty or so to a gang, 'made the whole ship resound with their merry choruses'.[38] Visiting the same city four years later Archduke Maximilian of

Austria (1832–67), soon to become the ill-fated emperor of Mexico but meanwhile pursuing his botanical studies in the Brazilian forests, found it 'interesting to see the black people passing through the streets with baskets full of the most splendid fruit, always crying it for sale as they go'. But what he heard did not impress him: 'Their hoarse tones roll forth without intermission like those of a rough mill-wheel ... The voice does not come naturally and in full tones from the chest, but appears rather to be an artificial acquirement, lacking modulation.'[39]

Ewbank wrote briefly about a kind of work music to be heard in Rio that does not seem to be mentioned elsewhere: a building worker hammering 'a kind of melody' on a wooden plank or piece of metal and gradually slowing down the rhythm as a signal that the shift was about to begin or was coming to an end. Ewbank described the sound, which reached to a great distance, as 'two, sometimes three, sonorous and startling knocks – a roll of raps tapering down to an inaudible rattle – the roll repeated in inverted order, and closing with a triple and emphatic menace'. (Similar 'work music', using tools as musical instruments, has been reported from Liberia and Dar es Salaam.) Ewbank also heard, on a building site, 'eight negroes ... yelling an African virelay [i.e. song] for nearly half an hour' while lifting a large stone by means of a chain running over a block.[40]

A tantalisingly brief mention of the rowing songs sung by black oarsmen in Guanabara Bay (the bay on which Rio stands) is given by the American traveller Luther Melanchthon Schaeffer, who heard them in 1849 as they rowed him ashore from his ship: 'Our oarsmen were black as night, and they would rise up when they pulled their oars, and dance, and sing, and whistle for the breeze to spring up.'[41]

Travellers' accounts of urban worksongs heard in places other than Rio de Janeiro and Salvador are relatively sparse, but one exists relating to the north-eastern port of Recife, two relating to the northern port of Pará, or Belém. The French visitor Louis-François de Tollenare (1780–1853), arriving in Recife in 1816, heard black porters 'cheering each other up with a simple and monotonous song', while black women 'wander through the streets, offering for sale handkerchiefs and other stuff, which they carried in baskets on their heads. Their cries mingle with those of the black porters.'[42] When John Esaias Warren, who later served as US attaché in Spain, visited Pará in the 1840s, he

> met with a party of some thirty or forty blacks, each one of them bearing a large basket of tapioca on his head. They were perfectly naked to their waists, and wore only a pair of pantaloons of very coarse material. They marched on at a slow and measured pace, chanting at the same time a singularly monotonous air, to which they beat time with their hands.
>
> We learned that they were free blacks, and called themselves 'Ganhadores'. Their business was that of loading and unloading vessels; horses and carts being but little used in Para.[43]

The naturalist and travel writer Alfred Russel Wallace (1823–1913) also heard 'the loud chanting of the Negro porters' in Pará in 1852, but gives no further information.[44]

Transcriptions of three early-twentieth-century Brazilian street cries (*pregões*) will be found in Renato Almeida's path-breaking *História da Música Brasileira* (second edition, 1942): one, in a pentatonic scale, collected from a Recife vender of *pamonha*, a sweet made largely from green corn paste; another, with a heavy stress on a flattened leading note, sung by a Bahia vender of sweets and fruit; the third, collected from a Rio vender of ice-cream.[45]

The countryside

All over the New World, Africans and their descendants sang as they worked in the fields. Singing helping them to sweeten and pace their labour to some extent, and to endure a working day that in Brazil lasted fourteen, sixteen, sometimes even eighteen hours a day, six days a week. But the worksongs had another function: they were often vehicles for social comment and, in particular, songs of protest. That was particularly the case with worksongs in riddle form, known as *jongos*. The *jongo* worksongs of slaves on coffee plantations in Rio de Janeiro state in the second half of the nineteenth century have been described by Stanley J. Stein, whose interviews with former slaves elicited valuable information that is not accessible anywhere else:

> Slave gangs often worked within singing distance of each other and to give rhythm to their hoe strokes and pass comment on the circumscribed world in which they lived and worked – their own foibles, and those of their master, overseers, and slave drivers – the master-singer (*mestre cantor*) of one gang would break into the first 'verse' of a song in riddle form, a *jongo*. His gang would chorus the second line of the verse, then weed rhythmically while the master-singer of the nearby gang tried to decipher ... the riddle presented. An ex-slave, still known for his skill at making jongos, informed that 'Mestre tapped the ground with his hoe, others listened while he sang. Then they replied.' He added that if the singing was not good the day's work went badly. Jongos sung in African tongues were called *quimzumba*; those in Portuguese, more common as older Africans diminished in the labor force, *visaría*.

Jongos, sung both as worksongs and at *jongo* and *caxambu* dances (for the *jongo* as a dance with sung riddles, see pp. 104–5), were primarily songs of protest – a protest that was, in Stein's words, 'subdued but enduring':

> Jongo form – that of the riddle – lent itself well in phrasing the slaves' reactions, for, as with all riddles, the purpose was to conceal meaning with words, expressions, or situations of more than one possible interpretation. Words were often African, undoubtedly more so in the nineteenth century ... Persons were

replaced by trees, birds, and animals of the forest. There was a premium on terseness; the fewer the words, the more obscure the meaning, the better the jongo, one not readily deciphered by contesting jongueiros, or one which could be repeated to depict a multitude of situations.

Stein quotes a typical *jongo* worksong, which he suggests may have been an allusion to the practice of chaining together recaptured fugitive slaves:

> Pretty little canary, kept in a cage,
> Why the little chain on your leg, please tell why?

Or, in a semi-transparent alllusion to the mistreatment of slaves, the *jongueiro* might sing about an ill-treated monkey:

> Monkey doesn't die by lead,
> He dies in a noose while they're thrashing him.

An 'aged ex-slave' told Stein that a slave who had informed on his fellows would be made the butt of this *jongo*:

> He's got a loose tongue.
> The little bird has a tongue.
> Look at that Angola bird with a loose tongue.

On a less sombre note, *jongos* might joke about sexual relations, as in this allusion to a man whose wife is visited by another man while he is out working in the fields:

> I don't know why mama
> Is playing tricks on papa.
> Ramalhete is yoked up,
> Jardim is in the stable.[46]

Foreign travellers in Brazil occasionally reported worksongs heard in the countryside. In 1844, somewhere near Nova Friburgo, in the state of Rio de Janeiro, Dr Yvan heard 'a group of negroes, with hatchets, who sang wild songs' as they cleared a path through the forest.[47] When the English chemist C. B. Mansfield, who seems to have been a very unusual Englishman indeed, heard singing coming from a barn in the countryside near Petrópolis in the 1850s and found black workers threshing corn, he promptly joined in both the work and the singing, about which unfortunately he has little to tell. The threshers were 'six Negroes armed with long straight poles, with which they alternately belaboured the corn, in two sets of three, striking alternately, and chanting a queer monotone in time'.[48] In 1866 the American ship's captain John Codman (1814–1900) heard gangs of black slaves 'generally singing cheerfully' as they went to work on a plantation growing cotton, sugar cane and cassava about 50 miles from the city of Rio de Janeiro.[49]

In 1883 the English visitor Hastings Charles Dent (b. 1855) was charmed by worksongs he heard free black agricultural workers singing near the Camapuão river in Mato Grosso:

> The singing in harmony of the blacks at their work of weeding the young maize plantations on the other side of the valley was extremely pretty, softened by distance. These blacks work about eleven hours a day, and get a milreis; they are mostly freed slaves ... they are fine, stalwart, pure-blooded negroes.[50]

Stein quotes a writer in the newspaper *O Vassourense*, in 1882, describing black washerwomen rhythmically beating clothes 'to the tune of mournful songs'.[51]

The songs of the miners

Two nineteenth-century visitors to a Brazilian gold mine, at Morro Velho in Minas Gerais, left brief accounts of the singing of the black miners there. In 1874 Count Charles d'Ursel (1848–1903), a French diplomat, heard songs that 'seemed to issue from the very bowels of the earth'.[52] The American traveller, collector and author Frank Vincent (1848–1916), who went down the same mine in 1885, found

> about fifty men engaged in drilling and loading the bucket with the ore. They were singing a wild refrain, keeping good time with the heavy blows of their sledges ... They paused for a moment to salute our party with a double '*Viva!*' and then the banging, clanging, and strange though not unmusical singing, continued.

As Vincent and his companions went back up to the surface, 'the negroes in the car entertained us with some more of their half-barbaric songs'. Though the miners looked 'quite robust ... that scourge of most miners, consumption, decimates them here as elsewhere'.[53]

The songs of the diamond miners of São João da Chapada, near Diamantina (formerly Tijuco), a mining town in Minas Gerais, were quite unlike the worksongs sung anywhere else in that state, even in other mining centres such as Mariana, Ouro Preto and São João del Rei. Their singularity was due to the extreme isolation of the diamond industry for reasons of security. Outside contacts were few, thanks to 'the zeal of an administration whose only purpose was to secure the major benefits for the Portuguese crown'. Known as *vissungos*, the miners' songs were sung in a language that was based on Kongo-Angola languages but included also a few West African elements and a few Portuguese words, mainly fragments of prayers and Christian greeting formulas. These songs 'represent one of the most genuine examples of African contribution to Brazilian folk music'. Combining protest and satire, they added also, as many worksongs must have done in the slavery era, the resistance function of transmitting clandestine messages. There were songs for each phase of mining work and special songs for different times of day: morning, noon and evening. There were songs for welcoming the rare visitors from outside the area. There were songs, by these chronically undernourished slaves, demanding food. There were songs claiming the contribution (*multa*) traditionally levied on every newcomer; once this had been handed over there was a dance of thanks, with rhythms beaten out on buckets with spades or pickaxes. There were even songs to register the very moment the master was leaving the house and setting out for the mine.

There were songs to accompany the task of carrying the corpse of a dead comrade in a hammock to a far-off cemetery. Unlike some of the *vissungos* sung during work, which were normally accompanied by the singers striking their tools together in rhythm, these funerary songs were never accompanied. Their 'constantly developing beautiful melodic lines' were often based on paternosters and the Ave Maria.

Some *vissungos* were accompanied by the Angola-derived friction drum known as *cuíca* or *puita*, but drums proper were never used. Some *vissungos* were solo songs, known as *boiados*; others, called *dobrados*, were cast in call-and-response form. All displayed 'extreme melodic richness'.[54]

What seems to be the earliest reference to the songs of the diamond miners is a passage by the French botanist Augustin Prouvençal de Saint-Hilaire (1779–1853), who travelled through Brazil in the years 1816–22 and later published a detailed multi-volume account of his travels. He was struck by the miners having to do their hard and ceaseless work with their legs constantly in water and by the poor food they were given, two circumstances which led to their physical decline: 'Joined together in very large numbers, these unfortunate men amuse themselves in their work; they sing in chorus the hymns [*cantiques*] of their native land.'[55]

Vissungos recorded in 1944 by the composer and musicologist Luiz Heitor Corrêa de Azevedo (1905–92) have recently been issued on a compact disc.[56] Dr Morton Marks, in the accompanying booklet, describes them as 'some of the most African-sounding music in all of Brazil'; they provide, he adds, 'a rare window into colonial Brazil'. This is no exaggeration. They are poignant, evocative and haunting: a song for carrying the dead in hammocks; a call for water, reminiscent of African-American fieldworkers' calls to the 'water-boy';[57] and a song greeting the dawn. The latter includes two brief passages sung in fourths. Students of the African musical heritage in Brazil are fortunate to have these recordings, made in the nick of time, when the tradition was all but extinguished. Much has been lost for ever. The son of a slave told an enquirer that his father taught him many of the *vissungos*, but not all: 'Some of them my father would not sing to anyone.' It is not hard to imagine why. These were songs that kept hope alive. They brought the only gleam of light into the lives of men who possessed nothing else. They were precious and, in some sense, sacred. When slavery came to an end in 1888 the diamond miners were offered paid work. But those bosses who had banned *vissungos* could not persuade a single former slave to work for them.[58]

In the strongest possible stylistic contrast to the *vissungos*, the same CD includes a stone-cutters' song by three men, recorded in Minas Gerais in 1944. Here, melody and vocal tone alike make more than a nod in the direction of Portugal.[59]

4

Brazil's Dramatic Dances

Brazil once had a large number of what the musicologist Mário de Andrade, who wrote a magisterial three-volume survey of them, called 'dramatic dances'.[1] These were more than just dances: they were traditional plays or pageants, with music, song and dance. Nowadays all but one of them are rarely if ever performed. Those incorporating African traditions within a European framework included the *Congos* performed in north-eastern and northern Brazil and the similar *Congadas* of central and southern Brazil. The *Quilombo*, celebrating the free republic of Palmares, established by fugitive slaves in the seventeenth century, was performed in the states of Alagoas and Minas Gerais. Despite its name, there is some dispute about the origin of the *Moçambique*, performed in the states of São Paulo, Goiás and Minas Gerais. But recent scholarship has established that Brazil's best-known dramatic dance, the widespread and still surviving *Bumba-meu-boi* (also known by many other names, such as *Boi-bumbá*), often supposed to be of Iberian origin, was created by African slaves in Brazil to poke fun at their Portuguese masters.

The *Congos* and *Congadas*, which generally featured the coronation of a king and queen of the Kongo, are thought to have been originated by the lay societies of black artisans that were formed in Brazil in the sixteenth and seventeenth centuries under the auspices of the Roman Catholic Church. So, before describing this dramatic dance, we first examine the contribution those societies made to the acculturation process.

Lay brotherhoods and danced processions

In 1696, watching a religious procession in Salvador, the Frenchman François Froger (b. 1676) was scandalised to see among the crosses, relics, and statues 'troupes of masqueraders, instrumentalists and dancers, who with their lewd [*lubriques*] attitudes disturbed the order of this holy ceremony'.[2] These were in fact groups of black people who practised various trades – smiths, tailors, tinsmiths, coppersmiths, and so on – organised in lay societies known as brotherhoods (*irmandades*), the first of which were formed by the first Jesuit missionaries in Pernambuco as early as 1552.[3] Rio de Janeiro followed suit in

1639; Salvador, Olinda and Belém in the 1680s. Similar black organisations existed also in Portugal and Spain from the fifteenth century onwards.[4]

In colonial Brazil the brotherhoods were attached to churches, convents and monasteries, and usually took Our Lady of the Rosary or Our Lady of Mercies as their patroness. There was one such organisation in almost every parish, forming a network that 'constituted a means of assembly and defence' for black people, enslaved and free alike.[5] These organisations did much to keep intact the African *nações* and to preserve African languages, religions and traditional music and dance, in the teeth of persecution.[6] They were also a significant, perhaps a decisive, step forward in the acculturation process. Through them black people took an active part in Brazilian popular life from the seventeenth century onwards, 'swarming through the streets whenever possible' with lamellophones, whistles, cane and bamboo flutes, *atabaque* drums and notched scrapers.[7] Black and white artisans would dance through the streets side by side.[8] Popular entertainment was sparse in that period: there were few theatres; radio, gramophone, cinema and television lay far in the future. Religious processions, with their rich costumes, masqueraders, musicians and dancers, gave the whole population, including the slaves, a chance to have some fun.

Black people in Brazil grasped that chance as often as they could. The practice of dancing near churches, if not actually inside them, was already quite familiar to the Portuguese settlers in Brazil; the German chronicler Gabriel Tetzel (d. 1479), scribe to the Bohemian traveller Leo of Rozmital (1426–85), noted it in 1466 as one of Portugal's 'strange customs'.[9] In both Portugal and Brazil, Africans adopted with great enthusiasm a custom that they found 'both readily comprehensible and appealing'[10] and, under a veneer of Catholicism, did much to set their distinctive stamp on it. In 1633 a Spanish visitor recorded in his travel diary how Lisbon's black community celebrated the day of Our Lady of the Snow (5 August):

> In Lisbon there are more than 15,000 black men and women slaves, and they all gather on the day of Our Lady of the Snow to celebrate her festival, and each puts on the costume of their land. Many go naked, with sashes on heads and arms and a piece of coloured cloth to cover the backside ...
>
> They go in procession through the town, and many sing, playing guitars, drums, flutes, and other instruments used in their lands, dancing with castanets the wild dances customary in their own lands, the women carrying on head, back or waist baskets of wheat or some other offering given them by their owners, which they take to the church of São Francisco da Cidade. Entering the church dancing Moorish dances and singing, they parade round the church two or three times. When they reach the side-altar where the mass is being sung for them, they offer what they have brought to the priest, who sits there robed, with deacon and sub-deacon, celebrating mass with the acolytes. All kiss the priest's hand. Leaving their offerings, they go away dancing as they came, and those offerings amount to 60 *fanegas* [*c.* 60–90 bushels] of wheat.[11]

In 1729 Le Gentil de La Barbinais, the first Frenchman to sail round the world, included in the book recounting his journey a drawing of a group of five black people dancing just outside an open church door in Bahia. It was 4 February, the festival of St Gonzales (Gundisalvus) of Amarante – a saint around whom a dancing cult arose in Mexico as well as Brazil[12] – and the five are shown dancing to the sound of harps, pipes, drums and tambourines played by friars in a gallery inside the church the French traveller had visited in 1718. The church itself was thronged with dancers, some of them slaves:

> We found close to the church consecrated to St Gonzales an astonishing multitude of people dancing to the sound of guitars. These dancers blocked the way to the church in the name of St Gonzales of Amarante. As soon as the viceroy appeared, they picked him up and forced him to dance and jump – a violent exercise which hardly suited his age or disposition ... It was rather droll to see, in a church, priests, women, friars, gentlemen, and slaves dancing and jumping promiscuously, and shouting at the tops of their voices *Viva San Gonzalés d'Amarante*.[13]

This vivid picture of such an exalted and dignified figure as the Portuguese viceroy, no less, being compelled by a motley and excited crowd to 'dance and jump', gives some idea of how far the acculturation process had advanced in Brazil by the first half of the eighteenth century. The annual Dance of St Gonzales was a living tradition in the Bahia town of Santa Brigida as late as the 1970s.[14]

A few years after the Portuguese viceroy's introduction to Brazilian merrymaking a Jesuit priest in Salvador, Plácido Nunes, was complaining that he could not understand why black people were allowed 'dances in their manner, and with instruments they use in their native lands, in the streets and public squares of the cities'. Many of these were 'dances and songs in the language of Angola'.[15] Another Salvador dignitary, Luís dos Santos Vilhena, regius professor of Greek, complained in 1802 about the black men and women who danced through the streets to the beat of drums and used African languages:

> It does not seem very prudent, politically speaking, to tolerate crowds of Negroes of both sexes performing their barbarous *batuques* through the city streets and squares to the beat of many horrible *atabaques*, indecently dancing to pagan songs [*dansando deshonestamente canções gentilicos*], speaking various languages, and that with such frightful and discordant clamour as to cause fear and astonishment.[16]

But the brotherhoods had always taken care to secure official sanction for such celebrations. In 1786 the Brotherhood of Our Lady of the Rosary in Salvador petitioned the Portuguese Queen Maria I (1734–1816), seeking permission to dance and to sing in 'the language of Angola' on the feast day of their patroness.[17] A Dominican friar, Domingos de Loreto Couto, had written in 1757 of the corresponding brotherhood in Recife that

> On the second Sunday of October they celebrate Our Lady with great solemnity and, to make their devotion more ardent, they engage in dances and other lawful amusements, with which they devoutly gladden the people ... Every Saturday and on the first Sunday of each month they go through the streets singing Our Lady's chaplet with such euphony and concordance of voices that a sweet harmony results which is at once pleasing and edifying.[18]

Unfortunately this source tells us nothing about the language used in the songs sung by black participants in festivities and processions, but it is certain that by the late 1720s, if not earlier, not all such songs were in African languages. By then there were also to be heard in Salvador what the historian José Ramos Tinhorão calls 'the first authentically Brazilian creations'.[19] This is made clear in a contemporary description of festivities in Salvador in 1729 to celebrate a wedding of Portuguese and Castilian royals, with a procession consisting of eight sub-processions, each with its dances, brotherhoods and statues carried on wooden frameworks. These 'Brazilian creations' are referred to as 'the airs and songs [cantigas, e modas] of the land, which are plentiful in this country'.[20]

Some priests and professors might tut, but the Brazilian public found black dancing delightful. The Salvador senate, knowing what went down well with the crowds, would set aside entire days for the black contribution to festivities. In the mid-eighteenth century black dances there were being hailed as 'great fun [muitas divertidissimas] ... all most exquisite [primorissimas] both in the opulence of the costumes and in the concepts of the dances themselves'.[21] In return for permission to perform their traditional dances, the brotherhoods would sometimes undertake to tone them down somewhat, 'to conform more closely to Portuguese religious values'.[22]

In Chapter 6 we shall look more closely at Brazil's black secular dances before emancipation. Here it is important to stress both the key role the Catholic Church played in the entire acculturation process in Brazil, and the two-sided nature of that process. Both sides made concessions, and both sides gained thereby. By permitting a certain degree of Africanisation of its procedures, the Church gained at least nominal converts; by embracing Catholicism, at least nominally, the slaves not only protected essential aspects of their culture but also saw that culture winning wider and wider acceptance – becoming in many respects Brazilianised, without surrendering its African essence. By 1860 the process had reached a stage which shocked and astounded the future Mexican Emperor Maximilian. Worth quoting at length is his description of what he called a 'wild bacchanalian orgy' – a Catholic ceremony, in fact – which he attended in that year at the church of Our Lady of Bomfin in a Salvador suburb. For, though it tells us nothing about music or dance, this passage does provide, in Robert Edgar Conrad's words, 'vivid impressions of the blending of African and European cultures and religious practices which had taken place in Brazil during centuries of contact and Catholic indoctrination':[23]

> The road brought us to the hill of Nossa Senhora do Bom Fin ... In the square and round the church all was confusion, as though it were a fair-day; black people in their gayest holiday attire were passing to and fro, and chattering noisily ... glass cases, filled with eatables, hovered above the heads of the crowd; little groups of people selling cachaça formed, as it were islands in the sea of people; a wooden stage ... announced marvels for the coming afternoon ... we pressed through a side door ... and found ourselves in a long, cheerful, handsomely ornamented gallery ... Mirth and gaiety pervaded the hall. Many young damsels were seated in rows by the wall; their dusky charms not concealed, but enhanced by kerchiefs of transparent light-coloured gauze. In the most graceful and becoming attitudes, and amid incessant chattering, they were selling all kinds of reliques, amulets, torches, and eatables, partly from their baskets and partly from glass cases. To a good Catholic the whole of this proceeding could not but appear most blasphemous; for at this festival the blacks mingled heathen notions to a most improper extent with their ideas of pilgrimage. All went on merrily in the hall: the negro crowd pressed round the saleswomen, laughing and joking; the latter jested in return, behaved in a very coquettish manner, and ogled at the black clowns. The whole scene presented a wild, oriental appearance, though mixed with a certain amount of civilisation ...
>
> We ... reached a spacious apartment filled with rich ornaments; the furniture of which showed it to be a sacristy. A jovial, yellow-faced clergyman was leaning on a chest, with a chasuble and chalice close beside him, and was talking to some senhoras in a lively and agreeable strain ...
>
> The stream of people again carried us on ... into a spacious hall ... An atmosphere of festivity seemed to pervade the place; a joyous expectation; as though nothing were wanting in this brilliant hall but the drums and fiddles for the dance. It was crammed with black, brown, yellow figures; with lovely women, sometimes complete giantesses, whose bare necks and beautifully formed shoulders were ornamented with beads, coral, gold chains, and amulets. These women all had shrill voices, rendered mirthful by the influence of cachaça; and for festal trophies, they carried ornamented brooms.
>
> This was an excellent opportunity for studying dusky complexions and negro costume. The negroes were holding their saturnalia; slavery had ceased for the moment; and by the unrestrained movements and the wild merriment of both blacks and mulattoes, by their rich and picturesque attire, one could see that they were, for this day, perfectly happy. There were specimens of every size, every form of the negro race; from the matron, with her gilt ornaments, her almost portly figure and proud gait, to the graceful, joyous, gazelle-like maiden, scarce yet developed; from the white-headed, ape-like, good-tempered old negro, to the roguish chattering boy.
>
> All moved hither and thither in a confused mass. Here, were two acquaintances greeting and kissing each other; there, two negro slaves from distant parts of the town were shaking hands; here a matron shouted 'Good day', over the heads of those around her, to an approaching Amazon; there groups of people had collected and were chattering merrily over the events and love-adventures

of this happy day. Mirth and unrestrained happiness reigned everywhere; one could see that it was a long-looked-for festival, at which the negroes felt quite at home ...

I was gazing here and there with curiosity, anxious to impress on my mind ... all the scenes of this black witches' sabbath; when at the farther end of the hall my eye was attracted to a figure on a daïs, who continually looked anxiously up and down in a book, then cast a glance around him ... It was the yellow-complexioned priest, who was going through the ceremony of the mass (I cannot call it celebrating mass), as though he were giving an oration at this public festival. I could no longer doubt; we were in the church; the large, mirthful dancing-hall was a Brazilian temple of God, the chattering negroes were baptized Christians, were supposed to be Catholics, and were attending mass.

The Brazilian priests maintain that it is necessary to lead the negroes into the paths of religion by these means: that they understand nothing higher, and can only be brought to the church by mirth and gaiety and when plied with cachaça ...

The proper object of this festival is a pilgrimage of the women to this church in order that by washing the entrance on the terrace and the stone pavement, they may obtain the blessing of children; hence the ornamented broom that each woman brings with her, and the emptying of water and cheerful sweeping which, to our amusement, we noticed everywhere among the crowd ... These saturnalia are really only occasions of public rejoicing.[24]

The American sea captain John Codman also noted the high degree of syncretism at a church service he attended in 1866, about 20 miles from Rio de Janeiro, though he described it in hardly less coarse terms than did the emperor-to-be. But, unlike the latter, he made special mention of singing, handclapping and foot-stamping. In 'uncouth ceremonies', about a hundred slaves sang

a chattering song, which must have been first sung in their native wilds. Sitting upon their haunches, ... they clapped their hands, wagged their heads, and rolled their eyeballs to this savage melody. The words were African, with the exception of the chorus of 'Sancta Maria, ora pro nobis' ...

Music again, and that always vocal, while the congregation, standing, beat time both with hands and feet.[25]

A remarkable survival of an Africanised dance procession in a Brazilian church was recorded in Minas Gerais in 1944, and this recording has recently been issued on a compact disc. The dance was called *catopê* (or *catupé*). The beautiful song accompanying it, in honour of Our Lady of the Light, is sung in a church by two men, one of whom plays a *pandeiro* tambourine.[26] The refrain is sung in thirds. There is a contemporary description of a *catopê* in honour of Our Lady of the Rosary, danced in the same state a few years earlier:

Dressed in vividly coloured sateen robes, wearing pectoral crosses decorated with knots of ribbons, with chintz shawls over their backs and plumed and sequined head-dresses, they were led by the Master of Ceremonies wearing a cardboard mask and playing a notched scraper [*reco-reco*], assisted by the Sub-Master playing a tambourine [*pandeiro*]. Master and Sub-Master performed unceasingly a lively dance, followed by the other blacks and by the royal court, whose Queen, clad in costly silks, wore on her head a silver crown together with another of artificial roses, set on a curled wig made from agave thread.[27]

Here the Africanised church procession, with its perambulating royal court, converges with the Kongo-derived coronation tradition which has been called 'one of the most beautiful Afro-Brazilian-Roman-Catholic ceremonies',[28] and to which we now turn.

Coronation ceremonies

An African-derived coronation ceremony is at the heart of both the *Congos* of north-eastern and northern Brazil and the similar *Congadas* of São Paulo, Goiás, Mato Grosso and Minas Gerais. These dramatic dances are said to have been first organised by the black lay brotherhoods early in the seventeenth century.[29] One authority holds that the *Congadas* are simply an adaptation of the twelfth-century *Chanson de Roland*, oldest of the *chansons de geste* recounting the legendary deeds of Charlemagne and other French feudal chiefs, and that '[i]n spite of black participation in the *congada* dance and the presence of remnants of customs from the slavery period, the *congada* is not considered to be of African origin'.[30] And, to be sure, Charlemagne and the Paladins, his warrior companions, are a frequent element in the *Congadas*, as is the struggle between Christians and Moors. Evidently, just as they did with the church processions, the lay brotherhoods laid hold of an existing tradition and skilfully adapted it to their own purposes.

From 1674 onwards, throughout the eighteenth century and into the nineteenth, African kings and queens were elected each year by the lay brotherhoods in Recife and Salvador.[31] They were crowned symbolically by a priest at the door of a church, after which there was a procession, with songs and dances, through the streets. Henry Koster described in 1816 the election of a king of the Kongo in Pernambuco:

> The Congo negroes are permitted to elect a king and queen from among the individuals of their own nation; the personages who are fixed upon may either actually be slaves, or they may be manumitted negroes ... [T]heir chief power and superiority over their countrymen is shown on the day of the festival. The negroes of their nation ... pay much respect to them. The man who had acted as their king in Itamaraca ...for several years, was about to resign from old age, and a new chief was to be chosen ... I proceeded to the church with the vicar. We were standing at the door, when there appeared a number of male and female negroes, habited in cotton dresses of colours and of white, with flags flying and

drums beating; and as they approached we discovered among them the king and queen, and the secretary of state. Each of the former wore upon their heads a crown, which was partly covered with gilt paper, and painted of various colours. The king was dressed in an old fashioned suit of divers tints, green, red, and yellow; coat, waistcoat, and breeches; his sceptre was in his hand, which was of wood, and finely gilt. The queen was in a blue silk gown, also of ancient make ...

The Brazilian Kings of Congo worship Our Lady of the Rosary, and are dressed in the dress of white men; they and their subjects dance, it is true, after the manner of their country; but to these festivals are admitted African negroes of other nations, creole blacks, and mulattos, all of whom dance after the same manner; and these dances are now as much the national dances of Brazil as they are of Africa.[32]

Two Austrians, the zoologist Johann Baptist von Spix (1781–1826) and botanist Karl Friedrich von Martius (1794–1868), who travelled through Brazil in the years 1817–20, described a 'solemn procession to the black people's church' in the then frontier province of Mato Grosso:

Blacks carrying a banner lead the way; others follow carrying images of the Saviour, of St Francis, of the Mother of God, all portrayed as black; then comes a band of music whose members, in red and purple cloaks adorned with big ostrich feathers, express joy to the sound of tambourines and rattles, the hissing *canzá* [shaker] and the murmuring marimba [lamellophone]; there follows a black man in a black mask, like a major-domo, sabre in hand; then the princes and princesses, whose trains are carried by pages of both sexes; the king and queen of the previous year, still with sceptres and crowns; finally, the newly-elected royal couple, adorned with diamonds, pearls, coins, and precious objects of all kinds that have been borrowed for this festival; the end of the retinue is made up of black people carrying large burning candles or canes covered with silver paper. Arriving at the church of the black Mother of God, ... the retiring king hands over his sceptre and crown to his successor, who then with his whole court pays a formal visit, in his new rank, to the superintendent of the Diamantino district ... The choir noisily sings its respects to the superintendent ...

On a later day, the musicians paraded before the king and queen, making a 'frightful clamour' with drums, pipes, tambourines, rattles and marimba, while dancers leapt and capered.[33]

The most detailed and informative description of such an Afro-Catholic ceremony in Brazil in the nineteenth century was written by the Austrian botanist Johann Pohl. Travelling through Goiás in June 1819, he witnessed a festival, presided over by a black 'Emperor' and 'Empress', in honour of St Iphigenia, said to be an Ethiopian maiden of the first century AD, converted by the apostle and evangelist St Matthew himself. Though it is by no means certain that Pohl fully understood the significance of what he was seeing, the many vivid details he supplies – how, for instance, a high mass with European church music was immediately followed by African music, singing and dancing, performed inside the church – make this extraordinary passage worth quoting almost in full. Fourteen days before the festival, permission having been asked for and granted,

> several Negroes in Portuguese uniform took to horse – these animals being decorated with bells and ribbons – first prancing up and down the narrow streets and finally riding to church. Out of the church they fetched a banner with the likeness of their saint and hoisted it on a high flagpole in front of the church door as a sort of signal for the holding of the festival. All this was accompanied by the continuous firing of fireworks and muskets. Thereupon they rode around the church, and then the same procession went to the presbytery, on the open space in front of which several evolutions were performed with the greatest skill. And so it wended its way from house to house with much mutual wishing for a happy festival. Accompanied by constant drumming and the sound of national instruments from the Congo, the firing of muskets, and other noise, the night is then spent in the Emperor's house (for an Emperor is also elected for this festival). One Negro keeps calling out 'Bambi', and the full chorus responds 'Domina', which is supposed to mean, more or less: 'The King rules over all.' This wonderful cry, which echoed up to where we were, kept us from getting a wink of sleep all night ...
>
> The following Sunday the Emperor, who was chosen by lot, went from house to house, accompanied by his wife and two drummers, to collect donations for this festival. Before him was carried a small chest with a little bust of the saint carved in the wood, which was offered to passers-by to be kissed. The noise, drumming, singing, etc. also lasted all this night until daybreak. Finally, on 23 June, the eve of the festival of St John, which falls on the same day the other saint is celebrated, a bonfire was lit in front of every house. The outside of the church was completely illuminated with lamps and several bonfires also blazed on the open space in front of it ... In the church itself there was singing and prayer. The so-called Empress was so kind as to present me with a plate of stewed fruit, and even came to me that evening to request that I should not become impatient that night if the Negroes' noise should become somewhat riotous. Prepared in this manner, I awaited what was to happen not without some curiosity. And indeed the noise that night did become incredible. Several mobs of Negroes paraded through the narrow streets from 11 o'clock until daybreak to the sound of the drums and the repulsive tones of [notched scrapers and tambourines]. Their clamour and the incessant firing of fireworks and guns added to the really deafening din. Bonfires were lit by every house, and they blazed up high. And when, to boot, crowds of mulattoes and whites joined the Negroes somewhat later, and their cries and the tones of European musical instruments were added to the noise-making, the whole really fused into an unspeakable chaotic din. Towards noon on the 24th the white natives gathered in the house of the so-called Empress, where all those connected with the festival had already arrived, and the procession to the church began. It was led by some twenty Negroes with their instruments. They were dressed according to the custom of the country. Ostrich feathers adorned their heads; around their loins were draped short skirts of red velvet embroidered with gold; their arms were adorned with

gold chains and ornaments, etc. They were followed by the whole white population walking in pairs. Then came the black Prince and Princess of the festival, he in Portuguese military uniform, she in a long white dress and – which was most strange to see – with heavily powdered hair. She too was almost covered in golden ornaments. Both carried a bouquet of flowers in one hand and in the other a long cane with a big silver knob, like our porters' staffs. There then followed the so-called Emperor and Empress, he also in Portuguese uniform, she too in a long embroidered dress. Both wore a crown and carried a sceptre and in the other hand also a long silver-knobbed cane. With music and song, and the continuous cry of 'Bambi' and 'Domina' ... this fantastic procession, which had a very picturesque appearance, moved on to the church, the Negroes marching before it, constantly dancing in their manner. Their slow, monotonous song accompanied this dance in which they partly crossed their feet and partly stretched them forward and back and contorted their bodies in the most varied and adventurous directions. Inside the church there were two raised thrones at the foot of the altar for the monarchs of the day and two stools for the so-called Prince and Princess. As they entered the church they were offered holy water by the priest amidst the greatest ceremonies, and the high mass began as soon as they had taken their places. From time to time incense was wafted towards these leading characters in the festival. The quality of the music far exceeded my expectations. At the end of the high mass the names of those persons on whom the lot had fallen to occupy these honourable positions the following year were read out in front of the altar. The thrones and stools were then placed in the church, and, as soon as the dignitaries had resumed their seats, the Negro musicians crowded in through the church door, threw themselves to the ground, and immediately began an African dance accompanied by singing. Once this had ended, the black monarch rose and in a loud voice commanded them to start the celebration of the festival of St Euphigenia with song and dance. Then a Negro stepped forward who played the role of military commander in the festival and called out, with wild gaze and much expression, that he had seen a suspicious stranger in the distance, upon which the so-called Emperor ordered him to take the field against this enemy and meet him in combat, begging St Euphigenia for her assistance in the struggle. He thereupon blessed with his sceptre the military commander kneeling before him. The latter then drew his sword and with warrior-like gestures pushed his way through the surrounding Negroes. At this moment the stranger referred to stepped forward in person. All the Negroes rushed upon him and threatened him with death. He, meanwhile, knelt before the throne and begged for an audience ... [H]e declared that he was the ambassador of a distant king, that he did not come with evil intent or to create disorder or hostility, but that his lord and master had heard that the festival of St Euphigenia was to be celebrated in this country and had sent him to take part in it. His request was granted. Now a song was intoned, dances were performed, the Emperor blessed his kneeling vassals with the sceptre, the name of St Euphigenia was repeatedly invoked, and, amid loud singing and music and the same ceremonials which had accompanied its entry, the procession now prepared to depart. Once at home, the dignitaries continued to celebrate the day with a feast in which beans and sugar-cane spirit played the main roles ...

I received an invitation to the company which was to gather that evening at the so-called Emperor's house. It lasted until midnight, was very noisy, the singing and music not falling silent for a moment, and sweetmeats [*Confituren*] and *Catschas* [i.e. *cachaça*] or sugar-cane spirit were handed round. The whole performance ... was done in fairly bad Portuguese verse in which many African words were mixed. There is nothing of the spirit of Camões to be found in this poetry. However, the Negroes are extremely keen on this festival, during which they can show themselves in their greatest finery, and there could be no surer way to hurt and insult them than to refuse them permission to hold this festival, which in so many respects reminds them of their homeland.[34]

Rugendas' vigorous picture of a coronation procession organised by the Brotherhood of Our Lady of the Rosary in Salvador (Fig. 8), dating from between 1821 and 1825, has all the immediacy of a photograph. The Kongo king and queen are central figures, but there is a wealth of supporting detail that calls

FÊTE DE Sᵗᵉ ROSALIE, PATRONE DES NÈGRES.

Figure 8 Black members of the lay brotherhoods in Brazil elected each year a king and queen of the Kongo, who are seen in the centre of this illustration by Rugendas (*c.* 1821–25). On the right is a band of four musicians, playing cylindrical drum, side-blown flute, what seems to be a Portuguese bagpipe, and marimba (lamellophone). (Rugendas, *Malerische Reise in Brasilien*)

for close study: e.g. the two Portuguese spectators on horseback on the left; the Portuguese priest on the right; and the four musicians playing stick-beaten cylindrical drum, side-blown flute, lamellophone, and what is probably a Portuguese bagpipe.

The cultural continuum that linked the black community in Brazil with that in Lisbon ensured that until the second half of the nineteenth century black people in Lisbon also had a ceremonial king or queen, whose entourage included a royal guard carrying halberds and black women dancers who performed 'their Congo dance'.[35]

The pristine form of the Brazilian *Congos*, as they were staged in the eighteenth century, is thought to be preserved in the Recife carnival groups called *maracatus rurais* (otherwise known as *maracatus de baque virado*). These associations are also referred to as *naçoes*, but only 'Cambinda Star' and 'Old Cambinda' have names resembling any of the traditional names of African *naçōes* in Brazil; other *maracatus* are called, for instance, 'Bright Star', 'Imperial Crown', 'Crowned Lion' and 'Elephant'. While the songs of these *naçōes* are sung, a royal couple (*Reis do Congo*) are crowned in a ceremony which perpetuates 'the coronation tradition of African kings as this has been reinterpreted and restaged in Brazil'.[36] The dancers symbolise the procession of the royal couple and their retinue.[37]

Traditionally the proceedings began with dancing at the door of a church, a custom which was popularly, and probably correctly, attributed to the early connection between the *maracatus* and the brotherhoods. The characters represented in the *maracatus* are King, Queen, Princes, Maids of Honour, Ambassador (standard-bearer), *Dama-do-Passo*, *Baliza* (drum majorette), and dancers known as *Baianas*, who wear white gowns and white head-dresses and are in effect ladies-in-waiting. In the earliest *maracatus* the King and Queen processed under a multi-coloured parasol, constantly spinning, decorated with mirrors and with tassels or lace and topped by a coloured sphere and a half-moon. In front of the procession a *balisa* (literally, 'boundary-marker') opens a pathway through the crowd. The *Dama-do-Passo*, the main figure in the retinue, is so called because she is an expert dancer of the *passo*, the capoeira-like dance of Recife mentioned in Chapter 2 (p. 29). It is she who brings forth the *kalunga*, a cloth doll dressed in white and sometimes also in a blue cloak.

The *kalunga* is in effect a kind of sceptre: a symbol of royal authority and a solemn link with Kongo-Angola religious beliefs and practices. Essentially it represents the sea;[38] the word often has that meaning when it appears in Brazilian folktales. In various Bantu languages it means death, the grave, destruction, and fate[39] – or, at a deeper level, 'God's perfection and completion (*lunga*) of all being'.[40] In the Kimbundu language of Angola a *lunga* (plural: *malunga*) is a sacred relic which can assume various shapes but usually takes the form of a human figure carved from wood. The *malunga*, which are extremely ancient, are closely associated with rain and water and also with 'the success of agriculture and hence with life'. The Mbundu say the *malunga* came originally from *Kalunga*, the 'great water'.[41]

In the Recife *maracatus* the *kalunga* is passed around the *Baianas*, each of whom dances with it in her arms before it is placed reverently on a table that serves as an *ad hoc* altar. The accompanying music is played on large deep-voiced *bombo* drums, *onguê* iron bells and rattles, by ensembles of up to 30 musicians. *Baque virado*, meaning literally 'spun beat', refers to the rapid spinning of the drumsticks before they strike the drumhead. Three *maracatu* songs accompanied by two unspecified drums, *cuíca* friction drum, shaker and *onguê*, recorded in Ceará in 1943, have recently been issued on a compact disc.[42]

Another danced procession, by women of mixed ethnicity (*mulatas*) dressed in white, in nineteenth-century style, and wearing ribbons, necklaces and ear-rings, was known as *Taieiras*. Perhaps originally an offshoot of the *Congos* dramatic dance, it was staged in Bahia, Sergipe, Alagoas, Pernambuco and Minas Gerais on 6 January each year in honour of St Benedict and Our Lady of the Rosary.[43]

Like the English folk play and morris dance, the *Congos* and *Congadas* contain much whose significance is lost. There is an overlay, often heavy, of Christian iconography. But, like the *maracatus*, these dramatic dances usually feature a royal court and the coronation of a king or queen or both. Another frequent but not obligatory element is the sending of an ambassador either on a peace mission or to declare war. An historical figure who appears in a Paraíba version as Zinga Nbângi, elsewhere as Queen Ginga, has been identified as Queen N'Zinga or Ginga Bândi (*c.* 1581–1663), who reigned as 'sovereign of Dongo, Matamba and Luanda' in the seventeenth century – and did in fact send a peace mission to the Portuguese governor, João Correia de Sousa, in the year 1621.

Oneyda Alvarenga distinguishes three versions of *Congos*:

1) *A simple royal court, with songs and dances that portray a battle.* This, described in the nineteenth century as being performed in Bahia and Sergipe, is probably the original version. The participants were drawn up in two lines and there was a simulated sword fight. Between the two lines stood three queens, and one group tried to seize the crown of one of them, Queen Perpétua, while the other group defended her. Queen Perpétua's name is thought to indicate that she held the office for life, the other two queens being elected periodically. The *Congadas* of certain parts of Goiás, São Paulo and Minas Gerais were formerly more complex but later conformed to this simple version, being limited to a royal court with war dances.

2) *A royal court with an embassy of peace.* This version was performed in the Minas Gerais town of Tejuco in the early nineteenth century, and was collected about 100 years later in the Goiás town of Goiânia. Here the principal characters are the King of the Kongo and Queen Ginga.

3) *A royal court followed by a war expedition.* This third version, which was richest of all in historical references and in allusions to Kongo traditions, was performed in the states of Paraíba, Rio Grande do Norte and Ceará.[44]

An alternative name for *Congada* in São Paulo was *Cayumba.* Under this name it was danced in the town of Campinas in 1837 by Congo, Benguela and Moçambique slaves; and in 1857 a São Paulo newspaper carried an advertisement for a piece of sheet music for piano called *A Cayumba*, which was described as 'Negro dance, original music in a completely new style'.[45]

According to José Jorge de Carvalho, the musical material of the *Congos* and *Congadas* is 'not as deeply rooted African' as that of candomblé; it varies from state to state, and often 'combines quite openly Western musical structures and instruments with Afro-derived rhythmic patterns'.[46] A 1977 recording of the *Congos de Saiote*, in the town of São Gonçalo de Amarante (Rio Grande do Norte), accompanied by *rabeca* fiddle, *pandeiro* tambourine and rattles, includes a song beginning *Óia, Nossa Rainha foi coroada* ('Listen, our Queen was crowned').[47]

Palmares and the Quilombo

Slave resistance in Brazil took many different forms. Widespread was a kind of go-slow, whereby an individual household slave would claim, 'That's not my work' or, pretending to be stupid, would ask the master or mistress to repeat each new detail several times. There were individual acts of vengeance and attempts at suicide and abortion.[48] There were frequent slave insurrections, the most serious of which took place in 1720, 1806, 1809, 1814, 1822, 1827, 1835 and 1838.[49] But the most common form of slave resistance in colonial Brazil was flight.[50] A large number of the Africans transported to Brazil fled from captivity as soon as possible after their arrival in the New World. Fugitives hunted down and recaptured endured an array of punishments that make horrifying reading. These included the *palmatório*, a kind of ferule; thumbscrews; handcuffs; ball and chain; a tin mask; a heavy iron stock (*tronco simples*) that imprisoned the legs; the *tronco duplo*, a stock which forced the victim to sit hunched forward, arms against ankles, or to lie on one side; a metal neck-ring with long chains or hooks; and the *chicote*, a five-tailed metal-tipped whip known as the 'codfish'. Ingenious planters devised a labour-saving 'codfish' by whose means a whip fixed to a revolving water-wheel lashed the backs of slaves bound to a bench. A mixture of pepper, salt and vinegar was rubbed on open wounds, and floggings were sometimes sadistically spread over several days to reopen wounds and leave deeper scars.[51]

Knowing what a hell to expect if they were recaptured did little to discourage fugitives from fleeing but did make them more than ever determined not to be caught. And many succeeded in evading recapture. Individual runaways built themselves shelters in the forest and grew corn and beans on a small plot, or else raided nearby plantations for supplies.[52] Fugitive groups, like their 'maroon' counterparts in Jamaica, the Guianas and elsewhere, established self-governing liberated territories. From about the beginning of the seventeenth century there were to be at least 25 of these liberated territories in the Brazilian interior. They were known in the Portuguese language as *quilombos*. The word *quilombo*, meaning 'refuge for fugitive slaves in the forest', strongly suggests – though it may not be directly derived from – the Kimbundu word *kilombo*, 'capital, town, confederation', which originally meant 'male initiation camp' (i.e. circumcision camp) and later 'male military society'. The Portuguese word *mocambo* (sometimes *mocana*), which is synonymous with *quilombo*, is probably derived from the Kimbundu *mukambo*, 'hideaway'.[53]

The *Quilombo* dramatic dance celebrates in particular the free state of Palmares, held by runaway slaves for the best part of the seventeenth century – from c. 1605 to 1697 – in the teeth of everything the Portuguese colonial administration threw against them. Palmares means literally 'palm groves', from the proliferation of wild palms in the coastal forest zone. But those who lived there called it Angola Janga (from Kimbundu *ngola iadianga*, 'first Angola'). Straddling the then captaincies – now Brazilian states – of Pernambuco and Alagoas, Palmares was a swath of land about 50 kilometres across, stretching south-westwards for approximately 200 kilometres, from about 40 kilometres south-west of the port of Recife to about 50 kilometres south-west of the town of Macaco. First established around 1605, it grew substantially in size and population from 1630 as a result of the Dutch invasion of north-east Brazil in that year. Captive Africans lost no time in taking advantage of the Europeans' internecine strife, and there was an immediate and substantial increase in the number of fugitives.

The people of Palmares left no written records, but we know something about their culture and way of life from the accounts by raiding Portuguese soldiers, who generally found the settlements deserted, the inhabitants having been warned of the imminent expeditions by spies posted in the coastal towns and on the sugar plantations.

Palmares was not a single community, but rather a cluster of settlements united to form a neo-African polity. Nine such settlements are known: Acotirene (or Arotirene), Amaro, Andalaquituche, Dambrabanga, Macaco, Osenga, Subupira, Taboas and Zambi. Macaco, the main town, is reported to have had over 1,500 houses, and, like the other settlements, was fortified by a palisade with embrasures, caltrops and pitfalls. In Subupira, the second town, there were more than 800 houses. It would be wrong to suppose that only Africans lived in Palmares. Its population, estimated at about 11,000 in the mid-seventeenth century, also included black people born in Brazil, people of mixed ethnicity, Amerindians, and even some white people.[54] Palmares in many ways represented an adaptation of African social and political practices to the Brazilian colonial situation.[55] For instance, as in many African societies in that period, a form of slavery existed: those who went to Palmares of their own free will became free citizens; those captured in raids were enslaved. Free citizens addressed each other as *malungo* (cf. Kikongo *mu alungo*, 'in the ship'). This was the word, meaning 'comrade' or 'foster-brother', used by slaves who had arrived in Brazil together on the same ship; it had the same emotional force as the cognate *malongue* in Trinidad, *batiment* in Haiti, 'shipmate' in Jamaica, and *sippi* (or *sibi*) and *mati* in Suriname.[56]

Palmares is sometimes wrongly referred to as a kingdom, but its political system had nothing in common with that of any seventeenth-century European kingdom. It is not to idealise Palmares to call it an 'egalitarian, fraternal, and independent republic'.[57] Those who were not slaves practised a form of democracy the likes of which would not be seen in Europe until the French revolution of 1789 overthrew monarchical absolutism. Political power was based on local assemblies which decided questions by majority vote. Palmares had a paramount chief known as Ganga-Zumba, who was elected by an assembly of local chiefs. All sources agree that the paramount chief was elected, but it is not clear whether the election was for life or for a limited period.[58] It is thought that Ganga-Zumba was a title rather than a personal name; in Angola the *nganga a nzumbi* was a priest who functioned as a psychiatrist by dealing with the spirits of the dead: 'One whose responsibilities included relieving sufferings caused by an unhappy spirit of a lineage ancestor'.[59] Under the paramount chief of Palmares was a military commander known as Zumbi: it is unclear whether this was a proper name, a praise name or a title.

Most of the inhabitants of Palmares lived by agriculture, but crafts were practised, including work in metal – there were at least four smithies – as well as in straw, gourds and ceramics. There was at least one church, with religious observances that fused Christian and African elements, although 'there may have been far more African features than observers realized'.[60]

Throughout its history, Palmares was never free from attack for long. The Dutch, who controlled the north-east coast for 24 years, sent three expeditions against it: all three were beaten back. Between the expulsion of the Dutch in 1654 and the eventual destruction of Palmares in 1694 Portuguese military expeditions were frequent – sometimes more than one a year. But between these raids Palmares carried on trade with its Portuguese neighbours, who seem to have had no qualms about exchanging arms, munitions and salt for foodstuffs and craft products. Like his Jamaican maroon counterpart Cudjoe in 1739, the Ganga-Zumba decided in 1678 to start peace negotiations with a new governor of Pernambuco. Hardly had peace terms been agreed than the Portuguese violated them, and there was a revolt in Palmares, led by Zumbi, nephew of the Ganga-Zumba; the latter was overthrown and put to death.

The defenders of Palmares are described as 'masters of guerrilla warfare, adept at the use of camouflage and ambush'.[61] Eventually the Portuguese turned to Amerindian mercenaries and professional slave-catchers from São Paulo. Backed up by local troops, these began operations in 1692 and slowly pushed back the defence perimeters. In February 1694 came the last battle, in which 200 defenders were killed, 500 were captured and 200 killed themselves rather than surrender. Zumbi was wounded but escaped. On 20 November 1695, with a small band of his supporters, he was ambushed and killed. The Portuguese cut off his head and put it on display.

As a symbol of daring and uncompromising resistance, Zumbi the warrior-chief has become a legend and a Brazilian national hero. Brazilians of African descent had never quite forgotten him or the free republic he led: as long ago as 1927 a civic centre in São Paulo adopted the name Palmares, and Jorge Amado's novel *Tenda dos Milagres* (1969) tells of an *afoxé*-like carnival group (*grêmio*) in 1920s Salvador that honoured Zumbi.[62] But it was not until the 1970s that Palmares and Zumbi emerged into national prominence. One of the first signs of this was the hit song 'Zumbi' by the pop singer Jorge Ben (Jorge Duílio Lima Meneses, b. 1942), released in 1974:

> I want to see what will happen
> When Zumbi arrives.
> Zumbi is the Lord of war,
> Zumbi is the Lord of demands.
> When Zumbi arrives
> It will be he who commands.[63]

Four years later black activists and artists in the state of São Paulo began celebrating the anniversary of Zumbi's death, 20 November, as Zumbi Day. They organised local 'Zumbi Festivals', with dances, street theatre, concerts and public readings. Rather than celebrating emancipation, which they saw as a lie and a farce, they insisted that Zumbi Day was the real black holiday. Portraying Palmares with understandable exaggeration as a kind of pastoral idyll, the composer and singer Milton Nascimento (b. 1942) wrote a *Quilombo Mass*, hailing 'the *quilombos* of yesterday, today, and tomorrow' and expressing the hope of 'making Palmares again'. Brazil's then military government, anxious not to be outflanked by the Left, jumped on the bandwagon. In 1980 a Zumbi National Park was created in Alagoas, on what was thought to be the site of Palmares. Project Zumbi was launched in Rio de Janeiro with the aim of strengthening the teaching of African-Brazilian history and culture in the schools. In São Paulo, Project Zumbi developed into a yearly month-long programme of films, concerts, lectures and other activities. *Quilombo*, a powerful film by Carlos Diegues, was released in 1983. In the same year a *bloco afro* called 'Palmares', which had been founded in 1982 and claimed 500 participants, sang this carnival song by Ariosvaldo Manoel da Conceição:

> Palmares, a little village,
> Where the assembled blacks
> Debated their freedom.
> In sugar mills, hells of bad luck or good.

> The blacks sweated blood.
> Sometimes they preferred death.
> Zumbi, fearless wise black man –
> Never was his body in chains –
> He struggled armed to the teeth.
> And today black people
> Have their own freedom.[64]

In 1988 the Mangueira Samba School, in its prizewinning samba 'One Hundred Years of Freedom: Reality or Illusion?', summed up the aspirations of many Brazilians, and not only those of African descent, for whom Zumbi 'embodies the strongest resistance to the slave-based colonial regime and, consequently, the struggle for economic and political justice today':[65]

> I dreamed ...
> That Zumbi of Palmares returned.
> The blacks' misery ended;
> It was a new redemption.[66]

The tercentenary of Zumbi's death, 20 November 1995, was widely commemorated in Brazil, and Salvador chose him as the theme of its 1995 carnival. Today, as Robert Nelson Anderson has made clear, Zumbi is seen by many black Brazilians as more than a secular hero. He is an ancestor, whose immortal spirit is 'worthy of respect from those who consider themselves his descendants'.[67]

The *Quilombo* dramatic dance originated in Alagoas and spread through the north-east. With a cast about 50 strong which included warriors, spies and two kings, each with a secretary who functioned as ambassador, it featured a mock battle between Africans (*Pretos*) and Amerindians (*Caboclos*). One account has the Africans wearing blue cotton trousers of the type formerly worn by slaves, while their king wore a gorgeous coat of glittering green cloth.[68] Another says the dance was accompanied by the *adufe* frame drum, various kinds of tambourine, rattles, bamboo flutes, *zabumba* drums and trumpets made from the rolled-up leaves of the pindova palm (*Altalea compta*).[69]

The Cucumbi

Probably related to the *Congos* and *Congadas*, but in some ways apparently a variant of the *Quilombo*, is the *Cucumbi* dramatic dance, which seems to have originated in Bahia and to have survived longest in Sergipe. It was known as *Quicumbiz* in Pernambuco, and there is a report of it being performed there in 1745 – a 'famous and pleasing [*plauzivel*] dance', whose 13 performers were clad in black velvet, with petticoats of silk or embroidery or galloon, all trimmed with gold and silver.

To the sound of guitars [*violas*] and tambourines [*pandeiros*], singing and dancing in the Ethiopian manner, they intoned praises to St Gonzales ... A still warmer reception was accorded to a pagan instrument vulgarly called marimbas, which a Negro dressed in a lace petticoat played commandingly with remarkable skill ...

A little later, with the sweetest harmony, ears were refreshed by three flautists dressed in shirts of fine lace with lappets of the same material and of crimson damask.[70]

There exists a detailed contemporary description of an 1830 performance of the *Cucumbi* in Rio de Janeiro, where it is said to have been incorporated into the carnival tradition. The characters included a king and queen, the king's eldest son (*Mameto*), an Amerindian (*Caboclo*), an overseer (*Capataz*), an ambassador (*Língua*) and a magician (*Quimboto*), as well as princes, princesses and fortune-tellers. There were dances imitating snakes, jaguars and the swaying of ships, and there was a mock battle between blacks and Amerindians, which strongly suggests the final attack on Palmares.[71]

According to Chasteen, the '*Cucumbys*' reappeared on the Rio streets in the 1880s, a phenomenon he associates with 'the momentum of the abolitionist movement'.[72] As the *Ticumbi*, this dramatic dance was still being performed in São Mateus and Conceição da Barra, in the north of Espírito Santo, as recently as 1977. Here it was accompanied by a locally made traditional guitar with five double strings, twelve locally made tambourines and four swords with steel blades, which were used to reinforce the rhythm in the war dance.[73] Alceu Maynard Araújo calls the *Ticumbi* a 'simplified form of the *Congada*', in which two black kings fight, and King Bamba is defeated by King Congo.[74] In Rio Grande do Sul the *Cucumbi* was called *Quicumbi*.

The Moçambique

The *Moçambique* has been described as

a highly elaborate dance with some symbolic fighting, singing and playing of instruments such as guitars, drums, rattles and violins ... [The dance] has a sacred character, and its performance is a privilege reserved for the members of the confraternity of Saint Benedict, a black saint whose name is sometimes given to the dance.[75]

Béhague states that the music accompanying the *Moçambique* 'has no African traits and its origin was obscure'.[76] Not all writers on this dramatic dance agree with him, however; according to one, the music of the *Moçambique* had 'a marked African flavour'.[77] Apart from anything else, the *Moçambique* was noteworthy for two unusual instruments. The dancers held wooden sticks (*bastões* or *paus*), 90–100 cm long and 2–3 cm in diameter and possibly of

Amerindian provenance, and marked the rhythm by banging these together. And they wore a jingle called *paiá*, a device which has several alternative names: *macaquaias, matungo, conguinho* and *coquinho*. This could be either a shoulder-strap with brass bells attached, or else small cylindrical tubes, tied to legs or feet, containing little stones. The custom is thought to derive from the Angolan *jiuáua*, a wire thread that Lunda children wrap around their bodies; from it hang small thin strips that clash together as the dancers move.[78] In São Paulo a rattle called *pernanguma* or *prananguma* was used in the *Moçambique*: this is a two-handled round, flat tin containing lead shot; it is somewhat louder than the ordinary *ganzá* rattle.[79]

Bumba-meu-boi *and the power of satire*

The best-known of Brazilian dramatic dances, performed in the north-east each year from the middle of November to 6 January, was long supposed to be of mixed European, Amerindian and African origin but is now known to have been created by African slaves in Brazil as an expression of resistance. European and Amerindian features entered the tradition much later. In *Bumba-meu-boi* the slaves devised a way of ridiculing and satirising their masters. Characters and music alike are quintessentially Brazilian, and it has been described as 'the most unadulterated of the north-eastern popular spectacles'.[80] In Maranhão and Piauí there are three basic styles, known as *Boi de Zabumba, Boi de Matraca* and *Boi de Orquestra*. The first, by far the oldest, has African characteristics; the second, less than 150 years old, is largely Amerindian; the third and most recent is a Europeanised style developed about 40 years ago by Francisco Paiva, leader of a brass band in the Maranhão town of Axixa. These differences are apparent in the choice of musical instruments, costume design, rhythmic patterns and choreography.[81]

The origins of *Bumba-meu-boi* have been established by Kazadi wa Mukuna, who has cut through a tangle of earlier conflicting theories. According to one of these it was a version of Gil Vicente's first play, *Monólogo do Vaqueiro* (1502), which he wrote to amuse a Portuguese queen after childbirth; according to another it originated in Portugal as one of the *reisados*, dramatic dances celebrating Epiphany (6 January).[82] Mukuna shows that, on the contrary, *Bumba-meu-boi* was

> created by African slaves in colonial Brazil ... to denounce and ridicule colonial slave owners. Other styles [of *Bumba-meu-boi*] came into existence at later periods, created by other segments of the population in imitation of the African by maintaining the story line of the play and its dramatization without necessarily adhering to the original raison d'être; each of the new styles incorporated features which reflected its ethnic identity. The argument for African authorship of the Bumba-meu-Boi is also sustained by the chronology of appearance of the African

style called Boi de Zabumba, the Indian style known as the Boi de Matraca introduced in Maranhão in 1868, and the most recent style called Boi de Orquestra (1958) with strong European influence – as well as by musical instruments, rhythmic organization, costumes, and the format of dance presentation.[83]

The Brazilian origin of *Bumba-meu-boi* is no longer in dispute. Mukuna clinches matters by quoting 'A Friend of Civilization' who, writing in a Brazilian journal in 1861 – seven years before the *Boi de Matraca* style emerged and 91 years before the *Boi de Orquestra* style emerged – called *Bumba-meu-boi* 'the stupid and immoral merrymaking of slaves'.[84] Though how and when *Bumba-meu-boi* was first performed is unknown and likely to remain so, Mukuna refers to documents pinpointing, as its most likely cultural matrix, the valley of the São Francisco river and, in particular, the sugar plantations and mills of Bahia and Pernambuco in the seventeenth and eighteenth centuries. For Brazil, this was 'the golden period of the cattle cycle'; it was the colony's pastoral phase, during which the ox was an economic factor of supreme importance for the colonists. As cattle-raising spread into the states of Ceará, Piauí, Maranhão and Pará, *Bumba-meu-boi* followed, though with a certain time lag.[85]

There are many versions of the *Bumba-meu-boi* story, but in essentials it goes as follows. The slave Pai Francisco (or Mateus) and his pregnant wife Mãe Catarina live on a ranch owned by a Portuguese master, Amo, who has a favourite ox, variously called 'Royal Fame' (*Fama Real*) and 'Star Ox' (*Boi Estrela*). Mãe Catarina has an urge to eat an ox's tongue, and it has to be that of the master's favourite animal. Worried about the welfare of his unborn child, Pai Francisco takes the ox into the woods, kills it and takes the tongue to his wife, who cooks and eats it. The next day, missing his favourite ox, the master gathers together his cowboys and slaves and asks if anyone has seen it. One of them tells him that he had seen Pai Francisco leading it into the woods and had heard a gunshot soon afterwards. The woods are searched, and the ox's remains are found. Amo is very angry and orders Pai Francisco to bring his ox back to life or die himself. A Portuguese doctor tries several times to resurrect the ox, but fails. At length an Amerindian practitioner of traditional medicine is sent for. He lays his hands on the animal, which comes back to life. All dance happily through the night.[86]

The literal meaning of *Bumba-meu-boi* is 'something like "Wham! Swing your horns, bull!", an interjection expressing violent action and excitement, which is repeated in the songs accompanying the pageant'.[87] The onomatopoeic word *bumba* may be derived from the Kimbundu *bumbalakata*.[88]

It is wrong to suppose, as some have done, that the ox in *Bumba-meu-boi* has anything to do with Iberian bullfighting: 'It is, rather, a legitimate Brazilian bull accustomed to rural work, with its escort of cowboys, not related to bullrings, matadors and picadors. This bull is a burlesque animal that dances in certain processions to the sound of drums and whistles.'[89] Mukuna explains why it is precisely the ox that figures in a folk drama created by the slaves:

The ox, symbol of power and wealth ... is utilized in the drama as the catalyst for deep-seated satire against the ruling class ...

Subtle satire is incorporated into the roles of characters representing social authorities and into the manner in which these authorities are addressed in the play by those considered to be of the lowest order in the social hierarchy. Ridiculed characters vary from one region to another, but the most prominent in Maranhão are the priest, the Portuguese master (Amo), and the captain (Cavalo Marinho) who represent the ruling class and slave owners in colonial Brazil ...

[*Bumba-meu-boi* was] utilized ... by the oppressed members of the society as a means of challenging the authority of the ruling class ... [They] created a play in which despised authorities were caricatured and denounced.[90]

Mukuna points out that satire in song, addressed to a superior, is a widespread practice in African cultures, and quotes Alan Merriam ('in song the individual or the group can apparently express deep-seated feelings not permissibly verbalized in other contexts')[91] and Hugh Tracey (among the Chopi of Mozambique, 'You can say publicly in songs what you cannot say privately to a man's face').[92]

In the original *Boi de Zabumba* style, the accompaniment is usually played on percussion instruments. Chief among these is the *zabumba* (or *bombo*), a large cylindrical double-headed drum, 60–80 cm in diameter and 30–40 cm deep, both heads being made of goat- or ox-skin. Painted, and often decorated with geometrical figures or other motifs, it is played with two sticks and, during the *Boi de Zabumba* procession, is carried on two people's shoulders for the drummer to play. Any number of such drums may be heard in a single ensemble. Mukuna makes it clear that, though this drum resembles the European bass drum, it is here a modern substitute for a double-headed hollow-log drum of the West African type. It provides 'heavy straight beats', with variations resembling those of the *tambor-de-crioulo* (see pp. 17, 23). *Tambor-de-crioulo*, as was said above, is remarkable for the dancers' periodical rotations (*gingas*) as they dance counter-clockwise, and these spinning figures are also seen in *Boi de Zabumba*, whose drum variations resemble those of *Tambor-de-crioulo*.[93]

The Africanism of the Boi de Zabumba style is also corroborated by the use of the friction drum and the organization of the rhythmic material. In contrast to samba and other carnival manifestations in which this drum is referred to as cuíca, in the Bumba-meu-Boi it is known as Tambor Onça [literally, jaguar drum].[94]

The dancers wear large hats covered with ribbons or adorned with coloured glass beads and with long ribbons hanging down the back; those playing Amerindian characters sport hats with feathers or coloured paper and raffia.[95]

In various parts of Brazil *Bumba-meu-boi* is known by alternative names: *Boi-bumbá* and *Boi-de-reis* (Amazonas, Maranhão and Pará); *Boi-calemba, Bumba* and *Cavalo-marinho* (Pernambuco); *Boi-surubim* or *Boi-surubi* (Ceará); *Três-pedaços* (Pôrto de Pedras, Alagoas); *Boi-de-jacá* (Pindamonhangaba, São Paulo); *Folguedo-*

de-boi and *Reis-do-boi* (Cabo Frio, Rio de Janeiro); *Boi-de-mamão* (Paraná and Santa Catarina);[96] and *Boizinho* (Rio Grande do Sul). But wherever it is performed, and under whatever name, this is, as it always has been, 'the dramatic dance most intensely enjoyed by the Brazilian rural population'.[97] It should be added, however, that it does not nowadays 'carry a single identity but offers material that can be extended or reworked so that it constitutes a screen where different identifications can be projected'.[98]

Cambinda: *a festival of liberation*

The *cambinda* performed in the Paraíba city of Lucena on Easter Sunday was created to celebrate the emancipation of the slaves in 1888. This is the oral tradition passed on by João Marcos Chagas, 'King' of the group of fishermen who constituted the Cambinda Brilhante de Lucena and recorded some of its 50-odd songs in 1978.[99] Other characters played by this all-male group were Queen, *Dama-do-Passo*, Master, Crowned Lion, Standard-bearer (Ambassador), Director of the Scarlet Group, Director of the Blue Group, and Lancers (otherwise known as *Cambindas* or *Baianas*). Here, as in *cambindas* reported elsewhere in Paraíba and in the neighbouring state of Pernambuco, there is clearly a close connection with the Recife *maracatus*, but their exact relationship is uncertain. The *cambindas* may be direct copies and adaptations; but there may also be some connection with the *nação* known traditionally as Cambinda, after the Angolan port of Cabinda. Formed up in two files, with the royal family between them, the participants dance through the streets to the accompaniment of *zabumba* bass drums and shakers.[100]

5

Three Vanished Instruments

The lamellophone (marimba)

Few Europeans who went to Brazil in the early nineteenth century took a genuine interest in the musical activities and instruments of the African slaves there. One who did was the English botanist Clarke Abel, who was on his way to China in 1816 when the ship on which he was travelling called at Rio de Janeiro. Abel was so intrigued by the instrument he heard a slave playing that he bought it from the musician. This purchase, perhaps unique in that period, had an unexpected and still more intriguing result:

> Returning from my ride through the city of St. Sebastian [i.e. Rio de Janeiro], I fell in with a group of negro slaves who were assembled at the corner of a street, listening with great delight to one of their own tribe playing on a very rude [i.e. crude] musical instrument. It consisted of a few wires fixed to a small square frame, placed over a large segment of the shell of the coco-nut. I requested one of his companions to accompany the instrument with his voice, which he immediately did, in a monotonous, though not unpleasing tone. Another performer accompanied the last notes by wild and expressive gesticulations, in which he was followed by most of the bye-standers. It was more than probable that national remembrances animated both performers and auditors. Nothing less powerful, surely, could excite the strong emotion which agitated their frames; and I was, in some measure, confirmed in this opinion by what followed. Having bought the instrument, I slung it on my arm, and rode with it through the streets to the English hotel. Every slave whose eye caught my appendage uttered as I passed a cry of surprise: it was also one of joy and exultation. His dark countenance assumed the liveliest expression, and his whole attitude marked the strong sensation excited by the appearance of a stranger, a white and free man, bearing, perhaps, his national emblem, under such circumstances, reviving the recollection of that liberty and that home from which he had been impiously and for ever torn.[1]

The 'very rude' instrument that the Englishman bought, much used by Africans and their descendants in Brazil in the eighteenth and nineteenth centuries and without doubt earlier, but now extinct there, was a lamellophone, also known as *mbira*, *sanza*, hand piano, and plucked idiophone.[2] In Brazil it was usually called a marimba, which is a source of possible confusion since the resonator xylophone to be described later in this chapter was also called marimba. The lamellophone occurs in many forms all over sub-Saharan Africa, where traditionally it was the preferred instrument for self-delectation and was frequently played by people who had to walk long distances – though that was by no means its only function; among the Bena Luluwa of Angola and Congo-Kinshasa, for instance, the gourd-resonated *issanji* lamellophone is not used as a solo instrument, but, exceptionally for Africa, in orchestras of four or five players, sometimes with percussion instruments added.[3] 'The blacks are excessively fond of these instruments everywhere in Angola', wrote Joachim Monteiro in 1875, 'playing them as they walk along or rest, and by day or night a "marimba" is at all hours heard twanging somewhere.'[4] One of the Angolan prototypes of the Brazilian lamellophone was described by Herman Soyaux in 1879:

> At one end of a boat-shaped box or of a small board tied to a gourd, little strips of iron or of the bark of the leaf-stem of the raffia palm, of varying length and thickness, are fixed across a kind of bridge which, moved by both of the player's thumbs, is able to produce a scale of higher and deeper notes of a quivering and humming, but not unpleasant, sound.[5]

The lamellophone bought by Abel had a coconut shell as resonator; other kinds used a small wooden box, or a gourd – it was common practice to hold the instrument over a half-calabash of suitable size, as can be seen in Fig. 5 – or, more rarely, a turtle shell. The number of keys varied from four to a dozen or so. (The Angola *quissanje* may have up to 22 keys; other African lamellophones, some of which have two or even three manuals, may have an even larger number of keys, but such large instruments do not seem to have been used in Brazil.) As is common practice in Angola and elsewhere in Africa, beads or metal disks would often have been threaded on the keys to obtain the preferred slightly buzzing sound; a contemporary reference to the Brazilian instrument's timbre as 'sleepy' seems to denote this practice.[6]

The French visitor Louis-François de Tollenare described the lamellophone he saw in 1816–18 as

> a wooden box – which looked like those in which German haberdashery is sent – with four small strips, six or seven inches long, each fastened to it by one end. These strips rested on a small cross-piece that served as a bridge. When the musician lifted one of these strips and let it spring back, he drew from it a muffled sound which made the belly of the box ring. These four strips of different lengths were no doubt tuned, but I could not guess which notes of the scale they yielded. The musician, squatting near his box, seemed to be paying it great attention and ran through his four notes very smoothly.[7]

As seen in the previous chapter, the Austrian biologists Spix and Martius, watching a church procession in Mato Grosso in 1817–20, heard a 'murmuring marimba', played by a band which included tambourines and rattles and the 'hissing *canzá*' (shaker).[8] Another traveller, Alexander Caldcleugh (d. 1858), quoting an advertisement in a Rio de Janeiro newspaper in 1820 which offered for sale 'a slave fit for a coachman, who can play on the Piano and Marimba, and combines with a knowledge of music some acquaintance with the trade of a tailor', explained that the marimba was 'a musical instrument much used by the blacks, by whom it was introduced. It is formed of five small steel bars fastened over a half gourd. It yields rather a monotonous sound, but which, however, does not want admirers among the lower classes' (i.e. lower-class Brazilians of European descent).[9] The Austrian botanist J. E. Pohl was not one of the lamellophone's admirers; to his sophisticated ear it produced 'the feeble noise of thin iron rods fixed to a little board whose meagre sounds are heard when touched by the thumb'.[10]

The artist Rugendas showed a lamellophone being played in the 1820s as part of an orchestra of four players making music for a festival organised by one of the black brotherhoods (Fig. 8); the other instruments are a cylindrical drum played with sticks, a side-blown pipe or flute; and what seems to be a Portuguese bagpipe (*gaita-de-foles*).[11] Here, as in Rugendas's two other drawings of the lamellophone (Figs 11, 12), he shows the simple, box-like, instrument without gourd resonator.

Captain von Kotzebue of the Russian navy found in the 1820s that on Sundays and holidays the black inhabitants of Rio de Janeiro sang as they strolled about, the tunes having 'a more lively character' than the worksongs, 'and they sometimes accompany their voices on a little instrument composed of a few steel springs'; he gave no further description.[12] For that we must turn to the British artillery officer Lieutenant Henry Chamberlain, who was in Rio in 1819–20 and left many drawings. In one of these he portrayed a black man 'bearing a load of wood' and

> amusing himself along the road with his favourite Madimba de Btsché [*sic*], a Congo musical instrument; formed of a number of narrow thin flat pieces of Iron, a little bent at the end where struck securely fastened to a square piece of Board, on the under side of which is a Calabash, or Gourd, ornamented with a string of coloured Beads, or gaudy coloured Worsted. The pieces of Iron are of various lengths, and are played upon by both thumbs. The notes produced are agreeable and harmonious, and in the hands of some of the Performers the Musick is by no means despicable.[13]

Chamberlain's 'Btsché' is a misprint for 'Bitsché'; the Bantu word is *m'bichi*.

The German army officer Carl Schlichthorst, who lived in Rio in the 1820s, reported:

The marimba is a musical instrument consisting of a row of steel springs fixed to a little board; half a coco-nut shell serves as a sounding board. It is played with the two thumbs and is held by the other fingers. The marimba has a soft, melancholic tone, and is without doubt the best instrument to have been invented in Africa.

Schlichthorst added that

one man who played the marimba most skilfully I moved to tears by saying I had never heard anything in the world more beautiful. Later he related with great gusto how some African king had employed him as *Capellmeister* or court musician, always adding the word '*mor*', which means principal or first.[14]

Schlichthorst's encounter with a black woman street-vender playing a lamellophone is described in a later chapter (pp. 129–30).

Maria Graham enjoyed the small marimba's 'very sweet tone' and described the instrument as follows:

On a flat piece of sonorous wood a little bridge is fastened; and to this small slips of iron, of different lengths, are attached, so that both ends vibrate on the board, one end being broader and more elevated than the other. This broad end is played with the thumbs, the instrument being held with both hands.

This and several other instruments Graham mentioned were, she added, 'tuned in a peculiar manner, and with great nicety, especially the marimba'.[15] Another of the lamellophone's admirers, the Revd Robert Walsh, writing in 1830, compared its sound to that of a spinet, and described it as

half a calabash, containing within it a number of small bars of iron parallel to each other, with one extremity flat, presenting a surface like the keys of a harpsichord: this [the player] holds in both hands, and presses with his thumbs, in succession, the flat bars, which emit a tinkling sound like a spinet. This instrument is very universal. Every poor fellow who can, procures one of those; and as he goes along under his burden, continues to elicit from it simple tones, which seem to lighten his load, as if it was his *grata testudo, laborum dulce lenimen* [pleasing lyre, a sweet way to alleviate labour].[16]

Debret left a similar description of the instrument in the same period, alongside his picture of a gourd-resonated lamellophone accompanying a blind berimbau player (Fig. 5). He called it

a kind of harmonica [i.e. dulcimer with strips of metal], consisting of iron strips fixed on a small wooden board and kept in place with a support. Each strip vibrates when released from the pressure of the player's thumbs, which causes them to bend and produces a tuneful sound when they spring back. Part of a huge gourd, approximating to this instrument's sound board, lends it a deeper sound, very much like that of a harp.[17]

In 1833 a writer in a German musical journal described the lamellophone, which he called *Loangobania*, as 'a sort of Glockenspiel [*Stahl-harmonika*]' and 'the best perfected' of the musical instruments played by Africans in Brazil:

> It consists of a thin board to which between five and seven steel springs of various lengths are fixed side by side to one end, being separated about half an inch from the board by a wooden block thrust underneath. This arrangement is usually glued to half a coco-nut shell in such a way that the board forms the sound-box. The notes produced by this instrument are not unpleasant, and a skilled player is even able to imitate proper [*vollkommene*] music by moving the blocks and other tricks.[18]

About 30 years later the US navy's William Ruschenberger was walking around Rio when he saw

> a crowd of Negroes in the street, in the midst of which one was dancing to the sound of a rude instrument, accompanied by the voice. 'What is this?' I asked my companion.
>
> 'Nothing more than a few idle Negroes of the neighbourhood assembled together to dance the "guachambo", a sort of fandango, to the sound of the "marimba", which claims Africa as the country of its invention.' It is generally made of some light species of wood, and may be compared to the toe part of a shoe. On the flat side, or sole part, are secured, nearly in their centres, eight pieces of steel wire about six inches long; their ends curve upwards, and being of different lengths, form an octave. The longer ends of these keys play free, and, when touched, vibrate a sleepy sort of note, which can hardly be called disagreeable. The instrument is clasped between the hands, hanging down in front, and is played upon by the thumbs. There is another form of the 'marimba', in which the keys are placed on a thin piece of board; this is secured to a thinly-scraped cocoa-nut shell, and is the better kind, sounding much clearer and more musical. The servants (porters), who are always seated at the doors of private dwellings ... pass hours together, nodding over their own music, produced with about the same effort required to twirl the thumbs. Playing on the 'marimba' is just one degree beyond '*dolce far niente*' [delightful idleness].
>
> When we came up the dancing had ceased, and the Blacks were making way for us to pass, I called the musician, that I might examine his instrument ... At our request, he played a lively air, and accompanied himself with a short see-saw motion of the body.

Ruschenberger added that the entrance gate to each house in the city was 'constantly watched over by a Black slave in livery, who manages to keep awake by sliding his thumbs over a "marimba"'.[19] In 1856 Thomas Ewbank included in his book *Life in Brazil* an illustration of the lamellophone, providing also what appears to be the only description of the instrument in Brazil which distinguishes among those originating in various parts of Africa. Ewbank's account is also noteworthy for establishing that, by the 1850s, the lamellophone was used in Brazil to play not only 'African airs' but also 'a fashionable waltzing tune':

> This morning a slave came along with a load on his head and both hands in a large gourd, out of which he drew a fashionable waltzing tune. I took the opportunity of examining the popular *Marimba*. Every African nation has its own, so that a Congo, Angola, Minas, Ashantee, or Mozambique instrument is recognizable, but the differences are not great. A series of thin steel rods, from ten to fifteen, are fixed on a thin board, five or six inches square, in the manner of flute-keys, which they resemble. A long and a short one alternate; sometimes they diminish like Pan-pipes. The board is secured in the larger half of a dry calabash. Grasping it with his fingers beneath, and his thumbs on the keys, he produces, by pushing them down at one end and letting them fly back, a soft humming sound allied to that of the Jews'-harp. The city [i.e. Rio de Janeiro] is an Ethiopian theatre, and this the favorite instrument of the orchestra. Slaves are daily met playing African airs on it, and groups returning to the country have commonly one or two among them. In the preceding illustration, a couple are, like Jewish captives by the river of Chebar, reviving recollections of home in the songs of their native land.[20]

Kubik suggests three reasons for the disappearance of the lamellophone in Brazil. First, with the coming of modern transport, fewer people had to walk long distances, and there was less need for a 'pastime instrument'. Second, the instrument's rather quiet and often very subtle tones could not compete with the noise of motor traffic. Third, black people began to receive wages after emancipation in 1888 and guitars, more versatile than lamellophones, were now more accessible to them. However, the lamellophone may have survived in Rio de Janeiro as late as the 1930s.[21]

The pluriarc (compound bow-lute)

The pluriarc, or compound bow-lute (or multiple bow-lute), consists of several bows, often of bamboo, embedded in the same resonator: often but not always a shovel-shaped gourd. Each bow has a separate string. There may be metal jingles attached. This instrument is 'peculiarly African', being found only in the continent's western and central areas. It is – or was until quite recently – played from present-day Guinea down to Namibia, apart from a sizeable gap between the Ivory Coast and Nigeria: 'Its distribution is coastal, but there is deep penetration inland' in Congo-Kinshasa, Rwanda, Burundi and Botswana.[22] Still popular in Angola in the 1970s, the pluriarc is held horizontally, with the bows pointing away from the body, and is carried by means of a string attached near the mouth of the resonator.[23]

The *nsambi* pluriarc of Angola was seen in 1682 by the Capuchin friar Girolamo Merolla da Sorrento (d. 1697). A contemporary translation describes it as

> like a little Gittar, but without a head, instead whereof there are five little bows of Iron, which when the Instrument is to be tun'd, are to be let more or less into the Body of it. The Strings of this Instrument are made of the Thread of Palm-Trees: It is play'd on with the Thumbs of each Hand, the Instrument bearing directly upon the Performer's Breast. Tho the Musick of this Instrument be very low, it is nevertheless not ungrateful.[24]

Bahia-born Alexandre Rodrigues Ferreira (1756–1825) spent the years 1783–92 travelling nearly 40,000 kilometres through north and central Brazil, and made many detailed coloured drawings in the course of his nine-year journey. One of them shows a compound bow-lute with seven strings, held by two disembodied hands, the strings being plucked by the thumbs. Ferreira called the instrument 'Guitar which the Blacks play' (*'Viola q. tocão os Prétos'*).[25] In Brazil, as in Angola, it was often played by people out walking and is shown thus in Henry Chamberlain's 1822 book on Rio de Janeiro, where it is called 'Sambee'. His caption says of the musicians who played the pluriarc, and those who played the single-string bowed lute: 'Native Airs are generally preferred by them to all others, and when these Instruments are in the hands of Proficients, the Musick they are made to produce is by no means unpleasing.'[26] Needing great skill to make, if not to play, the pluriarc is now unknown in Brazil; presumably it was ousted by the guitar.

The xylophone (marimba)

The resonator xylophone – i.e. a xylophone with a series of graduated gourd resonators under the keys – is one of Africa's most widely distributed musical instruments. It is found right across the continent, from Senegal, the Gambia, and Mali to Mozambique.[27] The intricate music of the xylophone orchestras of the Chopi of Mozambique, one of the pinnacles of African traditional culture, is known to have existed in its present form for at least 450 years.[28]

In Brazil the resonator xylophone, like the lamellophone, was usually called marimba. Attempts have been made to pinpoint the region of Africa it came from. Hugh Tracey suggested that the resonator xylophone of the Tswa of Mozambique, whose xylophones 'are collectively called *Marimba*', 'is the prototype of the *Marimba* which was first taken to South America in the sixteenth century'. He admitted, however, that the historical evidence is slender,[29] and the Tswa are not the only ethnic group who use this word for this instrument.

There is not in fact a huge volume of evidence about the resonator xylophone in Brazil, though there is no doubt whatever about its use there. Mello Morais Filho (1843 or 1844–1919), writing in 1895 but quoting a contemporary account, listed it among the instruments used in Rio de Janeiro in 1830 in a performance of the *Cucumbi* dramatic dance.[30] A dozen or so years earlier, the Austrian scientists Spix and Martius, in their vivid drawing of '*Die Baducca, in S. Paulo*' (Fig. 10) portrayed two black couples dancing to the music of what is obviously a resonator xylophone – though because of the angle at which it is played only the gourds, not the keys, are visible – as well as a kind of notched scraper.[31]

A Frenchwoman who visited Brazil in the early 1880s saw what was evidently a kind of gourd-resonated xylophone, though her account of it is not altogether clear. She described it as

> a kind of huge calabash within which were six or seven of different sizes, on which was placed a small, thin board. With the help of little sticks, which he wielded very skilfully, the Negro obtained muffled [*sourds*] sounds whose monotony, it seemed, must induce sleep rather than anything else. The second musician, squatting on his heels, had in front of him a piece of hollow tree-trunk over which a dried sheepskin was stretched. Now and again he beat gloomily on this primitive drum to back up the singing.[32]

On the seaboard of São Paulo state, the resonator xylophone survived well into the twentieth century. A nine-key instrument was used, apparently as late as the 1950s, in the *Congada de São Francisco*, in the São Sebastião district, near the island of that name; a smaller one was used in the *Congadas de Caraguatatuba*, a town a few kilometres north of São Sebastião. Each was accompanied by two hollow-log drums (*atabaques*).[33]

6

The African Dance Heritage

African dance in Brazil

Foreign visitors to Brazil before the slaves won emancipation in 1888 had much to say about their secular dances. Reporting on his visit to Salvador in 1610, the French adventurer François Pyrard (*c.* 1570–1621) found it 'a great pleasure on feast-days and Sundays to see the slaves gather, men and women, dancing and enjoying themselves in public in the squares and streets; for on those days they are not subject to their masters'.[1] Zacharias Wagner's watercolour of *Xangô* dancers in Pernambuco (Fig. 1) dates from 1634–41; what is apparently the earliest portrayal of black musicians and dancers in Brazil in a secular context (Fig. 2) comes from the same region and is of only slightly later date. It appears in a vignette on a map of 'Northern Pernambuco with Itamaracá', completed in 1643 by the cartographer and astronomer Georg Marcgraf (1610–43) and part of the great Klenck Atlas. Though dated 1647, this map was in fact engraved between 1644 and 1646 by the atlas-maker Johan Blaeu (1596–1673) and would be considered the most accurate map of the area for the next 200 years. Near a water-powered sugar mill, a black man is holding a gourd rattle in his right hand and possibly playing a pipe, though the latter is far from clearly shown, while a group of six black people are dancing with raised arms and two others are standing by, one drinking from a bowl. The leading authorities on the picture of which this is a small part, P. J. P. Whitehead and M. Boeseman, say the whole scene 'is rendered in extraordinary detail', adding that very probably 'the scenes depicted were actually observed and although redrawn and recombined afterwards, they can be trusted as authentic records of negro ... life at this time'.[2]

Right up to emancipation, European and American visitors would be impressed by the slaves' eagerness to dance at every possible opportunity. In an age when lateral hip movements were largely unknown in European dances north of the Pyrenees, and in the staid dances familiar to Americans of European descent, many of these visitors were, or claimed to be, greatly shocked by the dancers' bodily movements, which they found both indecent and fascinating. One visitor to Brazil in the 1650s was convinced, or professed to be, that 'the lascivious movements of these black people, in their rude festivities' threatened the mental health of white people.[3]

But again and again, for all the prudery with which they are larded, observers' accounts testify to the central part played by music and dance in the slaves' lives; to the alacrity with which they grasped even the slightest chance of relaxing in such a way; to the tireless energy with which they threw themselves into the dance; above all, to the high value they placed on skilful and expressive dancing. Dancing was their main relaxation and means of entertainment. But it was more than that: it asserted and reinforced community and community values, and passed these on to the rising generation. Nothing, not even harsh and cruel punishment, was more bitterly resented by Africans in Brazil and their descendants than restrictions placed on their singing, making music, and dancing. It is significant that when the slaves on the large plantation of Engenho Santana, near Ilhéus in Bahia, rose in revolt in 1789, killing their overseer, seizing some machinery and running off to found a settlement in the forest, one of the clauses in the 'peace treaty' they drew up, setting out their conditions for going back to the plantation, read as follows: 'We shall be able to play, relax and sing any time we wish without your hindrance, nor will permission be needed.'[4]

Figure 9 Part of a vignette on a map of 'Northern Pernambuco with Itamaracá' in the great Klenck Atlas, completed in 1643. This is the earliest portrayal of black dancers and musicians in Brazil in a secular context. (Klenck Atlas)

To some foreign observers, the singing and dancing of the Africans in Brazil suggested that the advocates of emancipation were exaggerating the horrors of slavery. Some, like the English visitor Alexander Caldcleugh, went so far as to suggest that the slaves were the real rulers. On quitting the warehouse where they were put up for sale after disembarkation, wrote Caldcleugh,

> the slaves leave the greatest part of their miseries behind and without wishing it to be inferred that they lead an enviable life, nobody can affirm, on seeing them singing and dancing in the streets, that they are wretched and continually pining over their unhappy fate. In many cases they appear to do as they please, and completely rule their indolent masters.[5]

This rose-coloured view bore little relation to Brazilian reality. According to Sir William Ouseley, who spent a few days in Rio de Janeiro in 1810, slaves were not free to dance when and where they pleased but had to seek permission on certain holidays

> to assemble in bands of fifteen, twenty or more, according to their native districts and dialects ... Among the members of each group there were generally two or three musicians, who performed their national airs on different instruments, some rude [i.e. crude] and simple, others of a strange and complicated form. Those tones, however, seemed to delight the slaves, who sang, and danced with an air of heartfelt gaiety, so strongly, so naturally expressed, that I could not for one moment suppose it to have been affected.[6]

Most visitors, whether or not they they approved of slavery, agreed that the slaves were passionately devoted to music and dance. A German visitor, Theodor von Leithold, left this typical snapshot from the second decade of the nineteenth century:

> They particularly love music and dance, however simple. Their instruments consist of the jaw's harp [*Brummeisen*, *Maultrommel*; i.e. mouth bow, for which see p. 168] and a board with two strings stretched across it [probably the *côcho*; see p. 169] which they strum as they walk along the road. They will gather together at a bend in the road and dance to the strumming of such an instrument. As I passed by such a crew I saw several Negroes and Negresses perform a bad, indecent [*unanständigen*] dance, shouting and cheering the while. They were joined by an old hoary grey Negro carrying a heavy load upon his head, who, to my astonishment, joined in the dance for a whole quarter of an hour without putting down his burden. The other Negroes and Negresses were so delighted at the old man's dancing that on several occasions they danced round him cheering.[7]

This tells us much, as does the Austrian botanist Pohl's quaintly disapproving and not very closely observed account of dances he saw in Brazil in the same period which, like all actual national dances … consist of expressions of courtship. Of course, in the case of so savage a people as the Negroes, these expressions are portrayed with the utmost pungency in the dance. Our own waltz, which actually rests on the very same principle, even the fandango, which has remained so close to its character, are left behind by the obvious pantomime of an Angolan dance. One often sees Negroes dancing on the streets, usually in threes. Two represent the loving couple and the third tries to prevent their coupling. They become so caught up in the Bacchanalian frenzy of this dance that they do not give up until they collapse from exhaustion. Usually a dense circle of spectators immediately forms around the dancers.[8]

The French traveller Tollenare seems ambivalent towards the animal dance which he saw in Brazil in 1816–19: having treated the dancers to a tot of spirits, he raises his eyebrows when their show becomes 'more lively'. In any case, according to Bastide, Tollenare failed to grasp the real nature of the dance he was seeing, which was accompanied by two musicians, one playing a four-key lamellophone, the other a gourd rattle whose handle he struck against the lamellophone's wooden box:

A monotonous song, consisting of three similar words, completed the rustic harmony. Three dancers occupied the centre of a circle seven or eight feet in diameter, with about twenty interested onlookers around them. Two of the dancers played the parts of a man and a woman, or rather of a male and a female making love. They mimicked now the ardours of apes, now those of bears or some other animal. The male fondled the female grotesquely with his paw; she resisted a little, ran off, and at last yielded. Then the two dancers rolled over each other, and the roars of laughter showed the delight the spectators took in this rather coarse portrayal of the act of generation. The third dancer played a hunter; his stick served alternately as gun and as javelin, which he mostly thrust towards a young black woman among the spectators, who seemed delighted by his choice. But the pantomime of the three dancers would have been of little value without a piquant movement which accompanied it unceasingly. It was a lively and extra-ordinary shaking of all the body's principal muscles, and a very indecent movement of hips and buttocks. This shaking and this movement, produced by great muscular strength, call for much skill and much practice; the dancers vie with each other as to who can keep it going the longest, and the people's applause rewards those whose muscles are most sturdy and, above all, most mobile. A few glasses of *tafiá* [*cachaça*, sugar-cane spirit] that I had handed out made the show still more lively. My two dancers no longer portrayed the love-making of animals, but that of humans. Lavishing kisses, clasped in each other's arms, they moved their loins repeatedly in the lewdest way. The spectators were in raptures, and the women's eyes sparkled. I should however say in the latters' favour that they did show some semblance of shame when the dancers' attacks on them ceased to be play-acting and seemed to be actual assaults.[9]

On this Bastide comments that the 'gallant Frenchman' saw only sexuality in these dances, which in fact had quite a different character:

This is probably a dance which still exists in Africa and is believed by some ethnologists to be the source of black African theatre. It is known as the *Nanzéké*, and it pits a group of men dressed as hunters against a group of masked men disguised as animals. Nanzéké kills a taboo antelope, which weeps at having been killed. This causes the hunter's wife, 'keeper of the sacred objects', to intervene.[10]

A German joined the disapproving chorus in 1833 when he wrote 'Something about Music and Dance in Brazil' for a German music journal. After briefly describing both lamellophone and mouth bow, he continued:

In the evening, when their work is finished, especially on holidays, one can see various groups of Negroes in public places dancing around players of such instruments, if that is, mighty twisting of the body on one spot merits the name of dance. One of them directs the participants to the spot where they are to perform their gyrations, although there is no perceptible symmetry in them. With the music there also occurs a vocal accompaniment on the part of the dancers, consisting of a monotonous growl [*Brummen*] (apparently with African words) interrupted now and then by the uttering of a loud cry. By preference they choose places with piles of timber for such entertainments, so that some of them can reinforce the music by beating the rhythm on beams and hollow arrangements of boards ... the dance is devoid of any nobility of form and is remarkable only for the incredible twists of the body. The dancers stay on the same spot, raising their feet alternately up and down and at the same time moving the part of their body below the hips extraordinarily quickly in a horizontal plane to and fro in a circle. Simultaneously they shake the upper muscles of the shoulders and back constantly and with such ease that they appear to be only lightly attached to the body. These movements place such a strain on the dancers that they are bathed in sweat after a few minutes. At the utterance of a loud cry, a new dancer suddenly runs into the centre of the circle and all continue the movement uninterruptedly. Since the arms, as far down as the elbows, are pressed hard against the body, it is clear that each dancer plays his role solo. Black men and women love the dances so passionately that, should they meet a Loangobania [lamellophone] player, even in the heat of the midday sun, they lay down their loads to abandon themselves even for a few minutes to the pleasures of this dance.[11]

The reference here to 'beating the rhythm on beams and hollow arrangements of boards' is of interest, for what have been called 'percussion-beams' (*poutrelles frappées*) are widely used in Kongo traditional music.[12]

Adolphe d'Assier (b. 1828), a French mathematics teacher who travelled through South America in 1858–60, left a brief account of the Brazilian slaves' Saturday night dances. The orchestra consisted of youngsters (*négrillons*), who played hand-beaten hollow-log drums with dog-skin or sheepskin heads, held between the legs, and who generally sang 'to increase the racket':

Normally there is only one dancer in the midst of the group. He leaps, capers [*gambade*], gesticulates; then, when he feels his strength leaving him, he throws himself on one of the bystanders, whom he designates as his successor; generally a woman is chosen. She in turn enters the circle, indulges in all sorts of choreographic improvisations, then, tired, goes and chooses a man to take her place. The action continues thus until the participants' fatigue brings it to an end.[13]

Despite his intemperate language, much may be learnt from such an eyewitness as the Revd Charles Samuel Stewart, an American who had formerly been a missionary to the Sandwich Islands. In 1852, while walking in Rio de Janeiro on the day of the Epiphany, a public holiday, he was 'about halfway up the Larangeiras', when

> my attention was arrested by a large gathering of negroes within an enclosure by the wayside, engaged in their native, heathen dances, accompanied by the wild and rude music brought with them from Africa. I stopped to witness the scene ... Many of the principal performers, both among the dancers and musicians, were dressed in the most wild and grotesque manner – some, as if in impersonation of the Prince of Evil himself, as pictured with hoof and horns and demoniac mien. Many of the dances surpassed in revolting licentiousness anything I recollect to have witnessed in the South Seas; and filled my mind with melancholy disgust; the more so, from the fact, that a majority, if not all the performers, as was manifest from the crosses and amulets they wore, were baptized members of the Romish Church – Christians in name, but in habits and in heart heathens still. Exhibitions of this kind are far from being limited here to extraordinary holidays, or to the seclusion of by-places. I have seen them in open daylight, in the most public corners of the city, while young females even, of apparent respectability and modesty, hung over the surrounding balconies as spectators.
>
> I know not how long the revelry had now been going on; but either from the free use of *cacha* [sic], the vile rum of the country, or from nervous excitement, many seemed fairly beside themselves. These danced till ready to drop from exhaustion; while shouts of encouragement and applause followed the persevering efforts of those who were most enduring and most frantic in muscular exertion. The performers on the African drums and other rude instruments, who accompanied the monotonous beating and thrumming upon these with loud songs, in solo and chorus, of similar character, seemed especially to enter into the spirit of the revelry, and labored with hands and voice and a vehemence of action in their whole bodies, that caused the sweat to roll down their naked limbs as if they had just stepped from a bath of oil.[14]

Not the least significant feature of this passage is its reference to the interest that young white women 'of apparent respectability and modesty' were taking in black dance by the 1850s. These young women themselves no doubt already danced the *lundu* – Brazil's first national dance, to be discussed in the next chapter – and so, perhaps, had their mothers. Their daughters would dance the *maxixe*; their granddaughters, the urban samba. The acculturation process was irreversible.

According to an Englishman writing in 1838, whose account is exceptional in referring to Brazil's African *nações* by name, between 10,000 and 15,000 black people would gather every Sunday for amusement and recreation at the Campo de Sant' Anna. He called the venue 'an immensely large unfinished square in the suburbs of the town ... a sort of common ... covered with a short green sward'. It was 'a very singular spectacle':

> Here was the native of Mosambique, and Quilumana [i.e. Quilimane], of Cabinda, Luanda, Benguela, and Angola ... The dense population of the Campo de Sant'Ana was subdivided into capacious circles, formed each of from three to four hundred blacks, male and female.
>   Within these circles, the performers danced to the music which was also stationed there ... A master of ceremonies, dressed like a mountebank, presided over the dance ... Eight or ten figurantes [i.e. dancers] were moving to and fro in the midst of the circle, in a way to exhibit the human frame divine under every conceivable variety of contortion and gesticulation.[15]

A Belgian visitor to Brazil in the 1870s, Count Eugène de Robiano, reported of the slaves on a coffee plantation:

> They take advantage of the slightest opportunity to give themselves up to dancing, their favourite amusement. It is interesting then to see them gathered in a ring under open sheds or on the asphalt of drying-grounds, each in turn indulging in the most ludicrous leaps, doing so always to the same figure, to the sound only of drums made from skins stuck over hollow tree-trunks, with accompaniment from the lookers-on, who sing out of tune and clap their hands more or less in time.[16]

'Out of tune', of course, merely means not in the European concert scale, while 'more or less in time' probably alludes to the clapping of cross-rhythms, which often puzzles those hearing it for the first time.

Unlike the American ex-missionary, James Wetherell, the British vice-consul in Salvador, found black dancing 'highly amusing' – when the dancers were men. He wrote in 1842:

> The men form a ring, and one, two, and sometimes three, step into it and commence dancing, holding in their hands a long brush made of horse's hair, the others begin singing a kind of chaunt, low and monotonous, increasing in loudness as they become excited, and clapping their hands in time with the music. The dancing is highly amusing, and must be very fatiguing; it consists of moving the body slowly, and putting it into all kinds of postures and distortions. It is continued for a long time together, and when one dancer is tired, another takes his place. Pieces of copper money are occasionally given to the dancers, and which they again give to one of the drummers, to form a common fund. To all appearance this dancing is very exciting, nearly as much to the lookers on as to the dancers, and they seem to enter into it with a great deal of spirit.[17]

Nine years later, however, the vice-consul found himself unable to describe such dances when women also took part in them: 'The monotony of the negro chaunting, and its never-ending repetitions convey no idea of the melody of sweet sounds, and the less that is said about the dances exhibited by them to these tunes, the better.'[18] But the award for being at once ready to condemn and reluctant to describe must go to the Revd Hamlet Clark, who in 1856 watched slaves dancing while he sat out on the veranda after dinner: '[T]hey soon gave us quite enough; the whole affair was vulgar, and coarse, and silly.'[19]

Two of the most fascinating accounts of nineteenth-century black dancing in Brazil speak of shows put on in Minas Gerais to entertain foreign visitors. In the mid-1870s the French diplomat Count Charles d'Ursel saw on a plantation what he called 'a rather odd sight':

We saw the arrival of fifteen or twenty mysterious- and grave-looking negresses, all of a fair age and dressed in costumes more typical than complete. They formed a ring in the room where we were and broke into a chorus of a strange, almost savage, melody. Then each in turn entered the circle and, in the midst of her capering [gambadant] companions, indulged in quite bizarre contortions. Now it was the mariboundo [sic] (wasp) dance, recalling, with coarser gestures, the bee dance performed by the gracious almas [Egyptian dancing-women]; now it was the pé di [sic] patto, which consists in imitating the clumsy gait of the duck; or again the loundou, with skipping [sautillants] and jerky movements ... Seeing these poor old African women indulging in this kind of dance, it is impossible to question that these are the true principles of primitive choreography.

While accompanying themselves, some with a tambourine, others with an emptied coco-nut in which a small shot was shaken, several of these witches carried, tied on their backs, a child several months old. Their bundle seemed to hinder neither their dancing nor their cries, and the poor little darkies [moricauds] either slept peacefully or were already beating time with their little woolly heads to their strange mothers' macabre steps. Becoming more and more lively, the latter soon struck up a kind of litany interrupted by yells and by ridiculously plastic postures [poses grotesquement plastiques]. Then the most inspired member of the party, addressing each of us, improvised, always in the same tone, some welcoming compliment. The style was sparse but the intention excellent. I have remembered this artless sentence: 'You who come from the city have come by a fortunate road; may it be fortunate for you on your way back!'

This song, these shouts and dances, seem to be a prerogative of the eldest, a priesthood whom the others regard with respect. Where does this tradition come from? I believe that these Africans, transported onto the soil of America, have adapted their melodies and their national dances to the words and songs which the Jesuits have taught them; hence, no doubt, this mixture of the religious and the savage.

At mass on the Sunday I heard these same women chanting psalms in church in the same kind of tone, though I have to acknowledge that at the lectern they left out their queer postures.[20]

The *maribondo* (or *marimbondo)* survived well into the twentieth century as a popular comic dance in Goiás and São Paulo, accompanied by tambourine, shaker and notched scraper. The dancer balances a water jug on the head, resting it on a rolled and twisted cloth pad (*rodilha*) and, without spilling any water, slaps the body as if being stung by wasps. This is one of several adult dance-games known in various parts of Brazil.[21] The dance imitating the duck is untraced, but animal and bird dances abound in the traditional cultures of sub-Saharan Africa and, as was seen in Chapter 4, dances imitating snakes and jaguars were a feature of the *Cucumbi*.

At Morro Velho in 1885, the American Frank Vincent was amused by the dancing of a group of black people hired by a gold-mining company to entertain the latter's foreign guests. The group's repertory included a lively pantomime bull that charged straight out of *Bumba-meu-boi*, though its significance was lost on Vincent:

> One evening Mr. Chalmers had the colored people come up to the 'Casa Grande', the manor, to entertain us with some of their music, dancing, and games. About half of them were slaves, though only hired by the company, not belonging to it. They were all dressed in their smartest. The musical instruments they brought were two guitars, a flageolet [whistle flute], triangle, bells, and a tom-tom, like those used in western Africa, to whose accompaniment they sang, sometimes with a solo and chorus, sometimes all in concert. The dances were very amusing. In one of them the men occupied one half of a circle, and the women the other. A woman would then jump about and twirl around in the center of the ring, and suddenly stop in front of some man, or more likely run up against him, and then return to her place. This was regarded as a sort of challenge by the man, who would at once leave the circle and go through a similar performance, halting in front of some woman. The latter would repeat the performance, and so on, alternately. This odd proceeding constituted the whole of the dance. But the performers were all enthusiasm and excitement, and skipped about so energetically that I was afraid some of them would get injured ... A crowd of a hundred or so were looking on, some clapping hands to the rhythm of the music, and all greatly interested and amused. The music, singing, clapping, laughing, and shouting made a fearful hubbub. Frequently one of the musicians, instrument in hand, would enter the arena and dance as wildly as any of the others, without ceasing his playing for an instant. A favorite and diverting game was 'baiting the bull'. A very good imitation of a bull's head had been made from an actual head of bone covered with cloth. A man imitated a bull by secreting himself in the skin of one of these animals, and supported the artificial head in proper position. This 'make-believe' bull was then led in by two men, fantastically dressed, and wearing masks, who capered around the improvised animal without ceasing. The crowd followed the bull about the lawn, playing, singing, and dancing, as merry as children. Occasionally the bull would walk around in a circle, clearing a larger space for himself. All his movements were those of the genuine animal. Sometimes, with head down and slightly swinging from side to side, he would make a charge straight into the crowd, knocking men and boys 'head over heels', and causing the women and girls to run and scream ... The performance was

continued for some time, and appeared to afford the colored people as much amusement as it did ourselves. At the finish the crowd all marched away, following the music and still dancing. It was a vivid reminiscence of western Africa. These slaves perpetuate not only their original habits and customs, but their languages, which they frequently talk among themselves.[22]

Another American visitor, the naturalist Herbert H. Smith, saw in the 1870s 'a rustic dance among the people' in a sugar-cane-producing area called Taperinha, but his impressionistic description is unfortunately short on detail about both the dances and the music:

It begins in the orthodox Amazonian manner, with a singing prayer-meeting in the little chapel, to which worshippers are called by the monotonous beating of a great drum. Then, when the concluding *Pai-Nosso* is sung, and the saint's girdle is kissed, the leader turns master of ceremonies, and such nondescript dances follow as could only originate in the fertile brain of a negro. There is an indescribable mingling of weird and comic in the scene: the dark faces and arms, set off by white dresses; the octogenarian negro, striking his tambourine with a trembling hand; the half-naked babies, tumbling about under the feet of the dancers; the dim, flaring lamps, half lighting, half obscuring the moving figures. We sit and watch them until midnight, and then go away as one goes from a theatre, dropping out of dream-life into the dark street.[23]

Batuque *and rural samba*

Discussion of the dance called *batuque* is made no easier by a cluster of terminological problems which are typically Brazilian: problems of overlapping nomenclature, of the same name being used for different genres, of different regional or national names being used for the same genre. The *batuque* considered in the present chapter is not the African-Brazilian religious ceremony of that name in Pará and Amazonas; nor is it the *batuque* ceremony practised in Rio Grande do Sul and more properly called *pará*. Salvador candomblé is also sometimes called *batuque*, and the word is sometimes used to designate a form of capoeira in Salvador and Rio de Janeiro: these too lie outside our present purview.

We are left with two meanings of *batuque*. It is often used to refer to a secular dance which came to Brazil from the Kongo-Angola culture area. But the Portuguese word *batuque* was originally a generic term for any kind of black dance:[24] 'It had a generalized meaning referring to community dances with drums and other loud instruments, in contrast to the individual music for bows, spike tube lutes, lamellophones, pluriarcs ... as depicted in early nineteenth-century paintings from Rio de Janeiro.'[25] What most, if not all, dances referred to as *batuques* had in common was percussion accompaniment, which normally included handclapping. But the word is so commonly used in a vague way in the literature that it is often hard and sometimes impossible to decide whether the specific or the general sense is meant. And Kazadi wa Mukuna has strongly challenged the idea that there was ever a distinct Kango-Angola dance called *batuque*:

> An examination of the contributions of early explorers and traders ... who visited the Kongo-Angola area in the last quarter of the nineteenth century reveals that the word *semba* alone is used in that area to denote the same dance for which the term is employed here in Brazil. The use of the word *batuque* (probably of Portuguese origin, meaning 'hammering'), on the other hand, could be attributed to the linguistic ignorance of some of these old writers, who preferred to use the word to denote the same kind of dance that would be known in Brazil as *'umbigada* dance' and would be considered as the forerunner of the present-day samba.[26]

Certainly, when the military commander of Goiânia called in 1796 for the suppression of the *batuques* that black people were accustomed to stage in his town, he was using the word as a generic term, meaning any kind of black dance with drumming. The official reply was that black people ought not to be deprived of such an activity 'since for them it is the main pleasure they can have throughout their days of bondage'; they should be warned not to cause disturbances, however, on pain of severe punishment.[27] We saw in Chapter 4 that a Salvador professor complained in 1802 about the black men and women who performed 'their barbarous *batuques* through the city streets ... to the beat of ... horrible *atabaques*, indecently dancing to pagan songs [and] speaking various languages'.[28] The Count of Arcos (governor of Bahia, 1810–18) and his masters in Lisbon used the word in the same sense when the latter ordered him in 1814 to put a stop to the *batuques do Negros*; to enforce his predecessor's ban on slaves' gathering in groups of more than four; and to stop their being in towns at night without their owners' written permission. Violations of these bans were to be punished with 150 lashes. The Count warned, however, that banning black dances would indirectly promote unity among the slaves of different *nações*, with potentially dreadful consequences.[29]

In the first half of the nineteenth century many local authorities chose to ignore this sensible advice, doing their best to suppress black dances in various Brazilian towns. In 1833, a Rio de Janeiro magistrate demanded a ban on drumming in the city, because the sound of the drums drew slaves from outlying plantations, and from that time on slaves were often arrested for dancing to drums. In 1849 the Rio police broke up a group of over 200 black people who were dancing 'the *batuque*' to the sound of drums.[30] In 1836 the town of Itamaracá in Pernambuco prohibited *batuques* at any hour; in the same year Brejo in Pernambuco forbade *batuques* of any kind. *Batuques* and African royal ceremonies (*reinados africanos*) were banned in the Santa Catarina town of Desterro in 1845. *Batuques com algazarra* ('with clamour') which disturbed the neighbourhood were forbidden in Diamantina, Minas Gerais, in 1846, and people who defied the ban were thrown in jail for a day. Itajubá, in Minas Gerais, passed a by-law in 1853 permitting black dances (here called *quimbetes*, not *batuques*) and royal ceremonies, on condition that they were not held at night, and that a fee of two *milréis* be paid each time.[31]

So much for the wider sense of *batuque*. It has been claimed that the particular dance known by that name was called *batuco* in Angola. As Mukuna states, this word may have been borrowed from the Portuguese (*bater* means 'to beat', 'to strike', 'to hammer'; *batucar*, 'to hammer', 'to drum'), though African origins have also been suggested: the Bantu word *batukue* means 'they who have become excited'[32] and *batchuk* is the name of a dance among the Ronga of Mozambique.[33] Joachim Monteiro, a Portuguese who spent many years in Angola, described the two different forms the dance took there and in the Congo. The Angolans, he wrote in 1875, were very fond of the 'batuco', of which there were two kinds. This was how it was danced by the 'Ambriz blacks' (i.e. presumably the Musurongo and Sorongo peoples, and possibly also the Mbamba) and the people of the Congo:

> A ring is formed of the performers and spectators; 'marimbas' [lamellophones] are twanged and drums beaten vigorously, and all assembled clap their hands in time with the thumping of the drums, and shout a kind of chorus. The dancers, both men and women, jump with a yell into the ring, two or three at a time, and commence dancing. This consists almost exclusively of swaying the body about with only a slight movement of the feet, head, and arms, but at the same time the muscles of the shoulders, back, and hams are violently twitched and convulsed … There is nothing whatever indecent in [these dances].

The 'batuco' of the Bunda-speaking people of Luanda and the interior of Angola was different:

> [O]nly two performers jump into the ring at a time, a man and a girl or woman; they shuffle their feet with great rapidity, passing one another backwards and forward, then retreat facing one another, and suddenly advancing, bring their stomachs together with a whack. They then retire, and another couple instantly take their places. This performance might be called somewhat indecent, but I do not believe that the natives attach the most remote idea of harm to the 'batuco'.[34]

A more moralistic description of the *batuque*, as seen in the south Angolan district of Benguela, was published in 1881 by two Portuguese writers, Hermenegildo Carlos de Brito Capello (1841–1917) and Roberto Ivens (1850–98). Their English translator could not resist calling it 'the inevitable *batuque*' and characterising it as a 'degrading spectacle', though neither phrase occurs in the original:

> Beside a large fire are seated half-a-dozen or more musicians, while men and women standing in a vast circle keep up the most horrible din. They sing, they

shriek, they clap their hands and beat their drums, each endeavouring to outvie his neighbour, until the effect is indescribable. In the midst of it all from out the crowd issue alternately sundry individuals, who, in the ample space, exhibit their choreographic powers, and throw themselves into the most grotesque attitudes. As a general rule these are of the grossest kind, which the women, more particularly, try to make as obscene as possible, without grace, without *cachet*, but simply indecent, and fitted only to inflame the passions of the lowest of our sex. After three or four pirouettes before the spectators, the male dancer butts his stomach violently against the nearest female, who in turn repeats the action.[35]

A number of foreign visitors to Brazil described a dance they called the '*baduca*' or '*baducca*', but there are often elements in their descriptions which seem rather to correspond to the *lundu* – or, at any rate to the Luanda and south Angolan style described by Monteiro and by Capella and Ivens. It is impossible to lay down a hard-and-fast dividing line between the two dances in Brazil.

In 1815, in a small village in the state of Espírito Santo, Prince Maximilian of Wied-Neuwied was

> very agreeably entertained in the evening with music and dancing. The son of our host, who was very skilful in the art of making [traditional] guitars, played, and the other young people danced the *baduca*, making strange contortions with the body, beating time with their hands, and snapping two fingers of each hand alternately in imitation of the Spanish castanets.[36]

In their drawing of '*Die Baducca, in S. Paulo*' (c. 1817–20) the Austrian scientists Spix and Martius omit the whole of the surrounding circle of people – except for a solitary Portuguese soldier who looks on with folded arms as if to emphasise his refusal to respond to the rhythm. They show two black couples dancing to the music of a resonator xylophone and a notched scraper (Fig. 10). The drawing suggests extremely vigorous bodily movements: of the four dancers, one is waving both arms above the head and two are each waving one arm. One authority concludes from the position of the arms that the dance here depicted is in fact the *lundu*,[37] and the Austrian scientists' description of the 'baducca' they saw danced by white people in Minas Gerais, with its snapping of fingers and its guitar accompaniment, does sound very much like the *lundu*:

> The Brazilian has a lively and pleasure-loving disposition. Almost everywhere we arrived in the evening we were met by the buzzing sound of the [traditional] guitar (*Viola*), to whose accompaniment people sang or danced. At Estiva [near Villa Rica, now Ouro Preto], a lonely ranch with marvellous broad fields surrounded by distant mountains, the inhabitants were engaged in dancing the baducca. Hardly had they learned of the arrival of foreign travellers than they invited us to witness their festivities. The baducca is performed by one single male and one single female dancer, dancing alternately towards and away from each other, snapping their fingers with the most wanton movements and

licentious gesticulation. The main attraction this dance holds for Brazilians is to be found in rotations and artful twists of the pelvis, in which they are almost as expert as the East Indian tumblers. It often goes on for several hours on end to the monotonous chords of the guitar, sometimes alternating with improvised vocals or with folk-songs whose content corresponds to its crudity. Sometimes the dancers also appear in women's clothes. Despite its obscene character, this dance is nevertheless widespread throughout Brazil and is everywhere the property of the lower class of people, who refuse to be deprived of it even though it is banned by the church. It appears to be of Ethiopian origin and to have been transplanted to Brazil by Negro slaves, where, like many of their other customs, it has taken root.[38]

In his almost contemporary drawing of the 'Danse Batuca' (Fig. 11) the German artist Rugendas shows the circle, though he omits the nearer half of it. Within

DIE BADUCCA, IN S. PAULO.

Figure 10 This picture of two black couples dancing the 'baducca' in São Paulo was published by the Austrian scientists Spix and Martius, who spent the years 1817–20 in Brazil. The position of the dancers' arms suggests that this was in fact the *lundu* dance. The music is provided by a resonator xylophone and a notched scraper. (*Atlas zur Reise in Brasilien von Dr. v. Spix und Dr. v. Martius* [Munich, M. Lindauer, *c.* 1823])

the circle there are two male dancers. A musician crouches to play a lamel-lophone. Rugendas called the 'Batuca'

> the customary dance of the Negroes ... As soon as any of them gather together there is heard the rhythmical clapping of hands; this is the signal calling for and, as it were, provoking the dance. The Batuca is led by a principal dancer. It consists in certain bodily movements which are perhaps too expressive; it is the hips especially which are shaken. While the dancer clicks his tongue, snaps his fingers, and accompanies himself with a rather monotonous song, the others stand round him in a ring and repeat the refrain.[39]

The French naturalist Auguste de Saint-Hilaire (1779–1853), who spent the years 1816–22 travelling through Brazil, called the *batuque* an 'indecent dance much in use among the Brazilians' and gave this account of it, and of a Mozambique ring dance, as seen at Ubá in Minas Gerais:

Figure 11 The 'customary dance' of black people in Brazil: the 'Danse Batuca' as seen by the German artist Rugendas, *c.* 1821–25. The dancers are surrounded by a circle of clapping spectators, and, on the left, a musician crouches to play the marimba (lamellophone). (Rugendas, *Malerische Reise in Brasilien*)

The creole Negroes danced *batuques*, while one of them played on a kind of tambourine [*tambour de basque*] and another, rapidly sliding a small rounded piece of wood along the transverse notches of a stout stick, produced at the same time a noise rather similar to a rattle. In another corner of the yard some Mozambique Negroes formed a circle in the middle of which sat two or three musicians who began beating in strict time on small and not very loud drums. The dancers accompanied them with their songs; they jumped as they went round and round in the same direction, and each time round their movements became livelier. Knees bent, fists closed, forearms upright, they moved forward on prancing feet, and gave all their limbs a kind of convulsive shaking which must have been extremely tiring for men who had been working the whole day long. But ... it was not without the keenest regret that they saw the moment arrive for rest.[40]

Further north, near Lage in Bahia, Saint-Hilaire saw the *batuque* danced by white people whom he described as imitating the dances of their slaves:

Soon ... there began the *batuques*, those lewd [*obscènes*] dances which the inhabitants of Brazil have borrowed from the Africans. They were danced only by men to begin with. Nearly all were whites; they would not have wanted to fetch water or wood like their Negroes, but they did not think they were demeaning themselves by copying the ridiculous and uncouth contortions of the latter. The Brazilians show a good deal of indulgence to their slaves, with whom they mingle so often, who have perhaps contributed to teaching them the system of agriculture they practise and the way to extract gold from streams, and who moreover were their dancing-masters.[41]

Another foreign visitor who saw the *batuque* danced by white people was the German naturalist Georg Wilhelm Freyreiss (1789–1825). He found the 'Batuca' to be an 'exuberant' dance:

The dancers form a circle and, to the rhythm of a guitar, the dancer standing in the middle moves his lower abdomen against a person in the circle, usually of the opposite sex. At first the music is slow, as are the dancer's movements; however, both accelerate, and, as the music reaches its emotional peak, the dancer quickly presses his or her lower abdomen against somebody in the circle who then assumes his or her role, and so the dance goes on, often lasting whole nights. No more lascivious dance can be imagined ..., and consequently it has no lack of opponents, particularly among the clergy ... One of them refused absolution to those of his flock who insisted on dancing this dance and so put an end to the mischief, although, it must be said, there was the greatest ill-feeling. However, even quite recently this dance was performed on a festive occasion in a house in Villa-Rica [now Ouro Preto] full of all sorts of women, by half-naked actors to loud clapping and applause. Other dances are rarely to be seen in the countryside, while in the towns the English quadrilles [*Contre-tänze*] have driven out the Batuca.[42]

A Frenchwoman who visited Brazil in the early 1880s saw both '*batuco*' and *lundu* danced. The former dance, in the countryside, was accompanied by a kind of gourd-resonated xylophone and a hollow-log drum:

Three or four groups of dancers soon positioned themselves in the middle of the ring formed by their companions; the women moved rhythmically, waving their handkerchiefs and indulging in a strongly marked movement of the hips, while their black escorts revolved around them, jumping on one foot with the most ludicrous contortions, and the old musician went from group to group, speaking and singing while shaking his sticks with frenzy. He seemed by his words to want to provoke them to dance and make love. The onlookers accompanied the *batuco* with handclapping that emphasised the rhythm in a strange way.[43]

The last sentence is an unmistakable reference to the use of cross-rhythms by those clapping their hands.

The *samba de roda* (ring samba) which survived into the twentieth century is simply the *batuque* under a different name. Despite the identity of name, there is no direct link between *samba de roda* and modern samba, which, as we shall see, derives from the *lundu* by way of the *maxixe*. In a *samba de roda* recorded in Bahia an unspecified drum is played with call-and-response singing and handclapping.[44] Drumming and handclapping seem to have been the usual accompaniment when the *batuque* was danced by black people; when white people danced it, guitar and sometimes also tambourine were used[45] – and, as the passage from Spix and Martius indicates, what they danced would probably have been called the *lundu* in many parts of Brazil.

The most obvious difference between the traditional samba of Bahia and that of the state of São Paulo is choreographic. Whereas the former is danced within a circle of spectator-participants, the latter is danced in rows which alternately advance and withdraw. Here we rely on the classic description published by Mário de Andrade in 1937, based on fieldwork he carried out in 1933. Presiding over the festivities was a *dono-do-samba* ('samba-master') aged about 60. Andrade mentioned the *bumbo* bass drum which was the most important of the accompanying instruments; an essential non-musical accompaniment was an enormous jug of *cachaça*, holding two and a half litres. The singing was in call-and-response form. The drummer waited until the call-and-response pattern was well established before coming in strongly to reinforce the established rhythm. Immediately the other instruments entered and the dancing began. About 30 dancers took part, occupying a space of about five metres by five. The men who danced all played instruments. The people who took part called their dance indifferently samba and *batuque*.[46]

Samba: *the word*

Nowhere are the difficulties of Brazilian musical nomenclature more apparent, and more likely to pile confusion on confusion, than in the term 'samba'. It has been claimed that 'there are dozens of types of samba in Brazil, each with its own musical, choreographical, lyrical and sociocultural parameters'.[47] This is not the overstatement it might at first seem to be. We have already distinguished the ring samba from the line samba of São Paulo (both also known as *batuque*), and both of these from the modern urban samba, to which we shall return in Chapter 9. In 1988 it was shown that at least 31 present or past forms of samba had been identified in Brazil, in 21 of which there was *umbigada*,[48] the smacking together of dancers' bellies that normally signalled a change of partner. Artur Ramos, psychoanalytically oriented student of African-Brazilian traditions, suggested in 1935 that *semba* was an African term for *umbigada*, and that the word 'samba', 'at first taken as synonymous with *batuque*' was probably derived from *semba*.[49] Kubik confirms that *semba* in the Kimbundu and Ngangela languages of Angola means 'belly bounce'.[50] But the study of African languages has advanced somewhat since Ramos's day, and 'samba' and similar words are now known to be legion, and many of them mean something rather less specific than 'belly bounce'. For instance, in Kimbundu *samba* means 'to be very excited, to be boiling over'; in the Ngangela language of Angola, *kusamba* means 'jump for joy, skip, gambol'; to the Bangi of Congo-Brazzaville *somba* means 'to dance the divination dance'; among the Hausa of Nigeria the *sa'mbale* is 'a dance for young people'.[51] In the far north-east of Guinea-Bissau, *samba* is reportedly both a rhythm and 'the name of the singer and actor in a mime which represents a girl provoking a boy. The boy's name is Samba.'[52] The dance called *samba* on the island of São Tomé was said in 1895 to be 'very similar to the *semba* of Angola, but ... more erotic' (exactly what this meant in this context in the 1890s is not clear).[53]

In 1978 the scholar N'Totilu N'Landu-Longa came up with an alternative suggestion: that the word *samba*, as well as the dance of that name, derives from the Kikongo word *sáamba*, meaning originally the initiation group in which a person becomes competent for political, social and religious functions, and, by extension, the hierarchy of deities.[54] Early-nineteenth-century dictionaries of Kimbundu and Kikongo do in fact give *sánba* as the Kimbundu word for 'prayer' and 'pray', *mussámbo*, *cussámba*, and *nghi-ssámba* as Kikongo words of similar meaning.[55]

These various explanations do not, of course, necessarily exclude each other. Indeed, the very richness and multiplicity of these variants spread over a wide area of Africa may well have helped to establish the word 'samba' as the stock term for a cluster of dances, one of which is now, all over the world, synonymous with Brazil.

It is often said that samba was originally a part of the candomblé ritual,[56] but this is disputed. Gerard Béhague writes that 'it is erroneous to attribute ... a religious ritual origin to such rhythms and dances as the Brazilian *samba*'.[57]

Jongo *and* caxambu

The *jongo* of Rio de Janeiro, Espírito Santo, São Paulo and Minas Gerais was performed at night near a huge bonfire. This counter-clockwise ring dance was accompanied by four (or sometimes fewer) hand-beaten conical drums, three of which (*tambu*, *angona* or *candonguêro*, and *junior* or *cadete*) were straddled by the players, while the fourth (*guzunga*) hung from the player's shoulder by a leather strap. The largest drum was nicknamed Pai Tôco, Pai João or Guanazambu. It and the second largest were beaten with open hands. The two smallest drums were played gently, with the fingertips. The *cuíca* friction drum and a *guaiá* shaker, containing lead pellets or small stones, were also played. The dance featured a solo singer and dancer (*jongueiro*) who shook a basket rattle known as *angoía*, rather similar to the *caxixi* described in Chapter 2. His song included African words.

> After intoning a short invocation to the local saints, the *jongueiro* sings his first *desafio* (challenge) which is always a kind of riddle. After this, the people dance around the players while the last words of the song are endlessly repeated. Another *jongueiro*, who wishes to guess the riddle, may enter the circle in order to sing the reply. After an hour or so the participants as well as the listeners are taken by a delirious excitement which only ceases the next morning ...
>
> *Jongo* singers are often regarded as sorcerers whose magic power is sometimes traced back to their African ancestors. The most famous *jongueiros* are usually old men whose supernatural performances are still remembered.[58]

In Cunha, a small town in the state of São Paulo, there was a tradition from slavery days of lighting a big bonfire and dancing the *jongo* in a central square, and this tradition was kept up until at least 1945. The participants ate sweet potatoes and drank *quentão*, a hot cane spirit spiced with ginger, cinnamon and sugar. An elderly dancer said that his father, born in Angola, had told him that the dance was known there and that originally in Brazil only black people had danced it. The slaves had used the improvised songs (*pontos*) to arrange meetings, arrange escapes and criticise their masters; after emancipation the songs became vehicles for social and political comment.[59] Stanley J. Stein quotes verses from *jongos* sung in 1888 to celebrate emancipation:

> In the days of captivity, I swallowed many an insult.
> I got up early in the morning, they whipped me for no reason.
>
> But now I want to see the fellow who shouts to me from the hilltop:
> 'Say "God bless you, master".' No sir, your Negro is a freedman now.[60]

The *jongo* had various local names: *bendenguê* in Rio de Janeiro state, *tambu* and *corimá* in São Paulo state. In the late 1970s it was still being danced in the

Paraíba valley in São Paulo. Some accounts speak of guitar accompaniment, and a *jongo* played by two guitars was recorded commercially in 1929.[61]

The evidence is inconclusive, but it seems very probable that the *caxambu* was the *jongo* under another name.[62] On the coffee plantations of Rio de Janeiro, according to Stein, the *caxambu* was danced for three days and nights in 1888, to celebrate emancipation, and one *jongo* sung during those celebrations had the line:

> Arise, people, captivity is over.

Stein calls the *caxambu* dance 'lay in theme, yet built around African religious elements of drum, soloist, responding chorus, and dancers' and states that, danced on Saturday nights and saints' days, it occupied an intermediate position between religious ceremony and secular diversion.[63] In the 1830s planters tried more than once to restrict gatherings for the *caxambu* dance to slaves coming from a single plantation in case their assembling in large numbers gave the slaves a chance to organise 'occult societies, apparently religious, but always dangerous, by the ease with which some clever Negro may use them for sinister ends'. On the other hand, it was recognised that 'it is barbarous and unreasonable to deprive the man who toils from morning to night' of a chance to amuse himself, and that 'Africans in general deeply enjoy certain amusements'.[64]

The *caxambu* took its name from the deeper-voiced of the two drums that accompanied it; the smaller, higher-pitched drum was called *candonguero*. Sometimes a third drum was also used. Besides instrumentation, several other features of the *caxambu*, as Stein describes it, tend to identify it as a form of *jongo*. One such feature was the use of a bonfire. On one side of the fire sat the musicians, on the other side the old people whom one former slave called the 'people from Africa, wise persons' (using also the term *macota*, 'persons of prestige and influence'). Another *jongo*-like feature was the participation of *jongueiros*, or singers of riddles in verse. Stein gives the following unique and invaluable description of the *caxambu*, having gathered details 'by oral interrogation and observation of the infrequently held caxambús in the município of Vassouras':

A warm-up period generally preceded the caxambú. Drummers tapped out rhythms or beats with the flat and heel of the palm, experimenting with companion drummers while jongueiros (versifiers) hummed to themselves and the drummers the verses they would try out. To assure an even, high resonance, drummers hauled their instruments close to the fire briefly where heat tautened the leather top. Supervising the whole session, was the 'king (*rei*) of caxambú' sometimes joined by his 'queen'. On wrists and ankles king and queen alone wore *nguízu* which produced an accompaniment to the drumbeats when they danced. Participants walked first to greet the king and kissed his hand. Then the king began the caxambú. Dressed in what one ex-slave called a red flannel outfit and hat bearing a cross, the king entered the dancing circle (*roda*) and, approaching the drums reverently, knelt with bowed head and greeted them. Arising, he sang the two lines of his jongo riddle, the drummers swung into the batida [beat], while assembled slaves repeated the refrain, clapped hands, and entered the dancing circle. Male slaves, dressed in white pants and possibly a striped shirt, women in loosely-hanging blouses and full skirts, kerchiefs on their heads, danced around each other without physical contact. Dancers moved in a counterclockwise circle. As they tired, they danced toward members of their sex and invited them to take their places by touching the palm. Even children entered the circle to imitate the motions of their elders. With the first riddle sung, and drumming and dancing under way, the king withdrew into the background, leaving the circle to another jongueiro who would try to decipher the riddle with two more lines and to introduce his rhymed riddle ('one line weighed upon the other'). Yet if trouble sprang up between contesting versifiers, the king returned immediately and silenced the drums by placing his palms atop them. 'He did not wish to have any disturbance in the dancing circle,' the son of a rei de caxambú explained ...

Each new jongueiro stepped close to the drums placing a hand on the large drum or caxambú to silence it temporarily, and then began his verses. The drummer on the flatter sounding small drum, or candongueiro, experimented to catch the correct beat for the rhymed verses, and when he satisfied the jongueiro, the large booming caxambú was 'called' to join. Blending words and drum accompaniment was explained as 'The candongueiro sings first, to set the beat for the caxambú'.[65]

Elaborating on the resistance role of the *caxambu* dance before emancipation, Stein calls it 'a sanctioned opportunity to indulge in sly, deft, often cynical comment on the society of which slaves were so important a segment'. He adds:

the caxambú with its powerful rhythms, its almost complete lack of planter supervision, the use of African words to cover too obvious allusions, and occasional swigs of warm cachaça, gave slaves a chance to express their feelings towards their masters and overseers and to comment upon the foibles of their fellows.[66]

The coco

The *coco* ring-dance originated in Alagoas, spread through the north-east and north, was first reported in Ceará in 1865, and was popular there until at least the 1970s. Throughout the first half of the twentieth century it was probably the most cherished dance of all in the north-eastern countryside. The participants dance in a circle, making vigorous body movements while striking together the dried half-shells of coconuts, an instrument known as *quenguinhas*,[67] or clapping their cupped hands to create a timbre that is said to imitate the sound of coconut shells being broken.[68] Another instrument generally used in the *coco* is the African-derived shaker known as *ganzá* (cf. Kimbundu *nganza*, 'gourd') or *canzá* or *xeque-xeque*. Sometimes there are also solo dancers inside the ring. Occasionally the musicians providing the accompaniment – flute and percussion – join in the dance. Mário de Andrade suggested that the *coco* began as a worksong used by the inhabitants of the seventeenth-century liberated area of Palmares (see pp. 69–71) while breaking up coconuts for food.[69]

Eight field recordings of the *coco*, made in Paraíba in 1938 by the folklorist Luís Saia and three colleagues, have recently been issued.[70] Four are accompanied by the large *zabumba* double-headed stick-beaten drum and the *ganzá* rattle; the rest have *ganzá* accompaniment alone. The *coco* was also recorded in Fortaleza in 1975.[71] A dance called *toré* or *torem*, in the north-eastern states of Ceará, Paraíba and Alagoas, is musically and choreographically very similar to the *coco*.[72]

The calango

Whirling, voluptuous movements, and 'floppiness' (*desengonços*) are said to be features of this 'dance of African origin',[73] popular in the countryside in the states of Minas Gerais, São Paulo and Rio de Janeiro, but sometimes also performed in towns. It is a couple dance in which a man and woman dance while embracing. According to one account, it features steps familiar in the urban samba and the Brazilian tango.[74] The dance is characteristically accompanied by the eight-button *sanfona* accordion and the *pandeiro* tambourine, and by songs in call-and-response form which may be sung separately and sometimes involve challenge singing between two singers (*calango de desafio*). These songs are often learnt from *cordel* pamphlets, the street literature, still on sale in many parts of Brazil, in which traditional stories are retold. In the north-east of Brazil, *calango* songs are heard without the dance; in the state of Rio de Janeiro such songs sometimes serve as worksongs during weeding and other work in the fields.[75]

Several other African secular dances were formerly danced in Brazil but have disappeared. The Bahian *sorongo* is described as a kind of samba for solo dancer.[76] In Minas Gerais were danced the *quimbete*, another variant of the samba,[77] and the *sarambeque*. The latter dance came from Mozambique, where it was known in the Chuabo language as *saramba*, which means 'dance featuring swaying bodies and hips accompanied by amorous gestures to the rhythm of small bells and rattles', and also 'the small bells and rattles used in this dance';[78] the Nyungwe (Wangongwe) call it *sarama*, the Yao *salamba*, with the same meanings. In the first half of the seventeenth century it was popular in Portugal (where Francisco Manuel de Mello advised husbands that for a wife to know about this dance, and to carry castanets in her pocket, were sure signs of licentiousness),[79] and, as *zarambeque* or *zumbé*, in Spain (where dictionaries defined it as 'Very gay and rowdy strumming and dancing, which is very frequent among the blacks').[80] The dance was also popular in Mexico in the early eighteenth century.[81] In Lisbon it evolved into an aristocratic dance, later became a popular dance in the Corpus Christi processions, and lasted in various forms until about 1810.[82] This hybrid, linking Mozambique, Portugal, Spain, Brazil and Mexico, is an excellent if unusually far-flung example of the Atlantic dance tradition, to which we now turn.

7

Brazil's Atlantic Dances

The Atlantic dance tradition

As both dance and song, the Brazilian *lundu* is our main key to understanding the rise of Brazilian popular music. But the *lundu* must first be seen in context, as a particular expression – one among many – of a widely shared dance tradition whose first seeds were sown when Africans started arriving in the Iberian peninsula in the eighth century. Seven centuries later the Atlantic trade and cultural triangles started to function. Relatively suddenly there began a long process of exchange and intermingling of styles and influences. Reaching out from the Iberian peninsula to the New World that lay across the ocean, the Afro-Iberian dance tradition would now blossom into an Atlantic dance tradition.

For the past 500 years, throughout much of South and Central America and the Caribbean, and in the Iberian peninsula too, the Atlantic dance tradition has been passed on from generation to generation by black and white dancers alike. Often, but not always, performed by one woman and one man, the dance is typically a stylised, even ritualised, dance of courtship. In this shared tradition African, Arab and Iberian body movements are subtly blended, and the dancers respond to music that is rich in cross-rhythms or in systematised syncopation deriving from the use of cross-rhythms. In Portugal, Brazil, Argentina, Chile, Cuba, Martinique, Peru, Puerto Rico, Uruguay and elsewhere the dance has gone under many different names from time to time and has displayed many differences of detail. But Brazilian and Portuguese *lundu*, Chilean and Argentinian *cueca*, Haitian *chica*, Martinique *calenda*, Peruvian *marinera* and other such dances are national variants of what is essentially one and the same tradition. John Charles Chasteen, to whom we owe an excellent recent account of this tradition, gives the following summary of its shared elements, found 'from Buenos Aires to Rio de Janeiro to Havana to New Orleans':

The instruments were especially African drums, but also rasping instruments ... a variety of Iberian stringed instruments ... and handclapping ... One of the dancers often sang verses that elicited a refrain from those clapping the rhythm for the dancers ... The dancers themselves were usually one couple, male and female ... The dance emphasised the lateral movements of the hips ... which create the sinuous twists of the body below the torso, ... imparting to the dancer's movements a sort of gyroscopic glide ... These were shared elements in a variegated, evolving tradition, expressed to some degree wherever enslaved Africans and their descendants formed a part of the population.[1]

To uncover the deepest discernible roots of this tradition, we have to go back a couple of hundred years before Columbus crossed the Atlantic. Although, as has just been seen, there was an African presence in Spain from the eighth century, it would be another 300 or 400 years before there was a substantial number of Africans there,[2] and a further similar period would elapse before the first Africans were transported to Portugal. The main, and possibly the earliest, concentration of black people in Spain was in Seville, for long perhaps the world's leading centre of musical culture,[3] where they took part collectively in public ceremonies and where, in 1475, a royal decree appointed a special judge, himself a black person, for blacks and persons of mixed ethnicity (*loros*), slave and free alike.[4] From the fifteenth century there were also free black communities in Valencia, Granada, Cadiz and Jaen.

According to P. E. Russell, there is evidence that black music and song heard in Moslem Spain began to be reflected in Iberian literature as early as the thirteenth century. Russell quotes a satirical poem, written in Galician by the poet D. Lopo Lias (active possibly in the first half of that century) for a melody described as a '*son de negrada*'; this poem is 'remarkable for its unusual and irregular rhythms'.[5] Three poems attributed to the Spanish poet Rodrigo de Reinosa (active probably in the last years of the fifteenth century and the early years of the sixteenth) provide what scanty information there is about the black dances which were popular among the general population in Spain at that time. These poems, Russell believes, 'seem ... to have been written for performance in a musical context that points to the existence in Spain by Reinosa's time of a taste for the music, singing and dancing of Black Africa brought to Spain by the slaves' – the majority of whom, in that period, were Wolofs from Senegambia.[6]

The heading of one of Reinosa's poems specifies that it is to be sung to the melody of a dance called the *guineo*, which the lexicographer Sebastián de Covarrubias would describe in 1611 as 'a hurried dance of quick and hasty movements, possibly brought from Guinea [i.e. West Africa] and first danced by black people'.[7] This definition, Russell points out, 'makes it quite plain that, by his time, the *guineo* was not a dance peculiar to the negro minority in Spain'.[8] In another of Reinosa's poems an African character called Comba boasts that he can sing the 'sweet *undul* and *maagana*', whereupon a character called Jorge ripostes that he himself dances the *guineo* well. Its name suggests that the *undul* (a word perhaps derived from the Spanish verb *ondular*) was a dance in which the body was shaken; it could conceivably have been the same dance as the black dance later known in Spain as the *ye-ye*.[9] In any case, Russell takes the *undul* and *maagana* to be 'African song-and-dance routines of the time, probably particularly associated with negro women', adding: 'But exactly what they were is not yet satisfactorily established.'[10] *Maagana* may be a variant form of *mangana*, a word also used by Reinosa – and by the great Portuguese poet Luís de Camões (*c*. 1524–80), according to whom this song had 'a sad sound'.[11] A satirical song of the late fifteenth century asserted that a slave-trader called Fernão Gomes da Mina danced the *mangana*.[12] The word *magana* (or *macana*) can mean 'a thick stick', Russell points out, so the dance of that name in the Iberian peninsula 'just possibly represents a version of a West African stick-dance', though 'the evidence for this is rather thin'.[13] Russell suggests that African musical instruments, 'or very close imitations', were in use in the Iberian peninsula by the first half of the sixteenth century, and quotes a play of *c*.1530, the *Farsa theological* of Diego Sánchez de Badajoz (*fl.* 1525), in which a black woman sings in a Spanish-based creole (*habla de negro*) and accompanies herself by tapping out a rhythm on a metal wine pitcher.[14] By Reinosa's time, Russell concludes, black music and dancing had in Spain 'already secured an appreciative clientele outside the narrow confines of the negro community'.[15]

Much the same may be said of Portugal. According to Robert Stevenson, 'Sub-Saharan music heard *in situ* so fascinated Portuguese visitors during three centuries that exploration literature abounds in cordial accounts'. He quotes as examples Ruy de Pina (1440–1521), who remarked on the musical retinue of the Kongo king in 1491, and Duarte Lopes (*fl.* 1578), who a century later lengthily described Kongo court instruments including 'certain Lutes ... made after a strange fashion'. André Alvares d'Almada (*fl.* 1594), in his *Relação e descripção de Guiné*, published in 1733, reported admiringly on 'talking drums'.[16] Several other Portuguese travellers were impressed in particular by how sweetly flutes were played in Kongo, Angola and South Africa.[17]

In Portugal itself, black singers were first heard in 1444, when Africans taken to Lagos 'made their lamentations in song, according to the custom of their country'.[18] Black dance music was heard in Lisbon in 1451, during the celebrations honouring the ambassadors sent by the emperor Frederick III to fetch his bride, Princess Leonor; an African in a dragon mask was the high point of the reception.[19] A group of six black musicians, playing trumpets, trompeta bastarda, sackbut and bass shawm, is shown on a panel of the so-called Santa Auta altarpiece from the Madre de Deus monastery in Lisbon, painted in about 1520, one of whose wings depicts the mystical marriage of St Ursula and Prince Conan. This highly realistic painting, now in Lisbon's Museu Nacional de Arte Antiga, 'amounts to a photograph of a black orchestra in Portugal in the early sixteenth century'.[20] Black drummers greeted church dignitaries arriving in Vila Viçosa and Évora in 1571, and the woodcut of a black guitarist served as the frontispiece of several Portuguese plays.[21] In a seventeenth-century musical manuscript preserved at Santa Cruz de Coimbra, West Africans enter to sing in *fala de Guiné*, at which point 'the text takes on a highly picturesque aspect'.[22] As we saw in the Introduction, the *guineo* was danced in Portugal as well as Spain, and apparently still is.[23]

So when the first New World dances arrived in the Iberian peninsula they found extremely fertile ground. By the 1580s, some 60 years after the Spanish invasion of Mexico (1519–20), the galleons that set sail from Vera Cruz laden with gold and silver from the mines of 'New Spain' were also bringing to Europe the rhythms and tunes of the *chacona* and *zarabanda*, *jácara* and *tocotín* (or *toncotín*), the last named said to be an imitation of Aztec song and dance. These first choreographic fruits of Europe's conquest of America were already hybrids, mingling Amerindian, African and European features. And when they reached the Iberian peninsula they were warmly welcomed in Seville, from where they spread through Europe to become widely fashionable and, to various degrees, Europeanised.

When Cervantes called the *chacona* 'mulatto-like' (*amulatada*)[24] he was personifying this dance as a vulgar and sacrilegious woman of mixed ethnicity who is nevertheless a favourite with eveyone. It was, in other words, a dance with pronounced Amerindian and African ingredients, as well as 'touches of Spanish (the instruments perhaps)'.[25] Similarly, the Spanish poet and satirist Francisco de Quevedo (1580–1645) called the dance '*la Chacona mulata*';[26] and the Spanish poet and dramatist Lope de Vega (1562–1635) wrote that it had 'come to Seville by post from the Indies'.[27] The *zarabanda*, better known in English-speaking countries as the sarabande, also originated in Mexico: as the *çarauanda* it was sung and danced at Pátzcuaro, Michoacán, in 1569.[28]

The African influence on both *chacona* and *zarabanda* needs little explanation. Africans accompanied the Spanish *conquistadores*; one of Cortes's gunners was an African; and by 1580, while there were fewer than 15,000 Spaniards in New Spain, there were more than 18,500 Africans there, as well as almost 1,500 people of mixed ethnicity. Such a population balance could not but affect the colony's music and dance. One of the oldest and most popular black dances in the New World, a '*portorrico de los negros*', of Caribbean origin, is transcribed in a mid-seventeenth-century Mexican instruction book for the cittern, *Método de Citara*.[29] What Robert Stevenson called 'the powerful impress of the Negro in colonial dance types' is also clearly apparent in the '*cumbees*', subtitled 'songs in West African style', transcribed around 1740 in a Mexican manuscript, 'Tablatura de vihuela'. The player is instructed 'to hit his vihuela with a thump at certain odd moments'.[30]

The popularity of the *zarabanda* gave Spain's rulers some anxiety. In 1583, by royal decree, Spaniards who sang or danced this shocking transatlantic import were rendered liable to 200 lashes, plus six years in the galleys for men and banishment for women.[31] Philip II's ban seems to have had little effect, though, for in 1606 Father Juan de Mariana (1536–1624), in a chapter wholly devoted to the *zarabanda*, was denouncing this dance and song that had taken root in Spain within the past 20 years as 'so lascivious in its words and so unseemly [*feo*] in its motions that it is enough to inflame even very decent people'; its gestures and words were 'equal to the lewdest kisses and embraces used in brothels'.[32] In both Spain and Portugal, according to Chasteen:

[d]ancing *zarabanda*, *chacona*, and their transcultural cousins became an activity frequent enough and important enough to give prominence to some men of the popular classes, often gypsies or blacks, who danced particularly well … A handful even attempted to make a living at it …

Lisbon and Seville seem to have seen particularly enthusiastic 'dance crazes'.[33]

Europeans who witnessed any variant of this Atlantic dance, either in the Iberian peninsula or in the New World, were always fascinated and often horrified by what they saw, and their colourful descriptions frequently suggest a certain degree of exaggeration as well as prurience. In 1694 a French aristocrat, the baron de Lahontan (1666–1715?) wrote from Portugal that the dances of the humbler classes there were 'indecent, through the rude [*impertinens*] gestures of head and belly'.[34] The Dominican friar and traveller Jean Baptiste Labat (1663–1738), who went to Martinique as a missionary in 1694, published in 1722 a description, destined to be much plagiarised, of the dance which, according to him, most pleased the black slaves on the island and was most usual among them. He called the dance *calenda*, though in his description it bore little resemblance to the Trinidad stick-fighting dance of the same name. Accompanied by two drums, the dance used postures and movements which were most unseemly (*déshonnêtes*):

It comes from the Guinea coast and to all appearances from the kingdom of Arda [i.e. Ardra, on the then Slave Coast]. The Spaniards have learnt it from the Negroes and dance it all over America in the same way as the Negroes …

The dancers are arranged in two facing lines, the men on one side and the women on the other. Those tired of dancing, and the onlookers, make a circle round the dancers and the drums. The most skilful one improvises a song on any subject he considers appropriate, and the refrain, sung by all the onlookers, is accompanied by loud handclapping. The dancers hold their arms approximately like those who dance while playing castanets. They jump, spin round, approach to within two or three feet of each other, move back rhythmically until the drum signals them to come together by striking their thighs against each other, that is to say, the men against the women. By the look of them, they seem to be giving each other blows on the belly, though in fact the thighs alone bear the blows. Now they fall back, twirling round and round, and start the same movement again, with quite lascivious gestures, as many times as the drum gives the signal, which it often does several times in succession. From time to time they link arms and turn round two or three times, still striking each other's thighs and kissing each other. It will be seen from this short description how contrary to decency [*pudeur*] is this dance. For all that, it does not fail to be so much to the taste of the American-born Spaniards [*Espagnols Creolles de l'Amerique*] and is so much used among them that it makes up the better part of their amusements and is even a part of their devotions. They dance it in their churches and their processions, and the nuns rarely fail to dance it on Christmas night on a stage erected in their chancel, facing their grille, which is open so that the people may share in the delight these simple souls show in the birth of the Saviour. To be sure, they do not let men in to dance such a pious dance with them. I am willing to believe, indeed, that they dance it with an entirely pure intention, but how many onlookers are there who will not judge it so charitably as me?

The black slaves' passion for this dance, Labat added, was unimaginable, extending even to children who could scarcely stand up: 'It looks as if they had danced in their mothers' bellies.'[35]

Another French monk, Dom Antoine Pernety (1716–1801) sailed to the Malvinas in 1763 with the circumnavigator Louis-Antoine de Bougainville. When he went on shore at Montevideo early in 1764 he saw people dancing the *calenda*. His account clearly owed much to Labat, from whom he borrowed certain passages, including virtually word for word the story about the nuns (here omitted):

[O]ne of the Mulatoes, who looked very much like an Indian born of Spanish parents, took the negro woman by the hand, and they both of them danced together upwards of a quarter of an hour, the dance called Calenda. Travellers who speak much of this dance in their accounts, do not exaggerate, when they describe it as the most lascivious [*lubrique*] of all dances, at least judging of it by our manners.

It is thought, that this dance has been brought into America, by the negroes of the kingdom of Arda, upon the coast of Guinea. The Spaniards dance it as well as the natives, throughout all their establishments in America, without making the least scruple about it; although the dance is so very indecent as to astonish people who are not used to see it. It is so universally, and so much liked, that even children, as soon as they are able to stand, imitate in this particular persons more advanced in life ...

One may readily judge, how surprising such a dance must appear to French manners, and how much our modesty must be offended by it. Nevertheless we are assured from the accounts of travellers that it is so very agreeable even to the Spaniards of America, and is become so much an established custom among them, that it is even introduced among their acts of devotion.[36]

The French lawyer Médéric Moreau de Saint-Méry (1750–1819), who was in the Caribbean from 1772 to 1784, described in much the same terms as Labat and Pernety the *calenda* he saw danced in Haiti. Another black dance there

which is also of African origin is the *chica*, called simply *calenda* in the Windward Islands, *Congo* in Cayenne, *fandango* in Spain, etc. This dance has its own special tune, with a strongly marked rhythm. The dancer's talent consists in the perfection with which she can move her hips and the lower part of her back while keeping all the rest of her body in a kind of immobility without losing the slight waving of her arms as she swings the two ends of a handkerchief or of her petticoat. A male dancer approaches her, springs forward suddenly and drops down in rhythm, almost touching her. He moves back, springs forward again, and challenges her to the most seductive contest. The dance grows lively and soon presents a picture all of whose features, at first voluptuous, then become lascivious. It would be impossible to portray the *chica* in its true colours, and I will confine myself to saying that the impression it creates is so powerful that the African or Creole, of whatever shade, who felt no thrill at seeing it danced would be thought to have forfeited the last sparks of his sensibility.[37]

This dance tradition went round the Atlantic cultural triangle over and over again. There were many national and regional variants. In some the man flourished a handkerchief; in others he shook a rattle or clicked castanets; in others again he snapped his fingers. There were different local names. But everywhere this was in essence the same dance, and it evoked an identical response of enthusiasm and affection in places as far apart as Lisbon and Lima. The *lundu*'s hold on the Portuguese in the 1820s was described by a less than wholly approving English writer who reported how people hearing a 'big drum and fiddle' in the street outside, hurried to their verandas and windows

> to regale themselves with a sight of the lascivious and even frantic Landum, danced by a negro and negress, whose very gestures and looks would to more delicate people serve only to create the utmost sensations of disgust; but the Portuguese are themselves so fond of this dance, under certain decent modifications, that they never fail to contemplate it with pleasure, even when carried to extremes by its original inventors ...

This dance, 'originally a negro one', had formerly been danced 'in the best societies of Lisbon' by persons of both sexes:

> The parties placing themselves at opposite ends of a room, and the gentleman holding a white handkerchief, they advance towards each other with measured steps and wooing mien, and the lady appears disposed to sympathise with her admirer. But at the moment when he imagines her favorable to his suit, she turns away from him with a smile of contempt and astonishment at his presumption; he likewise turns away, but with far other feelings; the handkerchief now finds its way to his eyes; and with disappointment in every feature, he measures back his steps, looking occasionally behind him as if to excite compassion.
>
> His reiterated solicitations make her at length relax in her severity and appear pleased at his attentions; which he no sooner perceives than he treats her with disdain. She in her turn becomes the suppliant, and receives from him the same handkerchief, a token of grief, which she uses with the most fascinating grace-fulness. This pantomimic representation of a love-scene ends in the lady's throwing the handkerchief over the neck of her partner, as an emblem of her conquest and their mutual reconciliation and union. When this is well danced, it never fails to elicit the most thunderous applauses [*sic*]. What I have just endeavoured to describe is the landun of the better orders; but when danced by the canaille it is far from being either graceful or decent.
>
> The common people in Portugal are so fond of the landun that even at an advanced age they experience a strong sensation of delight on hearing the measure played on the guitar. I shall never forget having once seen a mummy-

like old woman of eighty years of age rise from the floor which she was scrubbing, on hearing a barber strike up the tune, and begin to accompany the air with contortions, to which age had left no other character than unmingled disgust ...

In the national theatre of Rua dos Condes the landun is frequently introduced in after-pieces; and on these occasions the house is always best filled, so great and powerful is the attraction. It is usually danced by a lacquey and a soubrette, who, although they confine themselves to very few gestures, and their whole performance does not perhaps last more than two to three minutes, have, nevertheless, so much the art of conveying significance in the merest looks and movements, that the performance is applauded with vociferous 'vivas' and 'bravos'.[38]

With these indications of the *lundu*'s popularity in Portugal may be compared Fernando Romero's account 60 years ago of the 'animated and enthusiastic' shouts to the dancers (*'¡Qué buena china!'*, *'¡Voy a ela!'*, *'¡Asi!'*, *'¡Vamos!'*, *'¡Qué bueno!'*, *'¡Jajá!'*, *'¡Entra!'*, *'¡Ahora!'*, *'¡Dale!'*, etc.) with which spectators punctuated the beloved Peruvian *marinera*.[39] In that Peruvian dance of courtship, known also in Chile and Argentina and originally called *cueca* or *zamacueca* or *zambacueca*,[40] both dancers wave handkerchiefs.[41]

The lundu: *Brazil's first national dance*

Writing in Salvador at the end of the eighteenth century, the Brazilian satirical poet Gregório de Mattos Guerra (1623?–1696) declared his 'great desire to see the *gandu* danced'.[42] Less than 40 years later the same dance was referred to in Portugal by the poet João José Cardoso da Costa (b. 1693), who wrote in a sonnet that 'to see someone as black as you one must enter the dark realms where the *Gandú* is danced'.[43] The Portuguese poet Fr Lucas de Santa Catarina (1660–1740) saw the *gandu* danced in religious festivals in the São Bento district.[44] It is likely, though not certain, that this dance of black people in Brazil and Portugal was the same as – or at least a close relative of – the dance known as the *lundu* but apparently not called by that name until 1780.

The German artist Johann Moritz Rugendas saw the *lundu* danced in Brazil in the early 1820s and published two drawings of it. In one it is danced by a black couple, accompanied by a lamellophone (Fig. 12); in the other it is danced by a white couple, accompanied by a guitar, with the man holding what I take to be castanets in each hand (Fig. 13). Rugendas, in the text of his book, refers to the dance as 'Zandu', which is plainly an error of transcription or a printing error (in the captions to his drawings it is 'Danse Landu'). He calls it 'another very well-known black dance, ... in use also among the Portuguese', adding, 'It is performed by one or two couples to the sound of the mandolin; perhaps the Spaniards' Fandango or Bolero is only an improved copy of it.'[45] But in fact the *lundu* owed much to the fandango, about which a word must now be said.

The word 'fandango' is used today in three distinct senses in Brazil. In Alagoas and elsewhere in the north-east it is a series of songs on nautical themes.[46] In the coastal area of São Paulo and the southern states, it is a suite of ring dances. In the interior of São Paulo state it is a series of dances representing aspects of rural life.[47] One authority lists 51 distinct fandango dances that are known in the state of São Paulo alone.[48]

DANSE LANDU.

Figure 12 A black couple dancing the *lundu*, c. 1821–25, as depicted by Rugendas. On the right, a musician is playing a marimba (lamellophone). (Rugendas, *Malerische Reise in Brasilien*)

The basic fandango style may have originated in the New World. A 1769 dictionary defined it as a 'kind of very lively dance, which the Spaniards have learnt from the Indians',[49] a statement which may mean no more than that it was a Spanish import from across the Atlantic. During the 60 years of Spanish rule over Brazil (1581–1640), the fandango was the most popular dance among Europeans in the colony. It was already to some extent Arabised and Africanised in the sixteenth century, when it added hip movement and the frontal approach of the dancers, with rhythmic advances and backward movements, feints, turns and *umbigada* ('belly-blow'), to the curving and waving of arms above the head, the snapping of fingers, the stamping of feet (*sapateado*). It was no doubt this partial Africanisation of the fandango which led an English army officer, Major William Dalrymple, seeing this 'lascivious dance' performed in a Madrid theatre in 1774, to suppose that it had been 'brought from the West Indies' and that it 'originally came from the coast of Guinea'. His first supposition may have been correct; nor was his second one wholly unreason-

DANSE LANDU.

Figure 13 A white couple dancing the *lundu* in the early 1820s, by which time visitors from abroad were calling this Brazil's national dance. On the right, a musician plays a guitar. (Rugendas, *Malerische Reise in Brasilien*)

able, for at Tetuan Dalrymple had seen 'the Emperor of Morocco's black soldiers dance, with casnets [*sic*] in their hands, in a manner very similar'.[50] The English writer Richard Twiss (1747–1821), who had seen the fandango danced at Mafra, in south Portugal, a year or two earlier, reported that '[e]very part of the body is in motion, and is thrown into all postures, frequently into very indecent ones. Stamping the time with the feet, and playing all the while with the *castañetas*, ... the dancers approach, turn, retire, and approach again.'[51]

Certain characteristic movements of the fandango then – notably the curving and raising of the arms and stamping of the feet – were incorporated into the *lundu* in the course of its development. This seems to have happened in both Portugal and Brazil – in the latter probably during the period of Spanish rule. Chasteen suggests that the fandango also contributed to the *lundu* 'the basic choreography of an encounter between one man and one woman',[52] but, judging from Joachim Monteiro's 1875 description, quoted in the previous chapter, courtship seems already to have been the basic theme of the Kongo-Angola dances on which the *lundu* was based – unless, as may well be the case, there was more Europeanisation (or, as it were, Atlanticisation) of those dances in nineteenth-century Angola than is generally supposed. Leaving aside this writer's preoccupation with 'indecency', it would be tempting to identify the first of the two dances Monteiro describes as the forerunner of the Brazilian *batuque* and the second as that of the *lundu*, but this would be an oversimplification. In Brazil these two dances were often confused in contemporary accounts. There was obviously a continuum of styles without any clearly defined dividing line and it would be misleading to try and disentangle them in terms of their African provenance. It is often held that the *lundu* was the 'direct descendant of the African *batuque*',[53] and it is true that before 1780 there are frequent references to black dances in Brazil, especially *batuques*, but no express mention of the *lundu*. The *lundu* is said to have been danced in Portugal from the sixteenth century, the *batuque* from the eighteenth, but for neither claim is the evidence entirely clear.[54] The Portuguese king Dom Manuel I (1495–1521) is supposed to have issued a royal decree prohibiting both, as well as a third African-derived dance called *charamba* (also danced in the Azores), as 'unseemly' (*indecorosas*). In 1559 black people were indeed banned from assembling, dancing and playing musical instruments in Lisbon, 'either at night or during the day, on feast days or during the week' and for a league – about three miles – around the city, on penalty of being arrested and fined. But there is no evidence that this seemingly ineffective ban was imposed on moral grounds, and there is no reference to specific dances.[55]

In Salvador and Rio de Janeiro, as in Lisbon, the black dances called *batuque* and *lundu* (or *lundum*) were adopted first by the poorest among the white population and then moved steadily and quite rapidly up the social scale, so that by the early nineteenth century foreign visitors would regard them as the national dances of Brazil.

In 1812 Henry Koster saw a dance at Jaguaribe, in the state of Ceará, which he did not name but was probably the *lundu*. It was danced by 'free people of colour', who

> held their merry-making at the door of one of their own huts. Their dances were like those of the African negroes. A ring was formed; the guitar player sat down in a corner, and began a simple tune, which was accompanied by some favourite song, of which the burthen [i.e. chorus] was often repeated, and frequently some of the verses were extempore, and contained indecent allusions. One man stepped out into the centre of the ring, and danced for some minutes, making use of lascivious atitudes, until he singled out a woman, who then came forwards, and took her turn in movements not less indecent, and thus the amusement continued sometimes until day-break.[56]

The French journalist Charles Ribeyrolles, observing the *batuque* in the late 1850s, commented on its 'lewd postures, which the *urucungo* [berimbau] speeds up or slows down'. There was also, he added,

> a crazy dance, with the provocation of eyes, breasts and buttocks – a kind of drunken convulsion that is called *lundu*.
> Coarse pleasures, nasty sensualities, licentious excitements: all this is vile and lamentable. Yet the negroes have a taste for these bacchanalia, and others profit from them. Is not this a means of brutalisation?[57]

In 1865 a more than usually observant American couple, who spent 19 months in Brazil, witnessed a dance by black people in Rio de Janeiro that they called the fandango, though their description shows that what they saw was almost certainly the *lundu*. They were the Swiss-born naturalised US citizen Louis Agassiz (1807–73), zoologist and professor of natural history, and his wife Elizabeth (1822–1907), who went to Brazil with six assistants on a scientific expedition. They took a boat to the Ilha das Enxadas in Guanabara Bay:

> As we landed, a group of slaves, black as ebony, were singing and dancing a fandango. So far as we could understand, there was a leader who opened the game with a sort of chant, apparently addressed to each in turn as he passed around the circle, the others joining in chorus at regular intervals. Presently he broke into a dance which rose in wildness and excitement, accompanied by cries and ejaculations. The movements of the body were a singular combination of negro and Spanish dances. The legs and feet had the short, jerking, loose-jointed motion of our negroes in dancing, while the upper part of the body and the arms had that swaying, rhythmical movement from side to side so characteristic of all the Spanish dances ... It was nearly dark when we returned to the boat, but the negroes were continuing their dance under the glow of a bonfire. From time to time, as the dance reached its culminating point, they stirred their fire, and lighted up the wild group with its vivid blaze. The dance and the song had, like the amusements of the negroes in all lands, an endless monotonous repetition.[58]

The French diplomat Count Charles d'Ursel saw the *lundu* danced in Minas Gerais in the mid-1870s.[59] The American traveller Frank Vincent described as 'a sort of *fandango* or *cachuca*' (*sic*) a 'lively national dance' – possibly the *lundu* but possibly its descendant the *maxixe* (see Chapter 9) – which he saw performed '[a]t nearly all the theatres' during the 1885 carnival. It was

> extremely popular. It consisted of wriggling and suggestive posturing rather than of dancing, and its evolutions were extremely vulgar, not to say indecent; but so strong is custom that those in the boxes, who were evidently ladies, watched without flinching, and with great interest, those upon the floor, who certainly were not ladies.[60]

In the course of time, in Brazil as in Lisbon, *batuque* and *lundu* were stylised in taverns and theatres in a way that rendered them morally acceptable to the middle and upper classes, if not to all foreigners, and the *lundu*, as has just been seen was fused to some extent with the fandango. Having been lightly sanitised – how will be seen shortly – the *lundu* in particular soon entered the salons of colonial society and became all the rage in the middle and even the upper classes. Two sources enable us to pinpoint the decade in which this attracted notice in Brazil. The first, dated 1780, is a letter to the Portuguese government from a former governor of Pernambuco, José da Cunha Grã Athayde e Mello, Count of Pavolide, referring to black dances in Brazil that had been denounced to the Inquisition tribunal. Making what is generally taken to be the earliest known reference to the *lundu* in Brazil, the ex-governor compares the '*lundum* of the whites and blacks' to 'fandangos in Castille and *fofas* in Portugal'.[61] Closer examination of the text suggests, however, that this may be a reference to the *lundu* danced in Portugal. Our second, rather more convincing, source is a satirical poem published anonymously in 1787 by the Portuguese poet Tomás Antônio Gonzaga (1744–1810), who became a magistrate in Brazil and got himself jailed for three years for sedition and was then deported to Angola. He observes that in Brazil the 'torrid' (*quente*) *lundu* and the 'low' (*vil*) *batuque* are no longer the preserve of black women and lower-class women of mixed ethnicity (*vis mulatas*), of rogues and vagrants (*marotos e brejeiros*), dancing barefooted in humble shacks (*humildes choupanas*), but have succeeded in entering respectable houses. And he describes such a dance, at night, in the wings of the palace of the governor of Minas, by a black woman who holds up her skirt and glides on tiptoe as she dances and a white male servant who shakes his backside, puts one hand on his head, the other on his hip, and snaps his fingers to the beat of the guitars.[62] This reference to 'rogues and vagrants' underlines Stanley J. Stein's reminder that by no means all Portuguese settlers in Brazil were rich; that lower-class Portuguese settlers 'arrived poor, clerked for meager wages ... or moved into the rural areas where they worked on railroads, public roads, or in the towns and on plantations ...'; and that, above all, they 'were in constant contact with Negro and mulatto women, slave and free'.[63] Sexual relations between Portuguese men and African women were indeed commonplace in Brazil in colonial times; relations between Portuguese women and African men were probably less frequent but were far from rare. By no means all of these relationships were episodic. Such 'constant contact' could not but foster and accelerate the acculturation process.

Fifteen years after Gonzaga's poem was published a disapproving English visitor, Thomas Lindley, who was in Salvador on a smuggling expedition, saw in respectable houses in that city what he called the 'enticing *negro dance*':

> On grand occasions ..., after coming from church, they visit each other, and have a more plentiful dinner than common ...; ... they drink unusual quantities of wine; and, when elevated to an extraordinary pitch, the guitar or violin is introduced, and singing commences; but the song soon gives way to the enticing *negro dance*. I use this term as best assimilating with the amusement in question, which is a mixture of the dances of Africa, and the fandangoes of Spain and Portugal. It consists of an individual of each sex dancing to an insipid thrumming of the instrument, always to one measure, with scarcely any action of the legs, but with every licentious motion of the body, joining in contact during the dance in a manner strangely immodest. The spectators, aiding the music with an extemporary chorus, and clapping of the hands, enjoy the scene with an indescribable zest. The orgies of the dancing girls of India never equalled the flagrancy of this diversion. It is not that minuets and country dances are not known, and practised by the higher circles; but this is the national dance, and all classes are happy when, throwing aside punctilio and reserve, and, I may add, decency, they can indulge in the interest and raptures it excites. The effect of this scene on a stranger can hardly be conceived; and though, as an amusement, it may be intentionally harmless, it certainly breaks down the barriers of decency, and of course paves the way to depravity and vice.[64]

'Scarcely any action of the legs' suggests a rather less vigorous dance by white people in Salvador than the one the Agassiz couple saw danced by black people in Rio 60 years later; this is the main difference summed up in the phrase 'lightly sanitised'.

Visiting Brazil around 1811–13, another Englishman, Henry Koster, wrote that the dances he saw there 'are now as much the national dances of Brazil as they are of Africa', adding that the masters were imbibing 'some of the customs of their slaves'.[65] Writing in Rio de Janeiro in 1817, the Austrian botanist Karl Friedrich von Martius drew a distinction between the 'elegant quadrilles' danced in refined circles and the dances of lower-class Brazilians, 'done with erotic gestures and contortions, as among the Negroes'.[66]

Foreign visitors found many Brazilian dances sexually suggestive and morally repugnant mainly because they involved a lateral movement of the hips and the notorious *umbigada*, whereby a dancer pushes the stomach against another dancer's stomach – a manœuvre which in fact has no specific erotic significance but is merely an invitation to dance or a gesture terminating the dance. Indeed, as a sober observer pointed out a third of a century ago, the sensual aspect of black dances in general 'has been much overstated', and 'in Brazil, of which I speak with the authority of an observer, it cannot be said that the African dances are inherently lewd'.[67] Nineteenth-century foreign visitors saw in them what they wanted to see, however, and on the whole their comments tell us more about the writers than about the dances. In 1817 the French visitor Louis-François de Tollenare, who saw the *lundu* danced in a Salvador theatre, called it 'the most shameless [*cynique*] dance imaginable – nothing more or less than the crudest representation of the act of carnal love'. He went on:

> The woman dancer provokes her partner with the most unambiguous movements; he responds in the same way; the fair one surrenders to the lustful passion she feels, the demon of pleasure possesses her, the hurried jerks [*trémoussements précipités*] of her loins show how hot is the fire that is prompting her, her raptures become convulsive, love's climax seems to take place, and she swoons into her partner's arms while pretending to conceal with her handkerchief the blush of shame and of pleasure. Her conquest is the signal for applause on all sides, the spectators' eyes are sparkling with the desires she has provoked, their shouts call on her to start the contest again, and what would hardly be allowed in a disorderly house is repeated as many as three times before the people of a great civilised city. There are ladies in the boxes; they do not blush at all, no one could accuse them of prudery. I must however say that women of the first rank seldom go to the theatre. I have no doubt whatever that the performance of the *landu* there is one of the main reasons. The *landu* is very like the dance of the Negroes; but, embellished by art, it bears the same relation to the latter that the figures of Aretino painted by Annibal Carrache [*sic*] bear to the coarse smuttiness of the guard-house.[68]

In the same year that Tollenare wrote those words, another French visitor, Ferdinand Denis (1798–1890) reported from Salvador that the '*landou*' was 'extremely well performed, but [its] indecency prevents one giving an account of it, although it is the delight of the Brazilian public'.[69] In his later book on Brazil, Denis included a short account of the Brazilians' 'national dances', which

> take place impromptu anywhere they can be sure of not being interrupted. The *batuca*, which expresses by turns the refusal of love and its delights; the *capoeira*, a sham fight; the *landou*, which has even moved over into the theatre and whose charm consists above all in a peculiar movement of the lower parts of the body, which no European could ever imitate: all these impassioned dances, described by travellers a thousand times, are performed in Rio de Janeiro, as they are in our colonies and as they will be performed wherever there are blacks, with merely a change of name.

In Salvador, Denis added, the '*landou*', a 'sort of original fandango, copied from the dance of the blacks, is in reality a national dance'.[70] The rector of

Finglas, who visited Brazil in 1828–29, and whom we have already found enjoying the *berimbau*'s 'sweet notes', enjoyed rather less an unidentified 'dance of love' he saw, which concluded with 'indecencies not fit to be seen or described'.[71]

There can be no doubt that the 'national dance' that shocked Thomas Lindley and the 'dance of love' that shocked the Revd Robert Walsh was the *lundu*, which held sway for about a hundred years as the most popular social dance of urban Brazil.[72] But it was not only foreign visitors to Brazil who found this dance morally objectionable. In 1836–37, under the governorship of Francisco de Souza Aragão Paraíso, there was a debate among some of Bahia's bigwigs as to whether or not the *lundu* should be danced in the Salvador theatres.The manager of the São João theatre asked the administrator of public theatres, Ignácio Acioli de Carqueira e Silva, if he would permit the dancing of the *lundu* by various amateurs in the intervals. Wishing, he said, 'to combat this decided taste for immoral dances', the administrator withheld his consent. In the following year the manager renewed his request, adding that the dance would omit contortions which, being indecent, offended morality, and that it would be confined to the intervals in comedies and would not be danced during tragedies. The authorities replied that the *lundu* must be avoided as immoral and offensive to family modesty, and it was banned from most of the city's theatres.[73] It is not clear how long that ban remained in force.

The Frenchwoman whose description of the '*batuco*' was quoted in the previous chapter also saw some Brazilian ladies, 'by general request', dance the *lundu* in the early 1880s. She called it

> the national dance, which consists in a kind of rhythmical walk, with a movement of hips and eyes, which does not lack originality, and which as a rule everyone has to accompany by snapping their fingers like castanets to beat out the rhythm. In this dance the man merely, as it were, revolves around the woman and woos her, while she indulges in all kinds of feline movements of the most alluring kind.[74]

In 1889 a French writer on Brazilian folklore published this description of the *lundu* dance in its heyday:

> The dancers are all sitting or standing. A couple get up and begins the entertainment. At first they hardly stir: they snap their fingers with a noise like castanets, raise or round their arms, sway indolently. Gradually the gentleman comes to life: he manœuvres around his lady as if he were going to clasp her in his arms. She, unresponsive, scorns his advances; he is twice as ardent, while she maintains her supreme indifference. Now they are face to face, gazing in each other's eyes, nearly hypnotised by desire. She shakes, she springs forward; her movements grow more jerky, and she jigs about in a giddy passion, while the violin sighs and the enraptured onlookers clap their hands. Then she stops, breathless, exhausted. The gentleman continues his manœuvre for a moment;

then he calls out another woman dancer, who leaves her place, and the fevered and sensual *lundu* starts again.

The *lundu's* charms, this writer added, turned the strongest heads. As for the sung *lundu*, it was bantering (*gouailleur*), disorderly, stunning (*abracadabrant*), as often as not with a sting of coarse irony.[75]

When the Brazilian botanist François Freire Alemão (1797–1874) visited the north-eastern state of Ceará in 1859 he saw a dance he called the *baiana* (literally, 'woman of Bahia'). It was danced in a thatched hut by young men only, to the music of the *viola* traditional guitar, and Alemão found it 'entirely similar to our fado'. The participants danced alone or in couples, 'making difficult and agile steps, with postures more or less graceful or grotesque, accompanied by singing'.[76] This dance is thought to have been a north-eastern variant of the *lundu*[77] and is usually known as the *baiano* or *baião*. Its regional origin may have led to its being called at first the *lundu baiano* (Bahian *lundu*), a term known to have been used at least once in the nineteenth century. It is said to incorporate challenge singing and to involve very rapid 'gymnastic' movements of legs and feet. Mário de Andrade compared its basic step – a rotary movement of the soles of both feet, with the heels lifted – to that of the African-American Charleston, except that the latter's basic step was 'more organised', with knees bent and formalised arm movements, whereas the *baião* was more individual and often dispensed with arm movements. Originally it was accompanied by the *viola* traditional guitar, to which were added the *pandeiro* tambourine in Sergipe, the *botijão* jug in Paraíba and the *rabeca* fiddle in Maranhão. But the accordion is nowadays the usual accompanying instrument, especially now that the *baião* is most frequently heard as one of the five sub-styles of *forró*, the most typical present-day dance music of Brazil's north-eastern states.[78] In Pernambuco, one of the *baião's* traditional strongholds, there is a popular rhyme:

> São Paulo for coffee,
> Ceará for tough guys,
> Piauí for wild cows,
> Pernambuco for *baião*.[79]

The *baião* is the dance of the rural poor of north-east Brazil; it is 'confined to persons of the proletarian class', wrote Mário de Andrade.[80] Unfortunately it seems to have been less frequently recorded in the first half of the century than were less rustic styles. So far it is not well represented on reissues of Brazilian music from the first half of the century, but there is an excellent example by the superb accordionist Luiz Gonzaga do Nascimento (b. 1912), recorded in 1946.[81] This piece does bear a close rhythmic resemblance to the recorded *lundu*.

It is often supposed that the *lundu* has disappeared in Brazil, but one of the remote areas in which it is still danced is Marajó, an island the size of

Switzerland in the mouth of the Amazon. There is a 1976 recording of a local dance band playing two *lundus*. Besides clarinet, violin and guitar, the band includes the four-string plucked lute that the Brazilians call *cavaquinho* and that we call the ukelele.[82]

The fofa *that came from Bahia*

The *fofa* was a dance very like the *lundu* and may in fact have been the *lundu* under another name. The earliest reference to it in Portugal dates from 1730, when it is mentioned as the *'forfa'* in a letter written in the Portuguese-based creole known as *fala de Guiné* or *língua de preto*, and printed in a periodical called *Folhas de antas Lisboas*.[83]

French visitors to Portugal in the second half of the eighteenth century described the *fofa*, however 'indecent' and 'lascivious' they considered it to be, as Portugal's national dance,[84] though it is not clear whether the Portuguese themselves thought of it in either of those ways. Major William Dalrymple of the British army, who visited Portugal in 1774 and saw the *fofa* danced by a black man and woman on the stage, found it 'the most indecent thing I ever beheld, and only calculated for the stews [i.e. brothels]'; yet no one in the audience 'seemed displeased; on the contrary, the women beheld it with calmness, and the men applauded the performance'.[85] The major mistakenly called the *fofa* 'a dance peculiar to this country'; he had no idea that the *fofa* was already a popular dance in some urban centres of Portugal's Brazilian colony[86] – in the north-eastern province of Pernambuco, for instance, where it was in vogue by 1761. So much is clear from Fr Bento de Capêda's account in that year of the 'lamentable state which the Society of Jesus has come to in this region of Brazil'. Writing of the Jesuits' community at Olinda, near the coastal town of Recife, he complained that, according to the canons of the cathedral there, one of its members, Fr Manoel Franco, had 'danced the *fofa* (which is an indecent [*deshonesta*] dance) with women of ill repute'.[87]

It was long supposed that this 1761 complaint was the earliest reference to the existence of the *fofa* in Brazil. But since 1966 it has been known that a *cordel* pamphlet (a piece of street literature) printed almost certainly in Lisbon in about 1752 claims that the dance had originated in Bahia and had spread to Portugal from there. A copy of this extremely rare pamphlet, entitled *Relação da Fofa, que veyo agora da Bahia, e o Fandango de Sevilha* ('Account of the *Fofa*, which comes now from Bahia, and the Seville Fandango'), was discovered in the early 1960s by the Rio de Janeiro bookseller Walter Geyerhahn[88] and was obtained in 1992 by that city's Biblioteca Nacional, in whose Music Section it is now on deposit.

In size, appearance, and style, the *Relacaõ da Fofa* is typical of the *cordel* literature of the period.[89] The handsome binding of the Biblioteca Nacional's copy encloses a wretchedly printed eight-page pamphlet with the usual long-winded title and jocular publication details. In the title the Seville fandango is said to be 'acclaimed as the best music there is to assuage melancholy'. The title goes on to refer to 'Cupid's cuckoo, arrived from Brazil as an Easter gift, for whoever wants to eat it'. It is 'all explained, in the Academy of Extremes [*Extromozos*], by C.M.M.B.', and 'printed at Catalumna, at the press of Francisco Guevarz'.[90] The section on the *fofa* reads as follows:

In the first place, the Bahia *fofa* is defined as music from Brazil appropriate to weddings and merry-making. It is crazy music: the music of gaming houses, of social outcasts, of I don't know how to put it. The best way to explain: it's the music of sailors, Galicians, and serving lads, of revelry and tumult, uproar and roguery.

The Bahia *fofa* is also, among the common herd, the best music there is. As soon as the black woman hears it played, there she is in the middle of the floor, dancing without stopping. As soon as the black man hears it, there he is dancing madly, like a spinning-top, nor does he stop until he leaves the dance-floor. So hurrah for the Bahia *fofa*, which incites the black man and black woman to dance.

As soon as a Bahia mulatto woman hears it played, she is no longer herself. At once she starts to fidget, until she loses her head and dances with little steps. As soon as the dandy hears this music, at once he is jumping happily. So hurrah for the Bahia *fofa*, for bringing all this about, proving that it is the finest music for making people dance.

Whatever music best accords with the harmony of people's voices is the finest there is for making them dance. The Bahia *fofa* is the music that best accords with the harmony of people's voices, so it is the finest there is for making them dance.

So hurrah! For the Alfama *outavado* is no match for it,[91] *Macau* music does not hold a candle to it,[92] and the Coimbra *filhota* does not surpass it.[93]

The Bahia *fofa* entices your heart, makes your body shake, and tears up your toenails by stealth; so hurrah! The Bahia *fofa* makes many people get married; it is a charming sound with the merit of starting friendships, of bringing bride and bridegroom together; so hurrah for the Bahia *fofa*!

Hurrah! for by being frolicsome it will conquer the loveliest woman, fascinate the most elegant [*Eres*], bring joy to the saddest, give pleasure to the wisest, and captivate the most stupid. So hurrah for the aforesaid *fofa*, since by being in such strict time [*taõ giribandera*] it subjugates not only the kitchen maid but also the simple young girl and the circumspect woman. For I don't know what sweetness it has to cause it to be on the lips of so many people, to attract and agitate them, to incite them to take the floor and dance; but it is certain that the *fofa* alone is extraordinary, beautiful, wonderful, and perfect, to be the cause of all this; so hurrah for the Bahia *fofa*, hurrah, hurrah![94]

Opening a rare window into mid-eighteenth-century Lisbon, this remarkable passage does much more than confirm the Brazilian origin of the *fofa*. It claims that the *fofa* was not only irresistible to black people but also extremely popular among the rest of Lisbon's 'lower orders': seafarers, porters, servants, professional gamblers, prostitutes, criminals, beggars – and migrants from the Spanish province of Galicia, whom the architect James Murphy found in 1789–90 to be 'the hewers of wood and drawers of water of this metropolis',[95] providing the city with many of its porters, water-carriers and servants.[96]

This pamphlet is not the only piece of *cordel* literature surviving from mid-eighteenth-century Lisbon that pays attention to the *fofa*. An eight-page pamphlet called *Relacaõ das cantigas da fofa* ('Account of the *fofa* songs'), attributing the invention of the dance to the 'remarkable and most renowned eccentric [*estapafurdio*] Manoel de Paços', declares:

> Hurrah for the well-warbled *fofa*
> Than which there is no better tune ...
> I only want to dance the *fofa* ...
> The *fofa* is a fine dance
> It makes you tap your feet
> And makes better harmony
> Than dancing the *cumbé* ...
> This famous *fofa*
> Makes everybody smile
> It is the best there is
> And surpasses the *arrepia*.[97]

A similar pamphlet refers to *viola* traditional guitar, *pandeiro* tambourine and '*marinbas*', on which a 'respected little black' plays music for the *oitavado*, *fofa* and *Zabel-Macau*, while another plays a '*Birinbáu*' (here, jaws harp). The close association of the *fofa* with Lisbon's black community is suggested by mentions of '*o pay Flancisco*' and '*a may Flancisca*' (i.e. Father Francisco and Mother Francisca, pronounced as black people were heard, or supposed, to speak) and of little black girls whose smiles display their teeth and whose dancing delights the people.[98]

The *fofa* is briefly mentioned in a play acted in a Lisbon theatre in 1770. Here, significantly enough, it is a sailor who suggests: 'Let's sing two *fofa* tunes before you go.' A woman from Colares replies: 'Not the *fofa*, no; if you want to sing, let it be a different song.'[99]

In the Azores, the *fofa*, noted for its restless rhythms and for the coarseness [*rudeza*] of the accompanying song, was 'a very old dance' which is said to have died out by the end of the nineteenth century, its choreography forgotten through disuse.[100] However, the *fofa* is included in recordings made by Professor Artur Santos in 1960–65 on the Azores island of San Miguel, under the auspices of the Instituto Cultural de Ponto Delgada.[101]

The fado in Brazil

The similarities, both musical and choreographic, between *lundu* and fado are so close that only one conclusion is possible: as a dance popular in Brazil some

20 years before it emerged as a song in Portugal, the fado was either a specific form of the *lundu* or a development of it. Whoever doubts the close musical resemblance of the two forms should make a careful comparison between some of the Portuguese fados published by Alberto Pimentel in 1904[102] and the Brazilian '*Lundum*' published in Mário de Andrade's *Modinhas imperiais* (1930).[103] There is the same 'perpetual motion' in semiquavers, the same systematised syncopation within the bar, and the same repeated figure, a sort of 'Alberti bass', in the left hand.

A supposed mid-eighteenth-century reference to the fado as a dance in Brazil should be regarded with caution. According to a history of Brazilian music published in Italy in 1926, an English visitor, invited by the Portuguese viceroy to attend a performance in a Rio de Janeiro theatre between 1763 and 1766, was surprised to see a black of mixed ethnicity (*un prete meticcio*) conducting the orchestra, dancing the fado and singing *modinhas*.[104] This seems an implausibly early date for both *modinha* and fado: it would be another 30 years before the former and another 60 years before the latter were reliably reported in Brazil.

In 1822 the Venetian geographer and statistician Adriano Balbi (1782–1848) included the fado, along with the *chioo* (*sic*: perhaps a printer's error for *chico* or *chiba?*), *chula* and *volta no meio*, in a list of 'the most common and most noteworthy dances of Brazil'.[105] To be sure, Balbi's information about Brazilian dances seems not to have been first-hand, but there is striking confirmation of the fado's popularity as a dance in Brazil in the 1820s in a book published in 1829 by Carl Schlichthorst, a German officer serving in the Brazilian imperial army. Schlichthorst, who was in Rio de Janeiro in 1825–26, called the fado 'the blacks' favourite dance'. According to him, it

> consists in a softly rocking, quivering movement of the body and expresses man's most deeply felt sensations in a manner which is as natural as it is indecent. The postures involved in this dance are so charming that one not infrequently sees them imitated by European dancers at the San Pedro de Alcântara theatre to the noisiest applause.[106]

In a positively Gauguinesque passage, Schlichthorst then tells how he was at the Rio de Janeiro beach called Praia Vermelha one day when

> quite near to me I heard the tones of the marimba. A lovely Negro girl stood before me, plucking the African glockenspiel [*Stahlharmonica*] and offering me her *doçes* (sweets, jams). Her companion lay not far off in the shadow of the church with that peculiar ease characteristic of African women. To please the charming child I bought some of her quince jelly [*Marmelade*], drank from her jug, and then asked her to dance. She was a good girl and did not need much coaxing. She called her friend, handed her the marimba, and to its melody started the fado, a dance which in Europe would be thought indecent but here is popular with young and old, white and black.

Imagine a maiden in the bloom of her youth, her limbs most marvellously shaped, black as the night, in an elegant muslin dress drooping negligently from one shoulder, her woolly hair hidden under a red turban, eyes like stars, a mouth fresh as a newly flowering rosebud and teeth which outdo pearls in gleaming whiteness. Imagine this girl in a softly rocking, quivering motion, beating time to this wonderful dance with hands and fingers. See beside her a well-nourished woman seated on the ground, to judge by her bulk a real African beauty, holding the marimba between her fleshy fingers. Hear the notes of this instrument and the song they accompany, then cast a glance on me, lying outstretched on the bench as easy as a West Indies planter, a cigar in my mouth, breathing out long plumes of aromatic smoke, and there you have the group I would like to portray. But the song the lovely Moorish child sang as she danced would go more or less as follows:

> There is no paradise on earth!
> But were my beloved fatherland
> On Carioca beach
> I would dream I was in paradise.
>
> There is no paradise on earth!
> But if I had money in my hand
> I would buy myself a pretty ribbon
> And think I was in paradise!

I fulfilled her modest wish upon the spot and made her happy with a handful of *vinténs* – a poor copper coin in that vaunted Eldorado which has a surfeit of paper money but where nothing is rarer than gold and silver coin.[107]

With Schlichthorst's engaging pen-portrait of the dancing vender of sweetmeats may be compared the slightly later description of a similar scene by the French journalist and travel writer Jean-Charles-Marie Expilly (1814–86), who wrote of 'a crowd of black women' he saw in Rio de Janeiro dancing in a way that reminded him of the Paris cancan:

You should see them when a foreigner comes in sight! While nibbling their questionable sweetmeats, they call out in caressing tones … Some, for his benefit, start an indolent or spirited dance – an African cachucha – which resembles either the *capoeira* fighting dance or the *batuca* dance of love. Picturesque and alluring, this dance has its distinctive style, as have the minuet and polka. The abrupt splits and indiscreet movements of the lively regulars of the Château-Rouge and Mabile offer only a pale imitation of the exercise indulged in by the black women opposite the Carioca's double row of arcades …

These half-naked black women, bare-bosomed, turban over one ear, vying with each other in suppleness and daring, provide a strange spectacle before which you pause in spite of yourself.

> Fortunately for them, the Rio police are not so easily offended as those of Paris ... In the capital of the South American Empire, you do not spend a night in the cells for so little.[108]

By the 1820s, as Schlichthorst tells us, white Brazilians as well as black were dancing the fado, and J. Friedrich von Weech, travelling through Brazil at much the same time as his compatriot Schlichthorst was in the country, described the fado, in terms that would exactly fit the *lundu*, as 'a dance imitated from the Africans' and as one of Brazil's 'national dances', which were

> performed by individual couples only; in place of castanets they snap the fingers of both hands with such skill that at a distance you would think you were hearing castanets. The fado, a dance imitated from the Africans, is performed by several together, the dancers singing the while. It consists in the dancers twisting their bodies and bringing them close together in a way which would be found highly indecent in Europe.[109]

Both of these German witnesses describe the Brazilian fado as sung as well as danced. A vivid pen-picture of how it was danced – and sung – in the 1820s, by native-born Brazilians of European descent, was drawn by Manuel Antônio de Almeida (1831–61) in his novel of manners, *Memórias de um Sargento de Milícias* ('Memoirs of a Militia Sergeant'). This began publication in 1852, a couple of years before gas lamps were first used in Rio de Janeiro. Almeida throws a brilliant light on the city's customs a generation earlier. We are at a christening party, guests of the godmother, and the fado has just begun.

> Everybody knows what the fado is, that dance so sensual, so frivolous, that it seems to be the offspring of the most careful study of the art. A simple guitar [*viola*] serves better than any other instrument for the purpose.
> The fado has different forms, each one more singular. In one, a man or a woman dances alone in the middle of the floor for some time, performing the hardest steps, striking the most graceful attitudes, at the same time snapping their fingers, and then gradually getting closer and closer to someone they've taken a liking to. They gesture alluringly and pirouette before the chosen person and at last clap their hands, which means that the chosen one is to take their place.
> So it goes around the circle until everyone has danced.
> At other times a man and woman dance together. Following the beat of the music with the greatest precision, they follow each other now with slow steps, now with quick. Now they spurn each other, now they approach each other. Sometimes the man woos the woman with nimble steps, while she, with a slight gesture of body and arms, draws back languidly. Once more it is she who solicits the man, who draws back in his turn, until at last they are dancing together again.
> There is also the circle in which many people dance, underlining some beats with handclaps and heel-taps that are sometimes loud and long-drawn-out, sometimes softer and briefer, though always uniform and in perfect time.

Besides these there are still more styles, of which we shall not speak. In each the music is different, though always played on the guitar. Often the player sings, in certain rhythms, a song of genuinely poetical imagination.

Once the fado begins, it is hard to end it. It always finishes towards dawn – if it is not strung out for whole days and nights on end.[110]

Three aspects of this passage deserve emphasis: the distinction that Almeida draws among three different styles of dancing the fado; the similarities between the dances that he describes and contemporary and near-contemporary descriptions of the *lundu*; and his use of 'fado' (rather as the word 'fandango' is often used in present-day Brazil) to describe, not just a single dance but a whole suite of dances. (The use of the word 'fado' by José Vieira Fazenda in 1896, to describe the song and dance of sedan-chair carriers in Rio 60 years before, shows it being used as a generic term for any kind of black dance.)[111]

In Lisbon too, in the early nineteenth century, the fado first appeared as 'fado dances' (*bailes do fado*). The sung fado developed a generation later. This was in a sense the culmination of the long process of cultural exchange between Portugal and its South American colony.[112] That process, as seen from the Lisbon end, was summed up as early as 1752 in an anonymous publication called *Anatómico Jocoso*, which has been described as 'a priceless repository of information on social life in Lisbon in the first decades of the eighteenth century'[113] and is often attributed to Fr Lucas de Santa Catarina. Referring to the key part played by the Alfama riverside quarter of Lisbon in the importation from Brazil of 'sounds' – i.e. of music and dance – the poet wrote, in a chapter called 'Survey of the Dances':

> From Brazil in procession
> The sounds arrive there barefoot,
> Breed there, grow up there,
> And from there they pass
> By degrees to the *chulas* [lower-class women],
> Step by step to the *mulatos*.[114]

It is significant that the earliest form of sung fado heard in Lisbon, and apparently the only kind sung there before about 1840, was known as the 'sailors' fado' (*fado do marinheiro*), which was popular among Portuguese seafarers and is said to have served as the model for the first fados played and sung in the Portuguese capital.[115]

In the late 1850s the word 'fado' was still in use in Brazil as an alternative name for the *lundu*. In 1859 the Brazilian botanist François Freire Alemão refers to the *baiana* as 'entirely similar to our fado' (and perfectly illustrates the confusion in Brazilian musical nomenclature when he remarks that 'still we could not see here [in the Ceará town of Pacatuba] a fado, which they call samba, in which different dances are danced').[116] In the same period the German physician and 'scientific explorer' Dr Robert Avé-Lallemant (1812–84) writes of the 'fado or lundum' he sees at an auction in the Bahia town of Cachoeira:

> As is usual throughout Brazil, on the evening both before and after a church festival, an auction was being held for the benefit of the church. In order to draw in (and at the same time draw money out of) a goodly crowd, the auctioneer was playing the clown. Doves, cakes and gewgaws were sold off at very high prices to the noisy populace, who accompanied each bad joke by the already hoarse and barking auctioneer with ringing laughter. Between each lot a loud band played passages of the fado or lundum, that irregular Negro *tarantella* in which each person makes as many twists and obscene movements as at all possible. The wilder the high spirits, the more stormy the applause.
>
> Suddenly all around turned silent and fell to their knees. The sacrament was being brought back from the bed of a dying man. Hardly had it been carried back into the church however than the people returned with a vengeance to their auction and their fado. Quantities of rockets sped up into the sky and until late in the night the Negro bacchanal in celebration of the Catholic Church festival raved on.[117]

The sung fado migrated from Portugal to that country's then colony of Mozambique and was said in the early 1970s to be 'enjoying tremendous popularity in Southern Africa, particularly in Johannesburg'.[118]

8

The Emergence of Brazilian
Popular Music

Brazil's slave orchestras

Almost as soon as there was an African presence in Brazil, the richer Portuguese colonists – and some of them were very rich indeed – started looking for musical talent among their slaves. As early as 1610, the French adventurer François Pyrard, guest of a Bahia sugar tycoon identified as João Furtado de Mendonça (who had been governor of Angola in 1594–1602), found that his host maintained a private orchestra and choir of black slaves, 20- to 30-strong, supervised by a French musician and 'making music day and night'.[1] For successful and prosperous colonists it was soon a matter of prestige to have a slave orchestra – and often a slave choir in the chapel, too. Such possessions entertained not only the plantation-owner but also his or her family. They could be put on show to entertain, and impress, their guests and visitors, including visitors from overseas. And they could be sent to take part in festivals and processions in nearby towns, at first as a personal contribution showing how grand the owner was and what good taste he or she had, in the nineteenth century as a source of extra revenue, too.

Foreign visitors with the slightest knowledge of music were always impressed, and often surprised, by the skill and versatility of the black musicians they heard. In 1748 the French priest René Courte de la Blanchardière (1712–94), putting in at Rio de Janeiro on his way to Peru, noted that

> Violins are heard in most of the houses: every master is careful to have his Negroes taught to play that instrument. There are many guitars; several trumpets are to be heard, too, which produce rather pleasant harmony. I sampled this pleasure one evening in particular, when the General came back by water from a country house at the far end of the bay and sailed alongside us with two blacks in the prow of his boat who played on that instrument with reasonable taste.[2]

A German who had lived in Brazil wrote in 1833: 'The Negroes appear to possess a high degree of aptitude for music. With a little training they quickly achieve some virtuosity on any instrument, as I can testify from more than once seeing completely raw Negroes being trained into corps bands.'[3] The American clergymen Kidder and Fletcher, when they visited a Minas Gerais plantation called Soldade in the 1840s, were told 'very humbly' by the owner that he had 'his own music now'. Expecting the worst, the visitors were astounded by what they heard:

> We desired to hear his musicians, supposing that we should hear a wheezy plantation-fiddle, a fife, and a drum ... An hour after vespers, I heard the twanging of violins, the tuning of flutes, short voluntaries on sundry bugles, the clattering of trombones, and all those musical symptoms preparatory to a beginning of some march, waltz, or polka. I went to the room whence proceeded these sounds; there I beheld fifteen slave musicians – a regular band: one presided at an organ, and there was a choir of younger negroes arranged before suitable stands, upon which were sheets of printed or manuscript music. I also observed a respectable colored gentleman (who sat near me at dinner) giving various directions. He was the *maestro*. Three raps of his violin-bow commanded silence, and then a wave of the same, *à la Julien* [i.e. in the manner of a celebrated French conductor of the time], and the orchestra commenced the execution of an overture to some opera with admirable skill and precision. I was totally unprepared for this. But the next piece overwhelmed me with surprise: the choir, accompanied by the instruments, performed a Latin mass. They sang from their notes, and little darkies from twelve to sixteen years of age read off the words with as much fluency as students in the Freshman year. I could scarcely believe my eyes and ears, and in order to try the accomplishments of the company I asked the maestro for the *Stabat Mater*: he instantly replied, '*Sim, Senhor*', named to the musicians the page, waved his *bâton*, and then the wailing and touching strains of *Stabat Mater* sounded through the corridors of Soldade. While at supper we were regaled by waltzes and stirring marches – among the latter 'Lafayette's Grand March', composed in the United States.[4]

In 1865–66 the rich Bahia landowner Raimunda Porcina de Jesus (known as 'Chapadista') was reported to have a well-organised slave orchestra with a competent conductor, himself a former slave, good instruments and a broad and varied repertory. She received payment for her orchestra's participation in the Bomfin festivals, and signed receipts.[5] Felisberto Caldeira Brant, wealthy owner of the Barro Duro gold mines in Minas Gerais, built a chapel beside his house and installed in it an orchestra to play on feast days: 'The performers were all captive blacks belonging to Brant, and they played satisfactorily "by ear".'[6] Another rich landowner, Mariana Barbosa, countess of Rio Novo, kept on her father-in-law's plantation in the Paraíba valley in Rio de Janeiro state an orchestra of 80 musicians and a choir of 70 'little blacks with melodious voices', who played and sang at family celebrations and in masses at the church of Our Lady of Glory.[7] On one Pernambuco plantation, Monjope, there was not only a band of black musicians but also an entire circus, complete with ponies, black clowns and black acrobats.[8]

Competent black musicians were greatly sought after by plantation owners. The author Valentim Magalhães (1859–1903), in his 1886 tale *Praça do Escravos*, describes a scene at a slave auction:

> 'And he says he's a musician too,' prompted Manduca Lopes, sitting astride an empty barrel.
> 'What the devil do you play?'
> 'I play clarinet [*requinta*], sir.'
> 'Then go and fetch one. I want to see this. If the lad's got the hang of the thing, I'll take him. I need him for a band I have over at the farm.'[9]

'In real life such scenes must have taken place often', comments Tinhorão. 'In fact the black lads [*moleques*] usually showed such skill that frequently the enraptured purchasers ended up paying dearly for their enthusiasm for the art of music.'[10] João Teodoro, a colonist in western São Paulo state, went so far as to exchange an entire farm for a slave violinist who specialised in '*modas de cateretê*' (i.e. tunes accompanying a dance which may have been of Amerindian origin).[11]

That black musicians were greatly in demand is shown also by the large number of early-nineteenth-century advertisements in Brazilian newspapers offering slave musicians for sale. One, already quoted in Chapter 5, advertised in 1820 a slave who could play the piano and marimba[12] (this probably means lamellophone rather than resonator xylophone). Another, in 1847, is described as 'a good black barber, blood-letter, tailor, who plays several instruments, all of which he does with notable perfection'.[13] As in North America, many of the advertisements asking for the apprehension and return of fugitive slaves made special mention of these runaways' musical skills. Advertisements of this kind in Pará newspapers included such identifications as 'plays violin, can read' and 'plays fiddle with left arm, is given to drink and a great lover of *reviras*' (probably another word for *batuques*).[14]

The acculturation process works both ways, at any rate in music. The nationwide flourishing of slave orchestras, besides training many black musicians to play 'erudite' music, also did much to validate and make widely acceptable the slaves' own approach to music-making. Black orchestras played 'classical' music with impressive skill. And when they were called on to play European dances, they tended to 'creolise' the rhythm, introducing a degree of syncopation, a 'beat' and 'swing' that Portuguese dancers, some at least of whom had already got used to such infectious rhythms in Portugal itself, found greatly to their taste. So far as popular music was concerned, this was the musical culture that their children were born into and took for granted.

How Brazilian popular music arose

We have seen that the African musical heritage in Brazil played a decisive part in the creation of a musical culture that is neither African nor Portuguese but distinctively Brazilian; and that the first and decisive step in the emergence of Brazilian popular music was the widespread and enthusiastic adoption, first by poor whites but before long by the urban middle class as well, of the *lundu* dance, which originated in the Kongo-Angola culture area, and the emergence of the sung *lundu*. This whole process is more easily understood if three things are borne in mind.

First, as was seen in the Introduction and again in the previous chapter, the black contribution to the emergence of Brazilian popular music continued and deepened a process of acculturation in the Iberian peninsula which had begun in the eighth century with the arrival of Arab conquerors in Spain and Portugal, and of African slaves in Spain, and had been reinforced from 1441 onwards by the arrival of African slaves in Portugal.

Second, the old 'one-way street' model of musical influence, leading simply from Africa to Brazil, must be discarded as inadequate. From the seventeenth century the Atlantic acted as facilitator or catalyst of a much richer and more complex musical exchange than that model suggests. By the middle of the eighteenth century Lisbon, far and away the leading Portuguese port in the Atlantic trades, was almost at the peak of its affluence and cosmopolitanism. Its pivotal role in European and world trade had been expanding steadily for at least 50 years; and the 'jewel in its crown ... was its colonial extra-European commerce, to some extent with Africa and Asia, but overwhelmingly with Brazil'.[15] This booming trade augmented Lisbon's black community with a constant stream of fresh arrivals, free blacks as well as slaves, from Brazil as well as Africa. That thriving port of Lisbon, with its large black community; the ports of Luanda and Benguela in Angola and later the port of Lagos in Nigeria (see Appendix C); the Brazilian ports of Salvador, Recife and Rio de Janeiro: these were musical melting pots, as were those other New World ports, New Orleans and Saint-Pierre in Martinique (the latter until it was destroyed by the eruption of Mont Pelée in 1902). The Portuguese, African, and Brazilian ports in fact made up a connected system of musical melting pots – a kind of super melting pot, in which new dances and new musical styles were transmitted around the cultural triangle within a matter of weeks. As Kubik writes,

> In Brazilian history the extent of cultural exchange with Black Africa is indeed remarkable. It was a continuous process of *exchange* and not a one-way cultural impact linked to a one-way dislocation of peoples known as the slave trade ... [I]n the periods of intensive contact with Africa it did not usually take a long time until a new dance, a new popular song or a new musical fashion coming up in Luanda or Lagos was known among the black population of Rio de Janeiro, Salvador or Recife.[16]

To this it should be added that a new dance or a new musical style developing in one of those Brazilian ports – or in one of those African ports – would soon be known among the black population of Lisbon, too. There was no radio then, and there were no gramophone records; but there were ships. On average, in fair weather, the voyage from Luanda to Recife took only about 35 days; to Salvador, 40 days; to Rio, two months or less.[17] Before Brazil gained independence in 1822 ships sailing between Angola and Portugal usually went via Brazil. The English smuggler Thomas Lindley tells us that in the early nineteenth century it was the custom for Portuguese merchant ships putting in at the Bahia port of Pôrto Seguro 'to have music on their arrival, at departure, and the first day of taking in cargo; which repeatedly gives us a little concert, and sounds charmingly from the water'.[18] We can assume that this custom was observed at other ports, too. And it was above all black seafarers, making music (giving 'little concerts') in African, Brazilian and Portuguese ports in turn, and often putting in at that Lusophone 'Crossroads of the Atlantic',[19] the Cape Verde archipelago, where the ships of all nations were serviced (see Appendix D) – it was black seafarers who did more than anyone else to spread music and dance around the triangle.[20] The *lundu* and the *fofa* are the two outstanding examples. We can be sure that any seafarer with musical skills would, on reaching port, seek out and participate in what today would be called jam sessions, in which tunes and dances, rhythms and riffs would be swapped, taught, learnt and passed on.

It would be a mistake to think that any one point of the triangle was either dominant or static. Musical taste and practice in Angola as well as in Brazil and Portugal were increasingly influenced by the Atlantic cultural triangle; indeed Portuguese musical influence can be traced in Angola from the seventeenth century and possibly even earlier (see Appendix A).[21]

The third thing that should be borne in mind in considering the emergence of Brazilian popular music is the dramatic effect on the Brazilian economy of the discovery, first of diamonds in the interior of Bahia in the first half of the seventeenth century, then of gold in Minas Gerais in 1693–95. Relatively suddenly, there was a great deal more money about, and an internal migration from the coastal regions to the central plateau ensured that it was more widely distributed. The discovery of diamonds gave Salvador major importance as a centre of trade and services; the discovery of gold did much the same for Rio de Janeiro, the natural outlet for the riches of Minas Gerais. Within a generation, an urban middle class had emerged with enough disposable income to buy its entertainment and its musical instruments. Brazilian popular music arose in the eighteenth century, first of all in Salvador and Rio de Janeiro, primarily to satisfy the cultural demands of that urban middle class. And it was black music and black dance that the Brazilian middle-class public, especially its younger members, enjoyed above all. Young ladies of respectable families learnt to play Rossini, Mozart and Beethoven on the piano,[22] but, as was seen in the previous chapter, they also enjoyed leaning over their balconies to watch black people dancing in the streets and squares below; and an ever-increasing number themselves danced the *lundu* or similar dances. Black musicians and musicians of mixed ethnicity dominated Brazil's upper- and middle-class music-making, from military bands to ballroom orchestras, and made an important contribution to concert and church music too. Brazil's colonial administrators drew extensively on black musical talent, as when Dr Diogo de Toledo Lara Ordonhes, a judge of the high court, celebrated his birthday in 1790. The festivities went on for two solid months, 'not ... in the ballrooms or society lounges of Rio de Janeiro or Salvador but in distant Cuiabá in the captaincy of Mato Grosso', and included a dance of black people (*dança dos pardos*) and mimes showing the activities of hunters of fugitive slaves (*capitaes-do-mato*).[23]

By the end of the eighteenth century, black musicians in Brazil were both highly esteemed and widely regarded as the providers of a new type of urban service: music for entertainment. Some slaves, known as *negros de ganha*, were sent out by their owners to sell fruit, vegetables, firewood, or cloth in the city streets or were hired out to others for that purpose. Traditionally, after selling their daily quota of merchandise, they would earn a little money for themselves by singing, dancing and telling stories in the streets. Maria Graham tells of a slave she befriended, who 'earns a small gratuity for himself by his tales, his dances, and his songs'.[24] Often these street performers would accompany themselves on the musical bow or lamellophone they had been using for, as it were, drumming up trade. By the start of the nineteenth century every restaurant had a fiddle player at the door, and that musician was usually a black slave, and sometimes a blind one.[25]

In Rio de Janeiro, Maria Graham reported in the early 1820s, '[t]he orchestra of the opera house is composed of at least one-third of mulattoes'.[26] The British 'sketcher' Robert Elwes made a similar comment a quarter of a century later. There was a good orchestra at the theatre, 'many of the performers being blacks or mulattos, who are excellent musicians'. Elwes added: 'The African race seem to like music, and generally have a pretty good ear. Both men and women often whistle well, and I have heard the washerwomen at their work whistling polkas with great correctness.'[27] The Austrian globe-trotter Ida Pfeiffer, who visited Rio de Janeiro in 1846, thought that the military bands she heard were 'certainly the best, and these are generally composed of negroes and mulattoes'.[28] About ten years later the French traveller F. Dabadie noted that the musicians taking part in the procession of St George were 'all Negroes, equipped with flutes, French horns, trumpets, and drums and repeating unceasingly the same march'.[29] For the British vice-consul in Salvador, writing in 1851, the pseudo-science of phrenology offered the best explanation for the African musical talent which so greatly impressed him:

It is said by phrenologists that the head of the negro above all others presents the greatest development of the organ of music, and certainly some of the blacks do play remarkably well. You hear little boys in the streets, who with great truth you might fancy could scarcely speak, whistling tunes with great correctness, and the negro dances show how admirably the science of 'time' is appreciated.[30]

Barbers' customers expected to be entertained with music, and the barbers, who also worked as surgeons, dentists, blood-letters and musicians, were often black slaves or freedmen.[31] Documents in the archive of the Salvador church of Our Lady of Vitória give the names of conductors of bands of barber-musicians that played at church events in the eighteenth century; for instance, Damásio Nunes was paid a small sum in 1774 for fiddles and kettledrums (*atabales*) played at the church door. Others played trumpets and oboes.[32] In 1805 the Englishman Thomas Lindley wrote of black musicians in the Bahian coastal town of Pôrto Seguro, who sat 'playing lively pieces' at church entrances, 'regardless of the solemnities going on within'. Numerous as they were, these musicians found 'constant employment'. They were 'trained by the different barber-surgeons of the city, who are of the same colour, and have been itinerant musicians from time immemorial; they always command a full band ready for service'.[33] So common were barber-musicians in Brazil's eighteenth- and early-nineteenth-century popular bands of percussion, stringed and wind instruments that such bands, whose services could be hired for both religious and secular functions, were known as *barbeiros*.[34] The Revd Robert Walsh wrote of Brazil's barbers in 1830:

> They are ... the musicians of the country, and are hired also to play at church doors during festivals. All the persons who compose the bands on these occasions are barbers. Over the middle of every shop is an arch, on which are suspended the different articles for sale. In a barber's shop, the arch is always hung round with musical instruments.[35]

In Salvador in the 1840s the barbers' bands, typically including 'raucous [*rouquenhas*] flutes' and a 'thundering bass drum', would play at church doors during festivals and novenas; their repertory included *lundus* and popular songs.[36] The American clergyman Daniel Kidder reported in 1845 that begging processions on Whit Sunday were preceded by 'the music of a band of tatter-demalion negroes, who, with the sound of their instruments, serve the church by day, and the theatre by night'.[37] He did not specify that this was a barbers' band, though, and possibly it was not, for such bands were often smartly turned out. One, consisting entirely of black slaves, and playing in the Glória festival in Rio, was described as wearing (*c*. 1860) elegant uniforms of white drill (*brim*), black trousers and high white hats – though they did walk barefoot.[38]

Unlike the slave orchestras on the plantations, which for the most part played concert music, these barbers' bands played in a popular style, with a repertory that included *lundus* and *chulas* (a popular dance of Portuguese origin), marching music (*dobrados*), quadrilles and fandangos,[39] as well as waltzes and French *contredanses* 'arranged, to be sure, in their own way'.[40] In other words, these European dances were Brazilianised. The barbers' bands were the immediate forerunners of the *choro* groups that first emerged in the 1870s and greatly flourished after emancipation in 1888, when they were joined – as were military bands and groups of itinerant musicians – by large numbers of freed musician slaves. Mário de Andrade called the music of these groups, as played and recorded in the 1920s and 1930s, 'the Brazilian equivalent of hot jazz'.[41]

Brazilian popular music was slower to take shape in Minas Gerais than in Salvador and Rio, largely because the church in that inland region, in the absence of other rich patrons, creamed off the best black musical talent. The musical activities of Africans in Minas Gerais were attracting attention as early as 1717. A document in the state archives bearing that date tells us that the slaves 'sang melancholy songs in the Bantu dialect' (*sic*) and 'invoked the protection of the *orixás* by means of dances like the *caxambu* [see pp. 105–6], accompanied by rattles [*chocalho*] and foot-stamping'. But in Minas the orchestras maintained by the various brotherhoods absorbed a high proportion of the most talented black musicians, who were kept busy as singers, instrumentalists and composers of church music.[42] The diligent German musicologist Francisco Curt Lange (1903–97), 'one of the superlative figures of twentieth-century Latin-American musicology',[43] rescued from obscurity the astonishing achievements of the 'school' of musicians of mixed ethnicity – singers, instrumentalists, conductors and composers – that flourished in the province of Minas Gerais in the second half of the eighteenth century and beyond. Lange 'revealed the musical scores and names of composers completely unknown to historians'.[44]

Among the many eighteenth-century 'mulatto' composers and conductors in Minas Gerais four were outstanding: the tenor Inácio Parreiras Neves (*c.* 1730–*c.* 1791); the trumpeter Marcos Coelho Neto (1746–1806), who played in the chapels of several brotherhoods; the cantor Francisco Gomes da Rocha (*c.* 1754–1808), of whose approximately 200 compositions no more than five have survived; and the central figure of this group, the organist José Joaquim Emérico Lobo de Mesquita (*c.* 1746–1805), a 'dark mulatto'[45] who was the son of a Portuguese by his slave Joaquina Emerenciana, and whose works Lange regarded as not inferior to those of the leading European composers of the period. A recent compact disc of Brazilian music from the colonial period, performed by Vox Brasiliensis under the direction of Ricardo Kanji, includes three works by Neves (one of them his *Salve Regina* for four voices, two trumpets, strings and figured bass, transcribed by Adhemar Campos Filho in 1997); Gomes da Rocha's *Novena de Nossa Senhora do Pilar* (1789), also for four voices, two trumpets, strings and figured bass, transcribed by Lange in 1951; and a work attributed to Lobo de Mesquita, *Ego enim accepi a Domino*, for soprano, two violas and violoncello, transcribed by André Cardoso in 1995.[46]

But the black composers of Minas Gerais were not the only Brazilian 'school' of black composers which flourished in the eighteenth century. There were others in the coastal cities of Salvador, Recife, and Rio de Janeiro: composers like the black priest, organist, and pianist José Mauricio Nunes Garcia (1767–1830), who was only 16 when he composed *Tota pulcra es Maria Consertada*, and whose *modinha* 'Beijo a Mão que me Condena', has recently been issued on a compact disc.[47] 'Not always remembered', Robert Stevenson points out, 'is the fact that some of these coastal mulattos won applause loud enough during their own epochs to be heard at faraway Évora in mainland Portugal.'[48]

The modinha *and the sung* lundu

Visiting Lisbon in 1774, Major William Dalrymple of the British army heard 'a young Brazilian' playing 'a kind of Brazil music' on the guitar, 'accompanying it with his voice'. The major commented that this Brazilian music, 'though solemn, is soothing and agreeable'.[49] Although we cannot be certain of the identity of the 'young Brazilian', a likely candidate is Domingos Caldas Barbosa (*c.* 1740–1800), one of the founders of the Lisbon Academy of Belles Lettres, or Nova Arcádia, in which he used the literary name Lereno Selenuntino: hence the title of his collected poems, the two-volume *Viola de Lereno* (1798–1826). Born in Rio de Janeiro, this son of a Portuguese father and an Angolan mother was not only a poet but also a composer, singer and player of the *viola* traditional guitar; and it was he who brought the *modinha* and the sung *lundu* to Lisbon in the mid-1770s, where he sang them to his own accompaniment at court soirées. His songs had a lulling, rocking, relaxed, melancholy style, and they enchanted and often surprised his listeners. Audiences must have been intrigued not only by his music but also by the exotic Brazilianisms that suffused his vocabulary: words of African origin like *angu* (firm dough of corn meal, manioc meal, or rice meal boiled in salt water; cf. Yor. *angu*, with the same meaning), *moleque* (young black boy: cf. Kimbundu *muleke*, 'urchin' and Kikongo *muleke*, 'child'), *quindim* (delicacy made from egg yolk, coconut and sugar: cf. Kimbundu *udinkinda*, 'coy, affected'), and *quingombó* (okra pod or plant; cf. Kimbundu *kingombo*, 'okra'),[50] as well as such creolised words as *nhanhá* and *nhanhazinha* (a respectful or affectionate form of address by a slave to a young unmarried woman).

The earliest literary reference to what he called 'the Brazilian *modinha*' was made in 1779 by the Portuguese satirical poet Nicoláo Tolentino de Almeida (1740–1811),[51] who probably had Barbosa's music in mind. Barbosa himself preferred to call his songs *cantigas*; in the whole of his *Viola de Lereno* the word *modinha* occurs only twice, and in the same verse.[52] In a farce written in 1786, *A rabugem das velhas* ('The bad-tempered old women'), Tolentino has a character refer to 'this new *modinha* that's been invented now', whereupon her grandmother flies into a rage and starts to extol the past.[53]

The Brazilian *modinha*, as sung in Lisbon in 1787, found a distinguished English admirer. In that year the wealthy William Beckford (1759–1844), author of *Vathek* (1786), heard 'a little square friar with green eyes' singing Brazilian *modinhas*, which he called 'an original sort of music different from any I ever heard, the most seducing, the most voluptuous imaginable, the best calculated to throw saints off their guard and to inspire profane deliriums'. Four months later, having heard 'two young fellows' singing 'an enchanting *modinha*' in a Lisbon theatre, Beckford wrote in his journal:

> Those who have never heard *modinhas* must and will remain ignorant of the most voluptuous and bewitching music that ever existed since the days of the Sybarites. They consist of languid interrupted measures, as if the breath was gone with excess of rapture, and the soul panting to fly out of you and incorporate itself with the beloved object. With a childish carelesness they steal into the heart before it has time to arm itself against their enervating influence. You fancy you are swallowing milk and you are swallowing poison. As to myself, I confess I am a slave to *modinhas*, and when I think of them cannot endure the idea of quitting Portugal. Could I indulge the least hopes of surviving a two months' voyage, nothing should prevent my setting off for Brazil, the native land of *modinhas*.[54]

However, the beautiful playwright Lady Elizabeth Craven (1750–1828), later Margravine of Brandenburg-Anspach and Bayreuth, greatly disliked the *modinha* – if in fact that is what she heard in Portugal in the summer of 1791 and described as 'horrid negro airs', adding, 'miawling of cats – door-hinges, or anything horrible, is preferable to such a diabolical noise'.[55]

This was not a generally held view. The Venetian statistician Balbi wrote in 1822 that *modinhas*, 'and particularly those called *Brazilian*, are filled with melody and feeling, and when they are well sung they pierce the very soul of whoever understands the meaning'.[56] Another English visitor to Portugal, hearing 'the Brasilian modinhas' in the 1820s, shared Beckford's high opinion of them. To the Revd William Morgan Kinsey (1788–1851) they were 'singularly beautiful and simple, generally expressive of some amatory, tender, or melancholy sentiment, the effect of which, when well accompanied by the voice and guitar, is often known to elicit the tears of the audience'.[57] In Brazil itself the French artist Debret extolled 'the expressive and melodious sounds' of the flautist in one his pictures, and the merits of 'a chromatic accompaniment improvised on [the] guitar, whose passionate or unaffected style colours [the] ingenious *modinha*'.[58]

The *modinha* was not a kind of traditional song. It was composed for, and first heard in, the salon. Renato Almeida, in his *História da Música Brasileira*, distinguishes erudite, semi-erudite and popular styles of *modinha*,[59] but the distinctions between these are not altogether clear. A more helpful distinction, perhaps, is that between the Portuguese and the Brazilian *modinhas*, as drawn by the Austrian botanist Martius in 1817: '*Modinhas* are of Portuguese or Brazilian origin. The Brazilian ones are distinguished from the Portuguese by the simplicity of words and music.'[60]

The *modinha* 'owed its origin and its character to the intensive reciprocal exchange between continent and colonies'.[61] It took as its model the melodic ornamentation of eighteenth-century Italian and Italianate arias; in the early *modinhas* in particular there can be traced the influence of Giovanni Paesiello (1740–1816) and Christoph Willibald von Gluck (1714–87), as well as of Haydn and Mozart.[62] In the *modinha* the European aria joined hands with African-Brazilian music.[63] The *modinha* in fact straddled the border between 'erudite' and popular music, and it 'can be studied on one or other side of [this] dividing line'.[64] Like the *lundu* – by whose sung version it was greatly influenced, and with which it overlapped to an increasing extent – it attracted the attention of Haydn's favourite pupil, the Austrian composer, pianist and scholar Sigismund von Neukomm (1778–1858),[65] who harmonised 20 *modinhas* composed by the self-taught Joaquim Manoel (*c*. 1780–*c*. 1840), a Brazilian of mixed ethnicity.

Two characteristic features of the *modinha* which show the early, though attenuated, influence of African musical norms in the Brazilian salon are its systematic use of syncopation in the vocal line, and its tendency to change from major to minor mode while remaining in the same key.[66] In addition, the seventh note of the scale (the leading note) is often flattened, and it is a reasonable assumption that this indicates the same influence. Of these three indicators of the specifically Brazilian character of the *modinha*, the systematisation of syncopation is the most important, as Gerard Béhague makes clear in his study of two manuscript collections of *modinhas* held by the Biblioteca da Ajuda in Lisbon. One of these manuscripts contains the words and music of 30 *modinhas*, most if not all of which, though they are anonymous, Béhague attributes to Domingos Caldas Barbosa. The texts of two can be positively identified as Barbosa's, since one was published posthumously, in a fuller form, in the second volume of his *Viola de Lereno*, while the other figures in a manuscript of his songs held by a Rio de Janeiro library. But in most of the rest 'one finds elements strongly suggestive of Caldas Barbosa's style'. Most of them have systematically syncopated vocal lines 'that can be associated with the "vulgar" style of Brazilian modinhas'. The eighth *modinha* in this manuscript, 'Quem ama para agravar', has the note: 'This accompaniment must be played around Bahia'. Béhague comments:

> It would ... be presumptuous to consider that this particular modinha represents a definitely Brazilian or typically Bahian-style modinha. The statement ... is a probability, not a certainty. Possibly the scribe commented on this accompaniment because he was struck with the systematic syncopation of the first four measures, serving as instrumental introduction.

This is a reference to a bouncy syncopated figure, ubiquitous in ragtime, where the second and third semiquavers of the first crotchet in the bar are tied, so that the first, second and fourth semiquavers are sounded. Béhague goes on to point out that the vocal line of another *modinha* in the collection systematises 'a rhythmic procedure much closer to the Brazilian musical vernacular'. This consists in 'a simple suspension (by ties over the barline) used at cadential points provoking feminine endings of the phrase'. In other words, phrases end on a weak stress rather than a strong one. Precisely this formula, Béhague adds, would later become 'the classical cliché of most early composed sambas'. That intriguing note saying 'This accompaniment must be played around Bahia' points to the 'early association of syncopations ... with the Afro-Brazilian tradition'. In short, systematisation of syncopation is 'the distinctive feature' of these early *modinhas*, which display 'the vital rhythmic drive which characterizes most of Brazil's urban popular music'.[67]

So popular was the *modinha* in Lisbon that a periodical devoted to it was published regularly there between 1792 and 1795. The *Jornal de Modinhas*, offering songs 'by the best composers' with harpsichord accompaniment, was edited by two Frenchmen, Francisco Domingos Milcent and Pedro Anselmo Marchal. Besides *modinhas*, it also, as we shall see, found room for the '*Moda do Lundu*' as well as for several '*Modas Brazileiras*' and a '*Modinha do Zabumba*' (i.e. bass drum).[68]

The *lundu*, the other foundation stone on which was erected the whole edifice of Brazilian popular music, shared with the *modinha* its systematic syncopation, its switches between major and minor, and its frequently flattened leading note. As has been said, the two forms overlapped – and were in fact so closely linked that by the end of the eighteenth century there was a certain convergence, *modinhas* being composed that sounded much like sung *lundus* and vice versa. In both of these musical forms there came about the meeting of two classes at opposite ends of the social scale. There was a reciprocal cultural exchange between rich and poor, by means of which the *modinha* was democratised and the *lundu* became the accepted song and dance of white Brazilians.[69]

The music which accompanied the *lundu* was, in the words of Oneyda Alvarenga, 'the first kind of black music accepted by Brazilian society, and through it black people gave our music some important characteristics, such as the systematisation of syncopation and the use of the flattened seventh'.[70] Before long there emerged a sung version of the music accompanying the dance; this was the first music with obviously African roots 'to be accepted by the whole of Brazilian society – black and white alike'.[71] In short, '*modinhas* were taken out of their courtly environment and democratised, while the *lundu* wormed its way into our upper-class ballrooms, divesting itself of its character of popular and sensual [*lasciva*] dance and turning into a white people's song'.[72]

The acceptance by educated musicians in both Portugal and Brazil of the Luso-Brazilian variant of the dance tradition that Chasteen describes, and of the music to which it was danced, is shown by three landmarks, two in Portugal, one in Brazil.

The first Portuguese landmark dates from 1779 or 1780, when the 'genial satirist' Nicoláo Tolentino de Almeida, who 'sheds a gentle light on the manners of the time',[73] referred in a poem to 'the sweet plaintive *londum*'.[74] The second came in 1792, when there appeared in the *Jornal de Modinhas* some *lundus* harmonised in a 'classical' manner, with harpsichord accompaniment. Two alleged *'Moda[s] do Londu'* (i.e. *lundu* songs) are without syncopation, which suggests that they are rather distant imitations of their model. More interesting, there is a *'xula carioca'* called 'Onde vas, linda Negrinha?' ('Where are you going, pretty black girl?'). *Carioca* means belonging to or coming from Rio de Janeiro, and *xula* (more commonly spelt *chula*) was a popular dance of Portuguese origin, but may mean in this context a *lundu* sung by black people.[75] Here there is syncopation, though it is confined to the melody and does not extend across bar-lines.[76]

Then, in 1819, came the Brazilian landmark: for the first time in musical history, a composer of concert music made use of the *lundu*. He was Haydn's pupil, Sigismund von Neukomm, who lived in Rio de Janeiro from 1816 to 1821 and while there wrote *O Amôr Brazileiro – Caprice pour le Pianoforte sur un Londû brésilien* (op. 38).[77] The *lundu* had arrived, in the sense that it was the first African-derived song form to enter the European concert tradition.

In a musical supplement to the three-volume account by the Austrian biologists Spix and Martius of their travels around Brazil in the years 1817–20, Martius included the melody of a *'Landum'*, which he called a 'Brazilian folk dance'.[78] A brilliant reconstruction of how this *lundu* might have sounded has been recorded by Ricardo Kanji and the Vox Brasiliensis orchestra as part of their monumental series of CDs on the history of Brazilian music.[79] As the accompanying booklet points out, Martius did not say what part of Brazil this *lundu* came from (though he is careful to state the provenance of each of the *modinhas* included in the same supplement). Nor did he reveal whether he heard it himself or transcribed it from a printed source. Edited by Paulo Castagna and arranged by Luís Henrique Fiaminghi and Ivan Vilela, it is played on *rabeca* fiddle, *viola* traditional guitar, and *pandeiro* tambourine, 'in an attempt to reproduce the climate of improvisation which probably existed around this dance in the eighteenth and nineteenth centuries'.[80] The result is a triumph of historical judgement and musical skill.

Salvador was home in the nineteenth century to an entire school of composers who wrote *modinhas, lundus* and much else. Besides a *modinha* called 'Tristes Saudades', Damião Barbosa de Araújo (1778–1856) wrote dramatic, sacred and military music and a comic opera, *A Intriga Amorosa*. José Pereira Rebouças (1789–1843) studied violin at the Paris Conservatory and, besides *modinhas*, wrote marches and variations on a theme by Vincenzo Bellini (1801–35). Domingos da Rocha Mussurunga (Domingos da Rocha Viana, 1807–56) wrote twelve *modinhas* and 'Onde Vai, Sr. Pereira de Moraes?', a *lundu* which passed into the folk tradition, being collected in Pernambuco some 50 years after the composer's death. Augusto Baltasar de Silveira (*c*. 1810–*c*. 1870) wrote a famous *modinha* called 'Lamentos'. José de Sousa Aragão ('Cazuzinha', 1819–1904) composed more than a hundred *modinhas*. Fr Maximiano Xavier de Santana (1825–83) composed both *modinhas* and sacred music. Manoel Tomé de Bittencourt Sá (1826–86) was a virtuoso flautist as well as a composer of sacred music and dance music. Three brothers called Pinto da Silveira Sales – Possidônio, Olegário and Fr Guilherme, whose dates of birth and death are unknown – all wrote *modinhas*. The most important of these Salvador composers was Xisto Bahia de Paula (1841–94), a man of mixed ethnicity who was singing his first *modinhas* and *lundus* in public at the age of 17. Although said to be musically illiterate, he composed music that was greatly esteemed during his lifetime and for many years after his death. In 1905 it was his *modinha*, 'Quis Debalde Varrer-te da Memória', backed by his *lundu*, 'Isto é Bom', with which the pioneering gramophone company Casa Edison launched its recordings of Brazilian popular music.[81]

Our understanding and appreciation of the early *modinha* are now greatly enhanced by the work of Ricardo Kanji and his colleagues. The CD which includes José Mauricio Nunes Garcia's 'Beijo a Mão que me Condena' includes equally illuminating performances of seven other *modinhas*.[82] Two of these are Portuguese. The music of 'Você Trata Amor em Brinco' (c. 1792–95) is by the Portuguese composer Marcos Portugal (1762–1830), though the fact that the words are by Domingos Caldas Barbosa provides a Brazilian connection. 'Marilia de Dirceu' (*c*.1800) is generally attributed to Marcos Portugal. The remaining five *modinhas* are Brazilian and have been adapted, with impressive skill and taste, from the musical supplement of Martius referred to above. Martius, who transcribed these melodies between 1817 and 1820, did not call them *modinhas*, but that is what they are. He stated the regional provenance of each. They are arranged on the CD, by accident or design, in such a way that the alert ear cannot fail to spot a marked increase in the use of systematic syncopation when we move from São Paulo to Bahia. Hearing this drives home, better than any words could, the meaning of that comment: 'This accompaniment must be played around Bahia'.

The African heritage in Brazilian popular music

We have seen that the *modinha* and the *lundu* incorporated three features in particular which made the music sound strange, exotic and attractive to most European ears: systematised syncopation, the frequent used of a flattened leading note, and switches between major and minor. The first was an adaptation of African cross-rhythms to European rhythmic norms; the second and third are adaptations of African scalar values to the European concert scale. Virtually all Brazilian popular music shares the first two of these features, and much of it displays its African heritage in other ways, too: in its emphasis on percussion and dance rhythms; in its percussive approach to all instruments, including the human voice; in the off-beat phrasing of melodic accents; in a preference for ' rich' or 'rough' rather than 'pure' tone (i.e. for a tone rich in upper harmonics, with a noise-to-sound ratio higher than the European norm); in a texture of contrasting timbres, often polyrhythmically arranged; and in the frequent use of call-and-response patterns, often overlapping.

But the enduring Brazilian passion for music and dance may owe rather more to Africa and its influence than this dry list of technical debts conveys. When we read of female slaves in the Bahia town of Olinda singing novena hymns with their mistress, a merchant's wife and 'several young men of respectability', we see one aspect of the acculturation process: slaves participating in their masters' culture. But when we read that this socially and 'racially' mixed group, in 1811, interspersed their hymn singing with rhythmic dance pieces, we see another aspect of the process, and it was one that surprised Henry Koster, who had arrived from Liverpool not long before:

> On this occasion the performance for the *novena*, or nine evenings, consisted of a piano-forte played by a lady, the wife of a merchant, and a guitar, and some wind instruments, played by several young men of respectability. The vocal music was also executed by the same persons, assisted by some female mulatto slaves belonging to the lady. I was somewhat surprised to hear the airs of country-dances and marches occasionally introduced.[83]

Many nineteenth-century visitors were impressed by the Brazilians' great love of music and dance, though few had enough insight or knowledge to trace this to its primary cause. One who had was the American sea captain John Codman, who wrote in 1867 that 'even the better classes are generally proficient only in music and in dancing', and speculated, 'Perhaps their taste for music is in a great degree attributable to the African element, and the graceful voluptuousness of their postures in the dance may be owing to the same cause.'[84]

Even before the nineteenth century, Brazil was gaining a reputation as a land of music. In 1787 John White (1757 or 1758–1832), on his way to New South Wales to become the settlement's surgeon-general, saw a stage erected outside a small church in Rio de Janeiro, 'on which was placed a band of vocal and instrumental performers, who exerted themselves with might and main to please the surrounding audience'. He added surlily, 'I cannot, however, say that they succeeded in pleasing me.'[85] From this it may be concluded that the music differed greatly from what he was used to hearing in Britain. By the first decade of the nineteenth century, the seafarer and mineralogist John Mawe (1764–1829) tells us, there were in Salvador 'few houses without the guitar, and all the more respectable families have piano-fortes'.[86] A few years later, a 'liberal and enlightened Catholic' told the naval surgeon Sir James Prior (c. 1790–1869): 'If fireworks and music form passports to heaven, the people of

St Salvador are sure to be saved.'[87] In 1815 Prince Maximilian of Wied-Neuwied found that, though 'the Portuguese' in Brazil had a great natural talent for music, the only instrument seen in the countryside was the traditional guitar. All the same, a 'love of music and dancing is general among the country-people'.[88] Another German visitor, Friedrich Ludwig von Rango, noted in 1819–20 that educated Brazilians loved music as much as the slaves did.[89] In Recife in 1821, entering a 'Portuguese' private house for the first time, Maria Graham saw 'a handsome piano of Broadwood's', and in every house she visited in Salvador later the same year, she saw 'either a guitar or piano, and generally both'.[90] Three or four years later Weech was finding that Brazilians of European descent often

> entertain themselves by singing, accompanied by the viola [traditional guitar], an instrument with six metal strings. Many of them are able to play this truly Moorish instrument with extraordinary skill and delicacy. Usually it is used to accompany *modinhas*, little national songs. Talented singers improvise them, often with truly admirable wit and great inventiveness. The softness and flexibility of the Portuguese language favour this beautiful talent enormously.[91]

A German writer reported in the early 1830s that in Rio Grande do Sul learning to play the piano was seen as 'an essential part of a good upbringing for the female sex. Quite often the player demonstrates skill and even feeling in her performance.' The writer added:

> The Brazilian has a great love of music in general, and nothing recommends the educated foreigner more than this art. The viola is a very common instrument. It would be hard to find a family in which at least one member does not play it. In the evening hours one hears its melancholy strains in almost every house. But rarely does one hear a vocal accompaniment. It is not that they do not like singing, or that there is any lack of occasion. All they lack is good poems and compositions.[92]

The Scottish botanist George Gardner (1812–49), who spent the years 1836–41 travelling through Brazil, found that in Rio de Janeiro '[m]usic is very much cultivated, and the piano, which ..., in 1817, was only to be met with in the richest houses, has now become almost universal. The guitar was formerly the favourite instrument, as it still is all over the interior.' There was an exception, however – São Romão, a town in Minas Gerais about 300 kilometres south-west of where Brasília would later be built:

> The first evening, as I walked through the town, I was surprised to hear one or more fiddles playing in almost every house; this is the instrument almost exclusively used by the barbers in Rio de Janeiro, and the other large cities and towns along the coast, but in the interior it is very seldom met with, the guitar being a greater favourite, and generally used both by ladies and gentlemen. In San

[sic] Romão, however, this usual fashion is departed from, no young ladies' [sic] education being considered complete unless she has learned to handle the bow.[93]

'In every family the young ladies play and sing', Ida Pfeiffer reported in 1850 – though she did not think highly of their musical skills: 'of tact, style, arrangement, time, &c., the innocent creatures have not the remotest idea, so that the easiest and most taking melodies are often not recognisable.'[94] The British vice-consul in Salvador was scarcely less critical in 1852: 'The Brazilians seem very fond of music', he wrote. 'You frequently hear them singing and playing the guitar, but the performers are seldom very scientific musicians. Their voices generally are shrill, and not very pleasing. The favourite songs are short ballads called "modinhas", the music of which is generally plaintive, but occasionally sportive.' Four years later he wrote that

> The Brazilians seem of late years to have cultivated a taste for music ... Pianofortes have become very general, and I am told these instruments are to be seen one hundred leagues [about 480 kilometres] up the country, whither they have been conveyed on the shoulders of blacks, no other mode of conveyance being practicable.[95]

And Gilberto Freyre confirms that in mid-nineteenth-century Brazil '[a] piano was seldom lacking ... Sometimes the master of the house, being a flute or violin virtuoso, would entertain his visitors. Most of the men in those days played the piano or the violin or the flute.'[96] The naturalist Alfred Wallace summed it up in 1853: 'Music, noise and fireworks are the three essentials to please a Brazilian population.'[97] In 1872, at Rio Preto, on the border between Rio de Janeiro and Minas Gerais, the Belgian traveller Walthère de Selys-Longchamps heard a piano played each evening. Pianos were everywhere, he wrote, though sometimes they were a little out of tune: 'Love of music certainly seems to be one of the traits of the Brazilian character.'[98] The education of young unmarried Brazilian ladies, wrote a former US consul-general, Christopher Columbus Andrews (1829–1922) in 1887, 'consists principally of a knowledge of the French language, music and embroidery'.[99] In Santos, the American visitor Alice Humphreys found a few years later that '[a]ll the ladies speak French fluently and their piano-playing is brilliant'.[100] 'Many of the women of the upper classes', agreed her compatriot Frank Vincent in 1890, '... take to music – singing and piano-playing.' A few became good pianists, he added, but most were 'wretched strummers'. At Piranhas, a 'turbulent, lawless' place in Bahia,

> The evenings, and half the nights, are generally noisy with the twanging of guitars and the warbling of love-ditties. Did one not hear so much of it, this music would be very pleasant. The voices are frequently good, and the songs quaint and plaintive, or sweet and gay. The guitar accompaniment, too, adds a coloring, which is odd and primitive to a foreign ear. Brazilians are exceedingly fond of such

harmony, and you will rarely see a dozen of them traveling together without at least one guitar.[101]

The French novelist Gustave Aimard (1818–83) heard altogether too much of the piano in Brazil. It made a din that grated on the ears from daybreak to midnight: 'These confounded *pédalistes* respect nothing.'[102]

As for dancing, the Austrian botanist Martius found in 1817 that, when hearing songs accompanied on the guitar, 'the Brazilian is easily stimulated to dance',[103] a judgement with which few present-day visitors to Brazil would disagree. The Italian statistician Balbi remarked that in Brazil

> not only the Negroes and the natives [i.e. Amerindians] but even the whites are very inclined to indulge in this kind of pleasure. In Rio de Janeiro, Bahia, and the other large towns are to be found a great many pupils of Italian and French masters – amateurs who, for the skill and grace with which they perform the most difficult dances, could pass for genuine dancing-masters.[104]

Weech tells us that dancing was the preferred occupation of the younger members of respectable families when they got together at evening parties, while their elders played long games of cards or backgammon. The same traveller vividly suggests the animated nature of the young Brazilians' most popular dances in the 1820s, and the degree to which African body movements were being imitated, when, immediately following the description of the fado quoted in the previous chapter ('a dance imitated from the Africans'), he goes on:

> Both sexes dance excellently, with a spirit and fire which makes the spectator an involuntary participant in their joy. It is with difficulty that one recognises in the dancing beauty with her flashing eyes and the incomparable liveliness of all her body's movements the woman one may have seen at home the previous day, resting languidly on her sofa, too limp to speak or even to open her eyes properly.[105]

A German visitor found the *modinha* danced at birthday parties in Rio Grande do Sul in the 1830s. Assuming that the *moreninha*, referred to below, was a mishearing, this is one of only two references to the *modinha* as a dance – here, indeed, 'the popular national dance'. So it may well be that what the German saw was in fact the *lundu* or the fado:

> People talk, eat well, and dance to an artless music. Quadrilles [*Contre-Tänze*] alternate with waltzes until the festivities reach their culmination in the popular national dance, the Meiadinha [*sic*], whose 4/4 rhythm sounds very simple. The dance is in many ways similar to an anglaise, except that the dancers' changes are accompanied rhythmically on castanets and often rendered more interesting by the singing of a verse under the music. Even older people lose their accustomed gravity on such occasions and the applause is loud if the dance is performed successfully.[106]

'Brazilians are graceful dancers', wrote the American naturalist Herbert H. Smith, who visited Brazil in the 1870s.[107] In the same decade, Count Charles d'Ursel saw at a wedding in Minas Gerais two dances apparently not described elsewhere: the *ferro-fogo* ('whose performance consists in rhythmically stamping feet and clapping hands') and the *moreninha* (probably, as suggested above, a mishearing of *modinha*). The latter was 'in polka time, interrupted by a bolero in which a clever snapping of the fingers replaces castanets', a description which suggests, again, the *lundu*. The count went on to make an interesting distinction between the generations: 'Just as the natives of the country, especially the women, excel in these languorous movements, so the settlers [*colons*] are unsuccessful in this kind of exercise, which, contrary to the melody, they try and turn into an Irish jig.'[108]

By the last quarter of the nineteenth century, it seems that native Brazilians had absorbed African cultural norms to such an extent that they enjoyed dance music even in church, at any rate in the countryside. In 1883, after being entertained with music – 'guitar, trombone and concertina' – near the town of Pitanguy in Minas Gerais, the English visitor Hastings Charles Dent asked a priest 'why they had no sacred music, only dance music in church; he said the people were not educated up to it yet, but he hoped in time to introduce it'.[109] In 1914, when gramophones were still in their infancy and radio had yet to become a medium of entertainment, an Englishman who had spent 40 years in Brazil reported that Brazilians were 'exceedingly fond of dancing'; in the southern state of Rio Grande do Sul it was 'an immensely popular form of recreation, even in those places where the only music to dance to may be an accordion purchased at the nearest "Venda" [grocery shop]'.[110]

The kind of dancing popular in the south of Brazil had been well described a generation earlier by the English visitor Thomas Plantagenet Bigg-Wither (1845–90), who wrote in 1878 of a 'fandango' ('a kind of ball') given in what is now the town of Teresa Cristina, in the southern state of Paraná. The villagers danced on a large mud floor in a room bare of furniture:

> Two banjos (*violas*) struck up ... [T]en couples ... formed a circle in the middle of the room, and the dance commenced.
>
> With slow and rhythmic beat the men first began to keep time to the violas, alternately advancing towards and retiring from the centre of the ring, the women also stamping with their feet, but not advancing. At the end of each dozen bars or so of the music, all with one accord, both men and women, gave three loud claps of the hands, which was the signal for the moment of a greater display of energy in the movements of the body, and a more vigorous stamping of feet upon the hard mud floor. All at once one of the men dancers, in a rich full voice, struck up an 'impromptu' stanza, in beautiful time and harmony with the music, the last words of which were taken up and repeated in chorus by all. Once more vocal silence, while the monotonous tum, tum, tum, of the '*violas*', and the noise of the stamping of feet went on as before. Then again, a second, wild, 'impromptu'

stanza burst forth from another of the dancers, again to be taken up in chorus by all ...

As the dance went on the excitement waxed stronger, the 'impromptu' shouts became yells, and once graceful swaying of the bodies of the performers was changed into violent contortions, and all the characteristics of a North American Indian war-dance came into play.[111]

Noteworthy here are the references to 'rhythmic beat', 'beautiful time', 'wild' call-and-response singing, 'monotonous tum tum tum' and 'violent contortions'. All five of these indicators point, not to a fancied 'North American Indian war-dance', but to the Atlantic cultural triangle that joined Brazil to Africa and the Iberian peninsula.

9

Maxixe and Modern Samba

The *lundu* has been called the 'fundamental link' in the transition from *batuque* to modern samba.[1] And, as we saw in the previous chapter, it was the *lundu* which pioneered the assimilation of black music into Brazil's towns and cities and therefore made a major contribution to the formation of the Brazilian musical tradition.[2] But between *lundu* and modern samba there was an important intermediate stage: the *maxixe*.

In 1845, at the peak of the European polka craze, the polka arrived in Brazil.[3] By the 1870s – danced by Brazilians brought up on the *lundu* for two or three generations, and drawing on the rhythm of the Cuban *habanera*, popular in Brazil from the 1860s – the polka evolved into a dance at first called tango (or *tango brasileiro*). It is often claimed that the first Brazilian composer to use the word 'tango' for a composition was Ernesto Nazaré or Nazareth (1863–1934). The same claim is made for Chiquinha Gonzaga (Francisca Edwiges Neves Gonzaga, 1847–1935). In fact the first Brazilian composer to do so was Henrique Alves de Mesquita (1830–1906). In 1871, eight years before Nazaré, he described as a 'tango' his 'Olhos Matadores', an adaptation of two *habaneras* that incorporated also elements of polka and schottische.[4] In 1879 Nazaré published his own first 'tango', the polka 'Cruz, Perigo!!', and in the following year Chiquinha Gonzaga followed suit with her 'Tango Brasileiro'.

Soon, however, this hybrid but essentially Brazilian couple dance had been renamed *maxixe*.[5] That word had at first denoted a way of dancing polka, *habanera*, or tango, with a dragging of the feet and a rippling movement of the hips.[6] Before long the *maxixe* had superseded the *lundu* as the most popular social dance in Brazil's cities, and was often seen on the stage – although, like the Argentinian tango, it was assailed for its sensuality by guardians of public morality.[7] That was no doubt because the dance 'involved very close contact between the bodies of the dancers, who sometimes pressed their foreheads together' as well as interlacing their legs as in the later *lambada*[8] (a dance which developed in the north of Brazil from a mixture of the *carimbó* dance of Pará and the *merengue* borrowed from the Dominican Republic).[9] Satirists lost no time in holding the moralists up to ridicule, as in this squib a Brazilian theatrical journal published in 1903:

So tasty is maxixe
That if he only knew
The Holy Father'd come from Rome
To dance maxixe too.[10]

It would be another ten years before the *maxixe* reached Europe, about a year after the tango. The Brazilian dance caused rather less consternation on this side of the Atlantic than the Argentinian dance had caused. The *Dancing Times* hailed it as 'a restful change to the Grizzly Bear and Turkey Trot' and advised its readers: 'The body must be kept very flexible, and the movement throughout is very undulating. It is an easy and graceful dance, and its languourous simplicity makes it a delightful change from the acrobatic gyrations of our American importations.'[11]

The *maxixe* constitutes 'a second missing link in the prehistory of samba':[12] it paved the way for the emergence of the urban samba. And not only as a couple dance: 'as a style of body movement to accompany polyrhythmic percussion, *maxixe* eventually became a main attraction of street carnival and in that sense, as well, the antecedent of modern samba'.[13] Mário de Andrade

Figure 14 The *maxixe*, successor to the *lundu* and forerunner of the urban samba, as portrayed in 1907. Guardians of public morality in Brazil attacked the dance for its sensuality, but the *Dancing Times* in London called it 'easy and graceful'.

sees what he calls the *maxixe-samba* as evidence of re-Africanisation, though he does not use that word:

> The evolution of the *maxixe* into the present-day samba appears to be ... a reaction of Brazilian black ethnicity [*negrismo étnico do brasileiro*] against the undue whiteness [*branquismo*] of the *maxixe*. ... The present-day samba ... is a black reaction against the *maxixe*, a return to purer sources, and a return to the roots [*reprimitivização*] of our urban dance, under direct black influence ....
> The ... composers of *maxixes* began to use the word [samba] again, to denote not the old Afro-Brazilian choreography but a regional kind of *maxixe*, '*maxixe*' referring to pieces of specifically Rio de Janeiro feeling and movement, '*samba*' to the *maxixe* of rural, especially north-eastern, origin and style.[14]

Before 1917 the word 'samba' was not used to designate a kind of music. It meant a kind of dance step and a social event.[15] In Rio de Janeiro it was a dance step and social event enjoyed primarily by the black inhabitants of the *morros*, the hills on which the *favelas* or shanty-towns stand. 'The samba was our family, our Sunday stroll, our movies, our theater', said one old-timer in the 1970s. 'It was all we really knew of happiness there on the *morro*.'[16] It was the 1917 carnival hit 'Pelo Telefone' by 'Donga' (Ernesto Woaquim Maria dos Santos, 1889–1974) and Mauro de Almeida (1882–1956) which put samba on the map.[17] It has stayed there ever since. 'Pelo Telefone', with its catchy melody and syncopated march-like rhythm of two beats to the bar, contained in its original version a sly dig at police corruption: the practice of warning the owners of gambling dens that they could shortly expect a police raid. This, however, was prudently toned down in the recorded version.[18]

'Pelo Telefone' was a pivotal recording. But it was not, as has often been claimed, the first music to be recorded under the name of samba, for a dozen or so others had used the term previously, including a piece called 'Brasilianas' (*c.* 1910), played on the piano by João Gualdo Ribeiro, and 'Urubu Malandro' (*c.* 1914), 'arranged from popular motifs' for clarinet, *cavaquinho* (ukelele) and guitar. 'Pelo Telefone' was simply the first piece of music to gain national success under the name 'samba'.[19] Danced originally by Brazilians of African descent, many of them recent settlers from Bahia living on the *morros* of Rio de Janeiro, the new urban samba brought one of the principal African dance rhythms into the heart of Brazilian popular music and made it an immediately recognisable musical symbol of Brazil. 'The most typical samba rhythm,' writes Kazadi wa Mukuna, 'can be met with in a general manner in many parts of Africa and occupies an important position in some cultures'.[20] To pound out these rhythms, a series of African musical instruments entered Brazilian popular music for the first time: *atabaque* drums; *agogô* clapperless double bell; and, adding an inimitable, often humorous, flavour, the friction drum known in Bahia as *cuíca*, in São Paulo as *puita* – and throughout a wide area of Angola as *pwita*[21] – and capable of emitting animal-like sounds ranging from a squeak to a roar.[22] The first samba 'schools' were formed in the 1920s, and in the following decade these dance groups, whose purpose is to prepare for public display in the annual carnival, 'became the prime exponents of ... samba as it rose rapidly to become the universally recognised cultural symbol of Brazilian identity'.[23]

> This new musical form ... was developed by the descendants of slaves, meeting in the so-called samba schools, for whom the word samba continued to signify ring dance, belly-blow, a rhythm similar to the macumba religious ceremonies. For them samba constituted a rhythm, a choreography, a genre very close to that of the invocations of the Afro-Brazilian cults.[24]

However, as José Jorge de Carvalho makes clear,

> it is only in appearance that Brazilian popular music has incorporated these cult rhythms. As a matter of fact, all the incursions we have seen so far show the adaptation of drum rhythms used in the more syncretic kinds of cult (such as *candomblé de caboclo*, *umbanda*, *macumba*, and so on), which are more compatible with the song structures used in popular music.[25]

The process of re-Africanisation that turned *maxixe* into urban samba was not widely recognised at the time for what it was, and the problem of assigning a correct label to 'Pelo Telefone' led to a celebrated exchange some years later between its creator and a rival composer. When Ismael Silva (b. 1905) said of 'Pelo Telefone', 'That's a *maxixe*', 'Donga' asked: 'Then what's a samba?' '"Se Você Jurar"', replied Silva, pointing to a 1931 hit of his own, written in collaboration with Francisco Alves (1898–1952) and Nilton Bastos (1899–1931). To which 'Donga' retorted: 'That's a *marcha*.'[26] It is now recognised that the celebrated 'sambas' written by the prolific and highly satirical composer Sinhô (José Barbosa da Silva, 1888–1930) – the catchy 'Não Quero Saber Mais Dela' (1927), for instance – were in fact *maxixes*.[27]

There is a certain irony in the fact that samba, a creation of the poorest of the poor, has become a tourist attraction. But, given the powerful wave of energy that sweeps over Brazil at carnival time, the spectacular nature of the groups' costumes and displays, and the irresistible pull of the music, it is hard to see how it could be otherwise. Every attempt to co-opt or marginalise samba comes up against the endlessly creative and innovative response of the samba schools and their composers, artists, and supporters.[28] So nowhere in Brazil is samba, or the annual carnival, only or even mainly a tourist attraction. After 500 years Brazil's heart still beats to powerful rhythms of resistance, and its people prove this afresh each year as they dance joyfully through their streets.

Appendix A

Continuity and Change in the Music of the Kongo-Angola Culture Area

> The white man came up
> Out of the waters.
> His grave is in the waters.

According to a 400-year-old tradition of the Ovimbundu of Angola, this song, called *We Ko Yava*, was sung when the first European ships arrived on the coast; it survived into the twentieth century as a boys' marching song.[1] Few African traditional songs are so long-lived – though some of the royal songs (*ncyeem ingesh*) of the wives of the Kuba king (*nyimi*) in Congo-Kinshasa, handed down from generation to generation in the closed world of the harem, may have survived since that kingdom was established in the middle of the sixteenth century.[2] But basic aspects of musical organisation, performance and style, throughout the whole Kongo-Angola culture area, have shown remarkable powers of persistence since they were first reported by European travellers from the fifteenth century onwards. And yet, at the same time, the everyday music of Angola – and in particular the music of the Kongo-Luanda area – has been greatly influenced by instruments and styles brought from Europe, and in the first place from Portugal.

What exactly is meant by the Kongo-Angola culture area? According to Robert Farris Thompson, traditional Kongo civilisation encompasses modern Congo-Kinshasa and neighbouring territories in modern Cabinda, Congo-Brazzaville, Gabon and northern Angola:

> The Punu people of Gabon, the Teke of Congo-Brazzaville, the Suku and the Yaka of the Kwango river east of Kongo in Zaïre, and some of the ethnic groups of northern Angola share key cultural and religious concepts with the Bakongo and also suffered, with them, the ordeals of the transatlantic slave trade.[3]

The ancient African kingdom of Kongo was 'bounded on the north by the river Zaïre (or Congo), on the south by the river Dande, on the west by the sea, and by the river Kwango on the east'; Angola 'may be taken as the area between the Dande and Longa rivers, with a hinterland stretching several hundred miles into the interior'.[4]

The uniformity of major cultural concepts across such an immense area led to a striking uniformity in the approach to music-making. Gerhard Kubik points out that Angola is one of the few states in southern Africa where detailed written data on music are available, in Portuguese, Italian, Dutch, English and other languages, covering the whole period of European contact. As was seen in Chapter 7, these accounts start with Ruy de Pina (1440–1521), who reported that ivory trumpets were played at the Kongo king's reception of a Portuguese delegation in 1491. João de Barros (1496–1570) and Duarte Lopes (*fl.* 1578) added to the growing store of information. In 1648 the Italian missionary Giovanni Francesco da Roma described the Angolan xylophone; in 1654 the Capuchin monk and missionary Giovanni Antonio Cavazzi (d. 1692?) described and illustrated the xylophone and the *nsambi* pluriarc, or compound bow-lute; and in 1692 Girolamo Merolla da Sorrento, another Capuchin monk and missionary, illustrated the five-string *nsambi* and other local instruments.[5]

Portuguese cultural influence, according to Kubik, was especially strong in the sixteenth and seventeenth centuries. By the middle of the seventeenth century, Kongo musicians were playing with great skill the military drums brought over by the Portuguese. Nor was that the extent of such acculturation. Under Portuguese influence the side-blown ivory horns used at the Kongo court were transformed into end-blown trumpets with wooden mouthpieces, and these instruments were played in church in the king's presence. Kubik also refers to early Portuguese influence in the shape of

> bowed violins with three srings along the Luanda coast. The Portuguese term is *viola*, and in Angola they are played in two- and three-part harmony by celebrated musicians who often sing with a head voice. In the Lunda region the *viola* is often accompanied by a long vertical scraper of the type known in Portugal as the *reque-reque*.[6]

After some 200 years of such acculturation, Herman Soyaux, who had spent three years in Angola, could write in 1879:

> the concertina [*Harmonika*], flute and tin penny-whistle have become naturalised in the colony thanks to merchants and sailors. The military bands made up of Negroes and mulattoes, and usually led by a white, play the pieces popular in Europe, and many a Negro has become a virtuoso on his instrument. As proof of the Negro's excellent musical ear and memory, it must be said that everywhere in Angola, even in the interior, men, women and children can immediately and correctly whistle and sing the melodies played by the military bands.[7]

If there seems to be a contradiction between the essential musical conservatism of the Kongo-Angola area and its ready acceptance of military drums, military bands, concertinas, flutes, tin whistles and other European contributions, it is a contradiction that from a very early date underpinned and speeded up the acculturation process in Brazil. As time went on, fewer and fewer of the millions of Africans transported to Brazil from Kongo or Angola would have remained untouched by the musical innovations in their homelands. Kongo-Angola musicians held fast to certain basic organising principles in their music (they sought above all a texture of contrasting timbres arranged polyrhythmically); but whatever aspects of the music lay outside those basic principles were open to innovation, borrowing, experiment and change. And this dialectic of continuity and change largely determined the shape that Brazilian popular music would take, up to and including the modern samba.

Appendix B

African Musical Instruments in Brazil

This appendix does not try to give a comprehensive list of African and African-derived musical instruments in Brazil. Three of these have been described in Chapter 5; some others are mentioned, as appropriate, in the rest of the book. Here there is a short account of pioneering listings of such instruments, followed by some additional information about some of them.

The Brazil-born moralist Nuno Marques Pereira (1652–1728) seems to have been the first to make a list of African musical instruments in his country, but it was neither enthusiastic nor exhaustive. *Tabaques* (log drums), *botija* (jug), *canzá* (shaker), castanets, and *pés de cabras* ('goats' feet', an expression meaning 'crowbar' and here perhaps indicating a kind of striker) were all of them 'hellish instruments'. The proof was that when they were put on a bonfire, which was their fate after they had kept him awake all night, they caused loud explosions and gave off a smoke almost as black as night. Its unbearably horrid stink lingered until the Credo was recited, whereupon a cool breeze sprang up and scattered it.[1]

It would be some 200 years before any attempt was made to draw up a more comprehensive and rational list of musical instruments of African provenance in Brazil. This was the work of Manuel Raymundo Querino (1851–1923), self-taught son of poor black parents and one of Brazil's neglected pioneers of black studies. In a paper given in 1916 to the Fifth Brazilian Congress on Geography, and later republished several times, Querino listed nine musical instruments of African provenance in Brazil.[2] His list, reproduced and annotated in Table 1, was keyed to an accompanying photograph, in which nos. 2 and 3 were examples of the same instrument; the *batá-côtô*, unillustrated, was unnumbered.

The next attempt to compile a list of African musical instruments in Brazil was made by the composer and student of folklore Luciano Gallet (1893–1931). His list of 25 such instruments ('some already out of use') was published posthumously in 1934.[3] Unclassified, it is arranged more or less alphabetically, except that *Triangulo* – a European instrument unaccountably posing here as one of African provenance – comes at the end, as if it were an afterthought. Gallet's list, though confused, pre-scientific and far from complete, is often cited as an authority for the statement that Brazil has just 25 instruments which come from Africa.[4] But Gallet's work must be used with caution. For instance, one of the instruments on it (no. 2, *Adufe*) is of Arab origin and came to Brazil from Portugal. No description is known of another (no. 7, *Cucumbí*); yet another (no. 11, *Gongon*), similarly undescribed, may simply be an alternative name for the well-known *agogô* double clapperless bell. On the other hand, *Ganzá* or *Canzá* (no. 10) can mean three distinct instruments, and so can *Marimba* (no. 13). Table 2 briefly describes the instruments listed by Gallet.

Table 1

No.	Name as given by Querino	Description and function
1	Chéré or Chéchére	Usually spelt *xere*, this denotes several types of metal shaker. The one Querino illustrates, used in *Xangô* ceremonies, is a copper vessel containing pebbles.
2 and 3	Adjá	Small metal bell used in candomblé and *Xangô* ceremonies.
4	Batás	Small wooden drums of Yoruba origin, used in *Xangô* ceremonies.
5	Ilu	Large wooden drum, usually spelt *ilú*. Sometimes signifies the *batá-côtô* (see below) but more usually the *rum*, largest of the three *atabaques* used in candomblé ceremonies.
6	Afofiê	Small bamboo flute with wooden mouthpiece.
7	Tabaque médio e menor, played with baquetas (drumsticks)	Medium (*rumpi*) and small (*lé*) *atabaques* used in candomblé ceremonies.
8	Agôgô	Clapperless double bell, struck with metal stick. Used in candomblé ceremonies. Usually spelt agogô.
9	Agê	Large net-covered gourd shaker with shells attached to the net as external strikers. Usually spelt aguê.
10	Baquetas	Drumsticks
unnumbered	Batá-côtô	War drum

Table 2

No.	Name as given by Gallet	Description and function
1	*Atabáque*	Conical hand- or stick-beaten hollow-log drum of various sizes. Used in candomblé and similar ceremonies.
2	*Adufe*	Hand-beaten square frame-drum with jingles: an instrument of Arab provenance that came to Brazil from Portugal.
3	*Birimbau*	Gourd-resonated single-string musical bow. Accompanies capoeira.
4	*Agogó* or *Agogô*	Clapperless double bell, struck with metal stick. Used in candomblé and similar ceremonies.
5	*Carimbó*	Large hand-beaten hollow-log drum *c.* 1m long and 30cm in diameter, with deerskin head. Used in *carimbó* dance and *batuque* ceremonies in Pará.
6	*Caxambú*	Large drum of *atabaque* type, used in dance of same name (probably an alternative name for the *jongo* dance) in São Paulo, Minas Gerais and Goiás.
7	*Cucumbí*	No description known. Said to be used in dramatic dance of same name and in *Taieiras*.
8	*Chocalho*	Generic term for various types of shaker.
9	*Fungador*	Alternative name for *cuíca* friction drum.
10	*Ganzá* or *Canzá*	Name of three different percussion instruments: a) small wooden drum with ox-skin head (Amazonas); b) cylindrical or egg- or pear-shaped tin rattle; c) notched scraper (Bahia).
11	*Gongon*	No description known. May be another name for *agogô*.

continued

Table 2 *continued*

No.	Name as given by Gallet	Description and function
12	*Mulungú*	Large tambourine.
13	*Marimba*	Name of three different instruments: a) xylophone; b) lamellophone; c) berimbau (in north-east) .
14	*Puita*	Friction-drum, also called *cuíca*
15	*Piano de Cuia* (Balafon in Africa)	Large net-covered gourd shaker with shells attached to net as external strikers. (*Balafon* is the Manding word for resonator xylophone; the Yoruba word for the net-covered gourd shaker is *ṣẹ̀kẹ̀rẹ̀*).
16	*Pandeiro*	Tambourine.
17	*Quissango*	A type of lamellophone (cf. one Angolan name for this instrument: *quissanje*).
18	*Roncador*	Alternative name for *cuíca* friction drum.
19	*Pererenga*	Medium-sized drum used in the Maranhão ring-dance called *punga*.
20	*Socadôr*	Alternative name for *cuíca* friction drum.
21	*Tambôr* or *Tambú*	Drum used in *jongo* dance.
22	*Ubatá*	No description known. May be alternative name for *batá* drum used in some Recife *Xangô* ceremonies.
23	*Vuvú* or *vu'*	No reliable description known.
24	*Xequerê* or *Xêguedê*	This refers to four different kinds of shaker, including that listed above as *Piano de Cuia*.
25	*Triangulo*	Of Portuguese provenance.

Gallet adds to this list two supplementary lists that overlap with the first to some extent. One is of sub-Saharan African instruments collected in Brazil and preserved in the National Museum there. A conical drum (*bombo*), said to have belonged to an African king, is described as about 50cm high, resting on a three-legged stool, and 'of very rich appearance, covered with black and white leopard skin'. The list includes 'African tambourines'; musical bows (here called *cimbos*); an undescribed *'valica'* (which Mário de Andrade took to be the Malagasay *valiha* tube zither);[5] a large bell (*cincêrro*); small bells (*campainhas*) used on sheep and camels; various rattles; and a wooden flute.[6] The other supplementary list reproduces that of Manuel Querino.

Renato Almeida, in his *História da musica brasileira* (first published in 1926 and greatly revised for its second edition, 1942), reproduced the lists of Querino and Gallet and added three more names: *bansá* (small traditional guitar, usually spelt *banza*); *macumba* (probably another name for the *reco-reco* scraper); *matungu* (apparently a lamellophone with gourd resonator).

Taken together, these lists show how serious are the problems of overlap and nomenclature in this field. Above all, it is hard to say how many such separate instruments there have been. Following Gallet, the figure of 25 is commonly given, but this is very likely an underestimate. It is probably more helpful to say that musical instruments of African provenance account for some three-quarters of the popularly used instruments in the country,[7] though this too may be something of an understatement.

Wind instruments. The *afofié* (Yor. *afofie*) wooden or reed flute and the *cangá* cane or bamboo flute were widely used by Africans in Brazil, as in Africa.[8] Brazil's tradition of flute-and-drum or pipe-and-drum bands has Portuguese antecedents but may also have some connection with a similar tradition in Senegambia.[9] The Scottish botanist George Gardner was unimpressed by the pipe-and-drum band he heard at Crato in Ceará in the late 1830s. On the last night of the Festival of Our Lady of the Conception an immense crowd assembled on the terrace in front of the church, and 'at a little distance a band of musicians were playing, consisting of two fifers, and two drummers, but the music they played was of the most wretched description; there was also a display of fireworks, quite in keeping with the music'.[10] There are modern recordings of pipe-and-drum bands in Ceará, where such a band is called *banda cabaçal* and in Sergipe, where it is called *zabumba*.[11] In Alagoas the name *esquenta-mulher* is used.[12]

Stamping tubes, known among the Ga of Ghana and also in Colombia and Venezuela (*quitiplas*) as well as Haiti (*ganbo*), seem not to have been widely reported in Brazil. That such instruments did, however, exist in Salvador in the 1840s is shown by James Wetherell's reference to 'a short, hollow, thick piece of bamboo, a piece of which is taken in each hand and one end of which is struck against a stone, this gives a dull hollow sound'. Wetherell heard these instruments played for dancing, together with a large gourd rattle and a small hand-beaten drum: 'all these played together give a very singular and deafening kind of noise, without any apparent attempt at *tune*, but beaten in time'.[13]

Shakers of various kinds are extremely common in African traditional music, and many kinds of African rattle found a home in Brazil.[14] A black man is shown playing a gourd rattle on a mid-seventeenth-century map of part of north-eastern Brazil (Fig. 2). Prominent in candomblé is the large gourd rattle, covered with netting and shells, which the Yoruba call *agè* and *ṣèkèrè* and the Brazilians call *aguê, xequerê*, etc. In 1842 James Wetherell described it very accurately:

> a large calabash gourd, partly covered with a loose net-work, at each crossing of which was strung a glass bead, or a cowrie shell, and edged with a fringe. This gourd is held lightly in the hands, and is gently struck with first one and then the other palm: it emits a dull sound relieved by the sharper rattling of the beads.[15]

There is an important reference by Tollenare to the use of a gourd rattle to provide a supplementary rhythm, besides that of the gourd's shaken contents: the handle is struck on the wooden sound-box of a lamellophone, before whose player the percussionist kneels. This procedure is widespread in African traditional music; for Tollenare, who heard it in 1816–19, it was a 'racket' that spoilt the effect of the lamellophone. It was made by

> an eight-inch stick on whose end was fixed a small gourd in which some seeds were shaken. Rhythmically and in a very lively way [the player] struck the other end of the stick on the box. It was this rhythm which seemed to produce the orchestra's main effect, since according to whether it was more or less animated, the dancers displayed more or less fervour.[16]

The Angola-derived rattle known as *ganzá* (or *canzá* or *xeque-xeque*) is often made from a small, closed, tin-plated tube. That shakers were often made in Brazil *ad hoc* from such materials as lay to hand is suggested by a German visitor's observation in 1833: 'They are delighted when they are able to get hold of an old box, in which they place stones that fill out the sound when the box is shaken.'[17]

Notched scrapers or rasps are much played in African traditional music[18] and were much used by Africans in Brazil. The Austrian botanist Pohl heard in Goiás in 1819 'a piece of bamboo about a yard long into which are cut grooves and against which another piece of bamboo is drawn lengthways up and down, producing a quite unique and unpleasant sound which, however, the Negroes love to hear'.[19] A writer in a German musical journal, who called the instrument *Kerbestock* ('notched stick'), described it as a stave about three feet long provided with deep crosswise grooves, across which another stick is drawn. As far as I know this rasping kind of music is completely peculiar to them and the sounds they produce cannot be compared to any other kind of instrument, and it has a somewhat ghastly [*Schauerliches*] quality.[20]

Spix and Martius show (Fig. 10) a notched scraper accompanying a gourd-resonated xylophone.

Drums. A brief description of the hollow-log drum he saw in Jaguaribe, Ceará, in 1812, was given by Henry Koster, who called it 'a sort of drum, which is formed of a sheepskin, stretched over a piece of the hollowed trunk of a tree'.[21] The observant Maria Graham wrote of

drums made of the hollow trunks of trees, four or five feet long, closed at one end with wood, and covered with skin at the other. In playing these, the drummer lays his instrument on the ground and gets astride on it, when he beats time with his hands to his own songs, or the tunes of the gourmis [i.e. lute].[22]

Karasch refers to the large drum called *caxambu*, 'usually not seen and drawn by foreign artists, because police persecution led slaves to hide them and bring them out only at night in hidden locations'.[23] Stanley J. Stein describes how such a drum was made on the coffee plantations of Rio de Janeiro state, and his description probably holds good for many other African-type log drums in other regions of Brazil:

Great care went into the manufacture of the two or three drums used. First a red-leafed *mulungú* tree [coral-tree, *Erythrina*] was cut down and a section cut out. With an adze, the drum-maker hollowed out one end deep enough to hold castor oil which he then ignited. When fire had burned deep enough into the mulungú, it was extinguished and the inside scraped clean. Across the open end a piece of freshly dried and scraped cowhide was pulled taut and secured.[24]

The great war drum of the Egba people of Nigeria (a sub-group of the Yoruba), called *batá-côtó* in Brazil, was made from a large gourd, the upper part of which was covered with a piece of leather. It yielded a sound which some hearers described as 'hellish'. This drum played a major part in the slave insurrections in Salvador in the early years of the nineteenth century, and its importation into Brazil was forbidden after the insurrection of 1835.[25] A goblet-shaped drum with a long supporting leg and nail tension of the skin, called *quinjengue* in Brazil and found in southern Malaŵi and northern Mozambique, is used in *batuque* in Rio Grande do Sul.[26]

The Brazilian **friction drum** known as *cuíca* in the north-east, as *puita* in São Paulo (it has many other names: *roncador*, *socador*, *tambor onça*, etc.), adds its characteristic querulous sound to much ensemble playing. It is made and played in Brazil much as it is in Angola. A skin is stretched over a hollow cylinder and through the centre of the skin is pushed a stick or a leather strip which is rubbed with a moistened hand.[27]

The **mouth bow** – i.e. musical bow resonated in the mouth – is widely distributed in Africa.[28] The *benta* mouth bow, said to have been taken to Brazil by Ashanti slaves, was briefly described in 1833 in a German musical journal. It consisted of 'a rod some three feet long which is strung into a bow with vegetable fibre or gut. The player grasps one end of the string with his teeth and strikes the other with a chip of wood, producing a sound not unlike that of a jaw's harp [*Maultrommel*].'[29] The Angolan mouth bow known as *umgunga* was called *umcanga* in Brazil, where it was long supposed to be of Amerindian provenance. Theodor von Leithold, in a passage already quoted (p. 88) testified to the widespread use of the mouth bow in Brazil in the early years of the nineteenth century; he refers to it by two German words for jaws harp, *Brummeisen* and *Maultrommel*.[30] Schlichthorst wrote in 1829 of 'an instrument the Negroes frequently play, [consisting] of a single string stretching across a bow of flexible wood, one end of which is held against the teeth' and adds that jaws harps [*Maultrommeln*] 'are also very popular'.[31] According to Richard Graham, many African musical bows fell into disuse among people of African descent in the New World but entered Amerindian cultures, where their names reveal their African origins.[32] Kay Shaffer tells us that the mouth bow no longer exists anywhere in Brazil, not even in a museum. One was made for Shaffer in Sergipe, apparently in the 1970s, by a 73-year-old woman whose brother had formerly played the instrument. It consisted of a bow of flexible wood about a metre in length, with a string of imbe creeper, a wooden stick to strike the string, and a knife to stop it. It produced a reasonably loud sound. Two cuts were made at the ends of the bow where the string was fixed, and the end of the string was threaded through the cut, turned twice round the wood, and threaded through the cut again. At the other end the same procedure was used, except that before the string was threaded through the cut for the last time it was threaded above its own stretched part, so as to fasten it well. The finer the string, the better and sweeter the sound. The bow was placed on the left shoulder and held in the left hand, as was the knife. The stick with which the string was struck was held in the right hand. The player's head was turned to the left, and the string passed between his lips, his mouth acting as a sound-chamber. The string was never held by the teeth. Changes in pitch had nothing to do with the position or form of the lips, or of the mouth, or of the knife in contact with the string. The instrument, however simple, seems to have been capable of some flexibility, since the brother of Shaffer's informant could play on it the Brazilian national anthem and many other popular tunes.[33]

The **basin bow**, a kind of zither, is still met with in Brazil occasionally, according to Shaffer, who describes and provides an illustration of one consisting of a bow with a wire string placed above two large wooden blocks, which act as sound-chambers, and held in place by a helper. The player sits on the ground in front of the bow and slides a short cylindrical metal bar along the string with the left hand so as to produce the note of the desired pitch; the player's right hand holds another, slightly longer, metal bar with which the sound is produced. It is described as a pleasing sound, which consists not only of the melody but also of a percussive rhythm produced by the other metal bar hitting the wire. The melodic range is wide, and any tune can be played, depending on the player's skill. Often a basin is slid along the string; hence the name. The *berimbau de bacia* seen by Shaffer was used by a blind street performer for patriotic songs and popular tunes.[34] There is no clear evidence that this instrument is African-derived, but there is a striking African equivalent in the home-made zither (*kingwanda-ngwanda ia kikele*) played with a tin can, constructed by three young Babembe boys in Congo-Brazzaville;[35] both have an African-American analogue in the bow diddley (or diddley bow or jitterbug), a children's instrument common, or recently so, in Mississippi.[36]

Under the name *Gourmis*, Maria Graham described a two-string **plucked lute** which 'has ... the appearance of a guitar: the hollow gourd is covered with skin; it has a bridge and there are two strings; it is played with the finger'.[37] This may be the *côcho*, a lute whose soundbox and neck were made from a single piece of wood,[38] known in Angola as *cacoxe* (or *cacotxe*).[39]

Also called *Gourmis*, according to Maria Graham, was a single-string **bowed lute** which 'has but one string, but is fretted with the fingers'.[40] The Revd Robert Walsh described the single-string bowed lute as

a rude guitar, composed of a calabash, fasted [*sic*] to a bar of wood, which forms a neck to the shell; over this is stretched a single string of gut, which is played on by a rude bow of horse-hair; and by moving the finger up and down along the gut, three or four notes are elicited, of a very plaintive sound. The minstrel is generally surrounded by a group sitting in a circle, who all unite their voices as accompaniments to the music.[41]

Appendix C

The Brazilian Musical Heritage in Nigeria and Benin

Trade between Brazil and Lagos expanded greatly during the first half of the nineteenth century. A permanent Lagos embassy is thought to have been set up in Brazil in the 1830s.[1] Freed slaves from Brazil began arriving in Lagos in 1838. Many settled in the middle of Lagos Island, in a district known variously as Popo Aguda, Popo Maro, Portuguese Town, and the Brazilian Quarter. Others settled in Badagri, as well as Agoué, Cotonou and Porto Novo in Dahomey and Anécho in Togo.[2] These were Yorubas and *crioulos* (people born in Brazil) who had bought their freedom from their Brazilian owners. They were followed by freed slaves from Cuba. The Brazilians, known as Aguda or Amaro, took with them 'rich experience and expertise in craftsmanship', and their community contributed much to the development of Lagos. Within 50 years there were 3,221 Brazilians in Lagos, many of them skilled artisans:[3] masons, surveyors, carpenters, joiners, tailors, goldsmiths and barber-surgeons. The women among them were renowned as dressmakers and specialist cooks (*quituteiras*).[4] It was these resettlers who introduced the celebrated Brazilian architectural style to be seen in Lagos, Ibadan and Oshogbo, whose main features are 'flamboyant floral designs on doorways and portals, bas-relief decorations on the lower half of the outer wall, and a verandah in front of the house'.[5]

The resettlers also brought to Nigeria various Brazilian popular festivals, notably the *careta* masquerade celebrating Easter and Christmas;[6] the *Bumba-meu-boi* dramatic dance, lightly disguised as a masquerade called *burrinha*; and the Bonfin festival. In the 1880s there were complaints in Lagos about dances by 'semi-nude' women and 'bawdy' songs known as *Pandero*:[7] these too may have been introduced by the resettlers from Brazil, where the tambourine is called *pandeiro*. In neighbouring Dahomey towards the end of the nineteenth century, Francisco da Souza, 'wishing to revive Brazilian entertainments under African skies',[8] formed an orchestra called *Bourrillan* to provide the music for the Bonfin festival in Agoué, Ouidah and Porto-Novo. At the head of the procession went a torch topped by a star, followed by a series of wooden animals: bull, horse, camel, giraffe, elephant and ostrich. Then came the master of ceremonies, two singers and the musicians, playing three drums of Brazilian origin as well as a drum called *palma* and one or two pairs of *tchèkèlè* castanets. The Brazilian-derived drums were the *bane*, a double-headed drum 22cm high and 55cm in diameter, the *sinéga* small frame drum 15cm high and measuring 36cm along each side; and the *sámbà* drum, a hand-beaten single-membrane drum with a square or rectangular frame, 9.5cm high, 20cm long, and 11cm wide. Another Dahomey orchestra of Brazilian origin, called *Wolo*, which provided music for popular celebrations in Ouidah, consisted of one *bane* drum, two *sinéga* frame drums and one or two *gan* gongs.[9]

The most important of these drums that the Brazilians took to Nigeria, the *sámbà* frame drum was often used later in *jújù* music and sometimes also as part of the accompaniment in palmwine music.[10] Such drums are still made today – 'by carpenters and not by specialized instrument makers'.[11] Unlike, for instance, the *bàtá* drums used in the worship of S̀ọngó, the *sámbà* drum had no association with Yoruba traditional religion and accordingly, together with the tambourine, became the chief percussion instrument played in Christian churches in Nigeria.[12]

The *aṣikó* dance style, which preceded the emergence of *jújù* in the mid-1930s, used three *sámbà* drums, a wooden box struck by the player's heel and a wood-cutting saw that served as a notched scraper.[13] Christopher Waterman says that elderly informants, pointing to a relationship between *aṣikó* rhythms and the African-Brazilian samba, sometimes used the terms *aṣikó* and *sámbà* interchangeably.[14] According to Frank Aig-Imoukhuede, 'up till the 1940s in Lagos, the samba and many Brazilian dances were still prevalent'.[15] Waterman points out that *aṣikó* was 'a local variant of a type of syncretic street drumming found in port towns throughout Anglophone West Africa'; similar 'neotraditional dance musics using wooden frame drums (*kpanlogo*, *gombe*, *konkomba*) were also found in towns along the West African coast from Fernando Poo to Bathurst'.[16]

The Brazilian resettlers' musical influence in Nigeria was not confined to the *sámbà* drum or to African-Brazilian rhythms. 'From samba and Bonfin type celebrations', writes Aig-Imoukhuede, 'developed another musical form which later evolved into the highlife – a musical expression common to West Africa in which western popular forms got fused with traditional entertainment music'.[17] According to Waterman, they also 'introduced Catholic sacred music, Portuguese and Spanish song forms and guitar techniques', as well as such 'neo-African' dances as the *samba de roda*:

> Tambourines, guitars, flutes, clarinets, and concertinas were used to perform *serenatas*, *fados*, and polkas at weddings and wakes in the Brazilian Quarter. The most distinctive Aguda performance traditions were the *burrinha*, an adaptation of the Afro-Brazilian *bumba-meu-boi* ... tradition with elaborate masquerades called *calungas*, and the *caretta* or Fancy Dance, a syncretic fusion of West African ring dance and European country dance patterns which involved dancers gesturing with a handkerchief in their hand. The *caretta* was eventually adopted

by other black immigrant groups in Lagos, and became a mode of competition between various quarters of the city ... Although the Aguda constituted only a small part of the total population of Lagos by the outbreak of World War I, their syncretic musical styles profoundly influenced popular music in Lagos. The Brazilians and Cubans, along with other Afro-American migrants from the United States and British West Indies, introduced a range of mature syncretic styles, providing local musicians with aesthetic and symbolic paradigms that could be adapted to African urban tastes.[18]

The *caretta* was called 'Fancy Dance' to describe 'the flair and flamboyance embodied in the wearing of colourful costumes and often face masks'. With the *caretta*

came the band music developed in imitation of music supplied by members of the Hausa constabulary. Here, however, was free musical expression unhampered by the strictness of keeping to notated beat with which most popular musicians of the time were unfamiliar. The beat of the caretta or fancy group was the basic *kere-re-re gbamgbam*. This type was soon followed by the Calabar Brass Band whose repertoire included the most exciting pieces in which cornets and bugles were played with great verve as the Lagosians 'steamed' from one end of the island to the other. 'Steaming' was free – a sort of dance parade which gathered crowds as it went along and halted at road junctions to allow members of its procession to dance 'face to face' with handkerchiefs held high and waving in the air.[19]

Appendix D

The Music and Dance of Cape Verde

As a glance at the map on page xi might suggest, the ten islands and five islets that make up the Cape Verde archipelago were of

> central importance for the history of transatlantic shipping. The pattern of North Atlantic winds made it likely that every European sailing ship outward bound to destinations in the South Atlantic ..., would pass through the vicinity of the Cape Verdes ... [A] certain proportion of those ships passing through the archipelago's seas would find it possible, even desirable, to put in at a Cape Verdean port to procure beverages, victuals, or nautical supplies, or to undertake indispensable repairs.[1]

The archipelago was uninhabited when the Portuguese first arrived there in the fifteenth century, and the African slaves they took there, who came from diverse ethnic groups, developed a culture that blended African and European traditions in a unique way. Cape Verde has been described as a 'sea-isolated laboratory' in which there evolved 'a hybrid and syncretic society of unusual intellectual and historical interest', since '[A]t many levels of sensibility, and of social contact, African elements interpenetrate the imposed European patterns.' In traditional tales, for instance, 'the vicious, scheming wolf of European legend appears in semi-African guise, as a lovable, guitar-playing scamp'.[2] The islanders, while responsive to the styles of music and dance demonstrated to them by visiting seafarers, have maintained a fierce pride in their own musical traditions, which are extraordinarily rich and varied for such a small area. According to Susan Hurley-Glowa,

> The traditional musics of Cape Verde can be viewed as existing along a continuum with European influences on one end and African influences on the other. While all of the traditional musics are unique forms that have evolved over the 500 years that Cape Verde has been inhabited, the musics from São Tiago and Fogo ... have a stronger African influence while the musics from the Barlavento islands and Brava ... have more resemblance to Portuguese folk musics.[3]

At the African end of this continuum are worksongs used during sowing, hoeing and weeding, songs used to scare birds away and fishermen's songs.[4] In the islands of São Tiago and Fogo there are four traditional genres – *batuko*,

173

finaçon, funana and *tabanka* – all of which 'emphasize rhythm over melody, feature call-and-response structures, much repetition, simple harmonies, and an open, loud singing style without the use of vibrato. The dances have more in common with African and Afro-Caribbean traditions than European ones, especially the *batuko* style of dancing.'[5] The *batuko* and *finaçon* were tradition-ally accompanied by 'surrogate drums' in the form of rolled-up lengths of cloth covered with plastic bags and held between the legs;[6] this practice is said to have been a response to the banning of drums. Nowadays the *batuko* is normally accompanied by *tchabeta*, a slow beating of thighs with the palms of the hands.[7] To this may be added the *ferrinho*, an angle-iron struck with a knife, but the dance would once have been accompanied by a one-string fiddle called *cimbó* or *cimboa*. Now probably obsolete, the *cimbó*, whose resonator was made from a half-gourd or coconut shell covered with goatskin or sheepskin,[8] closely resembles a number of West African single-string bowed lutes;[9] its name is said to be of Manding origin.[10] Another African-derived stringed instrument formerly used in the archipelago was the berimbau, said in 1976 to be 'in the course of disappearing';[11] it is unclear whether it reached Cape Verde directly from the African mainland or was introduced from Brazil.[12] The *finaçon* combines an African-sounding melody with text said to be 'of Portuguese inspiration';[13] it includes 'compliments to party-givers, matrimonial advice, stern blame of loose behaviour, criticism against those in power, satire of pride, and saucy allusions'.[14] The *funana*, said to date back to the early nineteenth century, and possibly influenced by the Brazilian *choro*, is accompanied by diatonic accordion and *ferrinho*.[15] Since independence (1975) '*funana* and other musics from São Tiago have become symbols of Cape Verdean resistance to Portuguese domination and have become widely popular'.[16] The *tabanka*, which used conch-shell horns and drums, was associated with street parades and closed societies and was at one time officially banned, is said to be disappear-ing.[17] On the island of Fogo there is a special music for the *festa do pilão* or 'pestle festival', with two drums and singing accompanying the grinding of corn with pestles in large mortars.[18]

The acculturated *morna* is generally seen as Cape Verde's most typical musical and poetic form. It is 'often said to express the essence of the Cape Verdean soul'.[19] Usually a solo song, it was originally accompanied by *rabeca* fiddle and *viola* traditional guitar; nowadays modern guitar and *cavaquinho* plucked lute (ukelele) are also used, and often piano, clarinet, and flute or saxophone too. There is some dispute about the *morna*'s origins. Peter Manuel, who suggests that it first emerged on the island of Boa Vista in the mid-nineteenth century, shares the widespread view that it was 'possibly influenced by the Portuguese and/or Brazilian *modinha*'.[20]

It was obviously a dance squarely within the Atlantic tradition which a British visitor witnessed in the 1930s 'in a back street in Praia' on the Cape Verde island of Santo Antão and took to be the *coladeira*. He called it 'an extremely lubricious dance with very obscene verses':

There was a circle of excited blacks in the moonlight all clapping their knees with their hands and shrieking with joy. In the middle a man and a woman were mimicking the movements of courtship. First the woman would advance and shake her hips invitingly at the man. He would leap forward as though maddened with lust, and the woman would retire provokingly, only to return and vamp him once again when he had retreated baffled.[21]

Traditionally however, according to Manuel, the *coladeira* (also spelt *koladera*) was a line dance. The modern *coladeira*, he says, 'is of recent origin, emerging in the 1960s',[22] though some, like Luís Romero, date its emergence some 30 years earlier and say it was influenced by Brazilian samba, Cuban 'rumba' (i.e. *son*) and American ragtime.[23] Originally the name *coladeira* was used for an open-air processional dance, accompanied by drums and whistles; or it could mean 'one of a group of women who perform improvised topical verses in a lively call-and-response style during certain festivals, accompanied by male drummers'. The *coladeira*'s appeal 'lies in its fast, danceable rhythms'; its texts 'are generally simple, topical, light-hearted, and often satirical or humorous'.[24]

Cape Verde's focal position in the Atlantic cultural triangle led to many other forms of music and dance taking root there, though not all have survived. The list of dances which have established themselves in Cape Verde for longer or shorter periods is kaleidoscopic: tango, *maxixe*, foxtrot (*passo de raposa*), *contradanças*, quadrille (*quadrilha de lanceiros*), *modinha*, fado, samba, polka, *galope* and *cataretê* were all danced there,[25] and mazurka and waltz still are.[26] Of great interest, for the comparisons to be made with the Brazilian *lundu*, is a *lundum* recorded in Cape Verde in 1992.[27]

Appendix E

Relaçaõ da fofa que veya agora da Bahia: Extract

Description

RELAÇAÕ | DA | FOFA | QUE VEYO AGORA DA BAHIA, | E O | FANDANGO | DE SEVILHA, | *Applaudido pelo melhor som, que ha para diver-* | *tir malancolias* | E O | CUCO DO AMOR | *Vindo do Brasil por Folar, para quem o quizer comer.* | Tudo decifrado, na Academia dos Extromozos. | POR C.M.M.B. | CATALUMNA: | En la Imprenta de Francisco Guevarz
A^4. pp. [1–2] 3–8. 19.3 × 13.5 cm.
Single sheet, 28.8 × 19 cm, bound in at end, headed: Lista das Igrejas que sua magestade foy servido prover no Bispado da Guarda em quarta feira 20. de Setembro de 1752. Priores.

Extract

[p. 3:] A FOFA DA BAHIA
PRimeiramente se difine a *Fofa da Bahia: Som do Brasil com propriedade para vodas e galhofas:* He som desatinado, he som de Casa da Fortuna, he som de porhialem, e he som de naõ sey, que diga: E para o dicifrar melhor: he o som do marujo, do galego, do moço de servir, da inquietacaõ da balburdia, dos barulhos, e das traficancias.

He a *Fofa da Bahia* tambem o melhor som qne [*sic*] ha na maromba da chulice. Apenas a ouve tocar a Preta, já está no meyo da casa a baillar sem socego. Apenas a ouve o preto, já està, como doudo a dançar, como huma carapeta, e naõ socega tambem, sem sahir a terreiro. *Ora viva a Fofa da Bahia*, que faz desafiar o Preto, e a Preta, para dançar.

Apenas tambem huma Mulata da Bahia ouve o seu toque, já naõ está em si, jà toda se inquieta; até sahe fora de si a baillar as trepecinhas. Apenas o Casquilho ouve este som, já salta de contente; pois [p. 4:] viva *a Fofa da Bahia*; por ser a causa de tudo isto: provasse, que ella he o som mais excellente, para fazer saltar.

176

Todo o som, que mais suspende com a harmonia das suas vozes, he o mais excellente, que ha, para fazer saltar. A Fofa da Bahia he o som, que mais suspende com a armonia [sic] das suas vozes; logo he o mais excellente, que ha, para fazer saltar.

Ora viva; que nem o outavado d'Alfama lhe chega ao calcanhar, nem o som do Macau lhe dá pelo bico do pé, e nem a filhota de Coimbra lhe excede.

A Fofa da Bahia faz dezafiar o coraçaõ, tremer o corpo, e arrancar as unhas dos pés a modo d'osga; que viva. *A Fofa da Bahia* faz cazar muita gente, e he toque simpatico com prestimo, para atrahir a misades [sic], e unir noivos; que viva a *Fofa da Bahia*.

Viva; que por ser folgazona, renderá à mais guapa, captivará a mais Eres, alegratá à mais triste, dará gosto à mais entendida, e prenderá à mais tolla. Que viva a dita *Fofa*; que por ser taõ giribande-[p. 5:]ra renderà naõ só à fragona; mas à muchacha á tolla; e à discreta; porque naõ sey, que mel tem, para pôr pelos beiços a tanta gente, para a trahir [sic], e inquietar, mover a baillar, e tirar a terreiro; mas o certo he, que só esta *Fofa* he singular, bella, estupenda, e pefeita, para causar tudo isto; pois viva a *Fofa da Bahia*, viva, viva.

An English translation of this passage appears on p. 127 above.

Discography

Albums are compact discs unless otherwise stated. They are arranged here alphabetically under three headings: Brazil, Africa (including Cape Verde), and Other areas.

Brazil

Afro-American Drums. Folkways FE 4502 C/D. (12in. LP)
Includes 'Four Rhythms for Eshu' and 'Four Rhythms for Ogun', recorded in Salvador by Melville J. Herskovits and Frances S. Herskovits before 1955.
Afro-Brazilian Religious Songs. Lyrichord Stereo LLST 7315 (12in. LP)
Contains 14 recordings made by Gerard Béhague in 1967–75 at candomblé (Ketu and Gêge) ceremonies in and around Salvador. The songs are sung in Yoruba and Fon, with occasional exclamations in Portuguese. Music for the entry (*avaninha*) and departure (*saida*) of the initiates occupies three tracks. There are songs for Oxóssi, god of hunters; Oxumaré, who symbolises the rainbow; Ogun, god of iron and war; Orixalá, god of creation; and Exú, messenger of the gods, trickster, and guardian of crossroads, who is ritually sent away at the start of each ceremony. This LP also contains an example of the rhythm called *adarrum*, by means of which all the *orixás* are summoned at once; and an example of the music that accompanies the 'baptism' of the candomblé drums.
Amazônia: Festival and Cult Music of Northern Brazil. Lyrichord LYRCD 7300
Important collection of recordings of both religious and secular music of the north, made by Dr Morton Marks in and near Belém (Pará) in 1975. Two religious traditions are represented: *batuque* and umbanda. There are *batuque* songs to Exú and ceremonial songs (*doutrinas*). Some of the umbanda songs were recorded during the annual festival for Ogum Niká Befará; others honour Exú, Yemanjá and the *encantado* (spirit) João da Mata. This CD contains two splendid examples of *carimbó*, the Amazônia variant of ring samba, played by the Conjunto Tapayoara, whose instruments are three *carimbó* hand-beaten log drums, straddled by the players; *onça* friction drum; *reco-reco* notched

scraper; two rattles; *ganzá* metal shaker containing lead shot; *cavaquinho* plucked lute; banjo; and flute. The same group also contributes a rural samba.

Baianas/Alagoas. CDFB 021; Documentário Sonoro do Folclore Brasileiro no. 21 (7in. LP)

Recorded in Maceió, Alagoas, in 1977. Six songs, by Terezinha Oliveira and chorus, showing an evident mingling of influences that include *maracatus rurais* and the *coco* dance. The accompanying instruments are *bombo* bass drum and *ganzá* shaker.

Banda Cabaçal/Ceará. CDFB 023; Documentário Sonoro do Folclore Brasileiro no. 23 (7in. LP)

Recorded in 1976; this band from Crato, in the Cariri region of Ceará, comprises two side-blown seven-note flutes (*pifes*), *zabumba* bass drum and cymbals. Here it plays two marches, a *baião*, a hymn and two animal imitations: 'The Fight between the Dog and the Jaguar', and 'The Wedding of the Dove and the Sparrow-Hawk'.

Banda de Congos/ES. INF 033; Documentário Sonoro do Folclore Brasileiro no. 33 (7in. LP)

Recorded in 1980, these five songs typify the traditional music of rural Espírito Santo, whose subject-matter varies from recollections of slavery to Brazil's war with Paraguay (1865–70), from popular saints and mermaids to love, the sorrow of parting, and death. The rough heterophonic singing is accompanied by five large drums (*congos*), *caixa* small drum, *cuíca* friction drum, notched scrapers (here called *casacas*), *chocalho* rattle, and triangle. The *Banda de Congos* traditionally precedes processions on saints' days, when devotees pull, by means of long ropes, a two- or four-wheeled cart bearing the model of a ship.

Boi-de-Mamão/SC. CDFB 027; Documentário Sonoro do Folclore Brasileiro no. 27 (7in. LP)

Recordings made in 1976 of a variant of *Bumba-meu-boi* performed in the southern state of Santa Catarina. The singing is accompanied on accordion, *bumbo* drum, *pandeiro* tambourines and *reco-reco* notched scrapers. *Boi-de-Mamão* is said to take its local name from the children's custom of making a bull's head from an unripe papaw fruit (*Carica papaya*, called *mamão* in Brazil).

Brasil: A Century of Song: Folk & Traditional. Blue Jackel CD 5001–2

A mixed bag of tracks, some of them adaptations, more or less prettified, of traditional models, but including a Carmen Miranda song ('Ela Diz Que Tem', 1941); a virtuoso piece by the great accordionist Luiz Gonzaga ('Vira e Mexe', 1941); nearly nine minutes of berimbau and percussion; and a *samba de viola* from Bahia by *Mestre* Cobrinha Verde and his group. Uninformative booklet.

Brasil: A Century of Song: Carnaval. Blue Jackel CD 5002–2

There is much delightful music on this CD, but those seeking authenticity should listen with a cautious ear to some of it. However, Velha Guarda da Portela's 'Fui Condenado' (1989) is a little masterpiece. Uninformative booklet.

Brasil Chorinho: Alceu Maia. Columbia 283/002/1–464221. Academia Brasileira de Música, vol. 1 (12in. LP)

A pleasant enough collection of classical *choros*, played correctly but without much of a spark. No information about personnel and recording dates.

Brasile: Musica Nera di Bahia: Black Music of Bahia. Albatros VPA 8318 (12in. LP)

Eight recordings made in Salvador in 1975–76 by Massimo Somaschini and Chantal Peillex. They include capoeira; a candomblé ceremony for Yemanjá; and a carnival *frevo*.

Brazil: Forró: Music for Maids and Taxi Drivers. Globe Style CDORB 048

The best available introduction to the north-eastern dance-music tradition that is a latter-day development of the *baiano* or *baião*, itself probably the form the *lundu* took in the north-east. With its texture of contrasting timbres (basically: accordion, *zabumba* bass drum played with mallet and stick, and triangle) arranged polyrhythmically over a strong, lively beat, and with much use of call-and-response singing, the *forró* exemplifies the persistence in Brazil of the traditional African approach to music-making, and remains highly popular among the poor of Brazil's north-east. This CD comprises six tracks by Toninho de Alagoas, five by José Orlando, four by Duda da Passira, and two by Heleno dos Oito Baixos.

Brazil Roots Samba. Rounder CD 5045

A satisfying compilation of what Gerald Seligman's accompanying leaflet calls '*favela* samba', with eight tracks by Wilson Moreira (b. 1936), eight by Nelson Sargento (b. 1924) and three by the 13-strong Velha Guarda da Portela (who also sing on one of the Moreira tracks), all recorded before 1990.

Brésil: Choro – Samba – Frevo: 1914–1945. Frémeaux & Associés FA 077 (2 CDs)

A stunning collection of 37 tracks of Brazilian popular music. They range in time from a 1914 recording of the polka 'Sultana' written in 1882 by the prolific woman composer Chiquinha Gonzaga (Francisca Edwiges Neves Gonzaga, 1847–1935), with its lightly tripping flute, to the 1946 'Ixo' with Pixinguinha (Alfredo da Rocha Viana Filho, 1898–1973) on tenor saxophone and Benedito Lacerda (1903–1958) on flute. And they range in style from the pivotal urban samba (or was it?) 'Pelo Telefone' (1917), by 'Donga' and Mauro de Almeida (1882–1956), to Carmen Miranda's brilliant presentation with Dorival Caymmi (b. 1914) of a Salvador street-vender in 'A Preta do Acarajé' (1939) and the same couple's delicious 'O Que É a Bahiana Tem?', recorded in the same year. There are four other Pixinguinha tracks, including 'O Urubu e o Gavião' (1930), which Mário de Andrade called 'wonderfully performed' and 'one of the summits of Brazilian recording'.[1] There are four tracks by Noel Rosa (1910–37) and a 1930 recording of Ernesto Nazaré (1863–1934) playing, surprisingly stiffly, his own polka 'Apanhei-te, Cavaquinho' (here called a *choro*). An exceptionally rich and well-chosen collection, with an informative and generally accurate booklet by Philippe Lesage.

Calango–RJ. INF 44; Documentário Sonoro do Folclore Brasileiro, 44 (7in. LP)
Three sung *calangos* accompanied by accordion and tambourine, and one instrumental, all recorded *c*. 1986. The booklet includes brief but valuable notes by Rosa Maria Barbosa Zamith as well as the texts of the three songs.

Cambinda/Paraíba. CDFB 026; Documentário Sonoro do Folclore Brasileiro no. 26 (7in. LP)
Recorded in the Paraíba city of Lucena in 1978, this disc contains ten songs from the large repertory of the local Cambinda Brilhante group, who accompany their singing with *zabumba* bass drums and shakers.

Cana-Verde/Ceará. INF 037; Documentário Sonoro do Folclore Brasileiro no. 37 (7in. LP)
Six songs recorded in Fortaleza in 1975, accompanying a ring-dance that came to Brazil from Portugal, where it had already incorporated some African influences. The soloist, 73-year-old Paulino Elias de Oliveira, plays a *pandeiro* tambourine and is backed by a chorus. Especially popular in south and central Brazil, the *cana-verde* (also called *caninha-verde*) is known along the Ceará seaboard, where it is traditionally a favourite dance of fishermen.

Carmen Miranda 1930–1945. Harlequin HQ CD 94
Carmen Miranda: The Brazilian Recordings. Harlequin HQ CD 33
Portugal-born Carmen Miranda (Maria do Carmo Miranda da Cunha, 1909–55) went to Brazil when she was one year old and became Brazil's greatest twentieth-century woman singer of popular music – an achievement which, for many, has been obscured by her successes in the cinema. These two delightful CDs, containing 48 tracks altogether, showcase her alluring voice and flawless sense of rhythm. Few singers of European descent have rivalled either Carmen Miranda's confident grasp of black music or her creativity and originality within that genre.

Coco/Ceará. INF 032; Documentário Sonoro do Folclore Brasileiro, no. 32 (7in. LP)
Recorded in 1975 by a group of fishermen at Iguape, Aquirás, on the coast of Ceará, whose singing is accompanied by *ganzá* shaker, soap-box struck with two coconut shells, handclapping and *quenguinhas*: coconut shells fitted with small handles and banged together.

Congos de Saiote/RN. CDFB 025; Documentário Sonoro do Folclore Brasileiro no. 25 (7in. LP)
Recorded in 1977 in Rio Grande do Norte, this dramatic dance, staged in the city of São Gonçalo de Amarante, is accompanied by *rabeca* fiddle, *bandolim* mandolin and shakers. The five songs presented here have what the sleeve-note calls 'poignantly beautiful melodies and poetry'.

Dança do Lelê/MA. CDFB 028; Documentário Sonoro do Folclore Brasileiro no. 28 (7in. LP)
The *lelê* line dance is probably of Portuguese origin. On these recordings made in the Maranhão town of Rosário in 1976 it is accompanied by guitar, *cavaquinho* (ukelele), several *pandeiro* tambourines and castanets.

Danças do Marajó. CDFB 024; Documentário Sonoro do Folclore Brasileiro no. 24 (7in. LP)

Dance music from Brazil's far north, recorded in Soure, on the island of Marajó, in 1976. A band consisting of clarinet, guitar, *cavaquinho*, violin and unspecified drum plays two *lundus*, a polka and a mazurka.

The Discoteca Collection: Missão de Pesquisas Folclóricas. Rykodisc RCD 10403

Invaluable CD, providing 23 of the 234 acetate 78 r.p.m. recordings made in 1938 by the folklore research mission which São Paulo's Discoteca Pública Municipal sent to the states of Pernambuco, Paraíba, Ceará, Piauí, Maranhão and Pará. There is a song from a Recife *Xangô* ceremony; five *tambor-de-mina* songs from Maranhão; a *babaçuê* song; two *pagelança* songs; two harvest songs of a closed society of Pancaru Amerindians; eight songs from performances of the *coco* ring dance in Paraíba; a Paraíba rural samba, a berimbau playing for a *carimbó* dance in Maranhão; and brief extracts from *Bumba-meu-boi* performances in Maranhão and Pará.

Enciclopedia da Música Brasileira. Art Editora Ltda unnumbered (12in. LP)

A spoken tale by the writer Cornélio Pires (1884–1958), followed by twelve otherwise inaccessible songs, issued with only the barest minimum of information. Fascinating but frustrating.

Fandango/Alagoas. CDFB 022; Documentário Sonoro do Folclore Brasileiro no. 22 (7in. LP)

In Alagoas the fandango is a series of songs on nautical themes. On this disc, recorded in Pajuçara, Maceió, in 1957, there are seven such songs, accompanied by *rabeca* fiddle.

Fandango/SP. INF 035; Documentário Sonoro do Folclore Brasileiro no. 35 (7in. LP)

Recorded in Sorocaba, São Paulo, in 1981, this disc provides six examples of the fandango as dance and song (*moda de viola*) representing aspects of rural life. The performers are Os Tropeiros de Mata. As well as a locally made traditional guitar with five pairs of strings, the dancers' spurs provide a rhythmic accompaniment.

Fantastique Brésil. Barclay 920 160 (12in. LP)

Undated recordings of Rio de Janeiro carnival and macumba music, Salvador capoeira, a fishermen's song from Bahia, a song from Goiás and four tracks of Amerindian music.

História da Música Brasileira: Périodo Colonial I. Centro de Produções Editorais e Culturais 946137

História da Música Brasileira: Périodo Colonial II. Centro de Produções Editorais e Culturais 946138

These two CDs are the magnificent first fruits of an imaginative and flawlessly executed project. Of special interest on the first CD are an anonymous Christmas *vilancico*, dating from the early eighteenth century, which may be of folk origin; and works by the Minas Gerais composers Inácio Parreiras Neves (*c.* 1730–*c.* 1791), Francisco Gomes da Rocha (*c.* 1754–1808) and José Joaquim Emérico Lobo de Mesquita (*c.* 1746–1805). The second CD is a treasure house, with a triumphant reconstruction of an early-nineteenth-century *lundu*, and several *modinhas*, including five of those transcribed by Martius in 1817–20, in São Paulo, Minas Gerais and Bahia, as well as 'Beijo a Mão que me Condena' by José Mauricio Nunes Garcia (1767–1830). A solid achievement by Ricardo Kanji and Vox Brasiliensis.

In Praise of Oxalá and Other Gods: Black Music of South America. Nonesuch H 72036 (12in. LP)

Includes three recordings made in Salvador by David Lewiston, of capoeira, *samba de roda*, and part of a candomblé festival for Orixalá. Date of recording unstated.

Os Ingenuos Play Choros from Brazil. Nimbus NI 5338

Seventeen classics of the *choro* form expertly played by a Salvador group.

Levada do Pelô. Seven Gates SGDL 0021

The music of a typical Salvador *bloco afro*.

L. H. Corrêa de Azevedo: Music of Ceará and Minas Gerais. Rykodisc RCD 10404

Offers a selection of the outstandingly important field recordings made in the states of Ceará and Minas Gerais in 1943–44 by the musicologist and composer Luíz Heitor Corrêa de Azevedo, including *coco*, *rojão* (a variant of *baião*), *Congos*, *Xangô* and *maracatu* from Ceará, *coco*, waltz, *catopê* and *vissungos* from Minas.

Luiz Gonzaga: Quadrilhas e Marchinhas Juninas. Acervo Especial M60.050

North-eastern dance music by Brazil's master of the accordion. Uninformative leaflet.

Mais de Meio Seculo de Música Popular Brasileira, vol. 2 (1929–1939). RCA Camden 107.0211 (12in. LP)

Twelve commercial recordings by Nilton Bastos (1899–1931), Noel Rosa, Ismael Silva (b. 1905), Francisco Alves (1898–1952), Pixinguinha and other big names in 1930s Brazilian popular music.

Mestre Paulo dos Anjos: Capoeira da Bahia. BMG Ariola Discos 470.048 (12in. LP)

Probably the best introduction to the music of the berimbau.

Mineiro-Pau/RJ. CDFB 20. Documentário Sonoro do Folclore Brasileiro no. 20 (7in. LP)

Also called *Maneiro-Pau*, this is a traditional dance of country people in Rio de Janeiro state, performed at carnival time. The dancers mark the rhythm by clashing together the wooden sticks (known as *bastões*, *bastões-de-moçambique*, or *paus*) often used in the *Moçambique* dramatic dance. These are 90–100cm long and 2–3cm in diameter, and may be of Amerindian provenance. Also to be heard on this disc are a *bombo* large drum and a *sanfona* accordion. The songs are in call-and-response form.

Música Popular do Centro-Oeste/Sudeste (Mapa Musical do Brasil, 3). Discos Marcus Pereira MP 10045; Música Popular Brasileira, no. 3
Three *folias* (a kind of popular devotional song), three *calangos* (see p. 107) and two *cirandas* (a ring dance of Portuguese origin).
Música Popular do Nordeste (Mapa Musical do Brasil, 2). Discos Marcus Pereira MP 10044; Música Popular Brasileira, no. 2
Includes examples of Brazilian challenge singing by Severino Pinto and Lourival Batista (*quadra*), and by Otacílio Batista and Diniz Vitorino (*martelo agalopado, galope a beira-mar*, and *quadrão*), accompanied on guitar. The rest of the CD is devoted to *cirandas*.
Música Popular do Norte (Mapa Musical do Brasil, 4). Discos Marcus Pereira MP 10046; Música Popular Brasileira, no. 4
The richest collection in the Marcus Pereira series, this includes creolised dance music (polka, mazurka and schottische), *batuque* (the syncretised religion of Pará), *ciranda, caninha-verde*, and two tracks of Amerindian music.
Música Popular do Sul (Mapa Musical do Brasil, 1). Discos Marcus Pereira MP 10043; Música Popular Brasileira, no. 1
This CD, which includes creolised polka, mazurka and waltz, and several *gaúcho* songs, is perhaps most remarkable for the flawless accordion-playing of the elderly Moisé Mondadori, who first recorded in 1914, when he was 18 years old.
Musique du Nordeste, vol. 1: 1916–1945. Buda Musique 82960–2
Musique du Nordeste, vol. 2: 1928–1946. Buda Musique 82969–2
These two albums include 'Interrogando', a *jongo* played by João Pernambuco (João Teixeira Guimarães, 1883–1947) and Zezinho, guitars, and recorded in 1929; five recordings by Luiz Gonzaga from the 1941–45 period; several Recife *frevos* and carnival marches; and two of the brilliant *choros* of João Pernambuco.
Musique Folklorique du Monde: Brazil. Musidisque 30 CV 1383 (12in. LP)
Recorded by Maurice Bitter (date unstated), this disc includes a *baião*, an excerpt from a capoeira contest, two tracks of macumba music, three of carnival music, and four songs, two of them sung by children.
Olodum: Revolution in Motion. World Circuit WCD 031
A representative cross-section of the powerful drumming of Salvador's best-known *bloco afro*.
Pé de Serra Forró Band, Brazil. Haus der Kultūren der Welt/WERGO SM 1509–2 281509–2
Valuable disc of *forró* from the north-east, providing examples of all five sub-styles: *baião, xote, arrasta-pé, xaxado* and *forró* (a fast variant of *baião*). Exceptionally informative booklet, explaining in detail the drumming pattern used for each sub-style.
Raízes do Pelô. Braziloid BRD 4022
Another typical *bloco afro* in Salvador.
Reisado do Piauí. CDFB 19. Documentário Sonoro do Folclore Brasileiro no. 19 (7in. LP)

An excellent example of a tradition that came to Brazil from Portugal, its music being thoroughly Brazilianised in the process. *Reisados* are groups of musicians, singers and dancers who go from door to door between 24 December and 6 January, celebrating the Epiphany, i.e. announcing the coming of the Three Wise Men and the Messiah. The songs are accompanied by *viola* folk guitar, *rabeca* fiddle, banjo or *violão* guitar, *sanfona* accordion, *pandeiro* tambourine, *surdo* small conical drum and *reco-reco* notched scraper. *Reisados* are one of Brazil's most widespread traditional customs; this group was recorded in Teresina, Piauí.

Renato Borghetti. Somlivre (RBS) 402.0047 (12in. LP)
Typical village dance music from the far south of Brazil, played on the accordion.

Samba: Batuque – Partido Alto – Samba-canção 1917–1947. Frémeaux & Associés FA 159 (2 CDs)
Superb compilation of 38 recordings from the golden age of samba, including: three songs by the black singer Patrício Teixeira (1893–1972), 'Samba de Fato' (1932), 'Não Gosto dos Teos Modos' (1933) and 'No Tronco da Amendoeira'; five songs by Carmen Miranda, 'Canjiquinha Quente' (1937), 'Quantas Lagrimas' (1937), 'No Tabuleiro da Baiana' (1936), 'Gente Bamba' (1937) and 'Camisa Listrada' (1937); 'Pelo Telefone' (1917) by 'Donga' and Mauro de Almeida; Noel Rosa's 'Com que Roupa' (1930); and work by Sílvio Caldas (1908–98), Ciro Monteiro (1913–75), Mário Reis (b. 1926), Orlando Silva (b. 1915) and others.

Saudade em Samba: Brasil 1929–1942. Kardum 3004 084
Useful collection of 21 songs, including the famous two-part 'Aquerela do Brasil' (1939) by Ary Barroso (1903–64), sung by Francisco Alves; the delicious 'Alô Alô?' (1933) and three other Carmen Miranda songs; and 'Com que Roupa' (1933), sung by Noel Rosa.

Songs & Dances of Brazil. Folkways FW 6955 (10in.LP)
Recorded by Carlos Castaldi before 1957 at Mar Grande in Itaparica, the largest island in the bay that gives its name to Bahia, this is a disc of recreational music played on *cavaquinho* four-string plucked lute, guitar and tambourine. Several of the songs are *emboladas*, displaying great verbal dexterity.

Tempo de Bahia. Blue Moon BM 123 (12in. LP)
Collection of twelve songs by Salvador groups, recorded before 1990.

Ticumbi/ES. CDFB 029; Documentário Sonoro do Folclore Brasileiro no. 29 (7in. LP)
Dramatic dance accompanied by locally made traditional guitar with five double strings, twelve locally made tambourines, and the rhythmic clashing of steel swords during the war dance. Recorded in 1977.

Torém/Ceará. CDFB 030; Documentário Sonoro do Folclore Brasileiro no. 30 (7in. LP)
Recorded in 1975 by a group of descendants of Tremembé Amerindians from Almofala, Acaraú, in the state of Ceará.

Vieira e seu Conjunto: 'Lambada'. Sterns 2001 (12in. LP)
An engaging collection of early *lambada*, a north Brazilian dance which evolved from the *carimbó* dance of Pará, incorporating influences from the Caribbean, notably from the *merengue* of the Dominican Republic. Recorded before 1989.
Zabumba/SE. CDFB 031; Documentário Sonoro do Folclore Brasileiro no. 31 (7in. LP)
The Conjunto São João from Lagarto in Sergipe, recorded in 1977, is a flute-and-drum band, comprising two end-blown flutes, *zabumba* bass drum, two shakers, and triangle. They play *abrideira* (opening dance), two *marchas*, a *sambinha*, a *bendito* (i.e. a church song that has passed into the folk tradition) and an animal imitation: 'The Jaguar and the Puppy'.

Africa (including Cape Verde)

African Flutes. Folkways FE 4320 (12in. LP)
Recorded by Samuel Charters in the Gambia in 1976, this LP contains (side A) Fula music for two wooden four-hole flutes and shaker, and (side B) Serehule music for wooden four-hole flute and three drums of different sizes.
Cap Vert: Anthologie 1959–1992. Buda 92614–2 (2 CDs)
This ambitious attempt 'to tell the musical history of Cape Verde' from the beginning of professional recording in 1959 assembles 43 tracks of varying interest and merit. There are several examples of the archipelago's more familiar musical genres, as well as Conjunto Kola's 1976 'Tabanka' with Pericles Duarte on saxophone. There are five tracks by the popular group Os Tubarões and two by the inimitable Cesaria Évora, whose 'unforgettably deep, rich contralto voice and … silky smooth singing style' have made her the 'superstar of the Cape Verdean music industry'.[2]
Cap-Vert: Kodé di Dona. Ocora C 560100
Sixteen recordings, made in 1995, of songs by 'Kodé di Dona' (Grégorio Vaz, b. 1940), known as 'Father' of the *funana*, who accompanies his alllusive and elliptic singing on a diatonic accordion; his son plays the *ferrinho* angle-iron scraper.
Folk Music of Liberia. Folkways FE 4465 (12in. LP)
Recorded by Packard L. Okie before 1965, this disc includes a piece played by Pepa Kroma on a seven-string *gbegbetele* gourd-resonated pluriarc (compound bow-lute, here called a harp) with jingle attached.
Folk Music of the Western Congo. Folkways FE 4427 (12in. LP)
Recorded by Leo A. Verwilghen before 1953, in an area of Congo-Kinshasa just north of the Angola border, this disc includes recordings by Bapindi musicians of two different gourd-resonated lamellophones (here called sansas), with singing, and two examples of the Bapende resonator xylophone, one of which has 18 keys.

Iles du Cap-Vert – Les Racines. Playasound PS 65061
Recorded by Manuel Gomes in 1990, this CD includes a solo performance by 85-year-old Henrique on the *cimbó* one-string fiddle, by then rarely heard in the archipelago and now probably obsolete. There are also five *mornas*, three *coladeiras* and two recordings of the *festa do pilão*.

Juju Roots: 1930s–1950s. Rounder 5017 (12in. LP)
Compiled by Chris Waterman, this disc includes two tracks on which the *sámbà* drum is part of the ensemble: the Jolly Orchestra's 'Atari Ajanaku' (late 1930s), and 'Chief Ogunde' by Irewolede Denge and his Group (*c.* 1965).

Music and Musicians of the Angola Border: the Tshokwe. Lyrichord LLST 7311 (12in. LP)
Recorded by Dr Barbara and Wolfgang Schmidt-Wrenger in 1973–76, this important disc includes: solo performances by Yaf on the *ndjimba* 17-key resonator xylophone, accompanied by a gourd struck with a wooden stick; a xylophone duet in which Sakatanga Mwatshifi, who plays the *ndjimba* with one hand, shakes two *sangu* rattles with the other, and sings, while his son plays the *ndjimba kusaulwiya* 11-key resonator xylophone; two solos on the *tshisaji mutshapata* 17-key lamellophone by an unnamed musician from Angola ; and an example of the *kwita* friction drum, here accompanying the *Kalukuta* dance with two membrane drums (side A, track 5).

Music from Mozambique, vol. 3. Folkways FE 4319 (12in. LP)
Recorded by Ron Hallis and Gabriel Mondlane in 1982, this disc includes examples of the *shitendé* gourd-resonated musical bow and several xylophone performances, both solo and orchestral. One of the latter is a 20-minute performance by workers of the Maputo city sanitation department, whose xylophones have tin-can resonators.

Music from the Heart of Africa: Burundi. Nonesuch H 72057 (12in. LP)
The 11-key *ikembe* lamellophone is heard on three tracks, the *umuduli* gourd-resonated musical bow on five. This LP was recorded by Giuseppe Coter before 1975.

Music from Rwanda. Bärenreiter-Musicaphon BM 30 L 2302. Unesco-Collection – An Anthology of African Music, 2 (12in. LP)
The *munahi* musical bow of the Hutu is heard on one track, and the *likembe* lamellophone of the Hutu on another, of this LP recorded by Denyse Hiernaux-L'hoëst in 1954–55.

Music of the Dagomba from Ghana. Folkways FE 4324 (12in. LP)
Recorded by Verna Gillis and David Moisés Perez Martinez, *c.* 1978. On two tracks Yakubu Fuseni plays the *gingeli* (or *jinjelim*) gourd-resonated musical bow, accompanied by an empty soda bottle struck with a coin.

Music of the Kpelle of Liberia. Folkways FE 4385 (12in. LP)
Recorded by Verlon and Ruth Stone in 1970, this disc includes a song by Tokpa Peepee of Ponataa, playing the *gbegbetele* gourd-resonated pluriarc (compound bow-lute) with seven wire strings and with jingles attached. An empty beer bottle struck with a penknife provides an accompanying rhythm.

Musical Instruments 1. Strings. Kaleidophone KMA 1. The Music of Africa series (12in. LP)

Recorded by Hugh Tracey before 1973, this disc includes a song by Rosalina Ndhole and Juana Khosi, 'two elderly Swazi women' in Mataffin, South Africa, one of whom plays the *makeyana* (or *umakweyana*) single-string musical bow with gourd resonator.

Musical Instruments 2. Reeds (Mbira). Kaleidophone KMA 2. The Music of Africa series (12in. LP)

Recorded by Hugh Tracey before 1973, this disc provides examples of about 20 of over 100 different types of lamellophone known in Africa; six of these were played in the Kongo-Angola culture area.

Musical Instruments 5. Xylophones. Kaleidophone KMA 5. The Music of Africa series (12in. LP)

Recorded by Hugh Tracey before 1973, this disc includes dance music for two *marimba* resonator xylophones of the Kanyoka of south-east Congo-Kinshasa, one with 13 keys, the other with nine (as well as slit-drum, three membrane drums, and rattles); and a solo by Sandela Vilankulu on the *muhambi* treble xylophone of the Tswa of Mozambique.

Musique Bisa de Haute-Volta. Ocora OCR 58 (12in. LP)

The *dienguela* gourd-resonated musical bow of the Bisa (a people known also as Bussanga and Bussance) can be heard on one track. Two *kone* lamellophones, with five and six keys respectively, and each with a tin resonator containing seeds that rattle as the instrument is played, can be heard on another. These recordings were made by Charles Duvelle in 1961.

Musique de l'ancien royaume Kuba. Ocora OCR 61 (12in. LP)

Two songs accompanied by the *lakwemi* eight-string pluriarc (compound bow-lute) are on this LP, recorded by Benoit Quersin in 1970.

Musique du Burundi. Ocora OCR 40 (12in. LP)

Among these recordings made by Michel Vuylsteke in 1967 are a song by Bernard Kabanyegeye, accompanied by *umuduri* (or *umuduli*) gourd-resonated musical bow, and a song by Rtyazo, accompanied by *ikembe* 11-key lamellophone with a small wooden box resonator.

Musique Kongo. Ocora OCR 35 (12in. LP)

Recorded by Charles Duvelle in 1966, this disc has been described as 'the best recording of Bakongo music ever produced'.[3] It features a home-made zither (*kingwanda-ngwanda ia kikele*), constructed by three young Babembe boys and played with a tin can. Gabriel Bassoumba sings and accompanies himself on the *nsambi kizonzolo* five-string pluriarc (compound bow-lute), with raffia strings. The same musician sings and plays the *sanzi* lamellophone; the instrument has nine keys, on eight of which beads are threaded to serve as jingles.

Musiques Dahoméennes. Ocora OCR 17 (12in. LP)

This prize-winning disc includes Charles Duvelle's 1963 recording of a Nago (Yoruba) *Sakara* orchestra, one of whose instruments is the *agidigbo* five-key lamellophone with large wooden resonator and metal jingles.

Musiques du Gabon. Ocora OCR 41 (12in. LP)
Recorded by Michel Vuylsteke in 1967. Mounguengui di Doungou sings and accompanies himself on the five-string *nsambi* pluriarc (compound bow-lute), while several men strike with sticks a small wooden beam placed on the ground.
Sanza and Guitar: Music of the Bena Luluwa of Angola and Zaire. Lyrichord LLST 7313 (12in. LP)
Recorded by Dr Barbara and Wolfgang Schmidt-Wrenger in 1973–76, this disc is noteworthy for five remarkable performances by a lamellophone orchestra: four or five players of the gourd-resonated *issanji*, accompanied on two tracks by rattle and sticks used as clappers.
The Soul of Cape Verde. Tropical Music 68.978
Mostly *mornas* and *coladeiras* charmingly and often movingly sung and played by some of Cape Verde's leading musicians, among them Cesaria Évora, Bana and Titina. Of special interest for comparison with the Brazilian *lundu* is a '*lundum*' by Celina Pereira and Paulino Vieira.

Other areas

Les Açores/The Azores. Silex/Audivis YA 225710
Includes 15 minutes of Azores challenge singing (sung by Manuel de Sousa and Agostinho Guiomar, accompanied by Artur da Costa, *guitarra* long-necked lute with six double courses of metal strings, and João Botelho, guitar), recorded by Xavier Yerles on the island of São Miguel in 1994.
Afro-American Folk Music from Tate and Panola Counties, Mississippi. Library of Congress AFS L67 (12in. LP)
Largely recorded by David and Cheryl Evans in 1970–71, this LP includes a recording of a bow diddley (home-made zither, also called diddley bow and jitterbug) played by Compton Jones, who changes pitch by pressing or sliding a bottle on the string.
Ercília Costa with Armandinho. Heritage HT CD 32; Fado's Archives, vol. VI
Track 19 is an example of Portuguese verbal-contest singing: 'A Desgarrada', sung by Ercília Costa (1902–86) and António Menano (1895–1969), accompanied by Armandinho (Salgado Armando Freire, 1891–1946), *guitarra* long-necked lute with six double courses of metal strings, and João Fernandes, *guitarra*. This was recorded in 1930, probably in Madrid.
Musical Traditions of Portugal. Smithsonian/Folkways CD SF 40435; Traditional Music of the World, 9
Recorded by Max Peter Baumann and Tiago de Oliveira Pinto, this CD contains four women's songs accompanied by *adufe* square frame drums and three dances with accompaniment on bagpipes (*gaita-de-foles*) and drums.
The Music of Puerto Rico. Harlequin HQ CD 22
Compiled by Dick Spottswood, this CD includes an example of *controversia*: 'Un Jibaro en Nueva York', sung by Chuito (Jesús Rodríguez Erazo) and

Ernestina Reyes, accompanied by the Conjunto Tipico Ladi, recorded in 1947 in San Juan, Puerto Rico.

Negro Folk Music of Alabama, vol. 6: Game Songs and Others. Folkways FE 4474 (12in. LP)

Recorded by Harold Courlander in 1950, this includes a song to the water boy, 'Water on the Wheel', sung by Mrs Annie Grace Horn Dodson of Sumter County, Alabama, aged about 59, the daughter of a former slave.

Trinidad Loves to Play Carnival: Carnival, Calenda and Calypso from Trinidad 1914–1939. Matchbox MBCD 302–2

Compiled by John H. Cowley, this includes two *picongs,* or verbal-contest songs, both titled 'War'. One is sung by King Radio (Norman Span), The Tiger (Neville Marcano) and The Lion (Hubert Raphael Charles, afterwards Rafael de Leon), accompanied by Gerald Clark and his Caribbean Serenaders, recorded in New York in 1936. The other is sung by The Atilla (Raymond Quevedo), The Lion, The Executor (Philip Garcia) and The Caresser (Rufus Callender), with the same accompaniment, recorded in New York in 1937.

Notes

Unless otherwise stated, place of publication is London or, where the publisher is a British university press, the appropriate university city.

The following abbreviations are used in the Notes:

DFB   Luís da Câmara Cascudo, *Dicionário do folclore brasileiro*, 4th edn (São Paulo, Melhoramentos; [Brasilia], Instituto Nacional do Livro; 1979).

DMB   Mário de Andrade, *Dicionário musical brasileiro*, ed. by Oneyda Alvarenga and Flávia Camargo Toni (Belo Horizonte, Itatiaia; [Brasília], Ministério da Cultura; São Paulo, Universidade de São Paulo; 1989; Coleção Reconquista do Brasil, 2ª série, vol. 162).

EMB   *Enciclopédia da música brasileira: erudita folclórica popular*, ed. by Marcos Antônio Marcondes (São Paulo, Art, 1977).

HMB   Renato Almeida, *História da Música Brasileira*, 2nd edn (Rio de Janeiro, F. Briguiet, 1942).

MPB   Oneyda Alvarenga, *Música Popular Brasileira*, 2nd edn (São Paulo, Duas Cidades, 1982).

Introduction

1. In the state of Paraná challenge singing is also called *porfia* ('debate'), elsewhere, *cantoria* ('singing') and *peleja* ('battle').

2. An example can be heard on **Ercília Costa with Armandinho**, track 19 (for details of this and other albums, see Discography, pp. 178–90). For challenge singing in Portugal, see [João] Pinto de Carvalho (Tinop), *História do fado* (Lisbon, Empreza da Historia de Portugal, 1903), p. 80; Alberto Pimentel, *As alegres canções do Norte*, 2nd edn (Lisbon, Gomes de Carvalho, 1907), pp. 127–31; João do Rio [i.e. Paulo Barreto], *Fados, Canções e Dansas de Portugal* (Rio de Janeiro & Paris, H. Garnier, [1909]), p. 20; Paul Descamps, *Le Portugal: La Vie sociale actuelle* (Paris, Firmin-Didot, 1935), p. 86.

3. An example of challenge singing recorded in the Azores can be heard on **Les Açores/The Azores**, track 5. The Portuguese colonised Madeira in 1420, the Azores in 1437, and the Cape Verde islands in 1456. For the influence on traditional Madeira music and dance of the presence of African slaves, and of Madeira's links with the Canary Islands, North Africa and the West African coast, see Alberto Vieira, *Os escravos no arquipélago da Madeira: séculos xv a*

191

xvii (Funchal, Centro de Estudos de História do Atlântico, 1991), pp. 221–2, 226. For the music of Cape Verde, see Appendix D.

4. Earl W. Thomas, 'Folklore in Brazilian literature', in *Brazil: papers presented in the Institute for Brazilian Studies Vanderbilt University* (Nashville, Tenn., Vanderbilt University Press, 1953), p. 100; Luis da Camara Cascudo, *Vaqueiros e cantadores* (Belo Horizonte, Itataia; São Paulo, Universidade de São Paulo; 1984; Coleção Reconquista do Brasil, nova série, vol. 81), pp. 177–9. For examples of such debates, see *Medieval Debate Poetry: Vernacular Works*, ed. and trans. by Michel-André Bossy (New York and London, Garland, 1987; Garland Library of Medieval Literature, Ser. A, vol. 52).

5. Norman Daniel, *The Arabs and Mediaeval Europe*, 2nd ed. (London and New York, Longman; [Beirut], Librairie du Liban; 1979), p. 103; cf. also A. R. Nykl, 'L'Influence arabe-andalouse sur les troubadours', *Bulletin hispanique*, XLI (1939), pp. 305–15; Ramón Menéndez Pidal, *Poesía árabe y poesía europea: con otros estudios de literatura medieval* (Buenos Aires, Espasa-Calpe Argentina, 1941), pp. 13–67; Gustave Cohen, 'Le Problème des origines arabes de la poésie provençale médiévale', *Bulletin de la classe des lettres et des sciences morales et politiques* (Académie royale de Belgique), 5ᵉ sér., XXXII (1946), pp. 266–78; Gustave Cohen, *La Vie littéraire en France au moyen-âge* (Paris, Jules Tallandier, 1948), pp. 64–9; É. Lévi-Provençal, *Islam d'Occident: Études d'histoire médiévale* (Paris, G. P. Maisonneuve, 1948; Islam d'hier et d'aujourd'hui, vol. VII), pp. 285–304.

6. J. B. Trend, *The music of Spanish history* (Oxford University Press, 1926; Hispanic Notes & Monographs, X), p. 30.

7. H. G. Farmer, 'Music', in *The Legacy of Islam*, ed. by Sir Thomas Arnold and Alfred Guillaume (Oxford, Clarendon Press, 1931), p. 373; J. B. Trend, 'Spain and Portugal', in *The Legacy of Islam*, p. 17; Lois Ibsen al Faruqi, *An Annotated Glossary of Arabic Musical Terms* (Westport, Conn., and London, Greenwood Press, 1981), p. 357.

8. See Ewald Wagner, *Die arabische Rangstreitdichtung und ihre Einordnung in die allgemeine Literaturgeschichte* (Wiesbaden, Verlag der Akademie der Wissenschaften und der Literatur in Mainz; Abhandlungen der Geistes- und Sozialwissenschaftlichen Klasse, Jahrg. 1962, Nr. 8). Henri Pérès, *La Poésie andalouse en arabe classique au xie siècle: ses aspects généraux et sa valeur documentaire* (Paris, Adrien-Maisonnneuve, 1937; Publications de l'Institut d'études orientales, Faculté des lettres d'Algers, V) calls attention to the existence in eleventh-century Moslem Spain of 'a copious literature in prose and verse where a debate takes place between two flowers' (p. 183), and of debates on love resembling the 'courts of love' that flourished later in France (p. 423).

9. Cf. Nicolas J. Debbané, 'Au Brésil: L'influence arabe dans la formation historique, la littérature et la civilisation du peuple brésilien', *Bulletin de la Société khédiviale de géographie* (Cairo), VII série, no. 10 (1911), pp. 673–4. The Portuguese poet and statesman Teófilo Braga (1843–1924) seems to have been the first to suggest that Portugal owes its challenge singing to the Arabs; see Luis da Camara Cascudo, *Literatura oral no Brasil*, 2nd edn (Rio de Janeiro, Livraria José Olympio, 1978; Coleção Documentos Brasileiros, 186), pp. 358–9. For the effects of Moslem civilisation on Portugal and its influence

in Brazil, see: J. B. Trend, *Portugal* (Ernest Benn, 1957), pp. 42–56; Gilberto Freyre, *Casa-Grande e Senzala: Formação da Família Brasileira sob a Regime de Economia Patriarcal*, 5th edn (Rio de Janeiro and São Paulo, José Olympio, 1946; Coleção Documentos Brasileiros, 36), I, pp. 389–96; Gilberto Freyre, *The Masters and the Slaves: A Study in the Development of Brazilian Civilization*, trans. by Samuel Putnam (New York, Alfred A. Knopf, 1946), pp. 208–29.

10. Frederico de Freitas, 'O fado, canção da cidade de Lisbon; suas origens e evolução', in *Colóquio sobre música popular portuguesa: Comunicações e conclusões* ([Lisbon], Instituto Nacional para Aproveitamento dos Tempos Livres dos Trabalhadores, 1984), p. 9.

11. John Storm Roberts, *Black Music of Two Worlds* (Allen Lane, 1973), p. 81–2.

12. To be heard on **Musical Traditions of Portugal**, tracks 7–10. For the *adufe* in Portugal, see Ernesto Veiga de Oliveira, *Instrumentos musicais populares portugueses* (Lisbon, Fundação Calouste Gulbenkian, 1982), pp. 395–7 and figs. 62–75, 88, 278–84. It was introduced into the Iberian peninsula between the eighth and twelfth centuries. Played mainly by women and accompanying 'some of the most archaic songs known in the whole country', it is the most important popular instrument in Beira Baixa (Oliveira, *Instrumentos musicais populares portugueses*, p. 396).

13. Cf. William W. Megenney, *A Bahian heritage: An Ethnolinguistic Study of African Influences on Bahian Portuguese* (Chapel Hill, U.N.C. Department of Romance Languages, 1978; North Carolina Studies in the Romance Languages and Literatures, no. 198), p. 167. Debbané writes ('Au Brésil: L'influence arabe dans la formation historique, la littérature et la civilisation du peuple brésilien', p. 704): 'Brazil was colonised just at the end of Arab rule, so that those first settlers were still entirely imbued with, entirely steeped in, that oriental civilisation which they carried with them to the other side of the Atlantic.'

14. In 1551 the population of Lisbon was estimated at 100,000, of whom 9,950 were African slaves ([A. Braamcamp Freire], 'Povoação da Estremadura no XVI. século', *Archivo Historico Portuguez*, VI, 1908, p. 242). For the history of Portugal's black community, see A. C. de C. M. Saunders, *A social history of black slaves and freedmen in Portugal 1441–1555* (Cambridge University Press, 1982), and José Ramos Tinhorão, *Os Negros em Portugal: Uma presença silenciosa* (Lisbon, Caminho, 1988; Colecção Universitária, no. 31).

15. [Maria de Abreu] Caetano Beirão, *D. Maria I 1777–1792: Subsídios para a revisão da história do seu reinado*, 3rd edn (Lisbon, Emprêsa Nacional de Publicidade, 1944), p. 267. Lisbon's total population numbered *c.* 250,000 on the eve of the 1755 earthquake (José-Augusto França, *Lisboa Pombalina e o illuminismo*, 2nd edn, Lisbon, Bertrand, 1977, p. 20).

16. Roger D. Abrahams, 'Joking: the training of the man of words in talking broad', in *Rappin' and stylin' out: Communication in urban black America*, ed. by Thomas Kochman (Urbana, University of Illinois Press, 1972), pp. 216–17. For the so-called '*moqueries de villages*' of the Dogon, see: M. Griaule, 'L'Alliance cathartique', *Africa*, XVIII/4 (October 1948), pp. 242–58; C. Calame-Griaule, 'Les "Moqueries de villages" au Soudan français', *Notes africaines*, no. 61 (janvier 1954), pp. 12–15; Geneviève Calame-Griaule, *Ethnologie et langage: La parole chez les Dogon* (Paris, Gallimard, 1965), p. 257.

For abuse between age-mates among the Gogo, see Peter Rigby, 'Joking relationships, kin categories, and clanship among the Gogo', *Africa*, XXXVIII/2 (April 1968), p. 150.

17. B. Sinedzi Gadzekpo, 'Making music in Eweland', *West African Review*, XXIII/299 (August 1952), p. 819; Philip Gbeho, 'Music of the Gold Coast', *African Music*, I/1 (1954), p. 62. Camara Cascudo, *Vaqueiros e cantadores*, p. 182, makes the puzzling assertions that there is no African equivalent to the challenge singing of the Brazilian *sertão* and that there is no syncopation in the latter. Elsewhere, more puzzlingly still, he claims that 'challenge singing in Africa is an Arab extension [*projeção*]' (*DFB*, s.v. Desafio, p. 288).

18. An amusing example of *controversia* from Puerto Rico can be heard on **The Music of Puerto Rico**, track 23.

19. For the calypso 'wars' (*picongs*) of Trinidad, a 'now virtually defunct form of singing', see the booklet by John Cowley accompanying **Trinidad Loves to Play Carnival: Carnival, Calenda and Calypso from Trinidad 1914–1939**, and hear tracks 21 and 22 of that CD. See also: Errol Hill, *The Trinidad Carnival: mandate for a national theatre* (Austin, Tex. and London, University of Texas Press, 1972), pp. 76–8; and John Cowley, *Carnival, Canboulay and Calypso: Traditions in the Making* (Cambridge University Press, 1996), pp. 137, 175, 177, 178, 182.

20. For the African-American tradition of 'playing the dozens', see Abrahams, 'Joking', p. 217, and Roger Abrahams, 'Playing the Dozens', *Journal of American Folklore*, LXXV (1962), pp. 209–20, reprinted in *Mother wit from the laughing barrel: Readings in the Interpretation of Afro-American Folklore*, ed. by Alan Dundes (Englewood Cliffs, N.J., Prentice-Hall, 1973), pp. 295–309.

21. Heinrich Friedrich Link, *Bemerkungen auf einer Reise durch Frankreich, Spanien, und vorzüglich Portugal* (Kiel, neuen Academischen Buchhandlung, 1801–04), I, p. 217; Henry Frederick Link, *Travels in Portugal, and through France and Spain*, trans. by John Hinckley (T. N. Longman and O. Rees, 1801), pp. 203–4.

22. Júlio Dantas, *Os galos de Apollo*, 2nd edn (Lisbon, Portugal-Brasil, [c. 1928]), p. 93.

23. Mary C. Karasch, *Slave Life in Rio de Janeiro 1808–1850* (Princeton, N.J., Princeton University Press, 1987), p. 244.

24. Robert Stevenson, 'Some Portuguese sources for early Brazilian music history', *Yearbook*, Inter-American Institute for Musical Research, IV (1968), p. 21.

25. Frederico de Freitas, 'Lundum', *Enciclopédia Luso-Brasileira de Cultura* (Lisbon, Verbo, 1963–76), XII, p. 743; Freitas, 'O fado, canção da cidade de Lisbon; suas origens e evolução', p. 15.

26. Joanne B. and Ronald C. Purcell, 'Portugal, II. Folk music', in *The New Grove Dictionary of Music and Musicians*, ed. by Stanley Sadie (Macmillan, 1980), XV, p. 146.

27. Pedro Jaime Martelo (1665–1727), professor of literature at the University of Bologna.

28. Manuel Diégues Júnior, 'A poesia dos cantadores do Nordeste', in *Estudos e ensaios folclóricos em homenagem a Renato Almeida* (Rio de Janeiro, Ministério das Relações Exteriores, 1960), p. 635.

29. These formulas are set out in tabular form in *EMB*, s.v. desafio, I, p. 230. Gustavo Barroso, *Ao Som da Viola*, revised edn (Rio de Janeiro, Departamento

de Imprensa Nacional, 1949 [1950]) ,p. 467, conflates these styles into three: *ligeira*, *martelo*, and *natural*.

30. For the Portuguese *viola*, see Oliveira, *Instrumentos musicais populares portugueses*, pp. 182–200. For the *rabāb*, introduced into the Iberian peninsula in the eighth century, and its successor the *rabeca*, see Oliveira, *Instrumentos musicais populares portugueses*, pp. 224–6. For the *rabeca* in Brazil, see John Murphy, 'The Rabeca and Its Music, Old and New, in Pernambuco, Brazil', *Latin American Music Review*, XVIII/2 (Fall/Winter 1997), pp. 147–72.

31. Diégues Júnior, 'A poesia dos cantadores do Nordeste', p. 626; Faruqi, *An Annotated Glossary of Arabic Musical Terms*, p. 29. For the *pandeiro* in Portugal, see Oliveira, *Instrumentos musicais populares portugueses*, pp. 393–406.

32. *HMB*, pp. 113–14. Recordings of Brazilian challenge singing – *quadra*, *martelo agalopado*, *galope a beira-mar* and *quadrão* – can be heard on **Música Popular do Nordeste**, tracks 1–3. For Brazilian challenge singing see also: Leonardo Motta, *Sertão alegre (Poesia e linguagem do sertão nordestino)* (Belo Horizonte, Imprensa Official de Minas, 1928), pp. 214–17; *HMB*, pp. 90–9; Euclydes da Cunha, *Os Sertões (Campanha de canudos)*, 20th edn (Rio de Janeiro, Francisco Alves, 1946), p. 131; Barroso, *Ao Som da Viola*, pp. 467–82; Yvonne de Athayde Grubenmann, 'Música popular brasileira: a cantoria, uma arte com origens medievais', in *V Colóquio Internacional de Estudos Luso-Brasileiros, Coimbra – 1963: Actas* (Coimbra, 1964–68), IV, pp. 487–93; Leonardo Mota, *Cantadores*, 4th edn (Rio de Janeiro, Cátedra, 1976); Camara Cascudo, *Literatura oral no Brasil*, pp. 358–64; *DFB*, s.v. Desafio, pp. 287–8; *MPB*, pp. 297–306; Camara Cascudo, *Vaqueiros e cantadores*, pp. 172–232; *DMB*, s.v. Desafio, pp. 186–90.

33. Thomé de Sousa (d. after 1573), who founded Salvador in 1549. Properly called São Salvador da Bahia de Todos os Santos (St Salvador on All-Saints' Bay), this was the colony's capital and chief cultural centre until 1763.

34. A. J. R. Russell-Wood, 'Black and Mulatto Brotherhoods in Colonial Brazil: A Study in Collective Behaviour', *Hispanic American Historical Review*, LIV/4 (November 1974), p. 576 n. 15. Robert Edgar Conrad, *World of Sorrow: The Atlantic Slave Trade to Brazil* (Baton Rouge and London, Louisiana State University Press, 1986), p. 192, suggests an even earlier date: 1525.

35. Cf. A. J. R. Russell-Wood, *The Black Man in Slavery and Freedom in Colonial Brazil* (Macmillan, 1982), p. 3.

36. Pierre Verger, *Bahia and the West African trade 1549–1851* (Ibadan University Press for the Institute of African Studies, 1964), p. 3.

37. Melville J. Herskovits, *The myth of the Negro past* (New York and London, Harper & Brothers, 1941), p. 50, says the Brazilian records were 'burned to wipe out every trace of slavery when the Negroes were emancipated in that country', and that indeed was the declared object of Rui de Oliveira Barbosa (1849–1923), Minister of the Treasury, in his decree on the matter dated 14 December 1890 ('the Republic is compelled to destroy these vestiges for the honour of the Fatherland'); the full text of the decree is given in Francelino S. Piauí, *O Negro na Cultura Brasileira* (Campinas, São Paulo, 1974; Publicações da Academia Campinnense de Letras, no. 27), p. 8. Piauí comments that, however noble Barbosa's motive, the burning of the records has caused

historians 'huge confusion and terrible difficulties'. But the recent spate of research on slavery in Brazil makes it clear that by no means all the records were destroyed.

38. Conrad, *World of Sorrow*, p. 17.

39. Cf. George Reid Andrews, *Blacks & Whites in São Paulo, Brazil 1888–1988* (Madison and London, University of Wisconsin Press, 1991), p. 3.

40. Frédéric Mauro, *Le Portugal et l'Atlantique au xviie siècle (1570–1670): Étude économique* ([Paris], S.E.V.P.E.N., 1960; École Pratique des Hautes Études, VIe section: Centre de Recherches Historiques, Ports – Routes – Trafics, X), p. 173: a black man of between 15 and 25 years of age was valued as one 'piece'. Cf. C. R. Boxer, *Salvador de Sá and the Struggle for Brazil and Angola 1602–1686* (Athlone Press, 1952), p. 231.

41. Visconde de Paiva Manso, *Historia do Congo: obra posthuma (Documentos)* (Lisbon, Typografia da Academia, 1877), p. 287, citing António de Oliveira Cadornega, *Historia geral Angolana* (1680–81), III, p. 221. Boxer, *Salvador de Sá and the Struggle for Brazil and Angola*, p. 231, translates *tumbeiros* as 'undertakers'.

42. Philip D. Curtin, *The Atlantic Slave Trade: A Census* (Madison, Milwaukee, Wis. and London, University of Milwaukee Press, 1969), p. 49. Most modern historians accept this figure or one very close to it; see Mesquitela Lima, 'Da importância dos estudos bantos para a compreensão da problemática socio-cultural brasileira', in *V Colóquio Internacional de Estudos Luso-Brasileiros*, I, p. 346.

43. Conrad, *World of Sorrow*, p. 192 (and cf. p. 34).

44. By the author of *Diálogo das grandezas do Brasil*, as quoted by Conrad, *World of Sorrow*, p. 28. For 'Guinea' as a geographical designation, see Joseph E. Holloway, 'The Origins of African-American Culture', in *Africanisms in American Culture*, ed. by J. E. Holloway (Bloomington and Indianapolis, Indiana University Press, 1990), p. 2.

45. [Amédée François] Frezier, *Relation du voyage de la Mer du Sud aux côtes du Chily et du Perou, Fait pendant les années 1712, 1713, & 1714* (Paris, Jean-Geoffroy Nyon, 1716), p. 275; Frezier, *A voyage to the South-Sea and along the coasts of Chili and Peru* (Jonah Bowyer, 1717), p. 301.

46. Robert Southey, *History of Brazil* (Longman, Hurst, Rees, and Orme, 1810–19), II, p. 674.

47. James Lockhart and Stuart B. Schwartz, *Early Latin America: A History of Colonial Spanish America and Brazil* (Cambridge University Press, 1983; Cambridge Latin American Studies, 46), p. 372.

48. J. M. Pereira da Silva, *História da fundação do imperio brazileiro* (Rio de Janeiro and Paris, Garnier, 1864–68), IV, p. 261, commenting that these figures 'cannot be accepted as wholly accurate'. Adrien Balbi, *Essai statistique sur le royaume de Portugal et d'Algarve, comparé aux autres états de l'Europe* (Paris, Rey & Gravier, 1822), II, p. 229, using the same source, gives the total population of Brazil as 3,617,900, apparently because he omits the province of Cisplatina (Uruguay), which became part of Brazil in 1821 and declared its independence in 1825.

49 Clóvis Moura, 'Influência da escrivadão negra na estrutura e comportamento da sociedade brasileira', *Estudos afro-asiáticos*, nos 6–7 (1982), p. 249.

50. Clarke Abel, *Narrative of a journey in the interior of China, and of a voyage to and from that country, in the years 1816 and 1817* (Longman, Hurst, Reese, Orme & Brown, 1818), p. 15.

51. Otto von Kotzebue, *A new voyage round the world, in the years 1823, 24, 25, and 26* (Henry Colburn and Richard Bentley, 1830), I, p. 44.

52. Karasch, *Slave Life in Rio de Janeiro 1808–1850*, p. xxi and Table 3.6, p. 66 (this was the peak figure for slavery in Rio de Janeiro); Mary Karasch, 'From Porterage to Proprietorship: African Occupations in Rio de Janeiro, 1808–1850', in *Race and Slavery in the Western Hemisphere: Quantitative Studies*, ed. by Stanley L. Engerman and Eugene D. Genovese (Princeton, Princeton University Press, 1975), p. 376. Karasch's figures are derived from the 1849 census, 'the most accurate of any Rio census of the first half of the nineteenth century' (Karasch, 'From Porterage to Proprietorship', p. 373).

53. C. B. Mansfield, *Paraguay, Brazil, and the Plate: Letters written in 1852–1853* (Cambridge, Macmillan, 1861), p. 29. Mansfield gives the population of Recife as 70,000, a third of whom were slaves and a third free blacks (p. 74).

54. R. K. Kent, 'African Revolt in Bahia: 24–25 January 1835', *Journal of Social History*, III/4 (Summer 1970), p. 335.

55. Leslie Bethell, *The abolition of the Brazilian slave trade: Britain, Brazil and the slave trade question 1807–1869* (Cambridge University Press, 1970; Cambridge Latin American Studies, 6), p. xi.

56. Conrad, *World of Sorrow*, p. 179.

57. Robert Conrad, *The Destruction of Brazilian Slavery 1850–1888* (Berkeley, University of California Press, 1972).

58. Cf. Melville J. Herskovits, 'The southernmost outposts of New World Africanisms', *American Anthropologist*, n.s. XLV (1943), p. 496, reprinted in Melville J. Herskovits, *The New World Negro: selected papers in Afroamerican studies*, ed. by Frances S. Herskovits (Bloomington and London, Indiana University Press, 1966), p. 201.

59. Margaret Washington Creel, 'Gullah Attitudes toward Life and Death', in *Africanisms in American Culture*, ed. by Holloway, p. 92 n. 6.

60. Cf. José Jorge de Carvalho, 'Music of African Origin in Brazil', in *Africa in Latin America: Essays on History, Culture, and Socialization*, ed. by Manuel Moreno Fraginals, trans. by Leonor Blum (New York, Holmes & Meier; Paris, Unesco; 1984), pp. 227–8; Gerhard Kubik, *Extensionen afrikanischer Kulturen in Brasilien* (Aachen, Alano, Herodot., 1991; Forum, Bd. 13), p. 44. According to Herskovits, 'The southernmost outposts of New World Africanisms', p. 497, reprinted in Herskovits, *The New World Negro*, p. 201, 'whole villages of Negroes in the states of Rio de Janeiro and Espirito Santo were imported from Maranhão'.

61. Gerhard Kubik, *Angolan traits in black music, games and dances of Brazil: A study of African cultural extensions overseas* (Lisbon, Junta de Investigações Científicas do Ultramar, Centro de Estudos de Antropologia Cultural, 1979; Estudos de antropologia cultural, no. 10), p. 10. For the relative imprecision of terms distinguishing slaves by region or port of embarkation, see Daniel

C. Littlefield, *Rice and Slaves: Ethnicity and the Slave Trade in South Carolina* (Baton Rouge and London, Louisiana State University Press, 1981), pp. 22–3.

62. José Honório Rodrigues, *Brazil and Africa*, trans. by Richard A. Mazzara and Sam Hileman (Berkeley, Los Angeles, University of California Press, 1965), p. 41.

63. Roberts, *Black Music of Two Worlds*, p. 19.

64. Unattributed press comment, as quoted by Lisa Peppercorn, *Villa-Lobos*, ed. by Audrey Sampson (Omnibus Press, 1989), p. 85.

65. Ann Livermore, '[The arts in Brazil,] (iii) Music', in *Portugal and Brazil: an introduction*, ed. by H. V. Livermore (Oxford, Clarendon Press, 1953), pp. 396, 397, 400.

66. Emílio Willems, 'Portuguese Culture in Brazil', in *Proceedings of the International Colloquium on Luso-Brazilian Studies: Washington, October 15–20, 1950* (Nashville, Tenn., Vanderbilt University Press, 1953), p. 70; the quotation is from Rodney Gallop, *Portugal: A Book of Folk-ways* (Cambridge University Press, 1936), p. 167.

67. There is a copious literature on this. An invaluable recent work is John T. Schneider, *Dictionary of African Borrowings in Brazilian Portuguese* (Hamburg, Helmut Buske Verlag, 1991).

68. Freyre, *Casa-Grande e Senzala*, II, pp. 724–36; Freyre, *The Masters and the Slaves*, pp. 459–70. Attempts were made in the early nineteenth century to de-Africanise and re-Europeanise the Brazilian upper- and middle-class diet, to which end seventeen French cooks and ten French bakers were hired for service in Rio de Janeiro between 1808 and 1822; see Rodrigues, *Brazil and Africa*, p. 46.

69. J[oão]. Lúcio de Azevedo, *História de Antonio Vieira: com factos e documentos novos* (Lisbon, A. M. Teixeira, 1918–21), I, p. 408.

70. Octávio Tarquinio de Sousa, *Bernardo Pereira de Vasconcelos*, 2nd ed. (Rio de Janeiro, José Olympio, 1957; História dos Fundadores do Império do Brasil, V), p. 247.

71. José Honório Rodrigues, 'The influence of Africa on Brazil and of Brazil on Africa', *Journal of African History*, III/1 (1962), p. 56; there is a similar statement in Rodrigues, *Brazil and Africa*, p. 45.

72. For Mário de Andrade, see Vasco Mariz, *Três musicólogos Brasileiros: Mário de Andrade, Renato Almeida, Luiz Heitor Correa de Azevedo* (Rio de Janeiro, Civilização Brasileira; [Brasília], Instituto Nacional do Livro; 1983; Coleção Retratos do Brasil, vol. 169), pp. 17–90.

73. Kazadi wa Mukuna, '*Sotaques*: Style and Ethnicity in a Brazilian Folk Drama', in *Music and Black Ethnicity: The Caribbean and South America*, ed. by Gerard H. Béhague (Miami, North-South Center, University of Miami, 1994), p. 207.

74. Cf. Kubik, *Angolan traits in black music, games and dances of Brazil*, pp. 9–10.

75. Robert Farris Thompson, 'Kongo influences on African-American Artistic Culture', in *Africanisms in American Culture*, ed. by Holloway, p. 149.

76. Cf. George Brandon, 'Sacrificial Practices in Santeria, an African-Cuban Religion in the United States', in *Africanisms in American Culture*, ed. by Holloway, p. 119.

Chapter 1

1. José Jorge de Carvalho, 'Black Music of All Colors: The Construction of Black Ethnicity in Ritual and Popular Genres of Afro-Brazilian Music', in *Music and Black Ethnicity*, ed. by G. H. Béhague (Miami, 1994), p. 188.

2. Roger Bastide, 'The Present Status of Afro-American Research in Latin America', in *Slavery, Colonialism, and Racism*, ed. by Sidney W. Mintz (New York, W. W. Norton, 1974), p. 115.

3. David B. Welch, 'A Yoruba-Nagô "Melotype" for Religious Songs in the African Diaspora: Continuity of West African Praise Song in the New World', in *More than drumming: Essays on African and Afro-Latin American Music and Musicians*, ed. by Irene V. Jackson (Westport, Conn. and London, Greenwood Press, 1985; Contributions in Afro-American and African Studies, no. 80), p. 148; Paul V. A. Williams, *Primitive religion and healing: A study of folk medicine in North-East Brazil* (Cambridge, D. S. Brewer and Rowman & Littlefield for the Folklore Society, 1979), p. 18.

4. Edison Carneiro, 'Candomblés de Baía', *Revista do Arquivo Municipal* (São Paulo), ano 7, vol. LXXIV (julho-agosto 1942), p. 128. But there was 'a wide scatter around this average, since some temple groups were old and famous and wielded enormous influence, while others were new and unimportant' (Ruth Landes, 'Fetish worship in Brazil', *Journal of American Folk-lore*, LIII/210, October–December 1940, p. 268).

5. Cf. Roger Bastide, 'Le Batuque de Porto-Alegre', in *Acculturation in the Americas: Proceedings and Selected Papers of the XXIXth International Congress of Americanists*, ed. by Sol Tax (Chicago, University of Chicago Press, 1952), p. 205; Melville J. Herskovits, 'The social organization of the candomblé', in *Anais do XXXI Congresso Internacional de Americanistas*, ed. by Herbert Baldus (São Paulo, Anhembi, 1955), I, p. 509, reprinted in M. J. Herskovits, *The New World Negro*, ed. by F. S. Herskovits (Bloomington, 1966), p. 230.

6. Cf. Pierre Verger, 'Yoruba influences in Brazil', *Odù* (Ibadan), no. 1 (January 1955), pp. 5–6. Even as late as 1938, African-Brazilian religions were subjected to police persecution; see the booklet accompanying **The Discoteca Collection: Missão de Pesquisas Folclóricas**.

7. Roger Bastide, *Les Religions africaines au Brésil: vers une sociologie des inter-pénétrations de civilisations* (Paris, Presses Universitaires de France, 1960), pp. 225, 380; cf. Roger Bastide, *The African Religions of Brazil: Toward a Sociology of the Interpenetration of Civilizations*, trans. by Helen Sebba (Baltimore and London, Johns Hopkins University Press, 1978), pp. 162, 272.

8. This is also the case elsewhere in the western hemisphere; cf. Melville J. Herskovits, 'African gods and Catholic saints in New World Negro belief', *American Anthropologist*, n.s. XXXIX (1937), p. 635, reprinted in Herskovits, *The New World Negro*, pp. 321–2. For a table showing the correspondences, in Brazil, Cuba, and Haiti, between various Catholic saints and various African deities, see: Herskovits, 'African gods and Catholic saints', pp. 641–2, reprinted in Herskovits, *The New World Negro*, pp. 327–8. There are similar tables in Roger Bastide, *Les Amériques noires: les civilisations africaines dans le nouveau monde* (Paris, Payot, 1967), p. 163; in Roger Bastide, *African civilisations in the New World*, trans. by Peter Green (C. Hurst, 1971), pp. 157–8; and in Octavio

Ianni, 'Social Organization and Alienation', in *Africa in Latin America*, ed. by M. M. Fraginals (New York and Paris, 1984), p. 50. A more elaborate table of correspondences in Bahia, Recife, Alagoas, Porto Alegre, Rio de Janeiro, Pará, Maranhão, Cuba, and Haiti, appears in Bastide, *Les Religions africaines au Brésil*, pp. 366–71, and Bastide, *The African Religions of Brazil*, pp. 264–7. For more detailed information, see Waldemar Valente, *Sincretismo religioso afro-brasileiro*, 2nd edn (São Paulo, Nacional, 1976; Brasiliana, vol. 280), esp. pp. 98–106.

9. Cf. Bastide, *Les Religions africaines au Brésil*, p. 379; Bastide, *The African Religions of Brazil*, p. 272.

10. Antônio Geraldo da Cunha, *Dicionário etimológico Nova Fronteira da língua portuguesa* (Rio de Janeiro, Nova Fronteira, 1982), s.v. candombe, candomblé, p. 146.

11. For a brief introduction to the vast literature on *vodoun*, see George Eaton Simpson, *Black Religions in the New World* (New York, Columbia University Press, 1978), pp. 64–70.

12. For *Santería*, see Simpson, *Black Religions in the New World*, pp. 86–94, and G. Brandon, 'Sacrificial Practices in Santeria, an African-Cuban Religion in the United States', in *Africanisms in American Culture*, ed. by J. E. Holloway (Bloomington, Indiana, 1990), pp. 119–47.

13. For Shango, see Simpson, *Black Religions in the New World*, pp. 73–9. A form of Shango also exists in St Lucia, where it is called *kele*; see George Eaton Simpson, 'The Kele (Chango) cult in St. Lucia', *Caribbean Studies*, XIII/3 (October 1973), pp. 110–16, reprinted in a shortened form in Simpson, *Black Religions in the New World*, pp. 103–6, and in George Eaton Simpson, *Religious cults of the Caribbean: Trinidad, Jamaica and Haiti*, 3rd ed. (Rio Piedras, Institute of Caribbean Studies, University of Puerto Rico, 1980; Caribbean Monograph Series, no.15), pp. 313–19. There is also a form of Shango in Grenada; see Simpson, *Black Religions in the New World*, pp. 82–3.

14. 'Zacharias Wagner', [ed. by Paul Emil Richter,] in *Festschrift zur Jubelfeier des 25jährigen Bestehens des Vereins für Erdkunde zu Dresden* (Dresden, A. Huhle, 1888), p. 86. Wagner's 'Thier Buch', sometimes referred to as 'Zoobiblion', containing watercolours of Brazilian wildlife, people, scenes and maps, is in the Dresden Kupferstich-Kabinett. *Garapa*, Wagner's *'Grape'*, is a drink made from the juice of sugar cane. An African origin for the word is possible, but has not been established; cf. J. T. Schneider, *Dictionary of African Borrowings in Brazilian Portuguese* (Hamburg, 1991), s.v. garapa, pp. 154–5.

15. As J. A. Gonsalves de Mello Neto was the first to point out, in 'Dois relatórios holandeses', *Revista Arquivo Público* (Recife), IV/4 (1949), p. 623. Cf. René Ribeiro, *Cultos afro-brasileiros do Recife: Um estudo de ajustamento social*, 2nd edn (Recife, Instituto Joaquim Nabuco de Pesquisas Sociais, 1978; Série Estudos e Pesquisas, 7), p. 29.

16. José Jorge de Carvalho and Rita Laura Segato, *Shango Cult in Recife, Brazil* (Caracas, Fundación de Etnomusicología y Folklore, 1992), pp. 9, 45. For *Xangô*, see also Bastide, *Les Religions africaines au Brésil*, pp. 265–70; Bastide, *The African Religions of Brazil*, pp. 191–4; Simpson, *Black Religions in the New World*, pp. 190–2.

17. Bastide, *Les Religions africaines au Brésil*, pp. 254–65; Bastide, *The African Religions of Brazil*, pp.183–91; Simpson, *Black Religions in the New World*, pp.177–84. For *casa das minas*, see also Nunes Pereira, *A Casa das Minas: Contribucão ao Estudo das Sobrevivências do Culto dos Voduns, do Panteão Daomeano, no Estado do Maranhão, Brasil*, 2nd edn (Petrópolis, Vozes, 1979).

18. Simpson, *Black Religions in the New World*, pp. 195–203; booklet accompanying **Amazônia: Festival and Cult Music of Northern Brazil**. For a detailed account of *batuque* in Belém, by an anthropologist and a historian, see Seth and Ruth Leacock, *Spirits of the Deep: A Study of an Afro-Brazilian Cult* (Garden City, N.Y., Doubleday Natural History Press for The American Museum of Natural History, 1972).

19. Roger Bastide, 'Le Batuque de Porto-Alegre', pp. 196–7. According to Bastide (p.196) the minor poet Achylles Porto-Alegre (1848–1926) referred to the Rio Grande do Sul *batuque* 'in the time of the Empire' (i.e. between 1822 and 1889) as simultaneously entertainment, form of worship and funeral ceremony. See also, for *pará*, Bastide, *Les Religions africaines au Brésil*, pp. 254–65; Bastide, *The African Religions of Brazil*, pp. 183–91; Simpson, *Black Religions in the New World*, pp. 177–84; *As Religiões Afro-Brasileiros do Rio Grande do Sul*, ed. by Ari Pedro Oro (Pôrto Alegre, Ed. Universidade/UFRGS, 1994).

20. Bastide, *Les Religions africaines au Brésil*, p. 287; cf. Bastide, *The African Religions of Brazil*, p. 206. See also Simpson, *Black Religions in the New World*, pp. 203–4.

21. Duglas Teixeira Monteiro, 'A Macumba de Vitória', in *Anais do XXXI Congresso Internacional de Americanistas*, ed. by H. Baldus (São Paulo, 1955), I, p. 469. Exú is known as Legba or Elegba in Fon-derived rituals.

22. R. F. Thompson, 'Kongo Influences on African-American Artistic Culture', in *Africanisms in American Culture*, ed. by Holloway, p. 156.

23. Cf. G. Kubik, *Angolan traits in black music, games and dances of Brazil* (Lisbon, 1979), p. 25.

24. Thompson, 'Kongo Influences on African-American Artistic Culture', p. 157. For umbanda, see also: Renato Ortiz, 'Ogum and the Umbandista Religion', in *Africa's Ogun: Old world and new*, ed. by Sandra T. Barnes (Bloomington and Indianapolis, Indiana University Press, 1989), pp. 90–102; Robert Farris Thompson, *Flash of the spirit: African and Afro-American Art and Philosophy* (New York, Random House, 1983), pp. 96–197; Simpson, *Black Religions in the New World*, pp. 159–63.

25. The primary meaning of *caboclo* is 'civilised' Amerindian; the word is applied also to persons of mixed African (or European) and Amerindian ethnicity. For *candomblé de caboclo*, see Williams, pp. 18–20, 134–40; Edison Carneiro, *Religiões Negras: Notas de etnografia religiosa*, 2nd edn / *Negros Bantos: Notas de etnografia religiosa e de folclore*, 2nd edn (Rio de Janeiro, Civilização Brasileira; Brasília, Instituto Nacional do Livro; 1981; Retratos do Brasil, vol. 153), pp. 62–70, 133–6.

26. J. J. de Carvalho, 'Music of African Origin in Brazil', in *Africa in Latin America*, ed. by Fraginals, p. 232. For *catimbó* and *pagelança*, see Bastide, *Les Religions africaines au Brésil*, pp. 241–54, 303–5; cf. Bastide, *The African Religions of Brazil*, pp. 173–83, 218–19. For *pagelança* as a dance, see Octavio de Costa Eduardo, *The Negro in Northern Brazil: A Study in Acculturation* (New York, J. J. Augustin, 1948; Monographs of the American Ethnological Society, XV),

pp. 49, 102–4. Two *pagelança* songs recorded in Belém in 1938, when it was still 'a heavily Amerindian ritual', can be heard on **The Discoteca Collection: Missão de Pesquisas Folclóricas**, tracks 8 and 9.

27. J. J. de Carvalho, 'Music of African Origin in Brazil', p. 244.

28. *EMB*, s.v. tambor-de-crioulo, II, p. 740.

29. A still useful general study is Edison Carneiro, *Candomblés da Bahia* (Bahia, Secretaria da Educação e Saúde, 1948; Publicações do Museu do Estado, no. 8). The 6th edn (Rio de Janeiro, Civilização Brasileira, 1978; Retratos do Brasil, vol. 106) unfortunately omits illustrations and musical transcriptions. See also Roger Bastide, *Le* Candomblé *de Bahia (Rite Nagô)* (Paris and The Hague, Mouton, 1958; Le Monde d'outre-mer passé et présent, première série, Études, V).

30. According to Carneiro, 'Candomblés de Baía', p. 128, an unspecified Kongo language was still spoken in 1942 in 'the sole candomblé of that *nação* existing in Bahia'.

31. Cf. Edison Carneiro, *Ladinos e crioulos (Estudos sôbre o negro no Brasil)* (Rio de Janeiro, Editôra Civilização Brasileira, 1964; Retratos do Brasil, vol. 28), pp. 164–7; Zora A. O. Seljan, *Iemanjá e suas Lendas*, 2nd edn (Rio de Janeiro, Gráfica Record, 1967; Atlântica, no. 14), reissued as *Iemanjá Mãe dos Orixás* (São Paulo, Afro-Brasileira, 1973); Edison Carneiro, 'A Divindade Brasileira dos Águas', *Revista Brasileira de Folclore*, VIII/21 (maio/agôsto de 1968), pp. 143–54; and (a strongly Jungian account) Pedro Iwashita, *Maria e Iemanjá: Análise de um sincretismo* (São Paulo, Edicões Paulinas, 1991).

32. Cf. Gerard H. Béhague, 'Notes on Regional and National Trends in Afro-Brazilian Cult Music', in *Tradition and renewal: Essays on Twentieth-Century Latin-American Literature and Culture*, ed. by Merlin H. Foster (Urbana, University of Illinois Press, 1975; Center for Latin American and Caribbean Studies, no. 2), pp. 72–3.

33. According to J. J. de Carvalho, 'Music of African Origin in Brazil', p. 232, *atabaque* drums are no longer used in *caboclo* ceremonies.

34. By the 1970s this baptism ceremony was 'perhaps not as elaborate and precise as in the 1930s' (Béhague, 'Notes on Regional and National Trends', p. 77).

35. Thompson, *Flash of the spirit*, pp. 160, 162.

36. Cf. Herskovits, "Drums and drummers in Afro-Brazilian cult life', *Musical Quarterly*, XXX/4 (October 1944), p. 482, reprinted in Herskovits, *The New World Negro*, p. 188.

37. In Pernambuco both *agogô* and *aguê* are also known as *xere*. In Cuba the latter instrument is called *atcheré* (also spelt *acheré*), *chequeré*, *obwe*, and *güiro*; in Haiti, *asón* (also spelt *asson* and *açon*).

38. Sheila S. Walker, *Ceremonial spirit possession in Africa and Afro-America: Forms, meaning and functional significance for individuals and social groups* (Leiden, E. J. Brill, 1972; Supplementa ad Numen, altera series, vol. 4), pp. 18–21.

39. John Miller Chernoff, *African Rhythm and African Sensibility: Aesthetics and Social Action in African Musical Idioms* (Chicago and London, University of Chicago Press, 1979), p. 145 (emphasis added).

40. Melville J. Herskovits, 'Drums and drummers', p. 477, reprinted in Herskovits, *The New World Negro*, p. 184.

41. **Afro-Brazilian Religious Songs**. Hear also the drumming for Exú and Ogun on **Afro-American Drums**, side B, tracks 19 and 20.

42. Cf. Béhague, 'Notes on Regional and National Trends', p. 78.

43. Cf. Welch, 'A Yoruba-Nagô "Melotype" for Religious Songs in the African Diaspora', p. 152.

44. Béhague, 'Notes on Regional and National Trends', p. 78.

45. Alan P. Merriam, 'Songs of the Ketu cult of Bahia, Brazil', *African Music*, I/3 (1956), pp. 53–67. A recent thorough study of the music of the Nagô tradition is Angela Lühning, *Die Musik in candomblé nagô-ketu* (Hamburg, Verlag der Musikalienhandlung Karl Dieter Wagner; Studien zur afrobrasilianischen Musik in Salvador, Bahia, Teil 1; Beiträge zur Ethnomusikogie, Bd. 24).

46. Béhague, 'Notes on Regional and National Trends', p. 75.

47. M. J. Herskovits and R. A. Waterman, 'Musica de culto afrobahiana', trans. by Francisco Curt Lange, *Revista de Estudios Musicales*, I/2 (diciembre 1947), p. 126. Jeff Todd Titon, *Early Downhome Blues: A Musical and Cultural Analysis* (Urbana, University of Illinois Press, 1977), pp. 155–6 n. 12, prefers not to use the term 'blue notes' but refers to a 'complex', containing 'the major, the minor, and a distinct pitch approximately halfway between them, sometimes closer to one, sometimes to the other, depending on its position in the phrase and the pitch that precedes it': in other words, the 'blue third' occurs in vocal blues 'not only as a single slur, but also in a variable sequence of pitch gradations', corresponding individually to each newly sung syllable, 'with slurs between the variations'. Several candomblé songs are transcribed by Gisèle Binon, 'La Musique dans le candomblé', in *La Musique dans la vie*, ed. by Tolia Nikiprowetzky (Paris, Office de Coopération Radiophonique, 1967), pp. 159–207.

48. Carvalho and Segato, *Shango Cult in Recife*, pp. 9, 37.

49. **The Discoteca Collection: Missão de Pesquisas Folclóricas**, track 1.

50. **L. H. Corrêa de Azevedo: Music of Ceará and Minas Gerais**, tracks 9–12.

51. **Amazônia: Festival and Cult Music of Northern Brazil**, tracks 2, 6, 9, 11.

52. **The Discoteca Collection: Missão de Pesquisas Folclóricas**, track 7.

53. Bastide, *Les Religions africaines au Brésil*, pp. 263–5 ; cf. Bastide, *The African Religions of Brazil*, pp. 190–1.

54. **The Discoteca Collection: Missão de Pesquisas Folclóricas**, tracks 2–6.

55. Bastide, 'Le Batuque de Porto-Alegre', p. 202.

56. Melville J. Herskovits, 'The southernmost outposts of New World Africanisms', *American Anthropologist*, n.s. XLV (1943), pp. 505–6, 496, reprinted in Herskovits, *The New World Negro*, pp. 210, 201.

57. Examples of macumba music recorded in or near Rio de Janeiro can be heard on **Fantastique Brésil**, side A, tracks 4–6, and **Musique Folklorique du Monde: Brazil**, side B, tracks 5 and 6.

58. J. J. de Carvalho, 'Music of African Origin in Brazil', p. 233; Béhague, 'Notes on Regional and National Trends', p. 76.

59. **Amazônia: Festival and Cult Music of Northern Brazil**, track 5.

60. Béhague, 'Notes on Regional and National Trends', pp. 75, 74.

61. Thompson, *Flash of the Spirit*, p. 96.

62. Kazadi wa Mukuna, '*Sotaques*: Style and Ethnicity in a Brazilian Folk Drama', in *Music and Black Ethnicity*, ed. by G. H. Béhague, p. 221.

63. John Charles Chasteen, 'The Prehistory of Samba: Carnival Dancing in Rio de Janeiro, 1840–1917', *Journal of Latin American Studies*, XXVIII/1 (February 1996), p. 38.

64. *Jornal de Notícias*, 12 and 15 February 1901, as quoted by [Raymundo] Nina Rodrigues, *Os Africanos no Brasil*, 4th edn, ed. by Homero Pires (São Paulo, Companhia Editora Nacional, 1976; Brasiliana, Série 5ª, vol. 9), pp. 156–7.

65. Goli Guerreiro, 'As trilhas de Samba-Reggae: a invenção de um ritmo', *Latin American Music Review*, XX/1 (Spring–Summer 1999), p. 117.

66. *O País*, 3 February 1913, as quoted by Chasteen, 'The Prehistory of Samba', p. 44.

67. By Nina Rodrigues, as quoted by Helena Theodoro Lopes, José Jorge Siqueira, and Maria Beatriz Nascimento, *Negro e Cultura no Brasil* (Rio de Janeiro, UNIBRADE/UNESCO, 1987), p. 98. The *afoxé* groups did not use the sacred *atabaque* drums, however (Goli Guerreiro, 'As trilhas de Samba-Reggae', p. 116).

68. Larry N. Crook, 'Black Consciousness, *samba reggae*, and the Re-Africanization of Bahian Carnival Music in Brazil', *The World of Music*, XXXV/2 (1993), pp. 96, 98, 95.

69. As quoted by Guerreiro, 'As trilhas de Samba-Reggae', p. 107.

70. As quoted by Guerreiro, 'As trilhas de Samba-Reggae', p. 113.

71. Guerreiro, 'As trilhas de Samba-Reggae', p. 124.

72. Crook, 'Black Consciousness, *samba reggae*, and the Re-Africanization of Bahian Carnival Music in Brazil', pp. 100–2, 91, 104. Grupo Olodum can be heard on **Olodum: Revolution in Motion**. Other Salvador groups of percussionists can be heard on **Levada do Pelô** and **Raízes do Pelô**.

73. Daniel J. Crowley, *African myth and black reality in Bahian carnaval* ([Los Angeles], Museum of Cultural History, UCLA, 1984; Monograph ser. no. 25), pp. 25, 28.

74. Guerreiro, 'As trilhas de Samba-Reggae', p. 133.

75. Kubik, *Angolan traits in black music, games and dances of Brazil*, p. 17.

76. The concept 'time line' was introduced by J. H. Kwabena Nketia, *The Music of Africa* (Gollancz, 1975), pp. 131–2. It is discussed in detail by Lühning, *Die Musik in candomblé nagô-ketu*, pp. 137 ff.

Chapter 2

1. J. Lowell Lewis, *Ring of Liberation: Deceptive Discourse in Brazilian Capoeira* (Chicago and London, University of Chicago Press, 1992), pp. xxiii, 1 (emphasis in the original), 13. For capoeira, see also: Renato Almeida, 'O Brinquedo do Capoeira', *Revista do Arquivo Municipal* (São Paulo), ano 7, vol. LXXXIV (julho–agosto 1942), pp. 155–62; Waldeloir Rego, *Capoeira Angola: Ensaio Sócio-Etnografico* ([Rio de Janeiro?], Itapuã, 1968); G. Kubik, *Angolan traits in black music, games and dances of Brazil* (Lisbon, 1979), pp. 27–32; *MPB*, pp. 282–9.

2. Kubik, *Angolan traits in black music, games and dances of Brazil*, p. 28.

3. Moritz Rugendas, *Malerische Reise in Brasilien* (Paris, Engelmann; Mülhausen, Ober-Rheinisches Dep^t; 1835; facsimile reprint, Stuttgart, Daco-Verlag, 1986),

4^e Div., pl. 18. For a useful guide to this great work of Rugendas, see Vendelino Lorscheiter, 'Os Escritos de João Maurício Rugendas', *II Colóquio de Estudos Luso-Brasileiros: Anais* (Tokyo, Associação de Professôres de Português, 1968), pp. 102–9.

4. For *calenda*, see: E. Hill, *The Trinidad Carnival* (Austin, Texas, and London, 1972), pp. 27, 58, 70–1; J. Cowley, *Carnival, Canboulay and Calypso* (Cambridge, 1996), *passim*.

5. Lewis, *Ring of Liberation*, p. 20; Kubik, *Angolan traits in black music, games and dances of Brazil*, p. 28.

6. Rugendas, *Malerische Reise in Brasilien*, 4.te Abth. 4.tes Heft. 16.te Lief, p. 26.

7. James Wetherell, *Brazil: Stray notes from Bahia: being extracts from letters, &c., during a residence of fifteen years*, ed. by William Hadfield (Liverpool, Webb & Hunt, 1860), p. 119.

8. Lewis, *Ring of Liberation*, p. 1.

9. Lewis, *Ring of Liberation*, p. 129.

10. Lewis, *Ring of Liberation*, p. 33.

11. *DFB*, s.v. Pernada, p. 611. Note also the *bate-coxa* of Piaçabuçu, Alagoas, considered to be a more violent variant of *capoeira* (*EMB*, I, s.v. bate-coxa, pp. 81–2).

12. *HMB*, pp. 194–6; *DFB*, s.v. Passo^2, pp. 587–8, s.v. Frevo, pp. 346–7. See also Valdemar, 'O Passo Pernambuco', in *Antologia do Carnaval do Recife*, ed. by Mário Souto Maior and Leonardo Dantas Silva (Recife, Fundação Joaquim Nabuco / Massangana, 1991), pp. 363–7; Leonardo Dantas Silva, 'O Frevo Pernambucano', in *Antologia do Carnaval do Recife*, pp. 193–208. Alvarenga, *MPB*, pp. 346–7 and Andrade, *DMB*, s.v. frevo, p. 233, draw attention to the influence of the *polca militar* (or *polca-marcha*) on the *frevo*, whose dancers 'perform wonders of audacity and elasticity of movement' (Alvarenga) and whose orchestras 'are rich in metal instruments, especially trumpets' (Andrade). See also, not least for its striking photographs, Valdemar de Oliveira, 'O frêvo e o passo, de Pernambuco', *Boletín Latino-Americano de Música*, VI (abril de 1946), pp. 157–92. Stunning examples of *frevo* can be heard on **Musique du Nordeste, vol. 1**, track 21; **Musique du Nordeste, vol. 2**, track 17; and **Brésil: Choro – Samba – Frevo**, CD 1, track 18; a *frevo* recorded outdoors in Salvador is on **Brasile: Musica Nera di Bahia: Black Music of Bahia**, side B, track 5.

13. For *ladjia* (sometimes called *ronpoin* or *kokoyé*) and *chat'ou*, see Josy Michalon, *Le ladjia: Origine et pratiques* ([Paris], Editions Caribéennes, 1987); the author suggests (p. 60) that the word *ladjia* derives from *kadjia*, the name of an ancient fighting game practised by the Batache people of Benin at the annual yam festival each July.

14. Fernando Ortiz, *Los bailes y el teatro de los Negros en el folklore de Cuba* (Havana, Cardenas, 1951), pp. 294 ff.

15. I owe this example to Robert Farris Thompson, Foreword, in Lewis, *Ring of Liberation*, p. xiv.

16. I owe this example to Thompson, in Lewis, *Ring of Liberation*, pp. xiii–xiv.

17. J. T. Schneider, *Dictionary of African Borrowings in Brazilian Portuguese* (Hamburg, 1991), s.v. capoeira, p. 104.

18. Kubik, *Angolan traits in black music, games and dances of Brazil*, p. 29.

19. Lewis, *Ring of Liberation*, p. 26.
20. Lewis, *Ring of Liberation*, pp. 127, 227 n. 10.
21. Kathleen O'Connor, review of **Capoeira Angola from Salvador, Brazil** (Smithsonian/Folkways SF CD 40465), *Ethnomusicology*, XLI/2 (Spring/ Summer 1997), p. 320. The building is the Forte de Santo António Além do Carmo, and the group is the Grupo de Capoeira Angola Pelourinho.
22. Lewis, *Ring of Liberation*, p. 25; see Edwin M. Loeb, 'Transition rites of the Kuanyama Ambo (A Preliminary Study), Part I', *African Studies*, VII/1 (March 1948), p. 27.
23. See Kazadi wa Mukuna, *Contribução Bantu na Música Popular Brasileira* (São Paulo, Global, [*c.* 1978]), p. 210.
24. Lewis, *Ring of Liberation*, pp. xix–xxii.
25. Etienne Ignace, 'Le fétichisme des nègres du Brésil', *Anthropos*, III (1908), p. 897.
26. *DMB*, p. 690, provides a chart showing no fewer than 35 synonyms for berimbau, though one at least of them refers in fact to another instrument. Andrade's '*sambi*' is the *nsambi* pluriarc (compound bow-lute) of Angola.
27. Richard Graham, 'Technology and Culture Change: The Development of the *Berimbau* in Colonial Brazil', *Latin American Music Review*, XII/1 (Spring/ Summer 1991), p. 3. For the berimbau, see also *DFB*, s.v. Berimbau-de-Barriga, pp. 120–1; Albano Marinho de Oliveira, 'Berimbau o arco musical da capoeira na Bahia', *Revista do Instituto Geográfico e Histórico da Bahia*, no. 80 (1956), pp. 225–64; Rego, *Capoeira Angola*, pp. 71–7; Kubik, *Angolan traits in black music, games and dances of Brazil*, pp. 32–6.
28. Cf. Graham, 'Technology and Culture Change', p. 5.
29. Kubik, *Angolan traits in black music, games and dances of Brazil*, p. 34. José Redinha, *Instrumentos musicais de Angola: sua construção e descrição: notas históricas e etno-sociológicas da música angolana* (Coimbra, Instituto de Antropologia, Universidade de Coimbra, 1984; Publicações do Centro de Estudos Africanos, no. 3), p. 54, gives one Angolan name as *cambulumbumba*, 'whose root *mbulumbumba* is common to the designation of [various] instruments of this kind'; he describes the *cambulumbumba* as an instrument played by a group of musicians (p. 107). In south-east Angola, he states, the gourd-resonated bow is called *embulumbumba* (p. 54). Elsewhere (pp. 105, 218) Redinha says the Muílas living around Sá da Bandeira in south Angola call this bow *ombulumbumba* while other, unspecified, ethnic groups call it *nbulumbumba*.
30. Gerhard Kubik, *Muziek van de Humbi en de Handa uit Angola* ([Tervuren], Belgische Radio en Televisie, 1973), pp. 75–6.
31. Kubik, *Angolan traits in black music, games and dances of Brazil*, p. 34 (emphasis in the original). See also Gerhard Kubik, 'Musical bows in south-western Angola, 1965', *African Music*, V/4 (1975–76), p. 99.
32. Fernando Ortiz, *Los instrumentos de la musica Afrocubana*, V: Los pulsativos, los fricativos, los insuflativos y los aeritivos (Havana, Cardenas, 1955), p. 20, with illustrations on pp. 17 (fig. 408), 19 (fig. 409), and 21 (fig. 410). Also called *buru-mbúmba* and *bruro-mumba*, this is said in Cuba to be an instrument that 'speaks with the dead' (Ortiz, *Los instrumentos*, V, p. 20).

33. Ladislaus Magyar, *Reisen in Süd-Afrika in den Jahren 1849 bis 1857*, trans. by Johann Hunfalvy (Budapest and Leipzig, Lauffer & Stolp, 1859), pl. following p. 450.
34. Ladislau Batalha, *Angola* (1889), as quoted by Kay Shaffer, *O Berimbau-de-barriga e seus Toques* (Rio de Janeiro, Funarte, [*c*. 1978]; Monografias folclóricas, 2), p. 10; Graham, 'Technology and Culture Change', p. 3, has a slightly different translation.
35. Ladislau Batalha, *Costumes Angolenses: Cartas de um judeu* (Lisbon, Companhia Nacional, 1890; Bibliotheca do Povo e das Escolas, no. 177), p. 18. Graham, 'Technology and Culture Change', p. 4, translates *negralhão* as 'little Negro'.
36. Redinha, *Instrumentos musicais de Angola*, p. 106.
37. Fernando Romero, 'Instrumentos Musicales de Posible Origen Africano en la Costa del Perú', *Revista afroamérica*, I/1–2 (Enero-Julio de 1945), as quoted by Juan Liscano [Velutini], *Folklore y Cultura* (Caracas, Avila Gráfica, [1950]), p. 111.
38. Redinha, *Instrumentos musicais de Angola*, p. 106..
39. Henrique Augusto Dias de Carvalho, *Ethnographía e historia tradicional dos povos da Lunda* (Lisbon, Imprensa Nacional, 1890), p. 370; cf. Arthur Ramos, *O Folk-lore Negro do Brasil: Demopsychologia e Psychanalise* (Rio de Janeiro, Civilização Brasileira, 1935; Bibliotheca de Divulgação Scientifica, IV), p. 156; Nina Rodrigues, *Os africanos no Brasil*, 4th edn, ed. by H. Pires (São Paulo, 1976), p. 160.
40. Redinha, *Instrumentos musicais de Angola*, p. 104.
41. Wilfrid D. Hambly, 'The Ovimbundu of Angola', *Publications of Field Museum of Natural History*, Anthropological ser. XXI/2 (1934), p. 225.
42. H. Capello and R. Ivens, *De Benguella as terras de Iácca: descripção de uma viagem da Africa central e occidental* (Lisbon, Imprensa Nacional, 1881), I, p. 294; H. Capello and R. Ivens, *From Benguella to the territory of Yacca: Description of a Journey into Central and West Africa*, trans. by Alfred Elwes (Sampson Low, Marston, Searle, & Rivington, 1882), I, p. 326, where it figures among 'articles of Ban-Gala workmanship'; Redinha, *Instrumentos musicais de Angola*, pp. 104–5 and fig. 17 (p. 116).
43. Joachim John Monteiro, *Angola and the River Congo* (Macmillan, 1875), II, pp. 139–40.
44. Herman Soyaux, *Aus West-Afrika 1873–1876: Erlebnisse und Beobachtungen* (Leipzig, F. A. Brockhaus, 1879), II, pp. 176–7.
45. Lewis, *Ring of Liberation*, p. 26.
46. **Musical Instruments 1. Strings**, side B, track 10.
47. **Music from Mozambique**, vol. 3, side A, tracks 1 and 2; **Musical Instruments 1. Strings**, side B, track 9.
48. **Music from Rwanda**, side B, track 2.
49. **Music from the Heart of Africa: Burundi**, side A, tracks 1, 2 and 6, side B, track 1; **Musique du Burundi**, side A, track 5.
50. **Musique Bisa de Haute-Volta**, side B, track 2.
51. **Music of the Dagomba from Ghana**, side B, tracks 1 and 2.
52. Henry Koster, *Travels in Brazil* (Longman, Hurst, Rees, Orme & Brown, 1816), p. 241.

53. Ferdinand J. de Hen, *Beitrag zur Kenntnis der Musikinstrumente aus Belgisch Kongo und Ruanda-Urundi* (Inaugural-Dissertation zur Erlangung des Doktorgrades der Philosophischen Facultät des Universität Köln, 1960), pp. 136–7, listing these and other local names for the musical bow.

54. Lieutenant [Henry] Chamberlain, *Views and costumes of the city and neighbourhood of Rio de Janeiro, Brazil* (Thomas M'Lean, 1822; facsimile reprint, [Rio de Janeiro], Kosmos, 1974), pl. [4] ('A Market Stall'), and caption.

55. Chamberlain's *Street Vendors* is reproduced in Dawn Ades, *Art in Latin America: The Modern Era, 1820–1980* (New Haven and London, Yale University Press, 1989), pl. 3.44 (p. 74).

56. J[ean]. B[aptiste]. Debret, *Voyage pittoresque et historique au Brésil, ou Séjour d'un Artiste Français au Brésil depuis 1816 jusqu'en 1831 inclusivement* (Paris, Firmin Didot Frères, 1834–39), II, pl. 41 (facing p. 127) and p. 129.

57. Johann Emanuel Pohl, *Reise im Innern von Brasilien* (Vienna, 1832–37), I, p. 70.

58. Maria Graham, *Journal of a voyage to Brazil, and residence there, during part of the years 1821, 1822, 1823* (Longman, Hurst, Rees, Orme, Brown & Green; and J. Murray; 1824), pp. 198–9.

59. Revd R. Walsh, *Notices of Brazil in 1828 and 1829* (Frederick Westley & A. H. Davis, 1830), II, pp. 175–6.

60. Redinha, *Instrumentos musicais de Angola*, pp. 137, 162, and fig. 74 (p. 161).

61. Graham, 'Technology and Culture Change', p. 2. For the *angolía*, a rattle similar to the *caxixi* but larger.

62. Wetherell, *Brazil: Stray notes from Bahia*, pp. 106–7.

63. Charles Ribeyrolles, *Brasil Pitoresco*, trans. by Gastão Pinalva, 2nd edn (São Paulo, Martins, 1976), II, p. 37.

64. Kubik, *Angolan traits in black music, games and dances of Brazil*, pp. 29–30.

65. Lewis, *Ring of Liberation*, p. 133.

66. O'Connor, review of **Capoeira Angola from Salvador, Brazil**, p. 321.

67. Rego, *Capoeira Angola*, p. 35; Shaffer, *O Berimbau-de-barriga*, p. 40; Kubik, *Angolan traits in black music, games and dances of Brazil*, p. 28.

68. Rego, *Capoeira Angola*, pp. 58–69.

69. Shaffer, *O Berimbau-de-barriga*, pp. 47–56.

70. Lewis, *Ring of Liberation*, p. 134.

71. Lewis, *Ring of Liberation*, p. 145.

72. Lewis, *Ring of Liberation*, p. 152.

73. **Mestre Paulo dos Anjos: Capoeira da Bahia.** The berimbau can also be heard on: **Brasile: Musica Nera di Bahia: Black Music of Bahia**, side A, track 1, side B, tracks 1 and 2; **In Praise of Oxala and Other Gods: Black Music of South America**, side A, track 4; **Fantastique Brésil**, side B, tracks 1 and 2; and **Musique Folklorique du Monde: Brazil**, side A, track 5. For a transcription of a capoeira song, see *HMB*, p. 111.

74. **The Discoteca Collection: Missão de Pesquisas Folclóricas**, track 21. For the *carimbó* dance, described as a solo dance 'suggesting what the primitive *lundu* must have been like before it was polished in contact with bourgeois society', see *MPB*, p. 194.

75. *DMB*, p. 690.

76. Juan Max Boettner, *Música y músicos del Paraguay* (Asúncion, Autores Paraguayos Asociados, [c. 1958]), pp. 31–2, with a sketch on p. 31 (see also

p. 195, where it is stated that *gualambau* is the only word of black origin in Paraguayan musical nomenclature); Isabel Aretz, 'Music and Dance in Continental Latin America, with the Exception of Brazil', in *Africa in Latin America*, ed. by M. M. Fraginals (New York and Paris, 1984), p. 202.

Chapter 3

1. M. Graham, *Journal of a voyage to Brazil* (1824), p. 155.
2. Mrs [Nathaniel Edward] Kindersley, *Letters from the island of Teneriffe, Brazil, the Cape of Good Hope, and the East Indies* (J. Nourse, 1777), p. 47.
3. Maximilian Prinz zu Wied-Neuwied, *Reise nach Brasilien in den Jahren 1815 bis 1817* (Frankfurt a.M., Heinrich Ludwig Brönner, 1820–21), I, p. 28; Prince Maximilian of Wied-Neuwied, *Travels in Brazil, in the years 1815, 1816, 1817* (Henry Colburn & Co., 1820), p. 26.
4. H. M. Brackenridge, *Voyage to South America, performed by order of the American government* (John Miller, 1820), I, p. 97.
5. Fr[eidrich]. Lud[wig]. von Rango, *Tagebuch meiner Reisen nach Rio de Janeiro in Brasilien, und Zurück: In den Jahren 1819 und 1820*, 2nd ed. (Ronneburg, Friedrich Weber, 1832), p. 145.
6. W[illiam]. H[enry]. B[ayley]. Webster, *Narrative of a voyage to the southern Atlantic Ocean, in the years 1828, 29, 30* (Richard Bentley, 1834), I, pp. 41–2.
7. J. P. and W. P. Robertson, *Letters on Paraguay: comprising an account of a four years' residence in that republic* (John Murray, 1838–39), I, p. 162.
8. William S[amuel]. W[aithman]. Ruschenberger, *Three years in the Pacific; containing notices of Brazil, Chile, Bolivia, Peru &c. in 1831, 1832, 1833, 1834* (Richard Bentley, 1835), I, p. 98.
9. Edward Wilberforce, *Brazil viewed through a naval glass: with notes on slavery and the slave trade* (Longman, Brown, Green and Longmans, 1856), p. 47.
10. John Luccock, *Notes on Rio de Janeiro and the southern parts of Brazil; taken during a residence of ten years in that country, from 1808 to 1818* (Samuel Leigh, 1820), pp. 108–9.
11. Lieutenant [H.] Chamberlain, *Views and costumes of the city and neighbourhood of Rio de Janeiro* (1822; facsimile reprint, [Rio de Janeiro], 1974), pl. [7] ('Pretos de ganho, or black porters'), caption.
12. M. C. Karasch, *Slave Life in Rio de Janeiro 1808–1850* (Princeton, N.J., 1987), p. 214. Cf. Alexander Caldcleugh, *Travels in South America, during the years 1819–20–21; containing an account of the present state of Brazil, Buenos Ayres, and Chile* (John Murray, 1825), I, p. 83: 'Neither is it any longer a crime in the negroes to converse in their native tongues.'
13. For *fala de Guiné*, see A. C. de C. M. Saunders, *A social history of black slaves and freedmen in Portugal* (Cambridge, 1982), pp. 89, 105, 168–9, 203–4 n. 66; John Thornton, *Africa and Africans in the making of the Atlantic world, 1400–1680* (Cambridge University Press, 1992), p. 214.
14. Sir William Ouseley, *Travels in various countries of the east; more particularly Persia* (Rodwell & Martin, 1819–23), I, p. 13.
15. O. von Kotzebue, *A new voyage round the world* (1830), I, p. 44.

16. [José Vieira Fazenda], 'Antiqualhas e memorias do Rio de Janeiro', *Revista do Instituto Historico e Geographico Brasileiro*, tomo 86, vol. CXL (1919), p. 60.

17. Theodor v. Leithold, *Meine Ausflucht nach Brasilien oder Reise von Berlin nach Rio de Janeiro* (Berlin, Maurerschen Buchhandlung, 1820), p. 75.

18. James Holman, *A voyage round the world, including travels in Africa, Asia, Australasia, America, etc. etc. from MDCCCXXVII to MDCCCXXXII* (Smith, Elder, 1834–35), I, p. 465.

19. J. B. Debret, *Voyage pittoresque et historique au Brésil* (Paris, 1834–39), II, p. 113.

20. Revd R. Walsh, *Notices of Brazil* (1830), II, p. 335.

21. Dr. [Melchior-Honoré] Yvan, *Romance of Travel, from Brest, to the Isle of Bourbon, Brazil, &c.* (James Blackwood, 1854), p. 67.

22. Revd Walter Colton, *Deck and Port; or, Incidents of a cruise in the United States frigate Congress to California* (New York, A. S. Barnes; Cincinatti, H. W. Derby; 1850), p. 89.

23. Comte de Suzannet, *Souvenirs de voyages: les provinces du Caucase, l'empire du Brésil* (Paris, G.-A. Dentu, 1846), p. 208.

24. Ida Pfeiffer, *Eine Frauenfahrt um de Welt* (Vienna, Carl Gerold, 1850), I, p. 34; Ida Pfeiffer, *A woman's journey round the world* (Illustrated London Library, [1852]), p. 17.

25. Le Cte Eugène de Robiano, *Dix-huit Mois dans l'Amérique du sud* (Paris, E. Plon, 1878), p. 32.

26. C. S. Stewart, *Brazil and La Plata: the personal record of a cruise* (New York, G. P. Putnam, 1856), pp. 72, 271–2.

27. R. Elwes, *A sketcher's tour round the world* (1854), p. 25.

28. Revd Daniel. P. Kidder, *Sketches of residence and travel in Brazil* (Wiley & Putnam, 1845), I, pp. 68–9; this passage was republished with little change in Revd D. P. Kidder and Revd J. C. Fletcher, *Brazil and the Brazilians, portrayed in historical and descriptive sketches* (Philadelphia, Childs & Peterson, 1857), pp. 29–30.

29. Dr [Karl] Hermann [Konrad] Burmeister, *Reise nach Brasilien, durch die Provinzen von Rio de Janeiro und Minas geraës* (Berlin, George Reimer, 1853), p. 89.

30. Thomas Ewbank, *Life in Brazil; or, A Journal of a Visit to the land of the cocoa and the palm* (New York, Harper & Brothers, 1856), pp. 92–3.

31. C. Ribeyrolles, *Brasil Pitoresco*, trans. by G. Penalva (São Paulo, 1976), I, p. 167.

32. [Auguste] F[rançois]. Biard, *Deux Années au Brésil* (Paris, L. Hachette, 1862), p. 90.

33. Herbert H. Smith, *Brazil: The Amazons and the Coast* (New York, Charles Scribner's Sons, 1879), p. 470.

34. Kidder, *Sketches of residence and travel in Brazil*, I, p. 177.

35. Kidder, *Sketches of residence and travel in Brazil*, II, pp. 20–1; Kidder and Fletcher, *Brazil and the Brazilians*, pp. 475–6.

36. Alexander Marjoribanks, *Travels in South and North America*, 5th edn (New York, D. Appleton, 1854), p. 46.

37. J. Wetherell, *Brazil: Stray notes from Bahia* (Liverpool, 1860), p. 53.

38. Revd Hamlet Clark, *Letters home from Spain, Algeria, and Brazil, during past entomological rambles* (John Van Voorst, 1867), p. 106.

39. Maximilian, *Aus meinem Leben* (Leipzig, Duncker & Humblot, 1867), VI, p. 48; Maximilian I, Emperor of Mexico, *Recollections of my life* (Richard Bentley, 1868), III, pp. 129–30.

40. Ewbank, *Life in Brazil*, pp. 186, 188; Wolfgang Laade, 'An example of hammer and chisel music from Liberia', *African Music*, I/4 (1956), pp. 81–2, and 'Editor's Note', p. 82.

41. L. M. Schaeffer, *Sketches of travels in South America, Mexico and California* (New York, James Egbert, 1860), p. 13.

42. Louis-François de Tollenare, *Notes dominicales prises pendant un voyage en Portugal et au Brésil en 1816, 1817 et 1818*, ed. by Léon Bourdon (Paris, Presses Universitaires de France, 1971–73), II, p. 316.

43. John Esaias Warren, *Para; or, Scenes and Adventures on the banks of the Amazon* (New York, G. P. Putnam, 1851), pp. 10–11.

44. Alfred R. Wallace, *A narrative of travels on the Amazon and Rio Negro* (Reeve, 1853), p. 390.

45. *HMB*, p. 89. For Renato Almeida (b. 1895), see V. Mariz, *Três musicólogos Brasileiros* (Rio de Janeiro and [Brasília], 1983), pp. 131–74.

46. Stanley J. Stein, *Vassouras: A Brazilian Coffee County, 1850–1900* (Harvard University Press, 1957; Harvard Historical Studies, vol. 69), pp. 163, 137, 207, 209. The word *quimzumba* is not recorded in J. T. Schneider, *Dictionary of African Borrowings in Brazilian Portuguese* (Hamburg, 1991). Stein gives the Portuguese texts of a number of *jongos* as well as English renderings, which I have not always followed.

47. Yvan, *Romance of Travel*, p. 133.

48. C. B. Mansfield, *Paraguay, Brazil, and the Plate* (Cambridge, 1861), p. 83.

49. John Codman, *Ten months in Brazil: with incidents of voyages and travels, descriptions of scenery and character, notices of commerce and productions, etc.* (Boston, [Mass.], Lee & Shepard, 1867), p. 84.

50. Hastings Charles Dent, *A Year in Brazil* (Kegan Paul, Trench & Co., 1886), p. 116.

51. Stein, *Vassouras: A Brazilian Coffee County*, p. 116.

52. Le Cte Charles d'Ursel, *Sud-Amérique: Séjours et voyages au Brésil, à la Plata, au Chili, en Bolivie et au Pérou* (Paris, E. Plon & Cie, 1879), p. 59.

53. Frank Vincent, *Around and about South America: Twenty months of quest and query*, 2nd edn (New York, D. Appleton, 1890), pp. 280–1.

54. This paragraph is largely based on Luiz Heitor Corrêa de Azevedo, 'Vissungos: Negro Work Songs of the Diamond District in Minas Gerais, Brazil', in *Music in the Americas*, ed. by George List and Juan Orrego-Salas ([Bloomington, Ind.], Indiana University Research Center in Anthropology, Folklore, and Linguistics; The Hague, Mouton; 1967; Inter-American Music Monograph Series, vol. 1), pp. 64–7, from which all quotations are taken. I have also used Aires da Mata Machado Filho, *O Negro e o Garimpo em Minas Gerais* (Rio de Janeiro, Livraria José Olympio, [1943]; Coleção Documentos Brasileiros, 42), pp. 61–8, with musical transcriptions of 65 songs, pp. 69–112.

55. Auguste de Saint-Hilaire, *Voyage dans le district des diamans et sur le littoral du Brésil* (Paris, Librairie-Gide, 1833), I, pp. 11–12.

56. **L. H. Corrêa de Azevedo: Music of Ceará and Minas Gerais**, tracks 24–6. For Corrêa de Azevedo see Mariz, *Três musicólogos Brasileiros*, pp. 91–130.

57. Hear 'Water on the Wheel', sung in Sumter County, Alabama in 1950 by Mrs Annie Grace Horn Dodson, issued on **Negro Folk Music of Alabama, vol. 6: Game Songs and Others**, side B, track 2; her song is transcribed in Harold Courlander, *Negro Folk Music, U.S.A.* (New York and London, Columbia University Press, paperback edn, 1970), pp. 86–7.

58. Machado Filho, *O Negro e o Garimpo em Minas Gerais*, pp. 63, 62. For *vissungos*, see also: *MPB*, pp. 264–5; J. J. de Carvalho, 'Music of African Origin in Brazil', in *Africa in Latin America*, ed. by M. M. Fraginals, trans. by L. Blum (New York and Paris, 1984), pp. 242–3.

59. **L. H. Corrêa de Azevedo: Music of Ceará and Minas Gerais**, track 27.

Chapter 4

1. Mário de Andrade, *Danças Dramáticas do Brasil*, 2nd edn, ed. by Oneida Alvarenga (Belo Horizonte, Itatiaia; Brasília, Instituto Nacional do Livro, Fundação Nacional Pró-Memória; 1982; Obras Completas de Mário de Andrade, XVIII).

2. [François] Froger, *Relation d'un voyage Fait en 1695. 1696. & 1697. aux Côtes d'Afrique, Détroit de Magellan, Brezil, Cayenne & Isles Antilles* (Paris, Michel Brunet, etc., 1698), p. 131. The popularity in Bahia of African masks would be noted in 1760 by Fr Manuel de Cerqueira Torres (Eduardo de Castro e Almeida, 'Inventario dos documentos relativos ao Brasil existentes no Archivo de Marinha e Ultramar', *Annaes da Bibliotheca Nacional do Rio de Janeiro*, XXXI, 1909, p. 411).

3. Patricia A. Mulvey, 'Black Brothers and Sisters: Membership in the Black Lay Brotherhoods of Colonial Brazil', *Luso-Brazilian Review*, XVII/2 (Winter 1980), p. 254.

4. They were founded by Dominican missionaries in Lisbon and Cadiz; in the sixteenth century brotherhoods were also formed in the Portuguese towns of Alcácer do Sal, Évora, Lagos, Leiria, Moura, Mugem and Setúbal. For black brotherhoods in Portugal, see António Brásio, *Os pretos em Portugal* (Lisbon, Agência Geral das Colónias, 1944; Colecção pelo Imperio, no. 101), pp. 73–104.

5. Julita Scarano, 'Black Brotherhoods: Integration or Contradiction', *Luso-Brazilian Review*, XVI/1 (Summer 1979), pp. 7–8.

6. Patricia A. Mulvey, 'Slave confraternities in Brazil: their role in colonial society', *The Americas*, XXXIX/1 (July 1982), pp. 40, 46, 48; A. J. R. Russell-Wood, 'Black and Mulatto Brotherhoods in Colonial Brazil: A Study in Collective Behaviour', *Hispanic American Historical Review*, LIV/4 (November 1974), p. 599.

7. José Ramos Tinhorão, *Música popular de Índios, Negros e Mestiços* (Petrópolis, Vozes, 1972), p. 47.

8. A. J. R. Russell-Wood, *The Black Man in Slavery and Freedom in Colonial Brazil* (1982), p. 100.

9. *The Travels of Leo of Rozmital*, trans. and ed. by Malcolm Letts (Cambridge University Press, 1957; Hakluyt Society, 2nd ser., no. 108), p. 113.

10. A. C. de C. M. Saunders, *A social history of black slaves and freedmen in Portugal* (Cambridge, 1982), p. 150.

11. Sloane MS. 1572, fols. 61 recto–62 recto. This document is described in the British Library's catalogue of Sloane MSS. as 'Diary of a traveller, written in 1633, during a journey from Brussels through France to Spain, returning through France and the Netherlands to London'. Our Lady of the Snow and Our Lady of the Rosary were also venerated by African slaves in Madeira; see A. Vieira, *Os escravos no arquipélago da Madeira* (Funchal, 1991), pp. 217–19.

12. J. C. Chasteen, 'The Prehistory of Samba: Carnival Dancing in Rio de Janeiro, 1840–1917', *Journal of Latin American Studies*, XXVIII/1 (February 1996), p. 35.

13. L[e]. G[entil]. de La Barbinais, *Nouveau Voyage Autour du Monde* (Paris, Briasson, 1728–29), III, pp. 216–17. The illustration is clearly an artist's reconstruction and not a sketch made at the time by the author, though he may of course have provided the artist with such a sketch.

14. Maria Isaura Pereira de Queiroz, *O campesinato brasileiro: Ensaios sobre civilização e grupos rústicos no Brasil* (Petrópolis, Vozes; São Paulo, Universidade de S. Paulo; 1973; Coleção Estudos Brasileiros, 3), pp. 137–56. For the Dance of St Gonzales, see also Alceu Maynard Araújo, *Folclore Nacional* ([São Paulo], Melhoramentos, [1964]), II, pp. 25–76.

15. As quoted by Luiz Viana Filho, *O Negro na Bahia*, 2nd edn (São Paulo, Martins, 1976), p. 43.

16. Luís dos Santos Vilhena, *Recopilação de notícias soteropolitanas e brasilicas Contidas em XX Cartas*, ed. by Braz do Amaral (Bahia, Imprensa Official do Estado, 1921), pp. 135–6.

17. *Inventário dos documentos relativos ao Brasil existentes no Archivo de Marinha e Ultramar de Lisboa*, ed. by Eduardo de Castro e Almeida (Rio de Janeiro, Officinas Graphicas da Bibliotheca Nacional, 1913–36), III, Bahia, 1786–98, no. 12, 235, p. 23.

18. D. Domingos de Loreto Couto, *Desaggravos do Brasil e glorias de Pernambuco* (Rio de Janeiro, Officina Typographica da Bibliotheca Nacional, 1904), pp. 158–9.

19. Tinhorão, *Música popular*, p. 49.

20. Joseph Ferreyra de Matos, *Diário historico das celebradides, que na Cidade da Bahia se fizeraõ em acçaõ de graças pelos felicissimos cazamentos dos Serenissimos Senhores Principes de Portugal, e Castella* (Lisboa Occidental, Na Officina de Manoel Fernandes da Costa, 1729), p. 14.

21. 'Inventário dos documentos relativos ao Brasil existentes no Archivo de Marinha e Ultramar', ed. by Eduardo de Castro e Almeida, I, Bahia 1613–1762, no. 5097 (annexe), *Annaes da Bibliotheca Nacional do Rio de Janeiro*, XXXI (1909), p. 413.

22. Mulvey, 'Slave confraternities in Brazil', p. 49.

23. Conrad, *Children of God's Fire*, p. 195.

24. Maximilian, *Aus meinem Leben* (Leipzig, 1867), VI, pp. 112, 106–11; Maximilian, *Recollections of my life* (1868), III, pp. 176, 170–5. *Cachaça* is a strong drink made by fermenting and distilling molasses. A similar drink is known as *kachasu* in Malaŵi and northern Mozambique; cf. J. T. Schneider, *Dictionary of African Borrowings in Brazilian Portuguese* (Hamburg, 1991), s.v. cachaça, p. 62. Revd David Clement Scott, *Dictionary of the Nyanja language*,

ed. by Revd Alexander Hetherwick (Religious Tract Society, [1930]), s.v. Kachasu, p. 168, translates the word as 'wine'.

25. J. Codman, *Ten months in Brazil* (Boston, 1867), pp. 90–1.

26. **L. H. Corrêa de Azevedo: Music of Ceará and Minas Gerais**, track 23.

27. João Dornas Filho, 'A influencia social do negro brasileiro', *Revista do Arquivo Municipal* (São Paulo), ano 5, vol. LI (outubro 1938), p. 109.

28. Araújo, *Folclore Nacional*, I, p. 201.

29. *HMB*, pp. 254–64; *DFB*, s.v. Congadas, Congados, Congos, pp. 242–5; *MPB*, pp. 99–118; Andrade, *Danças Dramáticas*, II, pp. 9–106, III, pp. 196–24; *DMB*, s.v. Congos, pp. 151–2. Note also a 'curious form of Afro-Brazilian tradition – the *pemba* from Minas Gerais, a cult which is exactly midway between a *congada* and a modern *umbanda* possession cult' (J. J. de Carvalho, 'Black Music of All Colors', in *Music and Black Ethnicity*, ed. by G. H. Béhague, Miami, 1994, p. 191).

30. Gerard Béhague, 'Brazil', in *The New Grove Dictionary of Music and Musicians*, ed. by S. Sadie (1980), III, p. 237.

31. Mulvey, 'Slave confraternities', p. 47; cf. A. J. R. Russell-Wood, *The Black Man in Slavery and Freedom in Colonial Brazil* (1982), pp. 96–7.

32. H. Koster, *Travels in Brazil* (1816), pp. 274–5, 411.

33. Dr. Joh. Bapt. von Spix and Dr Carl Friedr. Phil. von Martius, *Reise in Brasilien auf Befehl Sr Majestät Maximilian Joseph I. Königs von Baiern in den Jahren 1817 bis 1820 gemacht und beschrieben* (Munich, 1823–31), II, pp. 468–70.

34. J. E. Pohl, *Reise im Innern von Brasilien* (Vienna, 1832–37), II, pp. 81–7.

35. J. Ribeiro Guimarães, *Summario de varia historia* (Lisbon, Rolland & Semiond, 1872–75), V, pp. 147–9.

36. Tiago de Oliveira Pinto, 'The Pernambuco carnival and its formal organisations: music as expression of hierarchies and power in Brazil', *Yearbook for Traditional Music*, XXVI (1994), p. 24.

37. Tiago de Oliveira Pinto, 'Musical Difference, Competition and Conflict: The Maracutu Groups in the Pernambuco Carnival, Brazil', *Latin American Music Review*, XVII/2 (Fall/Winter 1996), p. 100.

38. D. T. Moreira, 'A Macumba de Vitória', in *Anais do XXXI Congresso Internacional de Americanistas*, ed. by H. Baldus (São Paulo, Anhembi, 1955), I, p. 469.

39. Cf. Winifred Kellersberger Vass, *The Bantu speaking heritage of the United States* (Los Angeles, Center for Afro-American Studies, University of California, 1979; Afro-American Culture and Society, a CAAS Monograph Series, vol. 2), p. 111.

40. Robert Farris Thompson, 'Kongo Influences on African-American Artistic Culture', in *Africanisms in American Culture*, ed. by J. E. Holloway (Bloomington, Indiana, 1990), p. 151. For the *kalunga*, see also Mário de Andrade, 'A calunga dos Maracutús', in *Estudos Afro-Brasileiros: Trabalhos apresentados ao 1º Congresso Afro-Brasileiro reunido no Recife em 1934* (Rio de Janeiro, Ariel, 1935), pp. 39–47, reprinted in *Antologia do Carnaval do Recife*, ed. by M. S. Maior and L. D. Silva (Recife, Fundação Joaquim Nabuco, Massangana, 1991; Série Obras de consulta, 11), pp. 261–9. A spirit (*encantado*) called Kalunga plays a prominent role in the traditional belief-system in the rural district of São António dos Pretos (Maranhão state), where worshippers

'constitute an informal religious organization' and observe a rain ritual (G. E. Simpson, *Black Religions in the New World*, New York, 1978, pp. 177–8).

41. Joseph C. Miller, *Kings and Kinsmen: Early Mbundu States in Angola* (Oxford, Clarendon Press, 1976), p. 59.

42. **L. H. Corrêa de Azevedo: Music of Ceará and Minas Gerais**, tracks 13–15. For *maracatus*, see also: *HMB*, pp. 266–70; Ascenso Ferreira, 'O Maracatú', *Boletín Latino-Americano de Música*, VI/1 (abril de 1946), pp. 125–39; Katarina Real, *O folclore no carnaval do Recife* (Rio de Janeiro, Ministério da Educação e Cultura, Campanha de Defesa do Folclore Brasileiro, 1967; Coleção 'Folclore Brasileiro', vol. 2), pp. 67–95; [César] Guerra Peixa, *Maracutus do Recife*, 2nd edn, ed. by Leonardo Dantas Silva (São Paulo, Irmãos Vitale, 1981; Coleção Recife, vol. 14); *DFB*, s.v. Maracatu, pp. 471–2; *MPB*, pp. 118–27; Andrade, *Danças Dramáticas*, II, pp. 17, 129–76; *DMB*, s.v. Maracatu, p. 305; Ascenso Ferreira, 'O Maracatu', in *Antologia do Carnaval do Recife*, ed. by Maior and Silva, pp. 51–64.

43. *HMB*, pp. 264–5; *MPB*, pp. 127–9; *DMB*, s.v. Taieiras, pp. 495–6.

44. *MPB*, pp. 99–118.

45. Maria de Lourdes Borges Ribeiro, 'O baile dos Congos', in *Estudos e ensaios folclóricos em homenagem a Renato Almeida* (Rio de Janeiro, 1960), p. 680.

46. J. J. de Carvalho, 'Black Music of All Colors', p. 189.

47. **Congos de Saiote/RN**, side B, track 1. For *Congos* and *Congadas*, see also Andrade, *Danças Dramáticas*, II, pp. 42–8; Luís da Câmara Cascudo, *Made in Africa (Pesquisas e Notas)* (Rio de Janeiro, Civilização Brasileira, 1965; Perspectivas do Homem, 3), pp. 25–32; Araújo, *Folclore Nacional*, I, pp. 193–201, 216–96.

48. Cf. S. J. Stein, *Vassouras* (1957), pp. 140, 141; Stuart B. Schwartz, 'The *Mocambo*: Slave resistance in colonial Bahia', *Journal of Social History*, III/4 (Summer 1970), p. 315.

49. J. H. Rodrigues, 'The influence of Africa on Brazil and of Brazil on Africa', *Journal of African History*, III/1 (1962), p. 56.

50. Cf. Stuart B. Schwartz, *Slaves, Peasants, and Rebels: Reconsidering Brazilian Slavery* (Urbana and Chicago, University of Illinois Press, 1992), p. 103.

51. S. J. Stein, *Vassouras* (1957), pp. 135–7; Richard Graham, 'Brazilian slavery re-examined: a review article', *Journal of Social History*, III/4 (Summer 1970), p. 447. See also Artur Rawos [i.e. Ramos], 'Castigos de escravos', *Revista do Arquivo Municipal* (São Paulo), ano 4, vol. XLVII (maio 1938), pp. 79–104.

52. Cf. Stein, *Vassouras*, pp. 141–2.

53. J. T. Schneider, *Dictionary of African Borrowings in Brazilian Portuguese* (Hamburg, 1991), s.v. quilombo, p. 250; s.v. mocambo, p. 210. Other Portuguese synonyms were *ladeiras* (literally, 'slopes') and *magotes* (literally, 'groups').

54. Cf. Schwartz, *Slaves, Peasants, and Rebels*, pp. 122, 123.

55. Cf. Schwartz, *Slaves, Peasants, and Rebels*, p. 124.

56. Cf. Sidney W. Mintz and Richard Price, *The birth of African-American culture: an anthropological perspective* (Boston, Beacon Press, 1992), pp. 43–4.

57. Décio Freitas, *Palmares: a guerra dos escravos* (Porto Alegre, Movimento, 1973; Coleção Documentos, vol. 3), p. 102.

58. Freitas, *Palmares*, pp. 100–1.

59. Robert Nelson Anderson, 'The *Quilombo* of Palmares: A New Overview of a Maroon State in Seventeenth-Century Brazil', *Journal of Latin American Studies*, XXVIII/3 (October 1996), p. 559. For the functions of the *nganga a nzumbi* among the Imbangala of the state of Kasanje in Angola, see Miller, *Kings and Kinsmen*, pp. 254–5.
60. Schwartz, *Slaves, Peasants, and Rebels*, p. 124.
61. Schwartz, *Slaves, Peasants, and Rebels*, p. 123.
62. There is a translation of *Tenda dos Milagres* by Barbara Shelby: *Tent of Miracles* (New York, Alfred A. Knopf, 1971; paperback edn, Collins Harvill, 1989).
63. As quoted by G. R. Andrews, *Blacks & Whites in São Paulo, Brazil* (Madison and London, University of Wisconsin Press, 1991), p. 217. The paragraph that follows owes much to Andrews's well-informed account.
64. Quoted in the original by D. J. Crowley, *African myth and black reality in Bahian carnaval* ([Los Angeles], 1984), p. 31.
65. Anderson, 'The *Quilombo* of Palmares', p. 545.
66. As quoted by Andrews, *Blacks & Whites in São Paulo*, p. 219.
67. Anderson, 'The *Quilombo* of Palmares', p. 545. For a useful 'Introdução ao conceito de Quilombo', see H. T. Lopes, J. J. Siqueira, and M. B. Nascimento, *Negro e Cultura no Brasil* (Rio de Janeiro, 1987), pp. 25–39. For Palmares, see (besides the sources cited above): Mario Mello, 'A Republica dos Palmares', in *Estudos Afro-Brasileiros: Trabalhos apresentados ao 1º Congresso Afro-Brasileiro reunido no Recife em 1934*, I (Rio de Janeiro, Ariel, 1935), pp. 181–5; Nina Rodrigues, *Os africanos no Brasil*, 4th edn, ed. by Homero Pires (São Paulo, 1976), pp. 127–60; Ernesto Ennes, 'The Palmares "Republic" of Pernambuco: its final destruction, 1697', *The Americas*, V/2 (October 1948), pp. 200–16; R. K. Kent, 'Palmares: an African state in Brazil', *Journal of African History*, VI/2 (1965), pp. 161–75, reprinted in *Maroon Societies: Rebel Slave Communities in the Americas*, ed. by Richard Price (Garden City, N.Y., Anchor Press/Doubleday, 1973), pp. 170–90 (this paper should be used with caution, especially as regards dates and translations from Portuguese). For *quilombos* other than Palmares, see R. Bastide, *Les Religions africaines au Brésil* (Paris, 1960), pp. 126–35; English translation, as 'The Other *Quilombos*', in *Maroon Societies*, ed. by R. Price, pp. 191–201, and in Bastide, *The African Religions of Brazil*, trans. by H. Sebba (Baltimore and London, 1978), pp. 90–6.
68. Araújo, *Folclore Nacional*, I, p. 387–8.
69. For the *Quilombo* dramatic dance, see also: *HMB*, pp. 270–3; *DFB*, s.v. Quilombo, pp. 653–6; *MPB*, pp. 132–5; *DMB*, s.v. Quilombo, pp. 419–20.
70. 'Soterio da Sylva Ribeiro' [i.e. Fr Manuel da Madre de Deus], 'Summula Triunfal da nova e grande celebridade do glorioso e invicto martyr S. Gonçalo Garcia', *Revista do Instituto Historico e Geographico Brasileiro*, tomo 99, vol. CLIII (1º de 1926), pp. 34–5.
71. [Alexandre José de] Mello Morais Filho, *Festas e tradições populares do Brasil*, ed. by Luís da Câmara Cascudo (Belo Horizonte, Itatiaia; São Paulo, Universidade de São Paulo; 1979; Coleção Reconquista do Brasil, vol. 55), pp. 109–16. For the *cucumbi*, see also *HMB*, pp. 262–4; *EMB*, s.v cucumbi^2, p. 213; *DFB*, s.v. Cucumbi, pp. 266–7, s.v. Ticumbi, pp. 749–50; *MPB*, pp. 135–9; *DMB*, s.v. Cucumbi, pp. 165–6.
72. Chasteen, 'The Prehistory of Samba', pp. 40–1.

73. **Ticumbi/ES**.
74. Araújo, *Folclore Nacional*, I, p. 216 n. 52.
75. Emilio Willems, 'Caboclo cultures of Southern Brazil', in *Acculturation in the Americas*, ed. by Sol Tax (Chicago, 1952), p. 240.
76. Béhague, 'Brazil', p. 238.
77. João Dornas Filho, 'A influência social do negro brasileiro', *Revista do Arquivo Municipal* (São Paulo), ano 5, vol. LI (outubro 1938), p. 108. This was a paper presented to the 1938 Minas Gerais Afro-Brazilian Congress, held in Belo Horizonte.
78. J. J. de Carvalho , 'Music of African Origin in Brazil', in *Africa in Latin America*, p. 235. The *paiá* is referred to in Alceu Maynard Araújo, *Cultura popular brasileira*, 2nd ed. (São Paulo, Melhoramentos, 1973), p. 51, with an illustration on p. 137, and in Araújo, *Folclore Nacional*, II, p. 426. For the *Moçambique*, see also: *DFB*, s.v. Moçambiques, p. 498; *MPB*, pp. 129–32; Andrade, *Danças Dramáticas*, III, pp. 243–67; *DMB*, s.v. Moçambique, pp. 339–42.
79. *DMB*, s.v. Pernanguma, p. 394.
80. Hermilio Borba Filho, *Apresentação do bumba-meu-boi*, [2nd edn] (Recife, Guararapes, 1982; Cadernos Guararapes, 5), p. 5.
81. Cf. Kazadi wa Mukuna, '*Sotaques*: Style and Ethnicity in a Brazilian Folk Drama', in *Music and Black Ethnicity*, ed. by G. H. Béhague, p. 214.
82. Maria Isaura Pereira de Queiroz, *O campesinato brasileiro: Ensaios sobre civilização e grupos rústicos no Brasil* (Petrópolis, Vozes; São Paulo, Universidade de S. Paulo; 1973; Coleção Estudos Brasileiros, 3), p. 158, states flatly that it 'probably derived from Portugal'.
83. Mukuna, '*Sotaques*', p. 207.
84. Mukuna, '*Sotaques*', p. 213.
85. Mukuna, '*Sotaques*', p. 215.
86. This summary is adapted from Mukuna, '*Sotaques*', pp. 211–12.
87. Schneider, *Dictionary of African Borrowings in Brazilian Portuguese*, s.v. bumba-meu-boi, p. 47.
88. Schneider, *Dictionary of African Borrowings in Brazilian Portuguese*, s.v. bumba-meu-boi, p. 47.
89. Schneider, *Dictionary of African Borrowings in Brazilian Portuguese*, s.v. bumba-meu-boi, p. 47.
90. Mukuna, '*Sotaques*', pp. 211–12.
91. Alan Merriam, *The Anthropology of Music* (Bloomington, Northwestern University Press, 1964), p. 190.
92. Hugh Tracey, 'The Social Role of African Music', *African Affairs*, LIII/212 (July 1954), p. 237.
93. Mukuna, '*Sotaques*', pp. 221, 218.
94. Mukuna, '*Sotaques*', p. 218.
95. Mukuna, '*Sotaques*', p. 218.
96. Extracts from a performance of this version in Santa Catarina can be heard on **Boi de Mamão/SC**.
97. Pereira de Queiroz, *O campesinato brasileiro*, p. 161.
98. Denis-Constant Martin, review of *Music and Black Ethnicity*, ed. by G. H. Béhague, *Latin American Music Review*, XVI/2 (Fall/Winter 1995), p. 257. For *Bumba-meu-boi*, see also: *HMB*, pp. 245–54; *DFB*, s.v. Bumba-Meu-Boi, pp.

150–4; *MPB*, pp. 41–57; Andrade, *Danças Dramáticas*, III, pp. 11–191; Kazadi wa Mukuna, 'Bumba-meu-boi in Maranhão', in *Welt Musik: Brazilien: Einführung in Musiktraditionen Brasiliens*, ed. by Tiago de Oliveira Pinto (Mainz, Schott, 1986), pp. 108–20; *DMB*, s.v. Boi, pp. 62–7. For a suggestion by Roger Bastide as to a possible African source of *Bumba-meu-boi*, see p. 220, n. 10, below.

99. **Cambinda/Paraíba**.
100. See *DFB*, s.v. Cabinda, pp. 164–5; *EMB*, s.v. cambindas, I, p. 132.

Chapter 5

1. C. Abel, *Narrative of a journey in the interior of China* (1818), pp. 13–14.
2. Nicholas M. England, *Music Among ... Peoples of Namibia, Botswana, and Angola* (New York and London, Garland, 1995), p. 61, suggests 'linguiphone' as 'a neutral term'.
3. Hear **Sanza and Guitar: Music of the Bena Luluwa of Angola and Zaire**, side A, tracks 2 and 4; side B, tracks 1 and 2.
4. J. J. Monteiro, *Angola and the River Congo* (1875), II, p. 139. For African lamellophones, see J. H. K. Nketia, *The music of Africa* (1975), pp. 77–9, 81, and hear, e.g., **Folk Music of the Western Congo**, side B, tracks 2 and 3; **Music and Musicians of the Angola Border: the Tshokwe**, side B, tracks 1 and 2; **Musique Kongo**, side A, track 6; **Musique du Burundi**, side A, track 6; **Musical Instruments 2. Reeds (Mbira)**, all tracks; **Musique Bisa de Haute-Volta**, side A, track 1; and **Musiques Dahoméennes**, side A, track 1.
5. H. Soyaux, *Aus West-Afrika 1873–1876* (Leipzig, 1879), II, p. 176.
6. W. S. W. Ruschenberger, *Three years in the Pacific* (1835), I, p. 35.
7. L.-F. de Tollenare, *Notes domincales prises pendant un voyage en Portugal et au Brésil*, ed. by L. Bourdon (Paris, 1971–73), II, pp. 470–1.
8. Dr J. B. von Spix and Dr C. F. P. von Martius, *Reise in Brasilien* (Munich, 1823–31), II, p. 468.
9. *Gazeta do Rio de Janeiro*, 8 July 1820, as quoted by A. Caldcleugh, *Travels in South America during the years 1819–20–21* (1825), I, p. 85 n.
10. J. E. Pohl, *Reise im Innern von Brasilien* (Vienna, 1832–37), I, p. 70.
11. For the *gaita-de-foles*, see E. V. de Oliveira, *Instrumentos musicais populares portugueses* (Lisbon, 1982), pp. 315–31. The Portuguese bagpipe can be heard on **Musical Traditions of Portugal**.
12. O. von Kotzebue, *A new voyage round the world* (1830), I, p. 45.
13. Lieutenant [Henry] Chamberlain, *Views and costumes of the city and neighbourhood of Rio de Janeiro* (facsimile reprint, [Rio de Janeiro], 1974), pl. [36] ('Largo de Gloria'), caption.
14. C. Schlichthorst, *Rio de Janeiro wie es ist: Beiträge zur Tages- und Sitten-geschichte der Haupstadt von Brasilien mit vorzüglicher Rücksicht auf die Lage des dortigen deutschen Militairs* (Hanover, Im Verlag der Hahn'schen Hofbuchhandlung, 1829), pp. 182–3.
15. M. Graham, *Journal of a voyage to Brazil* (1824), p. 199.
16. Revd R. Walsh, *Notices of Brazil* (1830), II, p. 336.
17. J. B. Debret, *Voyage pittoresque et historique au Brésil* (Paris, 1834–39), II, p. 129.

18. 'Etwas uber Musik und Tanz in Brasilien', *Allgemeine Musikalische Zeitung*, 35. Jahrgang (1833), no. 2, col. 20.

19. Ruschenberger, *Three years in the Pacific*, I, pp. 35–6, 97. The 'guachambo' does not appear to be referred to elsewhere.

20. T. Ewbank, *Life in Brazil* (New York, 1856), pp. 111–12.

21. Cf. G. Kubik, *Angolan traits in black music, games and dances of Brazil* (Lisbon, 1979), pp. 44, 45.

22. England, *Music Among … Peoples of Namibia, Botswana, and Angola*, pp. 119, 121. The five-string *nsambi kizonzolo* of Congo-Brazzaville, with raffia strings, resonator and wooden sound-board, can be heard on **Musique Kongo**, side A, track 5; a similar instrument, called *nsambi*, can be heard on **Musiques du Gabon**, side B, track 3. The seven-string gourd-resonated pluriarc of the Kpelle of Liberia, known as *gbegbetele* (in some areas, *kolo koning*), is recorded on **Folk Music of Liberia**, side A, track 5 and **Music of the Kpelle of Liberia**, side A, track 4.

23. Kubik, *Angolan traits*, fig. 31, caption.

24. Father Jerom Merolla da Sorrento, *A Voyage to Congo and several other Countries, chiefly in Southern-Africa… in the Year 1682*, as quoted by Frank Harrison, *Time, place and music: an anthology of ethnomusicological observation c. 1550 to c. 1800* (Amsterdam, Frits Knuf, 1973; Source Materials and Studies in Ethnomusicology, I), p. 96.

25. Alexandre Rodrigues Ferreira, *Viagem filosófica pelas capitanias do Grão Pará, Rio Negro, Mato Grosso e Cuiaba 1783–1792* (Rio de Janeiro, Conselho Federal de Cultura, 1971) I, fol. 54.

26. Chamberlain, *Views and costumes of the city and neighbourhood of Rio de Janeiro*, pl. [29] ('Sick Negroes'), caption.

27. For African resonator xylophones, see Nketia, *The music of Africa*, pp. 81–4. Xylophones used in the Kongo-Angola culture area are recorded on: **Folk Music of the Western Congo**, side B, tracks 5 and 6; **Music and Musicians of the Angolan Border: The Tshokwe**, side A, tracks 1, 2, and 7; and **Musical Instruments 5. Xylophones**, side A, track 7.

28. Hugh Tracey, sleeve-note to **Musical Instruments 5. Xylophones**; see also Hugh Tracey, *Chopi Musicians: their music, poetry and instruments* (Oxford University Press for International African Institute, 1948).

29. Hugh Tracey, sleeve-note to **Musical Instruments 5. Xylophones**.

30. [A. J. de] Mello Morais Filho, *Festas e tradições populares do Brasil*, ed. by L. da Câmara Cascudo (Belo Horizonte & São Paulo, 1979), p. 110.

31. *Atlas zur Reise in Brasilien von Dr. v. Spix und Dr. v. Martius* ([Munich, M. Lindauer, c. 1823]), pl. [36], ('Bilder aus dem Menschenleben').

32. [Adèle] Touissant-Samson, *Une Parisienne au Brésil*, 2nd edn (Paris, Paul Ollendorff, 1883), pp. 128–9; cf. the inaccurate and incomplete contemporary translation: [Adèle] Touissant-Samson, *A Parisian in Brazil*, trans. by Emma Touissant (Boston, [Mass.], James H. Earle, 1891), pp. 94–5.

33. Rossini Tavares Lima and others, *O Folclore do litoral norte de São Paulo*, tomo 1 – Congadas (Rio de Janeiro, Campanha de Defesa do Folclore Brasileiro, 1968 [1969]; Coleção 'Folclore Brasileiro', 3), pp. 60–2, 108–9, and the third illustration between pp. 28 and 29.

Chapter 6

1. François Pyrard, *Voyage de François Pyrard, de Laual: Contenant sa navigation aux Indes Orientales, Maldiues, Moluques, Bresil*, 3rd ed. (Paris, Samuel Thiboust & Remy Dallin, 1619), II, p. 339; *The voyage of François Pyrard of Laval to the East Indies, the Maldives, the Moluccas and Brazil*, trans. and ed. by Albert Gray and H. C. P. Bell (Hakluyt Society, 1887–90), II, pp. 319–20.

2. P. J. P. Whitehead and M. Boeseman, *A portrait of Dutch 17th century Brazil: Animals, plants and people by the artists of Johan Maurits of Nassau* (Amsterdam, North-Holland Publishing Company, 1989; Koninklijke Nederlandse Akademie van Wetenschappen Verhandelingen Afd. Natuurkunde, Tweede Reeks, deel 87), pp. 155, 159. Below the map's main title is a vignette with a decorative festoon that includes two or three drums, three single-string musical bows (erroneously called 'single-string cachimbos' by Whitehead and Boeseman, p. 156; a *cachimbo* is a pipe for smoking), two or three lute-like instruments, and a stick with two rattles at the top and one hung below. These look like African instruments but are not shown very clearly, and some of them may be Amerindian. According to Whitehead and Boeseman, 'It has been concluded, probably rightly, that the pictures [on the Marcgraf-Blaeu map] were derived from drawings by Frans Post [1612–80]' (p. 154); on the other hand, 'There is no object that can be matched with known representations by Post' (p. 185).

3. D. Francisco Manuel de Melo (1608–66), as quoted by J. C. Chasteen, 'The Prehistory of Samba', *Journal of Latin American Studies*, XXVIII/1 (February 1996), p. 34 and n. 15.

4. As quoted by S. B. Schwartz, *Slaves, Peasants, and Rebels* (Urbana and Chicago, 1992), p. 62.

5. A. Caldcleugh, *Travels in South America, during the years 1819–20–21* (1825), I, p. 83.

6. Sir W. Ouseley, *Travels in various countries of the East* (1819–23), I, p. 14.

7. T. V. Leithold, *Meine Ausflucht nach Brasilien* (Berlin, 1820), pp. 74–5.

8. J. E. Pohl, *Reise im Innern von Brasilien* (Vienna, 1832–37), I, pp. 70–1.

9. L.-F. de Tollenare, *Notes domincales prises pendant un voyage en Portugal et au Brésil*, ed. by L. Bourdon (Paris, 1971–73), II, pp. 471–2.

10. R. Bastide, *Les Religions africaines au Brésil* (Paris, 1960), pp. 192–3; cf. R. Bastide, *The African Religions of Brazil*, trans. by H. Sebba (Baltimore and London, 1978), pp. 138–9. Bastide goes on to suggest that this dance may be one of the sources of *Bumba-meu-boi*, but this does not accord with Kazadi wa Mukana's findings. For the *Nanzéké* or *Nanzégé*, see M. Prouteaux, 'Premiers Essais de théatre chez les indigènes', *Bulletin du Comité d'Études Historiques et Scientifiques de l'Afrique Occidentale Française*, XII (1929), nos. 3–4, pp. 448–75.

11. 'Etwas uber Musik und Tanz in Brasilien', *Allgemeine Musikalische Zeitung*, 35. Jahrgang (1833), no. 2, cols 20–1.

12. Bertil Söderberg, *Les Instruments de musique au Bas-Congo et dans les régions avoisinantes: Etude ethnographique* (Falköping, A. J. Lindgrens, 1956; Ethnographical Museum of Sweden, Monograph Ser., no. 3), pp. 42–8. There is an example of a 'percussion-beam' on **Musiques du Gabon**, side B, track 3.

13. Adolphe d'Assier, *Le Brésil contemporain: races. – mœurs.– institutions. – paysage* (Paris, Durand & Laurel, 1867), p. 94.

14. C. S. Stewart, *Brazil and La Plata* (New York, 1856), pp. 293–4. By *cacha* Stewart meant *cachaça*.

15. J. P. and W. P. Robertson, *Letters on Paraguay* (1838–39), I, pp. 164, 166–8.

16. Le Cte E. de Robiano, *Dix-huit mois dans l'Amérique du Sud* (Paris, 1878), pp. 54–5.

17. J. Wetherell, *Brazil: Stray notes from Bahia*, ed. by W. Hadfield (Liverpool, 1860), p. 6.

18. Wetherell, *Brazil*, p. 54. This passage was first published, in a slightly different version, in William Hadfield, *Brazil, the River Plate, and the Falkland Islands* (Longman, Brown, Green and Longmans, 1854), p. 131.

19. Revd H. Clark, *Letters home from Spain, Algeria, and Brazil* (1867), p. 128.

20. Le Cte C. d'Ursel, *Sud-Amérique* (Paris, 1879), pp. 69–71.

21. *DMB*, s.v. Maribondo, p. 308, s.v. Marimbondo, Sinhá, p. 310; EMB, s.v. maribondo ou marimbondo, I, p. 451, s.v. jogos coreográficos adultos, I, p. 385. Other adult dance-games in Goiás are the *dança-dos-quatis*, a men's dance imitating the coati, and three ring dances: *candeia*, in which one of the dancers carries a lighted candle; *piranha*, in which children also take part; and *canoa*. Note also the *jacundá* ring dance of Amazônia. Most of these dance-games seem to show a mixture of Amerinidian and African influences. The *bate-coxa* of Alagoas and the *pernada* of Rio de Janeiro are variants or derivatives of capoeira, which itself can also be classified as an adult dance-game, but is of course much more than that.

22. F. Vincent, *Around and about South America*, 2nd edn (New York, 1890), pp. 281–2.

23. H. H. Smith, *Brazil: The Amazons and the Coast* (New York, 1879), pp. 160–1. On a cassava plantation at Terra Preta, near Lake Turará, 'José takes his wire-stringed guitar, and some neighbor comes in with a fiddle, and the young people improvise a rustic dance, José's two pretty daughters taking part very gracefully, though they are barefooted and dressed in calico. Songs and stories fill out the evening: a bit of sociable country life that we shall see very often in our travels' (p. 276).

24. *DFB*, s.v. Batuque, p. 114.

25. Gerhard Kubik, 'Drum Patterns in the "Batuque" of Benedito Caxias', *Latin American Music Review*, XI/2 (Fall–Winter 1990), p. 115.

26. Kazadi wa Mukuna, *Contribução Bantu na Música Popular Brasileira* (São Paulo, [*c.* 1978]), p. 70.

27. Dr. Francisco Augusto Pereira da Costa, 'Folk-lore pernambuco', *Revista do Instituto Historico e Geographico Braziliero*, LXX (1907), pt ii, p. 205.

28. L. dos Santos Vilhena, *Recopilação de notícias soteropolitanas e brasilica*, ed. by B. do Amaral (Bahia, 1921), pp. 135–6.

29. Quoted by Nina Rodrigues, *Os africanos no Brasil*, 4th edn, ed. by H. Pires (São Paulo, 1976), pp. 253–4.; and cf. R. K. Kent, 'African Revolt in Bahia: 24–25 January 1835', *Journal of Social History*, III/4 (Summer 1970), p. 344.

30. M. C. Karasch, *Slave Life in Rio de Janeiro 1808–1850* (Princeton, N.J., 1987), p. 233.

31. R. E. Conrad, *Children of God's Fire* (University Park, Pa., 1995), pp. 260–5 *passim*.

32. W. K. Vass, *The Bantu speaking heritage of the United States* (Los Angeles, 1979), p. 106.

33. J. T. Schneider, *Dictionary of African Borrowings in Brazilian Portuguese* (Hamburg, 1991), s.v. batucada, p. 36, suggesting also a Yoruba source.

34. J. J. Monteiro, *Angola and the River Congo* (1875), II, pp. 136–8.

35. H. Capello and R. Ivens, *De Benguella as terras de Iácca: descripção de uma viagem na Africa central e occidental* (Lisbon, Imprensa Nacional, 1881), I, pp. 64, 234; H. Capello and R. Ivens, *From Benguella to the territory of Yacca: Description of a Journey into Central and West Africa*, trans. by Alfred Elwes (Sampson, Low, Marston, Searle & Rivington, 1882), I, pp. 70, 258.

36. Maximilian Prinz zu Wied-Neuwied, *Reise nach Brasilien in den Jahren 1815 bis 1817* (Frankfurt a.M., 1820–21), I, p. 192; Prince Maximilian of Wied-Neuwied, *Travels in Brazil, in the years 1815, 1816, 1817* (1820), p. 164.

37. L. da Câmara Cascudo, *Made in Africa (Pesquisas e Notas)* (Rio de Janeiro, 1965), p. 51.

38. Dr J. B. von Spix and Dr C. F. P. von Martius, *Reise in Brasilien* (Munich, 1823–31), I, pp. 294–5. Cf. the contemporary translation: Dr Joh. Bapt. von Spix and Dr C. F. Phil von Martius, *Travels in Brazil, in the years 1817–1820*, [trans. by Hannibal Evans Lloyd] (Longman, Hurst, Rees, Orme, Brown and Green, 1824), II, p. 114.

39. Rugendas, *Malerische Reise in Brasilien*, 4.te Abth. 4.tes Heft. 16.te Lief, p. 25.

40. Auguste de Saint-Hilaire, *Voyage dans les provinces de Rio de Janeiro et de Minas Geraes* (Paris, Grimbert & Dorez, 1830), I, pp. 40–1.

41. Auguste de Saint-Hilaire, *Voyage aux sources du rio de S. Francisco et dans la province de Goyaz* (Paris, Arthur Bertrans, 1847–48), II, p. 60.

42. G. Wilhelm Freyreiss, *Reisen in Brasilien* (Stockholm, Ethnographical Museum of Sweden, 1968; Monograph ser., no. 13), p. 82.

43. [A.] Touissant-Samson, *Une Parisienne au Brésil*, 2nd edn (Paris, 1883), pp. 127–32; cf. [A.] Touissant-Samson, *A Parisian in Brazil*, trans. by E. Touissant (Boston, [Mass.],1891), pp. 94–5

44. **In Praise of Oxalá and Other Gods: Black Music of South America**, side B, track 5.

45. *DFB*, s.v. Batuque, p. 114.

46. Mário de Andrade, 'O Samba rural paulista', *Revista do Arquivo Municipal* (São Paulo), ano 4, vol. XLI (novembro 1937), pp. 40–59 *passim*.

47. Philip Galinsky, review of Barbara Browning, *Samba: Resistance in Motion* (Bloomington, Indiana University Press, 1995), *1998 Yearbook for Traditional Music*, p. 144.

48. Marilia Trindade Barboza da Silva, 'Negro em roda de samba: Herança africana na Música Popular Brasileira', *Tempo brasileiro*, nos 92/93 (Janeiro–Junho de 1988), p. 107.

49. Arthur Ramos, *O Folk-lore Negro do Brasil* (Rio de Janeiro, 1935), p. 136.

50. G. Kubik, *Angolan traits in black music, games and dances of Brazil* (Lisbon, 1979), p. 18.

51. W. M. Megenny, *A Bahian heritage* (Chapel Hill, 1978), p. 149.

52. Edmundo Correia Lopes, 'Samba, dança o samba, folclore fulo-mandinga ... etc.', *O Mundo Português*, X/3 (Março de 1943), p. 627.

53. Almada Negreiros, *História etnográphica da Ilha de S. Thomé* (Lisbon, José Bastos, 1895), p. 169.

54. Ralph Waddey, 'Viola de Samba and Samba de Viola in the Reconcavo of Bahia (Brazil), Part II: Samba de Viola', *Latin American Music Review*, II/2 (Fall/Winter 1981), p. 276 n. 2.

55. Fr Bernardo Maria de Cannecattim, *Collecção de observações grammaticaes sobre o Lingua Bunda, ou Angolense* (Lisbon, na Impressão Regia, 1805), s.v. Oração, p. 197, s.v. Rezar, p. 206; Fr Bernardo Maria de Cannecattim, *Diccionario da Lingua Bunda, ou Angolense, explicada na Portuguesa e Latina* (Lisbon, na Impressão Regia, 1804), s.v. Rezo, Resar, p. 638.

56. E.g. Guillermo Abadia M. and David Lewiston, sleeve notes to **In Praise of Oxalá and Other Gods: Black Music of South America**: 'The samba stems from the dances used in candomblé rituals'; the booklet accompanying **Samba: Batuque – Partido Alto – Samba-canção 1917–1947**: 'The samba [was] originally a part of the candomblé ritual'; and the booklet accompanying **Saudade em Samba: Brasil 1929–1942**: 'The samba comes from these early sacred dance rituals.'

57. Gerard Béhague, review of Vernon W. Boggs, *Salsiology: Afro-Cuban Music and the Evolution of Salsa in New York City* (New York, Greenwood Press, 1993), in *Latin American Music Review*, XIV/1 (Spring/Summer 1993), p. 175.

58. E. Willems, 'Caboclo cultures of Southern Brazil', in *Acculturation in the Americas*, ed. by S. Tax (Chicago, 1952), p. 241.

59. Alceu Maynard Araujo, 'Jongo', *Revista do Arquivo Municipal* (São Paulo), ano 16, vol. CXXVIII (1949), pp. 45–54.

60. Stanley J. Stein, *Vassouras: A Brazilian Coffee County, 1850–1900* (Harvard, 1957), p. 258. The translation given here is slightly different from Stein's.

61. For the *jongo*, see also: *HMB*, pp. 201–30; *EMB*, s.v. jongo, I, p. 385; *MPB*, pp. 162–5; J. J. de Carvalho, 'Music of African Origin in Brazil', in *Africa in Latin America*, ed. by M. M. Fraginals, trans. by L. Blum (New York and Paris, 1984), p. 236; *DMB*, s.v. Jongo, pp. 273–4. The *jongo* recorded commercially in 1929 has been reissued on **Musique du Nordeste, vol. 1: 1916–1945**, track 9. A French writer referred in 1883 to 'those curious dances where the jongo, the caninha verde or other special dances are jigged all night long by mulatto women very often attractively dressed, at any rate always clean' (as quoted by Stein, *Vassouras: A Brazilian Coffee County*, pp. 206–7 n. 19). *Caninha-verde* (or *cana-verde*) is a ring dance of Portuguese origin; hear **Cana-Verde/Ceará**.

62. Cf. Araújo, *Folclore nacional*, II, p. 201.

63. Stein, *Vassouras: A Brazilian Coffee County*, pp. 257, 204.

64. As quoted by Stein, *Vassouras: A Brazilian Coffee County*, p. 204.

65. Stein, *Vassouras: A Brazilian Coffee County*, pp. 205–8 *passim*. The word *nguízu*, which apparently means 'jingles', is not recorded in J. T. Schneider, *Dictionary of African Borrowings in Brazilian Portuguese* (Hamburg, 1991).

66. Stein, *Vassouras: A Brazilian Coffee County*, p. 207.

67. *MPB*, pp. 165–9; *DMB*, s.v. Coco, pp. 146–8.

68. G. Béhague, 'Brazil', in *The New Grove Dictionary of Music and Musicians*, ed. by S. Sadie (1980), III, p. 241.

69. *DMB*, s.v. Coco, p. 146.
70. **The Discoteca Collection: Missão de Pesquisas Folclóricas**, tracks 12–19.
71. **Coco/Ceará.**
72. **Torém/Ceará.** An extremely thorough study of the *coco*, with numerous musical examples, is Mário de Andrade, *Os cocos*, ed. by Oneyda Alvarenga (São Paulo, Duas Cidades, 1984). See also Araújo, *Folclore nacional*, II, 239–41.
73. *DMB*, s.v. Calango, p. 82.
74. *EMB*, s.v. Calango, I, p. 128.
75. Examples of *calango* can be heard on **Música Popular do Centro-Oeste/Sudeste**, tracks 4–6, and on **Calango–RJ.**
76. *MPB*, pp. 185–6; *DMB*, s.v. Sorongo, p. 489.
77. *MPB*, p. 160; *DMB*, s.v. Quimbete, p. 420.
78. Schneider, *Dictionary of African Borrowings in Brazilian Portuguese*, s.v. Sarambeque, p. 267.
79. D. Francisco Manuel [de Mello], *Carta de Guia de Casados: Paraque pello caminho da prudencia se acerte com a Casa do descanso* (Lisbon, Officina Craesbecckiana, 1651), fol. 54 verso; D. Francisco Manuel de Mello, *Carta de Guia de Casados*, ed. by Edgar Prestage (Oporto, Edição de a 'Renascença Portuguesa', 1923), p. 75.
80. *Colleción de Entremeses Loas, Bailes, Jácaras y Mojigangas desde fines del siglo XVI á medíados del XVIII*, ed. by Emilio Cotarelo y Mori (Madrid, Bailly/Bailliére, 1911; Nueva Biblioteca de Autores Españoles, 17), s.v. Zarambeque, I, p. cclxxi.
81. Robert Stevenson, *Music in Mexico* (New York, Thomas Y. Crowell Company, 1952), p. 162.
82. *DFB*, s.v. Sarambeque, p. 697. Júlio Dantas, *Êles e elas: na vida – na arte – na história* (Oporto, Chardron, 1918), p. 181, calls the *sarambeque* 'hip-shaking' (*saracoteado, desnalgado*); the section on the *sarambeque* (pp. 181–4) was omitted from the 4th edition of this work (Lisbon, Portugal-Brasil [c. 1925]). Frederico de Freitas, 'Sarambeque', *Enciclopédia Luso-Brasileira de Cultura* (1963–76), XVI, p. 1478, calls the dance 'boisterous [*buliçosa*] and sensual'. *HMB*, p. 161, says the Bahia *sarambeque* (*sarambé, sorongo*) was another name for the samba. See also: *MPB*, pp. 186–7; *DMB*, s.v. Sarambeque, p. 464.

Chapter 7

1. J. C. Chasteen, 'The Prehistory of Samba', *Journal of Latin American Studies*, XXVIII/1 (February 1996), pp. 32–3.
2. Cf. Charles Verlinden, *L'Esclavage dans l'Europe médiévale*, I, Péninsule ibérique – France (Brugge, 'De Tempel', 1955; Rijksuniversiteit te Gent: Werken uitgegeven door de Faculteit van Letteren en W. jsbegeerte, 119ᵉ Aflevering), p. 226.
3. Cf. Julian Ribeira [Tarragó], *Music in Ancient Arabia and Spain*, trans. and ed. by Eleanor Hague and Marion Leffingwell (London, Oxford University Press; California, Stanford University Press; 1929), p. 5.
4. Verlinden, *L'Esclavage dans l'Europe médiévale*, I, p. 566.

5. P. E. Russell, 'Towards an interpretation of Rodrigo de Reinosa's "poesía negra"', in *Studies in Spanish literature of the Golden Age presented to Edward M. Wilson*, ed. by R. O. Jones (Tamesis Books, 1973; Colección Támesis, serie A: Monografias, XXX), p. 245 n. 41.

6. P. E. Russell, 'Towards an interpretation of Rodrigo de Reinosa's "poesía negra"', pp. 226, 241.

7. Sebastian de Cobarruuias Orozco, *Tesoro de la lengua castellana, o española* (Madrid, Luis Sanchez, 1611), s.v. GVINEO, fol. 457 verso.

8. Russell, 'Towards an interpretation of Rodrigo de Reinosa's "poesía negra"', p. 230.

9. *Colleción de Entremeses Loas, Bailes, Jácaras y Mojigangas*, ed. by E. Cotarelo y Mori (Madrid, 1911), s.v. Ye-ye, I, p. cclxv.

10. Russell, 'Towards an interpretation of Rodrigo de Reinosa's "poesía negra"', p. 234.

11. Luís de Camões, *Obras completas*, ed. by Hernandi Cidade, III, 'Autos e cartas' (Lisbon, Sá da Costa, 1946), p. 262.

12. A. C. de C. M. Saunders, *A social history of black slaves and freedmen in Portugal 1441–1555* (Cambridge, 1982), p. 105.

13. Russell, 'Towards an interpretation of Rodrigo de Reinosa's "poesía negra"', p. 234.

14. *Recopilación en metro del bachiller Diego Sánchez de Badajoz (Sevilla, 1554): reproducida en facsímile por La Academia Española* (Madrid, Tipografía de Archivos, 1929), fol. xv recto.

15. Russell, 'Towards an interpretation of Rodrigo de Reinosa's "poesía negra"', p. 236.

16. Cf. Robert Stevenson, 'Some Portuguese sources for early Brazilian music history', *Yearbook*, Inter-American Institute for Musical Research, IV (1968), pp. 21–2.

17. Saunders, *A social history of black slaves and freedmen in Portugal*, p. 106.

18. Gomes Eannes de Azurara, *Chronica do descobrimento e conquista de Guiné* (Paris, J. P. Aillaud, 1841), p. 133.

19. Robert Stevenson, 'The Afro-American Musical Legacy to 1800', *Musical Quarterly*, LIV (1968), p. 497 and n. 66.

20. Jean Devisse and Michel Mollat, *Africans in the Christian ordinance of the world (fourteenth to the sixteenth century)*, trans. by William Granger Ryan (Cambridge, Mass. and London, Harvard University Press, 1979); *The Image of the Black in Western Art*, ed. by Ladislas Bugner, II, pt 2), p. 195 and figs. 196 (p. 193) and 200 (p. 196).

21. Saunders, *A social history of black slaves and freedmen in Portugal*, p. 106.

22. Francisco Faria, 'O estilo concertante em Santa Cruz de Coimbra, *Bracara Augusta*, XXVIII (1974), p. 429.

23. J. B. and R. C. Purcell, 'Portugal, II. Folk music', in *The New Grove Dictionary of Music and Musicians*, ed. by S. Sadie (1980), XV, p. 146.

24. Miguel de Ceruantes Saauedra, *Novelas exemplares* (Madrid, Iuan de la Cuesta, 1613), p. 173.

25. José-Antonio Guzmán-Bravo, 'Mexico, home of the first musical instrument workshops in America', *Early Music*, VI/3 (July 1978), p. 355 n. 5.

26. Francisco de Quevedo, *Poesía completa* (Madrid, Biblioteca Castro/Turner, 1995), II, p. 692.
27. Lope de Vega, *El Amante agradecido*, in *Obras de Lope de Vega*, [ed. by Emilio Cotarelo y Mori] (Madrid, Real Academia Española, 1916–30), III, p. 123.
28. Robert Stevenson, 'The Mexican origins of the Sarabande', *Inter-American Music Bulletin*, no. 33 (January 1963), p. 7. Cf. also Robert Stevenson, 'The First Dated Mention of the Sarabande', *Journal of the American Musicological Society*, V/1 (Spring 1952), pp. 29–31; Robert Stevenson, 'The Sarabande: A Dance of American Descent', *Inter-American Music Bulletin*, no. 30 (July 1962), pp. 1–13.
29. Robert Stevenson, *Music in Mexico* (New York, 1952), pp. 96, 141, 162.
30. Stevenson, *Music in Mexico*, p. 162.
31. Daniel Devoto, 'De la zarabanda à la sarabande', *'Recherches' sur la Musique française classique*, VI (1966), p. 28.
32. Juan de Mariana, *Trabado contra los juegos públicos*, in *Biblioteca de autores españoles, desde la formacion del lenguaje hasta nuestros dias*, XXXI (Madrid, M. Rivadeneyra, 1854), p. 433.
33. Chasteen, 'The Prehistory of Samba', p. 33.
34. [Louis Armand de Lom d'Arce], *Supplément aux Voyages du baron de Lahontan* (The Hague, Fréres l'Honoré, 1703; Nouveaux Voyages de M. le baron de Lahontan, dans l'Amérique septentionale, t. III), p. 129; cf. Baron Lahontan, *New Voyages to North-America* (H. Bonwicke etc., 1703), II, p. 205. [Françisco Marques] Sousa Viterbo, *Artes e artistas em Portugal: contribuições para a história das artes e industrias portuguezes*, 2nd edn (Lisbon, Livraria Ferin, 1920), p. 265, misdates this letter 1794, and his error is copied by José Sasportes, *História da dança em Portugal* ([Lisbon], Fundação Calouste Gulbenian, [1970]), p. 173.
35. [Jean Baptiste Labat], *Nouveau Voyage aux Isles d'Amérique* (Paris, Pierre-François Giffart, 1722), IV, pp. 153–60. The many plagiarisms of Labat's account are listed in Lauro Ayestarán, *La Música en el Uruguay*, vol. I (Montevideo, Servicio Oficial de Difusión Radio Eléctrica, 1953), pp. 65–8.
36. Dom [Antoine Joseph] Pernety, *Journal historique d'un Voyage fait aux Iles Malouïnes en 1763 & 1764* (Berlin, Etienne de Bourdeaux, 1769), I, pp. 299–302; I have used the contemporary translation, [Antoine Joseph Pernety] *The history of a voyage to the Malouine (or Falkland) Islands, Made in 1763 and 1764, Under the Command of M. de Bougainville* (T. Jefferys, 1771), pp. 120–1.
37. M. L. E. Moreau de Saint-Méry, *Description topographique, physique, civile, politique et historique de la partie française de l'isle saint-Domingue* (Philadelphia, 1797), I, pp. 44–5. At least two other writers laid Labat under contribution. The anonymous English translator of a travel book by the German Anton Zachariah Helms (1751–1803) spiced up his translation with a reference, which is not in the original, to 'a lively and very lascivious dance ... called *calenda* in Montevideo' (Anthony Zachariah Helms, *Travels from Buenos Ayres, by Potosi, to Lima*, Richard Phillips, 1806, Appendix, p. 215). And the Frenchman Jullien Mellet claimed to have seen in 1813, in the Chile town of Qullota, a 'very lively and extremely lascivious dance ... called *lariate*, brought by the Negroes from Guinea' (Jullien M[ellet], *Voyage dans l'Amérique méridionale ... depuis 1808 jusqu'en 1819*, Agen, Prosper Noubel, 1823, p. 74.

38. A. P. D. G., *Sketches of Portuguese life, manners, costume, and character* (Geo. B. Whittaker, 1826), pp. 288–91.

39. Fernando Romero, 'De la "Samba" de Africa a la "Marinera" del Perú', *Estudios afrocubanos*, IV (1940), p. 119.

40. For *cueca* and *marinera*, see: Fernando Romero, 'De la "Samba" de Africa a la "Marinera" del Perú', pp. 82–120; Antonio Acevedo Hernandez, *La Cueca: Orígenes, Historia y Antología* (Santiago, Nascimento, 1953).

41. I was fortunate enough to see a spellbinding performance of the *marinera* in Lima in 1986, and described it in Peter Fryer, *Crocodiles in the Streets: A Report on Latin America* (New Park, 1987), pp. 57–8. A coloured picture of a black couple performing a handkerchief dance to the music of fife and drum is contained in a miscellany collected by Battasar Jaime Martinez Compañon in northern Peru between 1782 and 1785 and now preserved in Madrid.

42. As quoted by José Ramos Tinhorão, *Fado: dança do Brasil: cantar de Lisboa: o fim de um mito* (Lisbon, Caminho, 1994), p. 13

43. Joam Cardoso da Costa, 'A huma negra vendo-se a hum espelho', *Musa Pueril* (Lisbon, Miguel Rodrigues, 1736), p. 328. This is a free translation of the lines: 'Pois para tal negrura como tu / Nesse lugar he bem que verse vá / Lá nos Reinos escuros do Gandú.'

44. As quoted by Tinhorão, *Fado*, p. 13.

45. M. Rugendas, *Malerische Reise in Brasilien* (Paris and Mülhausen, 1835; facsimile reprint, Stuttgart, 1986), 4.te Abth. 4.tes Heft. 16.te Lief, p. 26. As already stated, M. C. Karasch, *Slave Life in Rio de Janeiro 1808–1850* (Princeton, N.J., 1987), p. 244, suggests that the word *lundu* might derive from Luanda. J. T. Schneider, *Dictionary of African Borrowings in Brazilian Portuguese* (Hamburg, 1991), s.v. lundu, p. 173, suggests 'Kimbundu *lundu* "consequence, that which follows an action", since the dance follows the act of collecting the harvest in the Congo', and adds: 'Another possible explanation would be the Umbundu *lundo* "a provocation", referring to the nature of the dance.'

46. For which see Théo. Brandão, 'Autos e Folguedos populares de Alagoas, I: O Fandango', *Revista do Instituto Histórico de Alagoas*, XXVII (1951–53), pp. 50–138.

47. For examples of some of the latter, hear **Fandango/SP**. For the fandango in Brazil, see also A. M. Araújo, *Folclore Nacional* [São Paulo, 1964], II, pp. 129–92; *EMB*, s.v. fandango², pp. 261–2; *DMB*, s.v. Fandango, pp. 215–19.

48. Alceu Maynard Araújo, *Documentário folclórico paulista* (São Paulo, Prefeitura do Município de S. Paulo, etc., 1952), pp. 27–30.

49. Francisco Cormon, *Sobrino aumentado, o Nuevo Diccionario de las lenguages española, francesca y latina* (Antwerp, los Hermanos de Tournes, 1769), s.v. Fandango, II, p. 6.

50. William Dalrymple, *Travels through Spain and Portugal in 1774; with a short account of the Spanish expedition against Algiers, in 1775* (J. Almon, 1777), p. 51.

51. Richard Twiss, *Travels through Portugal and Spain, In 1772 and 1773* (G. Robinson, T. Becket and J. Robson, 1775), p. 18.

52. Chasteen, 'The Prehistory of Samba', p. 33.

53. Mozart de Araujo, *A Modinha e o Lundu no Século XVIII (uma pesquina histórico e bibliográfica)* (São Paulo, Ricordi Brasileira, 1963), p. 11.

54. Theophilo Braga, *O povo portuguez no seus costumes, crenças e tradições* (Lisbon, Livraria Ferreira, 1885), I, pp. 397, 399.
55. J. R. Tinhorão, *Os Negros em Portugal* (Lisbon, 1988), p. 120, gives the text of the decree, and there is a translation in Conrad, *Children of God's Fire*, p. 247. Cf. Frederico de Freitas, 'Lundum', *Enciclopédia Luso-Brasileira de Cultura* (Lisbon, 1963–76), XII, p. 742; Frederico de Freitas, 'O fado, canção da cidade de Lisbon; suas origens e evolução', in *Colóquio sobre música popular portugues* ([Lisbon], 1984), p. 15. J. Dantas, *Os galos de Apollo*, 2nd edn (Lisbon, [c. 1928]), p. 93, citing 'MSS. Pombalina, códice 131', claims that the African-derived *chegança* was such an indecent dance that D. João V (1706–60) felt obliged to ban it; it has not been possible to verify this reference. Frederico de Freitas, 'A modinha portuguesa & brasileira (Alguns aspectos do seu particular interesse musical)', *Bracara Augusta* (Coimbra), XXVIII (1974), p. 435, states that both D. João V and D. José I (1750–77) prohibited some dances because of their sensual nature, but gives no reference.
56. H. Koster, *Travels in Brazil* (1816), p. 241.
57. C. Ribeyrolles, *Brasil Pitoresco*, trans. by G. Penalva (São Paulo, 1976), II, p. 37.
58. Professor and Mrs Louis Agassiz, *A journey in Brazil* (Boston, [Mass.], Ticknor & Fields, 1868), pp. 48–9.
59. Le Cte C. d'Ursel, *Sud-Amérique* (Paris, 1879), p. 70.
60. F. Vincent, *Around and about South America* (New York, 1890), p. 230.
61. Dr. F. A. Pereira da Costa, 'Folk-lore pernambuco', *Revista do Instituto Historico e Geographico Brazileiro*, LXX, pt ii (1907), p. 204. The ex-governor's letter is quoted in the booklet accompanying **História da Música Brasileira: Périodo Colonial II**, p. 5.
62. Tomás Antônio Gonzaga, *Poesias: Cartas chilenas*, ed. by M. Rodrigues Lapa (Rio de Janeiro, Ministério da Educação e Cultura, Instituto Nacional do Livro, 1957; Obras Completas de ... Gonzaga, I), pp. 249, 295.
63. S. J. Stein, *Vassouras: A Brazilian Coffee County* (Harvard, 1957), pp. 156–7.
64. Thomas Lindley, *Narrative of a voyage to Brasil* (J. Johnson, 1805), pp. 276–7. This account would soon be plagiarised by Andrew Grant, *History of Brazil, comprising a geographical account of that country, together with a narrative of the most remarkable events which have occurred there since its discovery* (Henry Colburn, 1809), p. 232.
65. Koster, *Travels in Brazil*, p. 411.
66. As quoted in the booklet accompanying **História da Música Brasileira: Périodo Colonial II**, p. 9.
67. Renato Almeida, *Danses africaines en Amérique Latine* (Rio de Janeiro, Ministério da Educação e Cultura, 1964), p. 14.
68. L.-F. de Tollenare, *Notes dominicales*, ed. by L. Bourdon (Paris, 1971–73), III, pp. 698–9. The so-called 'postures' for which Pietro Aretino (1492–1556) wrote sonnets were in fact the work, not of Annibale Carracci (1560–1609), but of Giulio Romano (c. 1499–1546).
69. Léon Bourdon, 'Lettres familières et fragment du journal intime *Mes Sottises quotidiennes* de Ferdinand Denis à Bahia (1816–1819)', *Brasilia* (Coimbra), X (1958), p. 210.
70. Ferdinand Denis, *Brésil* (Paris, Firmin Didot Frères, 1837), pp. 146–7, 239.
71. Revd R. Walsh, *Notices of Brazil* (1830), II, p. 338.

72. Chasteen, 'The Prehistory of Samba', p. 35.

73. R. Almeida, *História da Música Brasileira*, 2nd ed. (Rio de Janeiro, 1942), p. 77 n. 116; Luiz Americo Lisboa Junior, *A presença da Bahia na Música Popular Brasileira* (Brasília, MusiMed / Linha Gráfica, 1990), pp. 15–18.

74. [A.] Touissant-Samson, *Une Parisienne au Brésil* (Paris, 1883), p. 81; cf. [A.] Touissant-Samson, *A Parisian in Brazil*, trans. by E. Touissant (Boston, 1891), pp. 67–8.

75. F.-J. de Santa-Anna Nery, *Folk-lore brésilien* (Paris, Perrin, 1889), pp. 76, 78–9.

76. 'Os manuscritos do botânico Freire Alemão', ed. by Darcy Damasceno and Waldir da Cunha, *Anais da Biblioteca Nacional*, LXXXI (1961), p. 214.

77. *MPB*, pp. 178–9; *DMB*, s.v. Baianá, p. 34; s.v. Baiano, pp. 35–6; s.v. Baião, p. 36.

78. There is an example of *baião* on **Pé de Serra Forró Band, Brazil**, track 3.

79. *MPB*, pp. 179–80.

80. *DMB*, s.v. Baiano, p. 35.

81. **Musique du Nordeste, vol. 2: 1928–1946**, track 2.

82. **Danças do Marajó**, side A, track 1; side B, track 1. The clarinet is played with a broad vibrato that calls to mind the playing of the New Orleans clarinet-tist Sidney Bechet (1897–1959) and the Martinique clarinettist Alexandre Stellio (Fructueux Alexandre, 1885–1939).

83. Quoted by J. R. Tinhorão, *Os Negros em Portugal: Uma presença silenciosa* (Lisbon, 1988), p. 191.

84. [Charles François Duperrier Dumouriez], *État présent du royaume de Portugal en l'année MDCCLXVI*, (Lausanne, François Grasset & Comp., 1775), p. 172; *An Account of Portugal as it appeared in 1766 to Dumouriez* (London, C. Law & J. Debrett; Edinburgh, Elph. Balfour; 1797), p. 160; [Pierre-Marie-Félicité Dezoteux, Baron de Cormatin], *Voyage du ci-devant duc Du Chatelet, en Portugal*, [ed. by Antoine Sérieys] (Paris, F. Buisson, [1798]), I, pp. 33–4, 78. A German visitor, Heinrich Link, wrote that a *'foffa'* would sometimes be danced in Portuguese market-places 'and by travellers mistaken for the fandango' (H. F. Link, *Bemerkungen auf einer Reise durch Frankreich, Spanien, und vorzüglich Portugal* (Kiel, 1801–04), I, p. 230; H. F. Link, *Travels in Portugal, and through France and Spain*, trans. by J. Hinckley (1801), p. 215.

85. W. Dalrymple, *Travels through Spain and Portugal in 1774*, p. 150.

86. J. R. Tinhorão, *Música popular de Índios, Negros e Mestiços* (Petrópolis, 1972), p. 124; Bruno Kiefer, *A modinha e o lundu: duas raizes da música popular brasileira*, 2nd edn (Porto Alegre, Editora Movimento, 1986; Coleção Luís Cosme, vol. 9), p. 8.

87. Dr F. A. Pereira Costa, 'Folk-lore Pernambucano', p. 221. Some versions have *mulheres-damas* in place of *mulheres de má reputação* ; see, e.g., *DFB*, s.v. Fofa, p. 331 ; *EMB*, s.v. fofa, I, p. 282. The two expressions are identical in meaning.

88. Theophilo de Andrade, 'O samba nasceu da "Fofa da Bahia"', *O Cruzeiro*, XXXVIII/22 (5 March 1966), p. 67, making the rash claim that the *Relaçaõ da Fofa* 'may be the clue to discovering the origins of our samba'.

89. See the bibliographical description in Appendix E, pp. 176–7.

90. The 'Academy of Extremes' features in the title of a similar eight-page cordel pamphlet, *O Palmito do Amor, deffindo na Academia dos Estremozos, e o Follar*

do Amor ([Lisbon], 1752), many paragraphs of which also begin with the words '*Ora viva ...*'.

91. The *outavado*, more commonly spelt *oitavado*, was a popular dance in Lisbon in the first half of the eighteenth century. It is described as an 'extremely sensual and brazen' dance accompanied by guitar or mandolin ([J.] Pinto de Carvalho, *História do fado*, Lisbon, 1903, pp. 4–5; *DMB*, s.v. Oitavado, p. 368).

92. '*O som do Macau*' is almost certainly a reference to the *Zabel Macau*, a popular eighteenth-century Lisbon dance, or group of dances. It is said to have originated in Lisbon's black community and to have been one of the precursors of the fado (*DMB*, s.v. Zabel Macau, p. 577).

93. By *filhota* the author probably means the *filhota do compasso*, a dance popular in the Portuguese provinces in the eighteenth century (*DMB*, s.v. Filhota do compasso, p. 224).

94. *Eres* is defined in António de Morais Silva, *Grande Dicionário da língua portuguesa*, 10th ed., ed. by Augusto Moreno, etc. ([Lisbon], Confluência, [1949–50]), IV, p. 585, as 'ornaments of tortoise-shell and feathers in the head-dress of ladies'; the same source quotes Júlio Dantas: 'In dandies' slang *eres* means elegant.' My translation of *giribandera* is conjectural; I take the word to be derived from *giribanda*, 'martingale', with the slang sense of 'admonition' or 'holding in check' (*Diccionario Contemporaneo da Lingua Portugueza*, Lisbon, Imprensa Nacional, 1881, I, p. 863).

95. James Murphy, *Travels in Portugal; through The provinces of Entre Douro e Minho, Beira, Estremadura, and Alem-Tejo, In the Years 1789 and 1790* (A. Strahan & T. Cadell Jun. & W. Davies, 1795), p. 202.

96. H. F. Link, *Bemerkungen auf einer Reise durch Frankreich, Spanien, und vorzüglich Portugal* (Kiel, 1801–04), I, p. 220; H. F. Link, *Travels in Portugal, and through France and Spain*, trans. by J. Hinckley (1801), pp. 206. In 1797 there were said to be 40,000 Galicians in Lisbon (*Tableau de Lisbonne en 1796*, Paris, H. J. Jansen, 1797, p. 312), but this was probably an exaggeration.

97. *Relacaõ das cantigas da fofa: compostas pelo memoravel e celebrissimo estapafurdio Manoel de Paços* [Lisbon, *c.* 1750], p. 4. There is a different version of this pamphlet in *Histórias jocosas a cavalo num barbante: O humor na Literatura de Cordel Sécs XVIII–XIX* (Oporto, Nova Crítica, 1980; Colecção Outras Terras, Outras Gentes, 5). The *cumbé* is described as an 'extremely sensual' black dance that diffused from Portugal to Spain in the eighteenth century; the *arrepia* was popular in Portugal in the eighteenth and nineteeth centuries; see *DMB*, s.v. Cumbé, p. 167, s.v. Arrepia, p. 26; *EMB*, s.v. arrepia, I, p. 47.

98. *Relaçam curioza em que conta das danças e Carros Triufantes, e mais aprestes, que haõ de assistir ás devertidas tardes de Touros* [Lisbon, *c.* 1752], p. 6. There are also references to the *fofa* in *Mappa curiozo das vistozas entradas, e danças, que haõ de preceder dos combates de Touros* [Lisbon, *c.* 1750].

99. *Entremez da Peregrina, que se reprezentou no theatro do Bairro Alto* (Lisbon, José da Silva Nazareth, 1770), p. 8.

100. Francisco José Dias, *Cantigas do povo dos Açores* (Angra do Heroísmo, Instituto Açoriano de Cultura, 1981), p. 237.

101. José de Almeida Pavão Jr, *Aspectos de cancioneiro popular açoriano* (Ponta Delgada, Universidade do Açores, 1981), p.283. A *fofa* collected in the island of São Miguel is transcribed in Frederico de Freitas, 'Fofa', *Enciclopédia Luso-*

Brasileira de Cultura, VIII, col. 1116–17, and two other versions are transcribed in Dias, *Cantigas do povo dos Açores*, p. 241. The texts of *fofas* from the islands of Santa Maria, São Miguel, and Terceira are given in Armando Cortes-Rodrigues, *Cancioneiro geral dos Açores* (Angra do Heroísmo, Direcção Regional dos Assuntos Culturais, 1982), III, pp. 376–8.

102. Alberto Pimentel, *A triste canção do sul (Subsidios para a historia do fado)* (Lisbon, Gomes de Carvalho, 1904), pp. 86–7 ('Fado corrido', reproduced in *DMB*, s.v. Fado, p. 213), 183 ('Fado do conde de Vimioso'), and 226 ('Fado serenata').

103. Mário de Andrade, *Modinhas imperiais* (São Paulo, Livraria Martins, 1964), pp. 47–9.

104. Vincenzo Cernicchiaro, *Storia della musica nel Brasile dai tempi coloniali sino ai nostri giorni (1549–1925)* (Milan, Fratelli Riccioni, 1926), p. 50, citing the 'Effemèridi' of Varnhagen. It has not been possible to check this reference.

105. A. Balbi, *Essai statistique sur le royaume de Portugal et d'Algarve* (Paris, 1822), II, p. ccxvii.

106. C. Schlichthorst, *Rio de Janeiro wie es ist* (Hanover, 1829), p. 185.

107. Schlichthorst, *Rio de Janeiro wie es ist*, pp. 233–5.

108. Charles Expilly, *Le Brésil tel qu'il est* (Paris, E. Dentu, 1862), pp. 93–4.

109. J. Friedrich v. Weech, *Reise über England und Portugal nach Brasilien und den vereinigten Staatem des La-Plata-Stromes während den Jahren 1823 bis 1827* (Munich, Fr. X. Auer, 1831), II, pp. 23–4.

110. Manuel Antônio de Almeida, *Memórias de um sargento de milícias*, ed. by Cecília de Lara (Rio de Janeiro, Livrs Técnicos e Científicas, 1978; Biblioteca Universitária de literatura brasileira, Série C, vol. 2), p. 27.

111. [José Vieira Fazenda], 'Antiqualhas e memorias do Rio de Janeiro', *Revista do Instituto Historico e Geographico Brasileiro*, tomo 86, vol. CXL (1919), p. 60.

112. Cf. Tinhorão, *Fado*, p. 13.

113. Tinhorão, *Fado*, p. 14.

114. As quoted by Luiz Moita, *O fado: canção de vencidos: oito palestras na Emissora Nacional* (Lisbon, Oficinas gráficas da Emprêsa do Anuário Comercial, 1936), p. 254 n. 9, citing Manuel de Sousa Pinto, 'O Lundum avô do Fado', *Ilustração* (Lisbon), no. 6 (131), 1 Novembro 1931. There is a slightly different version in Tinhorão, *Fado*, p. 14, with the reference: *Anatomico Jocoso*, III, 209.

115. Cf. [João] Pinto de Carvalho (Tinop), *História do Fado* (Lisbon, 1903), p. 26.

116. 'Os manuscritos do botânico Freire Alemão', *Anais da Biblioteca Nacional*, LXXXI (1961), pp. 214, 219.

117. Dr Robert Avé-Lallemant, *Reise durch Nord-Brasilien im Jahre 1859* (Leipzig, F. A. Brockhaus, 1860), I, pp. 60–1.

118. Margaret D. Nunes Nabarro, 'The background and development of fado in Moçambique up to 1973', in *Miscelânea Luso-Africana: Colectânea de estudos coligidos por Marius F. Valkhoff* (Lisbon, Junta de Investigações Científicas do Ultramar, 1975), p. 263.

Chapter 8

1. *Voyage de François Pyrard, de Laual* 3rd edn (Paris, 1619), II, pp. 343–4; *The voyage of François Pyrard of Laval to the East Indies*, trans. and ed. by A. Gray

and H. C. P. Bell (1887–90), II, pp. 319–20; see also Robert Stevenson, 'Some Portuguese sources for early Brazilian music history', *Yearbook*, Inter-American Institute for Musical Research, IV (1968), pp. 20–1.

2. M. l'Abbé [René] Courte de la Blanchardière, *Nouveau voyage fait au Pérou* (Paris, Delaguette, 1751), pp. 190–1.

3. 'Etwas über Musik und Tanz in Brasilien', *Allgemeine Musikalische Zeitung*, 35. Jahrgang (1833), no. 2, col. 20.

4. Revd D. P. Kidder and Revd J. C. Fletcher, *Brazil and the Brazilians* (Philadelphia, 1857), pp. 441–2; a shorter version had appeared in Revd Daniel. P. Kidder, *Sketches of residence and travel in Brazil* (1845), pp. 29–30. Louis Antoine Julien or Jullien (1812–60), conducted popular Promenade Concerts in London long before Sir Henry Wood. The *Stabat Mater* (properly *Stabat mater dolorosa*), a sequence of the Roman Catholic liturgy, has had numerous composed settings. It has not been possible to identify 'Lafayette's Grand March'.

5. Marieta Alves, 'Música de Barbeiros', *Revista Brasileira de Folclore*, VII/17 (janeiro/abril de 1967), pp. 12, 11.

6. A. da N. Machado Filho, *O Negro e o Garimpo em Minas Gerais* (Rio de Janeiro, [1943]), p. 24.

7. As quoted by J. R. Tinhorão, *Música popular de Índios, Negros e Mestiços* (Petrópolis, 1972), p. 87.

8. G. Freyre, *Casa-Grande e Senzala*, 5th edn (Rio de Janeiro and São Paulo, 1946), II, p. 668; G. Freyre, *The Masters and the Slaves*, trans. by S. Putnam (New York, 1946), p. 411.

9. Valentim Magalhães, *Vinte Contos* (Rio de Janeiro, A Semana, 1886), p. 98. The word *requinta* can mean a *viola* traditional guitar with high-pitched strings, but in this context is more likely to mean a clarinet.

10. Tinhorão, *Música popular de Índios, Negros e Mestiços*, p. 78.

11. Tinhorão, *Música popular de Índios, Negros e Mestiços*, p. 77.

12. *Rio de Janeiro Gazette*, 8 July 1820, as quoted by A. Caldcleugh, *Travels in South America, during the years 1819–20–21* (John Murray, 1825), I, p. 85 n.

13. *Jornal do Commercio*, 20 November 1847, as quoted by Delso Renault, *O Rio Antigo nos Anúncios de Jornais 1808–1850*, 2nd edn (Rio de Janeiro, Francisco Alves, 1984), p. 275.

14. Vicente Salles, *O Negro no Pará* (Rio de Janeiro, Fundação Gétulio Vargas, Universidade Federal do Pará, 1971), pp. 321, 319.

15. Stephen Fisher, 'Lisbon as a port town in the eighteenth century', in *Lisbon as a port town, the British seaman and other maritime themes*, ed. by S. Fisher (Exeter University Publications, 1988; Exeter Maritime Studies, no. 2), p. 9.

16. G. Kubik, *Angolan traits in black music, games and dances of Brazil* (Lisbon, 1979), p. 11.

17. C. R. Boxer, *Salvador de Sá and the Struggle for Brazil* (1952), p. 231; F. Mauro, *Le Portugal et l'Atlantique au xviiᵉ siècle* ([Paris], 1960), p. 171.

18. T. Lindley, *Narrative of a voyage to Brasil* (1805), p, 71.

19. T. Bentley Duncan, *Atlantic islands: Madeira, the Azores and the Cape Verdes in Seventeenth-Century Commerce and Navigation* (Chicago and London, University of Chicago Press, 1972), p. 238.

20. In 1648 a Jesuit priest visiting Brazil wrote that there were in the crew of the ship that took him there, 'besides a couple of excellent trumpet-players, some fiddlers, to the sound of whose instruments the passengers danced frequently and with great satisfaction' (Afonso de Taunay, *Visitantes do Brasil Colónial (século XVII, XVIII)*, São Paulo, 1933, p. 48).

21. Note in particular Herman Soyaux's statement (p. 159 above) about the 'naturalisation' in Angola by the 1870s of concertina, flute and tin whistle.

22. 'Etwas über Musik und Tanz in Brasilien', col. 19.

23. A. J. R. Russell-Wood, *The Black Man in Slavery and Freedom in Colonial Brazil* (1982), pp. 100–1.

24. M. Graham, *Journal of a voyage to Brazil* (1824), p. 166.

25. Tinhorão, *Música popular de Índios, Negros e Mestiços*, pp. 99, 72.

26. Graham, *Journal of a voyage to Brazil*, p. 197.

27. Robert Elwes, *A sketcher's tour round the world* (Hurst & Blackett, 1854), p. 17. This passage was also published in William Hadfield, *Brazil, the River Plate, and the Falkland Islands* (Longman, Brown, Green and Longmans, 1854), p. 142 n.

28. I. Pfeiffer, *Eine Frauenfahrt um de Welt* (Vienna, 1850), I, p. 40; I. Pfeiffer, *A woman's journey round the world*, 2nd edn [1852], p. 20.

29. F. Dabadie, *A travers l'Amérique du sud* (Paris, Ferdinand Sartorius, 1858), p. 18.

30. J. Wetherell, *Brazil: Stray notes from Bahia*, ed. by W. Hadfield (Liverpool, 1860), p. 54.

31. M. Karasch, 'From Porterage to Proprietorship: African Occupations in Rio de Janeiro, 1808–1850', in *Race and Slavery in the Western Hemisphere: Quantitative Studies*, ed. by S. L. Engerman and E. D. Genovese (Princeton, 1975). p. 388.

32. Alves, 'Música de Barbeiros', p. 10.

33. Lindley, *Narrative of a voyage to Brasil*, pp. 71–2.

34. Vassberg, 'African Influences on the Music of Brazil', p. 45; Tinhorão, *Música popular de Índios, Negros e Mestiços*, pp. 107–12.

35. Revd R. Walsh, *Notices of Brazil in 1828 and 1829* (1830), I, p. 473.

36. 'Senex' [i.e. José Francisco da Silva Lima], *A Bahia de ha 66 Annos (Reminiscencia de um contemporaneo)* (Rio de Janeiro, Companhia Brasileira de Artes Gráficas, [c. 1983]), p. 24. These reminiscences first appeared in the Salvador newspaper *Jornal de Noticias* in 1906–07.

37. Kidder, *Sketches of residence and travel in Brazil*, I, p. 154.

38. [A. J. de] Mello Morais Filho, *Festas e tradições populares do Brasil*, ed. by L. da Câmara Cascudo (Belo Horizonte & São Paulo, 1979), p. 151.

39. Mello Morais Filho, *Festas e Tradições populares*, p. 117.

40. J. B. Debret, *Voyage pittoresque et historique au Brésil* (Paris, 1834–39), II, p. 50.

41. *DMB*, p. 136.

42. Cf. M[aria]. Conceição Rezende, *A música na história de Minas colonial* (Brasilia, Instituto Nacional do Livro; Belo Horizonte, Itatiaia; 1989), p. 566.

43. Gerard Béhague, *Latin-American Music Review*, XVIII/2 (Fall/Winter 1997), p. iii.

44. Luiz Heitor Corrêa de Azevedo, 'Music and Society in Imperial Brazil, 1822–1889', in *Portugal and Brazil in Transition*, ed. by Raymond S. Sayers (Minneapolis, University of Minnesota Press, 1968), p. 304.

45. Robert Stevenson. 'Some Portuguese sources for early Brazilian music history', *Yearbook*, Inter-American Institute for Musical Research, IV (1968), p. 22.

46. **História da Música Brasileira: Périodo Colonial I**, tracks 9–11, 15–21, 14. Robert Stevenson. 'Some Portuguese sources for early Brazilian music history', pp. 24–5 and p. 24 n. 89, following Lange, challenges the much-repeated assertion that either the Jesuits in the mid-eighteenth century or the Portuguese king João VI (1769–1826), who took the Portuguese court to Rio de Janeiro in 1806, founded a conservatory near Rio de Janeiro for the musical education of black people in Brazil. Stevenson accepts however that D. João's 'composer laureate', Marcos Portugal (1762–1830) wrote a musical farce, *A Salioa namorada* (1812), for performance entirely by black artists.

47. **História da Música Brasileira: Périodo Colonial II**, track 10.

48. Robert Stevenson, 'Some Portuguese sources for early Brazilian music history', p. 22.

49. W. Dalrymple, *Travels through Spain and Portugal in 1774* (1777), pp. 150–1.

50. Domingos Caldas Barbosa, *Viola de Lereno*, ed. by Suetônio Soares Valença (Rio de Janeiro, Civilização Brasileira, 1980; Coleção Vera Cruz (Literatura Brasileira), vol. 306), p. 422 n. 5. Cf. J. T. Schneider, *Dictionary of African Borrowings in Brazilian Portuguese* (Hamburg, 1991), s.v. angu 1, p. 14; s.v. moleque, p. 214; s.v. quindim, p. 254; s.v. quingombô, p. 254.

51. Nicoláo Tolentino de Almeida, *Obras poeticas* (Lisbon, na Regia Officina Typografica 1801), I, p. 198.

52. D. Caldas Barbosa, *Viola de Lereno*, I, p. 45.

53. Theophilo Braga, 'Sobre a poesia popular do Brazil', in Dr Sylvio Roméro, *Cantos populares do Brazil* (Lisbon, Nova Livraria Internacional, 1883), I, p. xxvi.

54. *The Journal of William Beckford in Portugal and Spain 1787–1788*, ed. by Boyd Alexander (Rupert Hart-Davis, 1954), pp. 69, 228–9.

55. As quoted by Rose Macaulay, *They went to Portugal* (Jonathan Cape, 1946), pp. 261–2. Macaulay comments (p. 261) that what Lady Craven heard 'sounds very like modern crooning and dance-music'.

56. A. Balbi, *Essai statistique sur le royaume de Portugal et d'Algarve* (Paris, 1822), II, p. ccxiii.

57. Revd W. M. Kinsey, *Portugal Illustrated; in a series of letters* (Treuttel, Würtz & Richter, 1828), p. 68.

58. J. B. Debret, *Voyage pittoresque et historique au Brésil* (Paris, 1834–39), II, p. 43.

59. *HMB*, p. 59.

60. As quoted in the booklet accompanying **História da Música Brasileira: Périodo Colonial II**, p. 9.

61. *Modinhas luso-brasileiras*, ed. by Gerhard Doderer (Lisbon, Fundação Calouste Gubenkian, 1984; Portugaliæ Musica, ser. B, vol. XLIV), p. viii.

62. Cf. M. de Araújo, 'Sigismund Neukomm: Um músico austríaco no Brasil', *Revista Brasileira de Cultura*, I/1 (julho/setembro 1969), p. 68.

63. Cf. *Modinhas Luso-Brasileiras*, ed. by Doderer, p. vii.

64. Luiz Heitor [Corrêa de Azevedo], 'As modinhas de Joaquim Manuel', in *Estudos e ensaios folclóricos en homenagem a Renato Almeida* (Rio de Janeiro, 1960), p. 609.

65. For Neukomm, see Luiz Heitor Correa de Azevedo, 'Sigismund Neukomm, an Austrian composer in the New World', *Musical Quarterly*, XLV/4 (October 1959), pp. 473–83; Mozart de Araújo, 'Um músico austríaco no Brasil', *Revista Brasileira de Cultura*, I/1 (julho/setembro 1969), pp. 61–74.

66. M. de Andrade, *Modinhas imperiais* (São Paulo, 1964), p. 11.

67. Gerard Béhague, 'Biblioteca da Ajuda (Lisbon) MSS 1595/1596: two eighteenth-century anonymous collections of modinhas', *Yearbook*, Inter-American Institute for Musical Research, IV (1968), pp. 54, 56, 59, 61, 62, 63, 68.

68. *Jornal de Modinhas*, [first ser.] (Lisbon, Na Real Fabrica e Armazem de Muzica no Largo de Jezus, [*c.* 1792–93]), no. 4, pp. 10–12; no. 11, pp. 26–7; no. 15, pp. 36–7; no. 22, pp. 54–5. These are *Modas Brazileiras*. The *Modinha do Zabumba* is no. 14, pp. 32–4.

69. This paragraph owes much to M. de Araujo, *A Modinha e o Lundu no Século XVIII* (São Paulo, 1963), pp. 11–12.

70. *MPB*, p. 172.

71. D. E. Vassberg, 'African Influences on the Music of Brazil', *Luso-Brazilian Review*, XIII/1 (Summer 1976), p. 46.

72. Araujo, *A Modinha e o Lundu no Século XVIII*, p. 12.

73. Aubrey F. G. Bell, *Portuguese Literature* (Oxford, Clarendon Press, 1970 reprint), p. 276.

74. N. Tolentino de Almeida, *Obras Poeticas* (Lisbon, 1801), I, p. 197; II, p. 56.

75. For the *chula*, see *HMB*, pp. 172–3; *MPB*, pp. 180–3; *DMB*, s.v. Chula, pp. 139–40. The word *chula* originally meant 'woman of the lower classes'.

76. *Jornal de Modinhas*, [first ser., *c.* 1792–93]), no. 21, pp. 52–3; [second ser., *c.* 1795], no. 13, pp. 30–2.

77. Dated 3 May 1819, this was published in Leipzig in 1825. It was to be another 50 years before a Brazilian composer, Brazilio Itiberê da Cunha (1846–1913), in *A Sertaneja* (1869), used in concert music a popular Brazilian theme: the Pará fandango *Balaio, meu bem balaio*.

78. Dr Carl Friedr. Phil. von Martius, *Brasilianische Volkslieder und Indianische Melodien* [Munich, 1823], no. IX, p. 11.

79. **História da Música Brasileira: Périodo Colonial II**, track 1.

80. Booklet accompanying **História da Música Brasileira: Périodo Colonial II**, p. 6.

81. For this paragraph, see the appropriate articles in *EMB*, and also Ary Vasconcelos, *Raízes da música popular brasileira (1500–1889)* (São Paulo, Martins; Brasília, Instituto Nacional do Livro; 1977), *passim*.

82. **História da Música Brasileira: Périodo Colonial II**, tracks 3–10.

83. H. Koster, *Travels in Brazil* (1816), p. 16.

84. J. Codman, *Ten months in Brazil* (Boston, 1867), pp. 171–2.

85. John White, *A journal of a voyage to Botany Bay, in New South Wales* (J. Debrett, [1790]), pp. 52–3.

86. John Mawe, *Travels in the interior of Brazil, particularly in the gold and diamond districts of that country* (Longman, Hurst, Rees, Orme & Brown, 1812), p. 281.

87. James Prior, *Voyage along The Eastern Coast of Africa … to Rio de Janeiro, Bahia, and Pernambuco in Brazil, in the Nisus frigate* (Sir James Phillips & Co., 1819), p. 103.

88. Maximilian Prinz zu Wied-Neuwied, *Reise nach Brasilien in den Jahren 1815 bis 1817* (Frankfurt a.M.,1820–21), I, p. 192; Prince Maximilian, of Wied-Neuwied, *Travels in Brazil, in the years 1815, 1816, 1817* (1820), p. 164.

89. F. L. von Rango, *Tagebuch meiner Reise nach Rio de Janeiro* (Ronneburg, 1832), p. 145.

90. Graham, *Journal of a voyage to Brazil*, pp. 127, 136.

91. J. F. v. Weech, *Reise über England und Portugal nach Brasilien* (Munich, 1831), II, p. 23.

92. 'Etwas über Musik und Tanz in Brasilien', cols 19–20.

93. George Gardner, *Travels in the interior of Brazil, principally through the northern provinces, and the gold and diamond districts, during the years 1836–1841* (Reese, Brothers, 1846), pp. 8, 414–15.

94. Pfeiffer, *Eine Frauenfahrt um de Welt*, I, p. 39; Pfeiffer, *A woman's journey round the world*, p. 20.

95. Wetherell, *Brazil*, pp. 62, 118.

96. Gilberto Freyre, 'Social life in Brazil in the middle of the nineteenth century', *Hispanic American Historical Review*, V (1922), p. 614.

97. A. R. Wallace, *A narrative of travels on the Amazon and Rio Negro* (1853), p. 19.

98. Walthère de Selys-Longchamps, *Notes d'un voyage au Brésil* (Brussels, C. Muquardt, Merzbach & Falk, 1875), p. 45.

99. C. C. Andrews, *Brazil: its condition and prospects* (New York, D. Appleton, 1887), p. 34.

100. Alice R. Humphreys, *A summer journey to Brazil* (New York and London, Bonnell, Silver & Co., 1900), p. 55.

101. F. Vincent, *Around and about South America* (New York, 1890), pp. 223, 333–4.

102. Gustave Aimard, *Mon Dernier Voyage: Le Brésil nouveau* (Paris, E. Dentu, 1886), p. 127.

103. As quoted in the booklet accompanying **História da Música Brasileira: Périodo Colonial II**, p. 9.

104. Balbi, *Essai statistique sur le royaume de Portugal et d'Algarve*, II, p. ccxxvij.

105. Weech, *Reise über England und Portugal nach Brasilien*, II, pp. 23, 24. There follows a serious warning: 'The foreigner who understands music and dance is a welcome guest, and if he is satisfied with the exchange of tender glances, dallying in words with a beauty, then he will have right good entertainment. However, if he thinks he can take the matter further, then he falls into the error all foreigners make, who are at first inclined to think that Brazilian women are easygoing.'

106. 'Etwas über Musik und Tanz in Brasilien', col. 20.

107. H. H. Smith, *Brazil: The Amazons and the Coast* (New York, 1879), p. 122. The musicians at a dancing party in Santarem, on the south bank of the Amazon, were 'very good in their way ... they play simple tunes; once we are astonished to hear a quadrille led off with "Pop Goes the Weasel", hardly a note changed' (p. 122).

108. Le Cte C. d'Ursel, *Sud-Amérique* (Paris, 1879), p. 65.

109. H. C. Dent, *A Year in Brazil* (1886), pp. 70–1.

110. Frank Bennett, *Forty years in Brazil* (Mills & Boon, 1914), pp. 205, 187.

111. Thomas P. Bigg-Wither, *Pioneering in south Brazil: Three years of forest and prairie life in the province of Paraná* (John Murray, 1878), I, pp. 253–5.

Something of the atmosphere of such a dance, complete with foot-stamping and handclapping, is captured on **Fandango/SP**.

Chapter 9

1. Nei Lopes, *O Negro no Rio de Janeiro e sua tradição musical: partido-alto, calango, chula e outras cantorias* (Rio de Janeiro, Pallas, 1992), p. 41.
2. Gerard Béhague, 'Biblioteca da Ajuda (Lisbon) MSS 1595/1596: two eighteenth-century anonymous collections of modinhas', *Yearbook*, Inter-American Institute for Musical Research, IV (1968), p. 44.
3. *HMB*, p. 185.
4. José Ramos Tinhorão, *Pequena história da música popular – da modinha ao tropicalismo*, 5th edn (São Paulo, Art, 1986), pp. 97–8.
5. But not by Ernesto Nazaré, who continued to give the name 'tango' to the *maxixes* he wrote for the piano; cf. *MPB*, p. 336. Gerard Béhague explains: 'Around 1890 the tango was still very similar to the habanera; in fact, in Brazil "tango" was the name given to the habanera itself ... [T]he habanera was also known as tango in Argentina and Uruguay around 1890. The tango had the same basic rhythmic pattern as the habanera but was slightly faster and used variants of the syncopation that also defined the maxixe. The tango [in Brazil] ... underwent rhythmic transformations under the influence of the maxixe to such an extent as to make it impossible to differentiate musically between pieces called diversely "Brazilian tango" and "maxixe"' (Gerard Béhague, *Music in Latin America: an introduction*, Englewood Cliffs, N.J., Prentice-Hall, 1979, p. 118).
6. Cf. Luiz Heitor, *150 Anos de Música no Brasil (1800–1950)* (Rio de Janeiro, José Olympio, 1956; Coleção Documentos Brasileiros, 87), p. 147.
7. See Jota Efegê [i.e. João Ferreira Gomes], *Maxixe: a dança excomungada* (Rio de Janeiro, Conquista, 1974; Temas Brasileiros, vol. 16), pp. 157 ff.
8. J. C. Chasteen, 'The Prehistory of Samba: Carnival Dancing in Rio de Janeiro, 1840–1917', *Journal of Latin American Studies*, XXVIII/1 (February 1996), p. 39.
9. Gerard Béhague, 'La afinidad caribeña de la música popular en Bahia', *Del Caribe* (Santiago de Cuba), no. 19 (1992), p. 92. For early *lambada*, hear **Vieira e seu Conjunto: 'Lambada'**.
10. As quoted by Chasteen, 'The Prehistory of Samba', p. 40.
11. *Dancing Times and Social Review*, n.s., no. 28 (January 1913), p. 263; no. 29 (February 1913), p. 331.
12. Chasteen, 'The Prehistory of Samba', p. 39.
13. Chasteen, 'The Prehistory of Samba', p. 40.
14. *DMB*, s.v. Maxixe, p. 324, s.v. Samba, p. 454.
15. Marilia Trindade Barboza da Silva, 'Negro em roda da samba: Herança africana na Música Popular Brasileira', *Tempo brasileiro*, nos 92/93 (janeiro–junho de 1988), p. 109.
16. As quoted by Alison Raphael, 'Samba Schools in Brazil', *International Journal of Oral History*, X/3 (November 1989), p. 258. Also quoted, in a slightly different form, by Alison Raphael, 'From Popular Culture to Microenterprise:

The History of Brazilian Samba Schools', *Latin American Music Review*, XI/1 (Spring/Summer 1990), p. 74.

17. 'Pelo Telefone' has been resissued on **Brésil: Choro – Samba – Frevo: 1914–1945**, CD 2, track 3, and on **Samba: Batuque – Partido Alto – Samba-canção 1917–1947**, CD 1, track 9.
18. See the booklet accompanying **Brésil: Choro – Samba – Frevo: 1914–1945**.
19. Cf. Barboza da Silva, 'Negro em roda de samba', *Tempo Brasileiro*, nos 92/93 (janeiro–junho de 1988), p. 110.
20. Kazadi wa Mukuna, *Contribução Bantu na Música Popular Brasileira* (São Paulo, [c. 1978]), p. 113.
21. Cf. G. Kubik, *Muziek van de Humbi en de Handa uit Angola* ([Tervuren], 1973), p. 68.
22. There are some good examples on **Brazil Roots Samba**.
23. Chasteen, 'The Prehistory of Samba', p. 44.
24. Barboza da Silva, 'Negro em roda de samba', p. 111.
25. J. J. de Carvalho, 'Black Music of All Colors: The Construction of Black Ethnicity in Ritual and Popular Genres of Afro-Brazilian Music', in *Music and Black Ethnicity*, ed. by G. H. Béhague (Miami, 1994), p. 188.
26. Barboza da Silva, 'Negro em roda de samba', pp. 112–13. 'Se Você Jurar' is reissued on **Samba: Batuque – Partido Alto – Samba-canção 1917–1947**, CD 2, track 6.
27. Barboza da Silva, 'Negro em roda de samba', p. 110. Sinhô's 'Não Quero Saber Mais Dela' is reissued on **Brésil: Choro – Samba – Frevo: 1914–1945**, CD 1, track 12.
28. Cf. Philip Galinsky, 'Co-option, Cultural Resistance, and Afro-Brazilian Identity: A History of the *Pagode* Samba Movement in Rio de Janeiro', *Latin American Music Review*, XVII/2 (Fall/Winter 1996), p. 122.

Appendix A

1. Laura Boulton, *The music hunter: The Autobiography of a Career* (Garden City, N.Y., Doubleday, 1969), pp. 81–2.
2. **Musique de l'ancien royaume Kuba**, side A, tracks 1 and 2.
3. R. F. Thompson, *Flash of the spirit: African and Afro-American Art and Philosophy* (New York, 1983), p. 103.
4. C. R. Boxer, *Salvador de Sá and the Struggle for Brazil and Angola 1602–1686* (1952), p. 224.
5. Gerhard Kubik, 'Angola', in *The New Grove Dictionary of Music and Musicians*, ed. by S. Sadie, I, pp. 431–2.
6. Kubik, 'Angola', p. 432.
7. H. Soyaux, *Aus West-Afrika 1873–1876* (Leipzig, 1879), II, p. 176.

Appendix B

1. Nuno Marquez Pereira, *Compendio narrativo do Peregrino da América*, [3rd edn] (Lisbon, Antonio Vicente da Silva, 1760), pp. 118, 122.

2. Manuel Querino, *A Raça Africana e os seus costumes* (Salvador, Livraria Progresso, 1955; Coleção de Estudos Brasileiros, Série Cruzeiro, vol. 9), pp. 97–8.

3. Luciano Gallet, *Estudos de folclore* (Rio de Janeiro, C. Wehrs, 1934), p. 59.

4. Though he does not cite Gallet, A. J. R. Russell-Wood, *A world on the move: the Portuguese in Africa, Asia, and America, 1415–1808* (Manchester, Carcanet, 1992), p. 194, makes the familiar claim that 'there are descriptions or pictures of some twenty different [African] instruments in colonial Brazil'.

5. *DMB*, s.v. valica, valiha, p. 548.

6. Gallet, *Estudos de folclore*, p. 60.

7. Cf. J. J. de Carvalho, 'Music of African Origin in Brazil', in *Africa in Latin America*, ed. by M. M Fraginals, trans. by L. Blum (New York and Paris, 1984), p. 233.

8. For flutes in African traditional music, see J. H. K. Nketia, *The Music of Africa* (1975), pp. 91–4.

9. Hear **African Flutes**.

10. G. Gardner, *Travels in the interior of Brazil* (1846), p. 195.

11. **Banda Cabaçal/Ceará; Zabumba/SE.**

12. *HMB*, p. 115.

13. J. Wetherell, *Brazil: Stray notes from Bahia* (Liverpool, 1860), p. 6. For the stamping tubes used in Ghana, see Nketia, *The music of Africa*, p. 76.

14. For African shaken idiophones, see Nketia, *The music of Africa*, pp. 70–2.

15. Wetherell, *Brazil*, p. 6.

16. L.-F. de Tollenare, *Notes domincales prises pendant un voyage en Portugal et au Brésil*, ed. by L. Bourdon (Paris, 1971–73), II, p. 471.

17. 'Etwas uber Musik und Tanz in Brasilien', *Allgemeine Musikalische Zeitung*, 35. Jahrgang (1833), no. 2, col. 21.

18. Nketia, *The music of Africa*, p. 75.

19. J. E.. Pohl, *Reise im Innern von Brasilien* (Vienna, 1832–37), II, p. 82.

20. 'Etwas uber Müsik und Tanz in Brasilien', col. 21.

21. H. Koster, *Travels in Brazil* (1816), p. 241.

22. Graham, *Journal of a voyage to Brazil*, p. 199.

23. M. C. Karasch, *Slave Life in Rio de Janeiro 1808–1850* (Princeton, N.J., 1987), p. 232.

24. Stanley J. Stein, *Vassouras: A Brazilian Coffee County, 1850–1900* (Harvard, 1957), p. 205 n. 18.

25. Querino, *A raça africana e o seus costumes*, p. 98; E. Carneiro, *Religiões Negras*, 2nd ed. / *Negros Bantos*, 2nd ed. (Rio de Janeiro and Brasília, 1981), p. 74; *DMB*, s.v. batacotô, p. 50.

26. Gerhard Kubik, 'Drum Patterns in the "Batuque" of Benedito Caxias', *Latin American Music Review*, XI/2 (Fall–Winter 1990), p. 145.

27. For friction drums in Africa, see Nketia, *The music of Africa*, p. 89; J. Redinha, *Instrumentos musicais de Angola* (Coimbra, 1984), pp. 163–4 and fig. 76. For the *kwita* friction drum of the Tshokwe or Chokwe of north-east Angola and south-west Congo-Kinshasa, hear **Music and Musicians of the Angola Border: the Tshokwe**, side A, track 5. For friction drums in Portugal, see E. V. de Oliveira, *Instrumentos musicais populares portugueses* (Lisbon, 1982), pp. 417–18.

28. Nketia, *The music of Africa*, p. 98, with illustration on p. 100.
29. 'Etwas uber Musik und Tanz in Brasilien', col. 20; K. Shaffer, *O Berimbau-de-barriga e seus Toques* (Rio de Janeiro, [c. 1978]), p. 19.
30. T. v. Leithold, *Meine Ausflucht nach Brasilien* (Berlin, 1820), p. 74.
31. C. Schlichthorst, *Rio de Janeiro wie es ist* (Hanover, 1829), p. 183.
32. R. Graham, 'Technology and Culture Change: The Development of the *Berimbau* in Colonial Brazil', *Latin American Music Review*, XII/1 (Spring/ Summer 1991), p. 5.
33. Shaffer, *O Berimbau-de-barriga e seus Toques*, pp. 18–19.
34. Shaffer, *O Berimbau-de-barriga e seus Toques*, p. 19.
35. **Musique Kongo**, side A, track 1.
36. Hear **Afro-American Folk Music from Tate and Panola Counties, Mississippi**, side B, track 2, and see the accompanying booklet by David Evans, p. 14, and also David Evans, 'Afro-American One-Stringed Instruments', *Western Folklore*, XXIX (1970), pp. 229–45.
37. Graham, *Journal of a voyage to Brazil*, p. 199. For African plucked lutes, see Nketia, *The music of Africa*, p. 103.
38. A. M. Araújo, *Folclore Nacional* [São Paulo, 1964], II, p. 421.
39. Redinha, *Instrumentos musicais de Angola*, pp. 56–7 and 116–19 (figs. 18–23) and foto 9.
40. Graham, *Journal of a voyage to Brazil*, p. 199. For African bowed lutes, see Nketia, *The music of Africa*, pp. 102–3.
41. Walsh, *Notices of Brazil*, II, pp. 335–6.

Appendix C

1. A. B. Aderibigbe, 'Early History of Lagos to About 1850', in *Lagos: The Development of an African City*, ed. by A. B. Aderibigbe ([Lagos], Longman Nigeria, 1975), pp. 15, 14.
2. Manuela Carneiro da Cunha, *Negros, estrangeiros: os escravos libertos e sua volta à África* (São Paulo, Brasiliense, 1985), p. 107.
3. Aderibigbe, 'Early History of Lagos', p. 22; P. D. Cole, 'Lagos Society in the Nineteenth Century', in *Lagos*, ed. by Aderibigbe, pp. 43, 46; Carneiro da Cunha, *Negros, estrangeiros*, pp. 101, 107; Afolabi Alaja-Browne, 'The Origin and Development of JuJu Music', *The Black Perspective in Music*, XVII/1, 2 (1989), p. 56.
4. Carneiro da Cunha, *Negros, estrangeiros*, p. 136.
5. *The city of Ibadan*, ed. by P. C. Lloyd, A. l. Mabogunje, and B. Awe (Cambridge University Press, 1967), p. 50.
6. For *caretas* in Brazil, see *MPB*, p. 42.
7. Frank Aig-Imoukhuede, 'Contemporary Culture', in *Lagos*, ed. by Aderibigbe, p. 210.
8. Clément da Cruz, 'Les instruments de musique dans le Bas-Dahomey (Populations Fon, Adja, Kotafon, Péda, 'Aïzo'), *Études dahoméennes*, XII (1954), p. 66.
9. Cruz, 'Les instruments de musique dans le Bas-Dahomey', pp. 66, 26.

10. Frank Aig-Imoukhuede, 'Contemporary Culture', in *Lagos*, ed. by A. B. Aderibigbe, p 213; Alaja-Browne, 'The Origin and Development of JuJu Music', pp. 55–6; Christopher Alan Waterman, *Jùjú: A Social History and Ethnography of an African Popular Music* (Chicago and London, University of Chicago Press, 1990), p. 46. For the *sámbà* drum in *Jùjú* music, hear **Juju Roots: 1930s–1950s**, side A, track 6, side B, track 8.
11. Waterman, *Jùjú*, p. 234 n. 7.
12. cf. Waterman, *Jùjú*, pp. 41–2.
13. Alaja-Browne, 'The Origin and Development of JuJu Music', p. 55.
14. Waterman, *Jùjú*, pp. 39–40.
15. Aig-Imoukhuede, 'Contemporary Culture', p. 213.
16. Waterman, *Jùjú*, p. 40.
17. Aig-Imoukhuede, 'Contemporary Culture', p. 214.
18. Waterman, *Jùjú*, p. 32.
19. Aig-Imoukhuede, 'Contemporary Culture', p. 214.

Appendix D

1. T. B. Duncan, *Atlantic islands* (Chicago and London, 1972), p. 158.
2. Duncan, *Atlantic islands*, pp. 195, 233.
3. Susan Hurley-Glowa, 'Music', in Richard Lobban and Marlene Lopes, *Historical Dictionary of the Republic of Cape Verde*, 3rd edn (Metuchen, N.J., and London, Scarecrow Press, 1995), p. 149.
4. Oswaldo Osório, *Cantigas de trabalho: Tradições orais de Cabo Verde* (Comissão Nacional para as Comemorações do 5° Aniversário da Independência de Cabo Verde – Sub-Comissão para a Cultura, [1980]), pp. 25, 37, 69 ff.
5. Hurley-Glowa, 'Music', p. 150.
6. Hurley-Glowa, 'Music', p. 150.
7. Nuno de Miranda, *Compreensão de Cabo Verde* (Lisbon, Junta de Investigações do Ultramar, 1963), p. 52; Iliídio do Amaral, *Santiago de Cabo Verde: A Terra e os Homens* (Lisbon, 1964; Memórias da Junta de Investigações do Ultramar, segunda série, no. 48), p. 218; João Lopes Filho, *Cabo Verde: apontamentos etnográficos* (Lisbon, Sociedade Astória, 1976), p. 54.
8. Lopes Filho, *Cabo Verde*, p. 52. There is a rare recording of the *cimbó* on **Iles du Cap-Vert – Les Racines**, track 15.
9. For African bowed lutes, see J. H. Kwabena Nketia, *The music of Africa* (1975), pp. 102–3.
10. Lopes Filho, *Cabo Verde*, p. 52.
11. Lopes Filho, *Cabo Verde*, p. 43.
12. Lopes Filho, *Cabo Verde*, p. 46, says it came to the archipelago from the African coast, but the evidence is inconclusive.
13. Amaral, *Santiago de Cabo Verde*, p. 218.
14. Booklet accompanying **Cap-Vert: Kodé di Dona**, p. 15.
15. **Iles du Cap-Vert – Les Racines**, tracks 3, 7, and 11.
16. Hurley-Glowa, 'Music', p. 151.
17. There is an example on **Cap Vert: Anthologie 1959–1992**, CD 1, track 18.

18. Hurley-Glowa, 'Music', p. 151; and hear **Iles du Cap-Vert – Les Racines**, tracks 5 and 12.
19. Hurley-Glowa, 'Music', p. 151.
20. Peter Manuel, 'Morna', in Lobban and Lopes, *Historical Dictionary of the Republic of Cape Verde*, p. 144.
21. Archibald Lyall, *Black and white make brown: An Account of a Journey to the Cape Verde Islands and Portuguese Guinea* (London and Toronto, William Heinemann, 1938), p. 58.
22. Peter Manuel, 'Coladera', in Lobban and Lopes, *Historical Dictionary of the Republic of Cape Verde*, p. 56. Ronnie Graham, *The World of African Music* (Pluto Press, 1992; Stern's Guide to Contemporary African Music, vol. 2), p. 95, suggests that it was influenced by the polka.
23. Luís Romano, *Cabo Verde – Renascença de uma civilização no Atlântico médio*, 2nd ed. (Lisbon, Edição da revista 'Ocidente', 1970), p. 127.
24. Manuel, 'Coladera', pp. 55–6.
25. Pedro Monteiro Cardoso, *Folclore caboverdiano* (Paris, Solidariedade Caboverdiana, 1983), p. 40; José Alves dos Reis, 'Subsídios para o estudo da Morna', *Raízes* (Praia Santiago), no. 21 (Junho 1984), p. 9.
26. Hurley-Glowa, 'Music', p. 150.
27. **The Soul of Cape Verde**, track 19.

Discography

1. *DMB*, p. 136.
2. S. Hurley-Glowa, 'Music', in R. Lobban and M. Lopes, *Historical Dictionary of the Republic of Cape Verde,* 3rd edn (Metuchen, N.J., and London, 1995), p. 153
3. Randall Fegley, *The Congo* (Oxford, Clio Press, 1993; World Bibliographical Ser., vol. 162), p. 132.

Index